P9-DBS-167

EntreCultures 2

Communicate, Explore, and Connect Across Cultures

Elizabeth Zwanziger
Florence Falloux
Erin Gibbons
Jan Hagedorn

Printed in the USA

5 6 7 8 9 10 KP 20

Print date: 1238

Hardcover ISBN 978-1-944876-96-8

Le Monde francophone

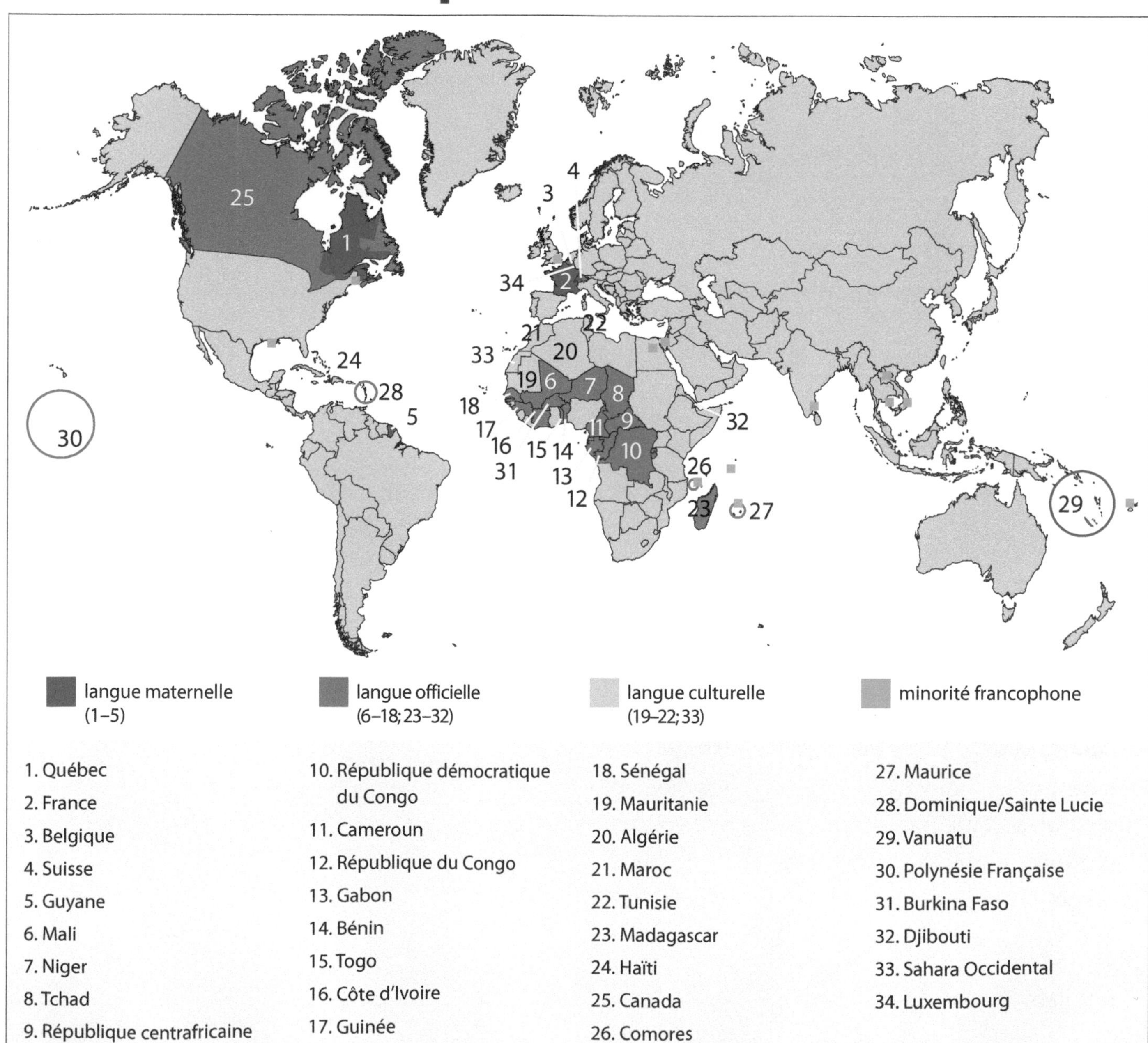

EntreCultures 2

Glossary of Classroom and Activity Instructions

Expressions pour les activités

ajoutez	add
associez	match
choisissez	choose
classez	classify/sort
cochez	check (the box)
créez	create
décrivez	describe
demandez	ask
dessinez	draw
discutez	discuss
écoutez	listen
enregistrez	record/film
entourez	circle
envoyez	send
expliquez	explain
identifiez	identify
indiquez	indicate
laissez un message	leave a message
lisez	read
mettez	put
notez	note
partagez	share
pensez	think
posez une question	ask a question
réfléchissez	reflect
regardez	watch
répondez	respond/answer
suggérez	suggest
trouvez	find
utilisez	use
un(e) autre élève de la classe	a classmate
une colonne	column
un nuage de mots	word cloud
un(e) partenaire	a partner
une phrase	a sentence
une représentation schématique	graphic organizer
un rôle	a role
à l'oral	out loud
avec	with
même	same
sans	without
suivant	following

Expressions pour travailler ensemble

Je sais...	I know...
Tu sais...?	Do you know...?
À quelle page?	What page?
C'est mon tour.	It's my turn.
C'est ton tour.	It's your turn.
Qu'est-ce que tu as trouvé pour...?	What did you find for...?
Tu as raison.	You're right.
Ce n'est pas correct.	That's not right.
J'ai dit...	I said...
C'est ici [dans le texte].	It's here [in the text].
Tu veux commencer?	Do you want to start?
Vas-y!	You go ahead.

Pour indiquer de qui ou à qui on parle

je	mon/ma/mes	moi
tu	ton/ta/tes	toi
il	son/sa/ses	
elle	son/sa/ses	
on	son/sa/ses	
nous	notre/nos	nous
vous	votre/vos	vous
ils	leur/leurs	
elles	leur/leurs	

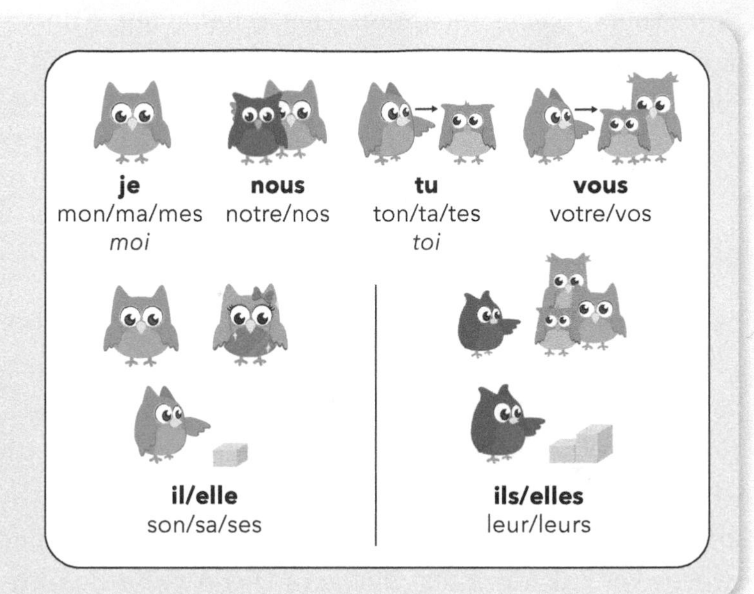

Descriptions d'emplacement – Où est le cercle?

sur

sous

dans

devant

derrière

à côté de

à droite de

à gauche de

loin de

près de

Acknowledgements

We are grateful to all who accompanied us on our path from start to finish on this edition of the ***EntreCultures*** level two program. We had the privilege of working with many talented and diligent professionals who steered our team along the way.

From this project's inception, Eliz Tchakarian, Editorial Project Manager, coached us to organize our thoughts and ideas to create an engaging, quality program for students of French. We also greatly appreciate Curriculum Coordinators Helen Small and Janet Parker's kind leadership and guidance throughout the journey. Kelsey Hare and Elizabeth Rench, Permissions Coordinators, were diligent in finding the owners of and acquiring permissions for authentic materials. We commend our outstanding editors, Eileen M. Angelini and Florian P. Croisé, whose advice and attention to detail were indispensible to the completion of this work. We also thank Ana-Maria M'Enesti for her assistance with the citations for authentic sources. Contributing Authors Anne Bastings, Nitya Viswanath, and Eliane Kurbegov enriched the content of our online presence. Our book would not have been as truly authentic nor as engaging without the generous contribution of our international video bloggers, incredible young people from across the Francophone world who shared their lives with our readers to help make a true connection to the French language and culture. Many thanks to Lou-Ann, Maxime, Éloïse, Élisa, Mathew, and Brenda for being the faces of ***EntreCultures*** level two, as well as our guest bloggers Diego, Gaïa Bomfin, Léo Falloux, Mylène Falloux, Lola, Corentin, Sylvain Ferey, Ndona Hansen, Édrige Oris, and Yngara Péhoua-Dupervil.

We thank Derrick Alderman and Rivka Levin at Bookwonders, our talented and artistic production team, who brought our manuscripts to life on the engaging and colorful pages of the completed product. We thank Wayside Publishing Sr. Graphic Designers Nathan Galvez, Shelby Newsted, Sawyer McCarron-Rutledge, and Jr. Graphic Designer Tawny Cantor who designed many of the beautiful graphics and graphic organizers used in both the print and online versions of this book. We extend our appreciation to Senior Tech Support Representatives Maddie Bonneau, James LeVasseur, and everyone else on the IT team led by Manager Deb Penham.

The Wayside Publishing Sales and Marketing team was led by director Michelle Sherwood, who was assisted by Marketing Manager Nicole Lyons, Professional Development Manager Jay Ketner and the entire Instructional Strategist team. We'd like to specifically thank all Instructional Strategists, and Marketing Specialists Stefanie Millette and Zsofia McMullin. In collaboration with the Wayside Publishing Sales and Marketing team, we are getting the word out to the French teaching community about ***EntreCultures***, a new instructional tool and innovative approach to developing students' intercultural communicative competence.

This project was made possible due to the leadership, wisdom, and vision of Wayside Publishing Manager, Product Development Steve Whitworth and President Greg Greuel, who supported and believed in our team to create this exciting project.

Elizabeth Zwanziger   Florence Falloux   Erin Gibbons   Jan Hagedorn

World-Readiness Standards For Learning Languages

GOAL AREAS	STANDARDS		
COMMUNICATION Communicate effectively in more than one language in order to function in a variety of situations and for multiple purposes	**Interpersonal Communication:** Learners interact and negotiate meaning in spoken, signed, or written conversations to share information, reactions, feelings, and opinions.	**Interpretive Communication:** Learners understand, interpret, and analyze what is heard, read, or viewed on a variety of topics.	**Presentational Communication:** Learners present information, concepts, and ideas to inform, explain, persuade, and narrate on a variety of topics using appropriate media and adapting to various audiences of listeners, readers, or viewers.
CULTURES Interact with cultural competence and understanding	**Relating Cultural Practices to Perspectives:** Learners use the language to investigate, explain, and reflect on the relationship between the practices and perspectives of the cultures studied.	**Relating Cultural Products to Perspectives:** Learners use the language to investigate, explain, and reflect on the relationship between the products and perspectives of the cultures studied.	
CONNECTIONS Connect with other disciplines and acquire information and diverse perspectives in order to use the language to function in academic and careerrelated situations	**Making Connections:** Learners build, reinforce, and expand their knowledge of other disciplines while using the language to develop critical thinking and to solve problems creatively.	**Acquiring Information and Diverse Perspectives:** Learners access and evaluate information and diverse perspectives that are available through the language and its cultures.	
COMPARISONS Develop insight into the nature of language and culture in order to interact with cultural competence	**Language Comparisons:** Learners use the language to investigate, explain, and reflect on the nature of language through comparisons of the language studied and their own.	**Cultural Comparisons:** Learners use the language to investigate, explain, and reflect on the concept of culture through comparisons of the cultures studied and their own.	
COMMUNITIES Communicate and interact with cultural competence in order to participate in multilingual communities at home and around the world	**School and Global Communities:** Learners use the language both within and beyond the classroom to interact and collaborate in their community and the globalized world.	**Lifelong Learning:** Learners set goals and reflect on their progress in using languages for enjoyment, enrichment, and advancement.	

The National Standards Collaborative Board. (2015). *World-readiness Standards for Learning Languages*. 4th ed. Alexandria, VA: Author.

Essential Features

SELF-ASSESSMENT

Learners maintain an online ***Mon dossier*** to self-assess, reflect, and upload evidence for each Can-Do statement displayed alongside activities in the Student Edition. Building their collections of artifacts allows learners to form vital habits leading them to efficiently continue learning beyond the classroom.

INTERCULTURALITY INTERCULTURALITY

Interculturality is at the heart of EntreCultures

AUTHENTICITY

With ***EntreCultures***, learners explore and compare Francophone communities to their own communities. Video blogs created by native speakers allow learners to compare their lives with those of their peers. Activities and assessments are based on authentic sources and set in real-life thematic and cultural contexts.

PERFORMANCE-BASED ASSESSMENT

Units include performance-based formative assessments, ***J'avance***, which solidify culturally appropriate communication skills relating to learners' communities. ***J'y arrive***, summative integrated performance assessments, engage learners in global intercultural contexts. Analytic rubrics that include intercultural and communicative learning targets accompany summative assessments.

Our vision is a world where language learning takes place through the lens of interculturality, so students can discover appropriate ways to interact with others whose perspectives may be different from their own.

RESOURCES FOR TEACHERS AND STUDENTS

The online **Explorer** provides all audio/video resources; scaffolding for Student Edition activities; vocabulary and grammar reinforcement, including flipped classroom videos; additional activities; formative and summative assessments; rubrics; and other teacher resources.

Appendices

In the Teacher Edition, you are provided with audio and audiovisual transcripts for authentic resources, answer keys, instructional strategies, Can-Do statements for each unit, and rubrics. Indices include a Grammar and Learning Strategies Videos Index as well as an index of grammatical concepts. All glossaries are also included in the program.

EntreCultures Mission and Vision

EntreCultures is a three-level, standards-based, thematically-organized program consisting of six in-depth units per level that provide learners with opportunities to interact and engage with authentic materials and adolescent speakers of the language. By learning in an intercultural context, students acquire communication skills and content knowledge while exploring the products, practices, and perspectives of French-speaking cultures.

EntreCultures Mission

EntreCultures aims to prepare learners to communicate, explore, and connect across cultures in order to foster attitudes of mutual understanding and respect.

EntreCultures Vision

Our vision is a world where language learning takes place through the lens of interculturality, so students can discover appropriate ways to interact with others whose perspectives may be different from their own.

Welcome to *EntreCultures 2*

Dear students,

Bienvenue à ***EntreCultures 2***!

In today's world, we all live *entre cultures*: that is, we all live around and among people and influences from a variety of cultures. As we live, learn, work and play in our communities and abroad, we interact in person and online with people whose experiences and perspectives may be different from our own.

The learning materials in the ***EntreCultures*** program were designed to help you communicate in French, and to develop the attitudes and habits of mind to interact appropriately with French speakers, respecting differences and recognizing the many things we share as human beings.

We are excited that you have decided to continue your discovery of French and the Francophone world. We hope that your journey will be a fun one as you continue to build upon your ability to communicate interculturally in French. *Bonne continuation!*

Elizabeth Zwanziger

Florence Falloux

Erin Gibbons

Jan Hagedorn

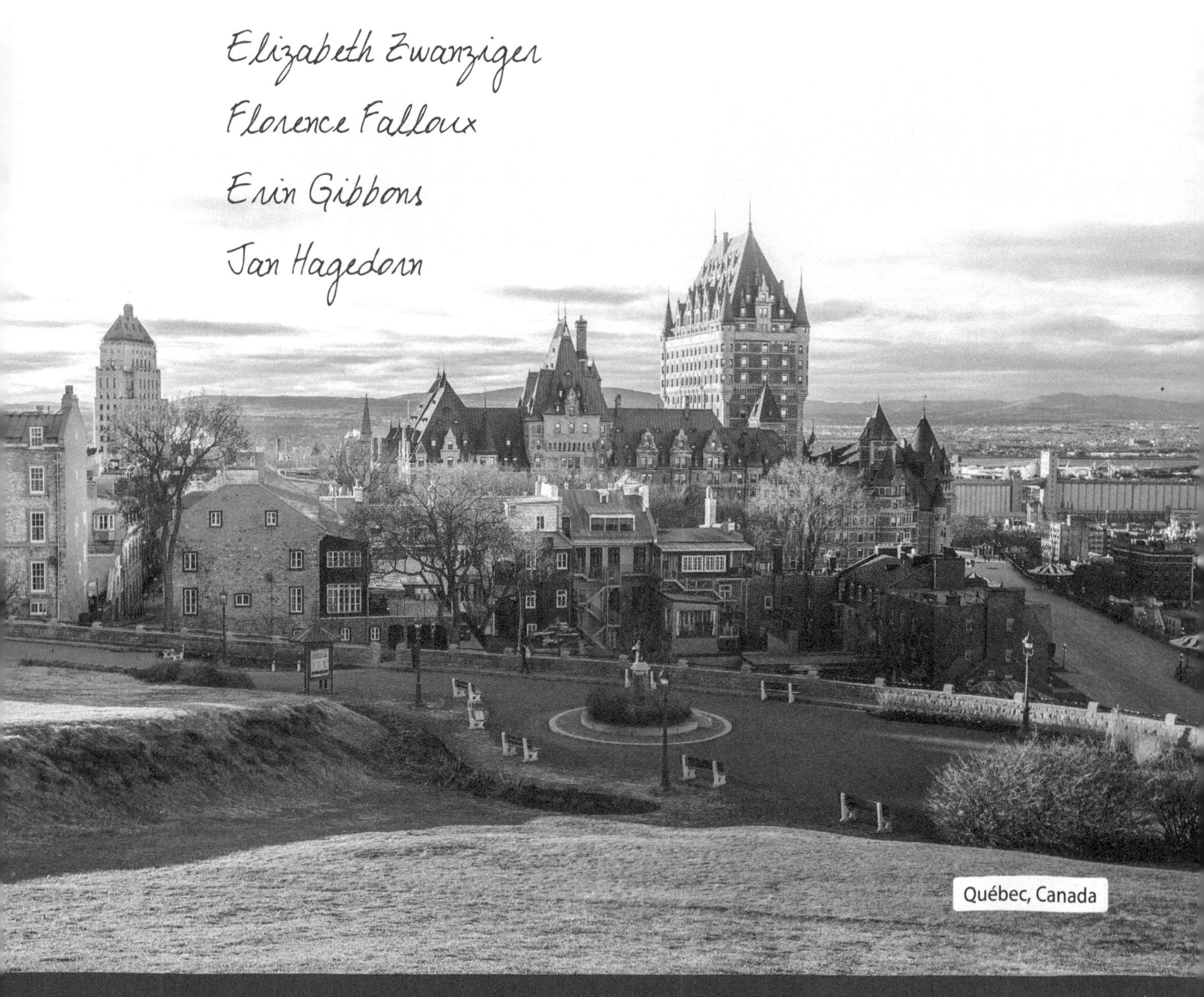

Québec, Canada

Unit Organization

Éléments supplémentaires

Prononciation
Détail grammatical
Détail linguistique
Rappel
Stratégies

Rencontre interculturelle

Rappelle-toi

Comment dit-on? 1
Expressions utiles
On peut aussi dire

Découvrons 1
- **Zoom culture**
  Connexions
  Réflexions
- **Réflexion interculturelle**
- **Mon progrès**
  Communicatif
  Interculturel

J'avance 1

Comment dit-on? 2
On peut aussi dire
Expressions utiles

Découvrons 2
- **Zoom culture**
  Connexions
  Réflexions
- **Réflexion interculturelle**
- **Mon progrès**
  Communicatif
  Interculturel

J'avance 2

Comment dit-on? 3
On peut aussi dire
Expressions utiles

Découvrons 3
- **Zoom culture**
  Connexions
  Réflexions
- **Réflexion interculturelle**
- **Mon progrès**
  Communicatif
  Interculturel

J'avance 3

J'y arrive!

Introduction to a Unit

 **Explorer**

EntreCultures 2 Explorer resources include video blogs, audio/video authentic resources, vocabulary, grammar and learning strategies videos, additional vocabulary practice, discussion forums, and more. You will collect evidence of growth in ***Mon dossier*** in Explorer, as well.

Objectifs de l'unité

Review learning targets for interpretive, interpersonal, and presentational communication as well as intercultural learning.

Questions essentielles

Connect day-to-day learning to bigger questions.

Rencontre interculturelle

Start with interculturality.

Rappelle-toi

Review previously learned material to activate background knowledge.

Communiquons

Integrate language and culture to communicate.

UNITÉ 1

C'est la rentré

Objectifs de l'unité

Exchange information about academic and extracurricular offerings at your school and schools in Francophone cultures.

Read, view, and listen to information about a variety of schools in Francophone cultures to draw comparisons with your own.

Present your school to a visiting student from a Francophone culture while giving advice on how to be successful in your school.

Investigate how schools in a Francophone culture promote learning and student involvement.

4

Questions essentielles

How do personal preferences and traits influence our choices in school?

What helps students engage in their school community?

What do schools in different cultural contexts provide to meet the needs of their students?

When you meet young people who speak French, you will want to talk about the classes and activities you do at school. In this unit, Lou-Ann will share her school experiences in ***la Réunion*** through her video blogs. Learning about schools and education in other cultures will help you welcome new students to your school and community.

UNITÉ 1 5

Comment dit-on?

Begin with the essential vocabulary chunks.

J'avance Formative Assessments

Check progress after each unit section.

Synthèse de grammaire et vocabulaire

Review the language needed.

J'y arrive

Apply learning in the final assessment.

Rencontre interculturelle/Interculturality

Rencontre interculturelle

You will be introduced to the Francophone world with the assistance of our teen video bloggers.

Blogger videos are available in Explorer.

UNITÉ 2 | À table!

Rencontre interculturelle

La Belgique

Nom: Maxime

Langues parlées: français, néerlandais, anglais

Origine: Floriffoux et Mornimont, Belgique

La Belgique a trois langues officielles: le néerlandais, le français et l'allemand. La plupart du pays est divisée en une région francophone (la Wallonie) et une région flamande (la Flandre ou Vlaanderen en néerlandais). La Belgique est aussi un des six pays fondateurs de l'Union européenne. Bruxelles, la capitale de la Belgique, est une ville importante dans l'Union européenne. On y trouve le Conseil européen et la Commission européenne.

La Belgique est un pays riche en traditions. On peut voir de l'architecture médiévale dans beaucoup de villes et il y a des festivals traditionnels comme le carnaval de Binche (qui ressemble un peu au Mardi Gras de la Louisiane aux États-Unis). Les gaufres sont une spécialité culinaire belge qui date du Moyen Âge. On fait du chocolat en Belgique depuis le dix-septième (17e) siècle.

La citadelle de Namur et la rivière Sambre

58

Rencontre interculturelle | UNITÉ 2

Les "Gilles", un costume traditionnel du carnaval de Binche

Voici Philippe, le roi des Belges, et la reine Mathilde. La Belgique est une monarchie constitutionnelle où il y a un roi mais également un gouvernement parlementaire.

Les drapeaux de l'Union européenne devant la Commission européenne à Bruxelles

Voilà comment on faisait des gaufres dans le passé!

UNITÉ 2 | Rencontre interculturelle 59

Rencontre interculturelle | UNITÉ 1

phrases de Lou-Ann	préférences	origines	nom
Je m'appelle Lou-Ann.			
Je vis sur l'île de la Réunion.			
J'adore étudier les mathématiques.			
J'aime beaucoup parler anglais.			
Information supplémentaire:			

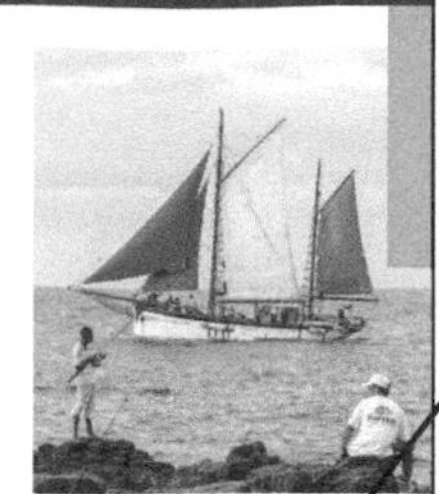

La côte de Saint-Paul à l'île de la Réunion

Étape 2: Écouter

Écoutez la vidéo de Lou-Ann. Levez la main quand Lou-Ann dit les quatre phrases de l'**Étape 1**.

Étape 3: Écrire

Écoutez et regardez la vidéo encore une fois. Puis, écrivez deux phrases avec des informations supplémentaires sur la vie scolaire de Lou-Ann qui ne sont pas mentionnées dans les **Étapes 1** et **2**.

Étape 4: Parler et comparer

Avez-vous les mêmes préférences que Lou-Ann? Formez un groupe avec trois ou quatre élèves.

a. Comparez les similarités et les différences entre vos opinions sur les cours.

b. Partagez vos réponses avec la classe.

Modèle

Lou-Ann vit sur l'île de la Réunion. Je ne vis pas à la Réunion.

Lou-Ann adore étudier les mathématiques. Moi aussi, j'adore étudier les maths!

Le cirque de Mafate, île de la Réunion

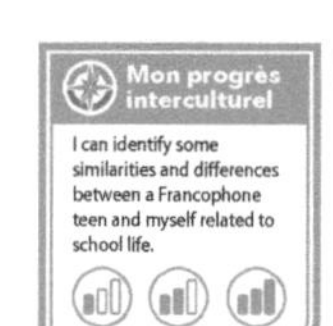

Réflexion interculturelle

What did you notice in the video about Lou-Ann's preferences at school? Are her preferences similar to or different from yours? Which aspects of her school life in ***la Réunion*** (e.g., schedules, classes, and activities) are similar to your school life? Which aspects are different? Answer the questions in the discussion forum in Explorer.

UNITÉ 1 | Rencontre interculturelle

Réflexion interculturelle

After a variety of experiences with cultural products, practices, and perspectives, you will reflect on your growing intercultural awareness.

You will share reflections in an Explorer discussion forum.

Mon progrès interculturel

This unique self-assessment feature makes intercultural goals explicit to you.

You will provide evidence of growth in ***Mon dossier*** in Explorer.

Communiquons | UNITÉ 1

Zoom culture

Pratique culturelle: La filière scolaire

Connexion

How do you choose which classes you will take each year? Which classes are already decided for you?

In France and the ***DROMs***, prior to their final two years, students' courses are mostly decided for them by the ***Ministère de l'éducation nationale***. During ***1re*** and ***terminale***, all students must take ***français, philosophie, histoire-géo, enseignement moral et civique,*** two ***langues vivantes, EPS,*** and ***humanités scientifiques et numériques***. However, students in these last two years of ***lycée*** get to choose from among ten ***disciplines de spécialité***.

The two ***spécialités*** a student chooses dictate parts of the ***baccalauréat***, which is the exit exam that determines if and where students can enroll in higher education. ***Les bacheliers*** are also required to pass tests in ***français, philosophie,*** and an oral exam. (***Le brevet*** is a comparable exam between ***collège*** and ***lycée***).

Réflexion

How do students' goals after high school determine the academic choices they make?

Réflexion interculturelle

Les cours obligatoires

Does your school offer the same classes as other schools in your area? What are your graduation requirements? Are they the same or different from other schools in your area? Search online to find the answers to these questions about your own culture.

Answer the questions in the discussion forum in Explorer.

UNITÉ 1 Communiquons | Comment dit-on? 1 23

Zoom culture

Knowing about cultural products, practices, and perspectives lays a foundation for intercultural reflections.

You will share reflections in the Explorer discussion forum.

Vocabulaire

Comment dit-on?

Essential vocabulary is presented visually in manageable chunks and authentic contexts.

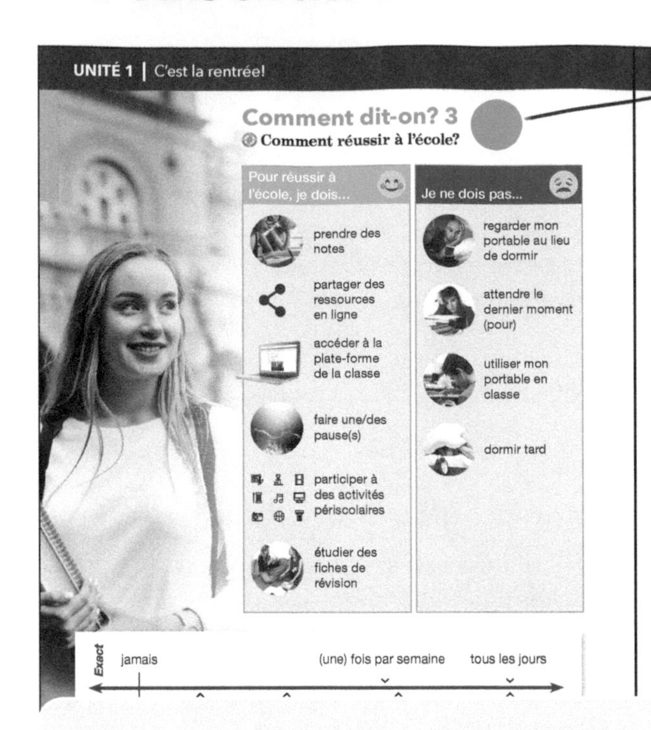

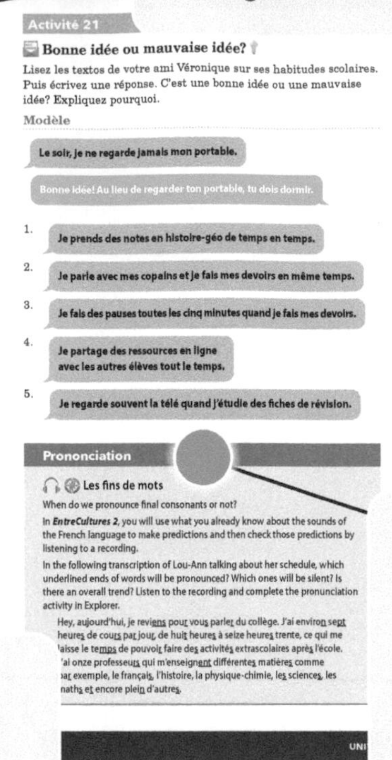

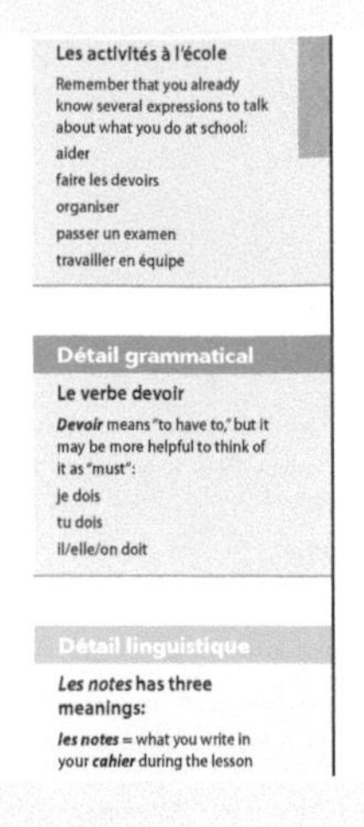

Prononciation

You will learn about sounds that occur in French and listen to them being modeled by a native speaker.

Pronunciation recordings and activities are available in Explorer.

For every vocabulary section, there are ***activités supplémentaires*** in Explorer which provide extra practice, if needed or desired. You do not need to complete all of these activities to be successful on ***J'avance*** or ***J'y arrive*** assessments.

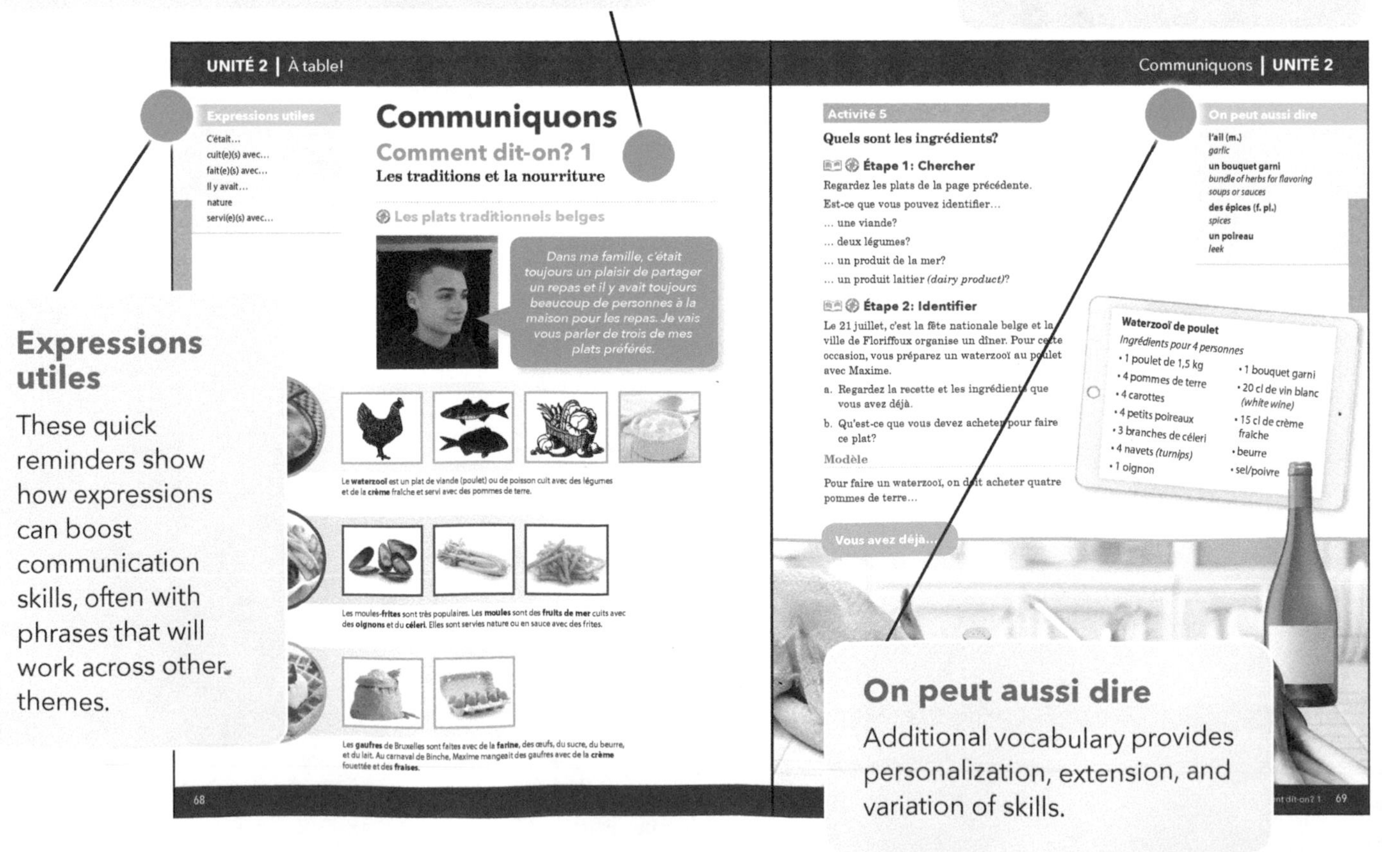

Expressions utiles

These quick reminders show how expressions can boost communication skills, often with phrases that will work across other themes.

On peut aussi dire

Additional vocabulary provides personalization, extension, and variation of skills.

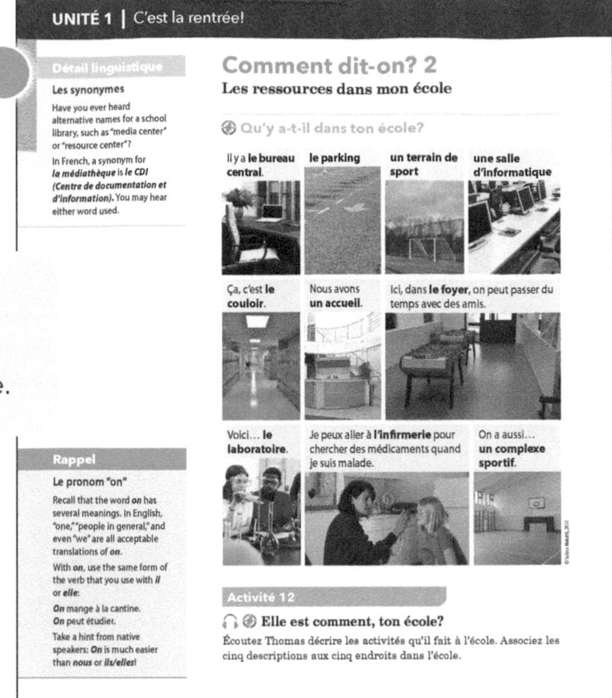

UNITÉ 1 | C'est la rentrée!

Détail linguistique

Les synonymes

Have you ever heard alternative names for a school library, such as "media center" or "resource center"?

In French, a synonym for *la médiathèque* is *le CDI (Centre de documentation et d'information)*. You may hear either word used.

Comment dit-on? 2

Les ressources dans mon école

Qu'y a-t-il dans ton école?

Il y a **le bureau central**. **le parking** **un terrain de sport** **une salle d'informatique**

Ça, c'est **le couloir**. Nous avons **un accueil**. Ici, dans **le foyer**, on peut passer du temps avec des amis.

Voici… **le laboratoire**. Je peux aller à **l'infirmerie** pour chercher des médicaments quand je suis malade. On a aussi… **un complexe sportif**.

Rappel

Le pronom "on"

Recall that the word *on* has several meanings. In English, "one," "people in general," and even "we" are all acceptable translations of *on*.

With *on*, use the same form of the verb that you use with *il* or *elle*:

On mange à la cantine.
On peut étudier.

Take a hint from native speakers: *On* is much easier than *nous* or *ils/elles*!

Activité 12

Elle est comment, ton école?

Écoutez Thomas décrire les activités qu'il fait à l'école. Associez les cinq descriptions aux cinq endroits dans l'école.

28

Détail linguistique

You will explore curious and useful details of the language.

Stratégies

Learning Strategies are briefly explained in the book.

All Learning Strategies videos from all three levels are available in Explorer.

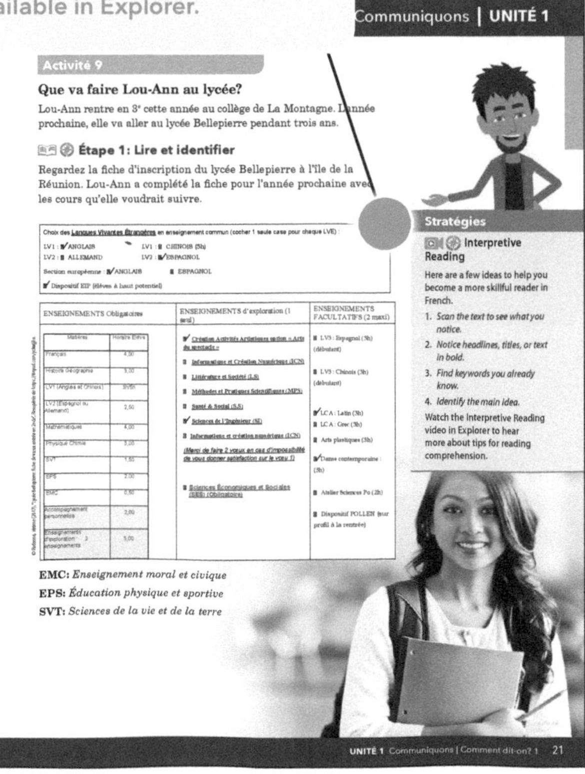

Communiquons | UNITÉ 1

Activité 9

Que va faire Lou-Ann au lycée?

Lou-Ann rentre en 3e cette année au collège de La Montagne. L'année prochaine, elle va aller au lycée Bellepierre pendant trois ans.

Étape 1: Lire et identifier

Regardez la fiche d'inscription du lycée Bellepierre à l'île de la Réunion. Lou-Ann a complété la fiche pour l'année prochaine avec les cours qu'elle voudrait suivre.

EMC: *Enseignement moral et civique*
EPS: *Éducation physique et sportive*
SVT: *Sciences de la vie et de la terre*

Stratégies

Interpretive Reading

Here are a few ideas to help you become a more skillful reader in French.

1. *Scan the text to see what you notice.*
2. *Notice headlines, titles, or text in bold.*
3. *Find keywords you already know.*
4. *Identify the main idea.*

Watch the Interpretive Reading video in Explorer to hear more about tips for reading comprehension.

UNITÉ 1 Communiquons | Comment dit-on? 1 21

Vocabulaire

These lists summarize the vocabulary studied in the unit.

You will find more practice in context in Explorer.

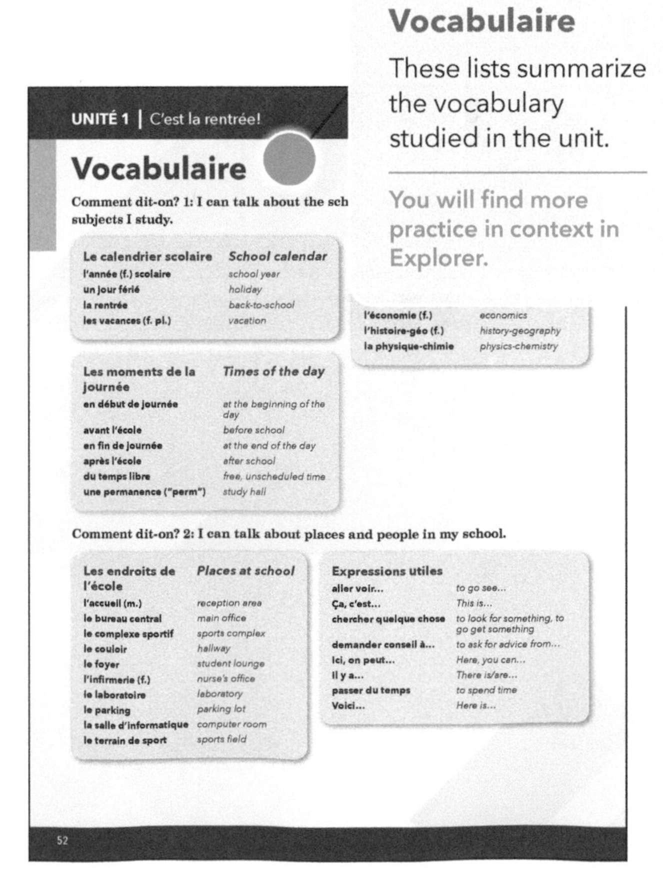

UNITÉ 1 | C'est la rentrée!

Vocabulaire

Comment dit-on? 1: I can talk about the sch… subjects I study.

Le calendrier scolaire	School calendar
l'année (f.) scolaire	school year
un jour férié	holiday
la rentrée	back-to-school
les vacances (f. pl.)	vacation

l'économie (f.)	economics
l'histoire-géo (f.)	history-geography
la physique-chimie	physics-chemistry

Les moments de la journée	Times of the day
en début de journée	at the beginning of the day
avant l'école	before school
en fin de journée	at the end of the day
après l'école	after school
du temps libre	free, unscheduled time
une permanence ("perm")	study hall

Comment dit-on? 2: I can talk about places and people in my school.

Les endroits de l'école	Places at school
l'accueil (m.)	reception area
le bureau central	main office
le complexe sportif	sports complex
le couloir	hallway
le foyer	student lounge
l'infirmerie (f.)	nurse's office
le laboratoire	laboratory
le parking	parking lot
la salle d'informatique	computer room
le terrain de sport	sports field

Expressions utiles	
aller voir…	to go see…
Ça, c'est…	This is…
chercher quelque chose	to look for something, to go get something
demander conseil à…	to ask for advice from…
Ici, on peut…	Here, you can…
Il y a…	There is/are…
passer du temps	to spend time
Voici…	Here is…

52

Rappelle-toi

Rappelle-toi
Use familiar vocabulary in context before learning new material.

Rappel
Quick reminders about vocabulary or structures you have seen before.

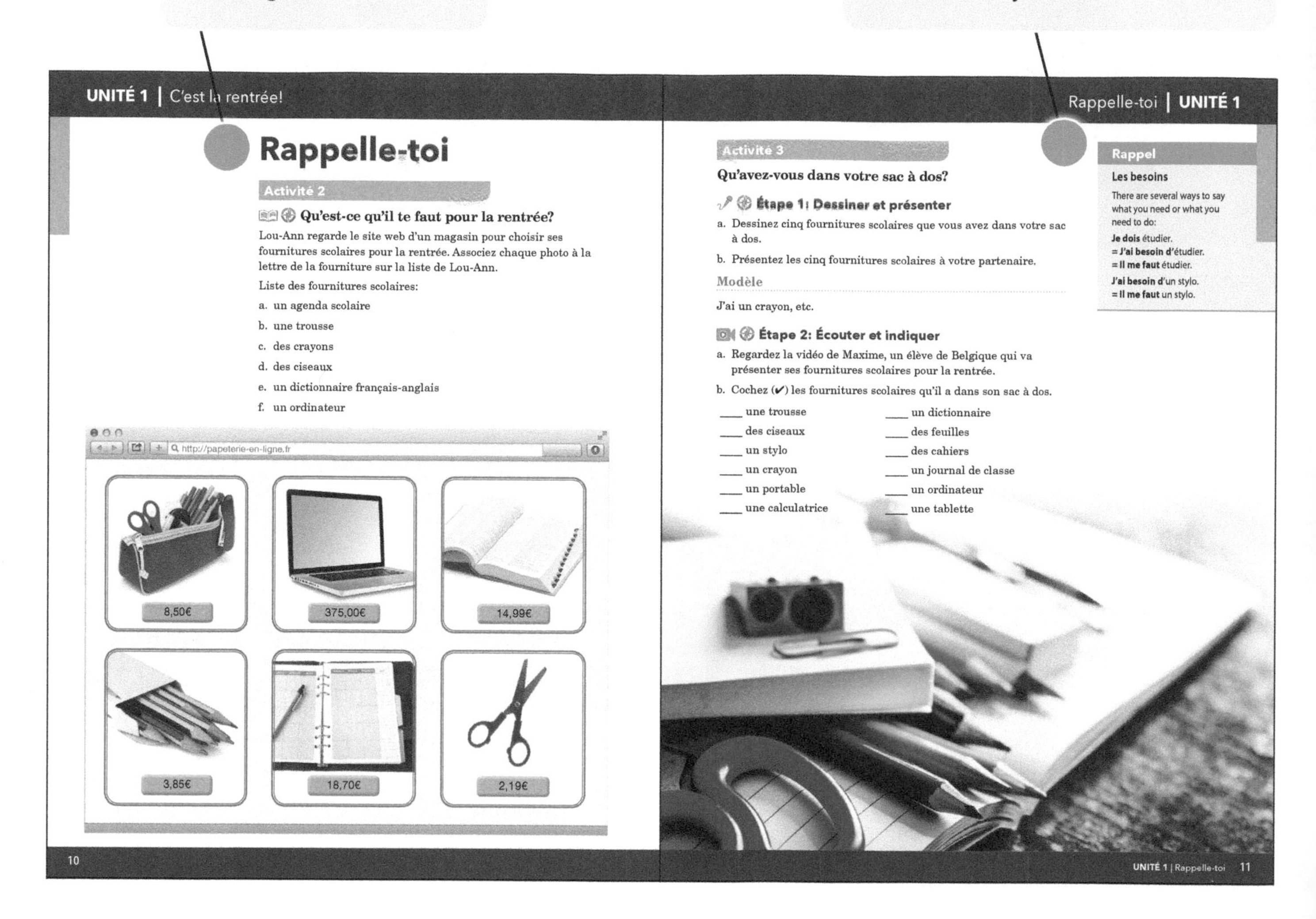

Grammaire

Détail grammatical

Timely grammar details will help you communicate.

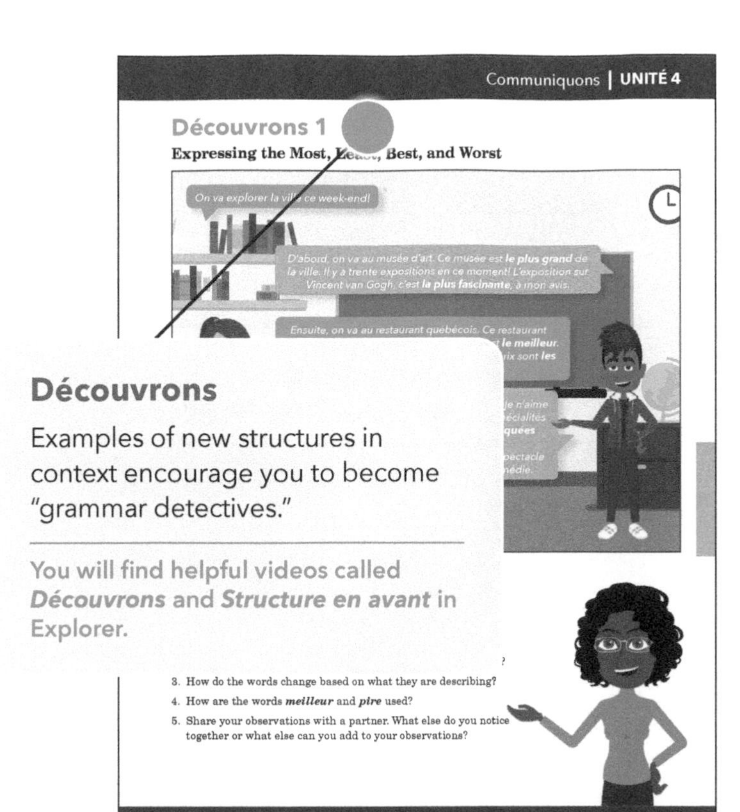

Communiquons | UNITÉ 4

Découvrons 1

Expressing the Most, Least, Best, and Worst

3. How do the words change based on what they are describing?
4. How are the words *meilleur* and *pire* used?
5. Share your observations with a partner. What else do you notice together or what else can you add to your observations?

UNITÉ 4 Communiquons | Découvrons 1 181

Découvrons

Examples of new structures in context encourage you to become "grammar detectives."

You will find helpful videos called ***Découvrons*** and ***Structure en avant*** in Explorer.

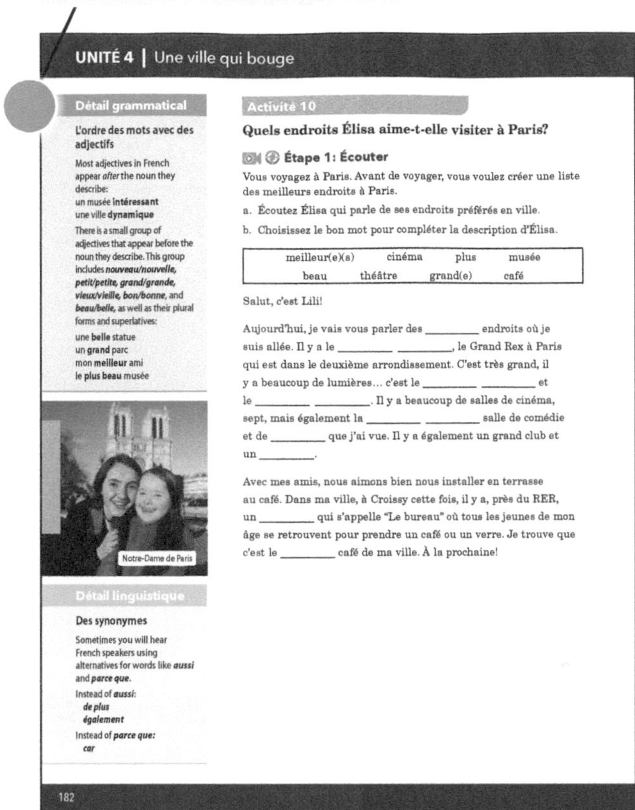

UNITÉ 4 | Une ville qui bouge

Détail grammatical

L'ordre des mots avec des adjectifs

Most adjectives in French appear *after* the noun they describe:
un musée **intéressant**
une ville **dynamique**

There is a small group of adjectives that appear before the noun they describe. This group includes *nouveau/nouvelle, petit/petite, grand/grande, vieux/vieille, bon/bonne,* and *beau/belle,* as well as their plural forms and superlatives:
une **belle** statue
un **grand** parc
mon **meilleur** ami
le **plus beau** musée

Notre-Dame de Paris

Détail linguistique

Des synonymes

Sometimes you will hear French speakers using alternatives for words like *aussi* and *parce que*.

Instead of *aussi*:
de plus
également

Instead of *parce que*:
car

Activité 10

Quels endroits Élisa aime-t-elle visiter à Paris?

Étape 1: Écouter

Vous voyagez à Paris. Avant de voyager, vous voulez créer une liste des meilleurs endroits à Paris.

a. Écoutez Élisa qui parle de ses endroits préférés en ville.
b. Choisissez le bon mot pour compléter la description d'Élisa.

meilleur(e)(s)	cinéma	plus	musée
beau	théâtre	grand(e)	café

Salut, c'est Lili!

Aujourd'hui, je vais vous parler des ________ endroits où je suis allée. Il y a le ________ ________, le Grand Rex à Paris qui est dans le deuxième arrondissement. C'est très grand, il y a beaucoup de lumières... c'est le ________ ________ et le ________ ________. Il y a beaucoup de salles de cinéma, sept, mais également la ________ ________ salle de comédie et de ________ que j'ai vue. Il y a également un grand club et un ________.

Avec mes amis, nous aimons bien nous installer en terrasse au café. Dans ma ville, à Croissy cette fois, il y a, près du RER, un ________ qui s'appelle "Le bureau" où tous les jeunes de mon âge se retrouvent pour prendre un café ou un verre. Je trouve que c'est le ________ café de ma ville. À la prochaine!

182

UNITÉ 1 | C'est la rentrée!

Synthèse de grammaire

1. Expressing Preferences and What You are Going to Do: *préférer/aimer + l'infinitif et le futur proche*

...u like or prefer something, you will use verbs like ...ently followed by another verb. In that case, it is ...at the first verb is conjugated according to the subject ...cond verb remains in its infinitive form, meaning that ...ding.

...çais.

...er de la guitare?

... expressing that something is going to happen soon, in ... *aller* changes according to the subject to convey the ...ing to" happen, but the second verb does not change,

...e *"étudier"*

nous allons étudier
vous allez étudier
ils vont étudier elles vont étudier

...sentence negative, your **ne...pas** will go around the

Je n'aime **pas** lire. Je **ne** vais **pas** étudier.

50

Synthèse de grammaire

This summary contains helpful explanations of grammatical structures.

You will find more practice in context in Explorer.

Synthèse de grammaire | UNITÉ 2

a. Professions: Many words for a person's job have a masculine form and a feminine form. In some cases, the same word will be used regardless of the person's gender.

masculin	*féminin*	*masculin ou féminin*
principal	principa**le**	entraîneur
surveillant	surveillant**e**	documentaliste
infirmier	infirmi**ère**	

Note: Do not forget to choose appropriately between *un/une* and *le/la/l'* when working with words for someone's profession.

b. Adjectives of personality: The same idea will be true for adjectives that describe someone's personality. There are common patterns of changes based on the endings of the words. This almost always changes the pronunciation of the word.

masculin	*féminin*	*masculin ou féminin*
dévoué	dévoué**e**	dynamique
créatif	créati**ve**	énergique
travailleur	travaill**euse**	sympa

3. Comparing How Much or How Often: *le comparatif des noms, des verbes et des adverbes*

When you want to compare how much you do something or how often something happens, you can use comparative structures:

plus — *more*
plus...que — *more...than*
plus de...que — *more (of something) than*

J'étudie **plus** au lycée. — *I study more in high school.*

Although it is possible to use *plus* on its own, your meaning is clearer if you add more information to your sentence.

J'étudie **plus que** mon frère. — *I study more than my brother.*
J'étudie **plus** souvent **que** mon frère. — *I study more often than my brother.*

Notice that the structure follows this pattern:

Item A + **PLUS** + (Expression of frequency) + **QUE** + Item B

If you are comparing how many of something (e.g. *examens, notes, activités*), you will need to add the word *de* before the nouns in the comparison:

J'étudie **plus de** jeux vidéo **que de** livres pour l'école!
I study more video games than school books!

UNITÉ 1 | Synthèse de grammaire 51

For every grammar section, there are ***activités supplémentaires*** in Explorer which provide extra practice, if needed or desired.

Évaluations

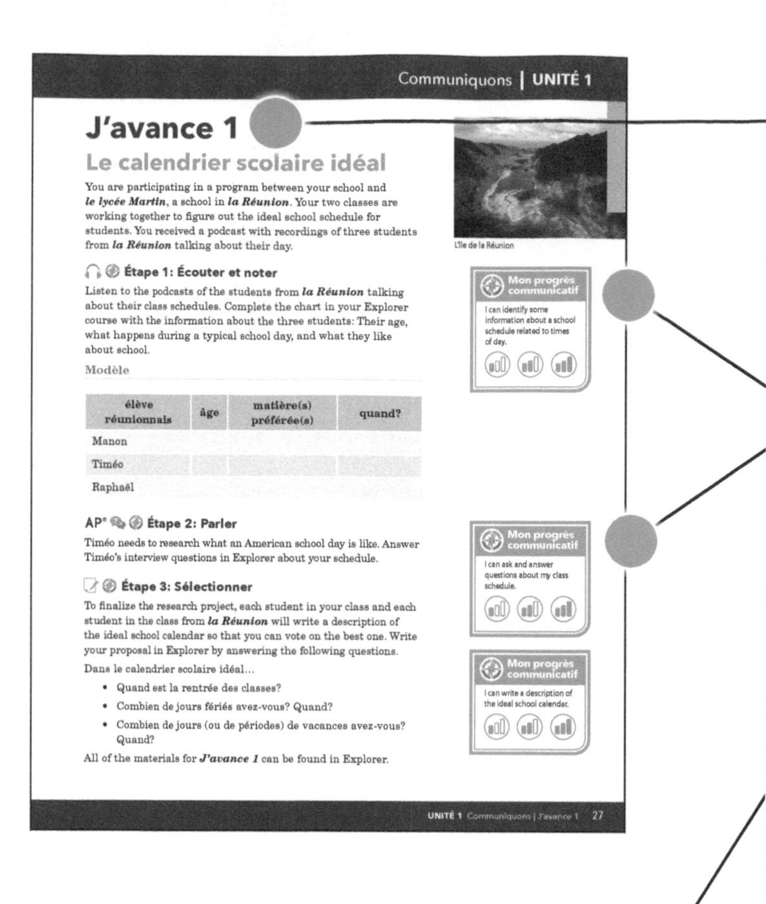

J'avance 1

Le calendrier scolaire idéal

You are participating in a program between your school and ***le lycée Martin***, a school in ***la Réunion***. Your two classes are working together to figure out the ideal school schedule for students. You received a podcast with recordings of three students from ***la Réunion*** talking about their day.

L'île de la Réunion

Étape 1: Écouter et noter

Listen to the podcasts of the students from ***la Réunion*** talking about their class schedules. Complete the chart in your Explorer course with the information about the three students: Their age, what happens during a typical school day, and what they like about school.

Modèle

élève réunionnais	âge	matière(s) préférée(s)	quand?
Manon			
Timéo			
Raphaël			

Mon progrès communicatif
I can identify some information about a school schedule related to times of day.

AP® **Étape 2: Parler**

Timéo needs to research what an American school day is like. Answer Timéo's interview questions in Explorer about your schedule.

Mon progrès communicatif
I can ask and answer questions about my class schedule.

Étape 3: Sélectionner

To finalize the research project, each student in your class and each student in the class from ***la Réunion*** will write a description of the ideal school calendar so that you can vote on the best one. Write your proposal in Explorer by answering the following questions.

Dans le calendrier scolaire idéal…

- Quand est la rentrée des classes?
- Combien de jours fériés avez-vous? Quand?
- Combien de jours (ou de périodes) de vacances avez-vous? Quand?

Mon progrès communicatif
I can write a description of the ideal school calendar.

All of the materials for ***J'avance 1*** can be found in Explorer.

J'avance

Formative assessments measure your progress towards unit goals.

Find supporting materials in Explorer.

Mon progrès communicatif

You will provide evidence of growing proficiency in ***Mon dossier*** in Explorer, which contains all Can-Do statements included throughout the unit.

J'y arrive

A final assessment set in an authentic intercultural context.

Find supporting materials in Explorer.

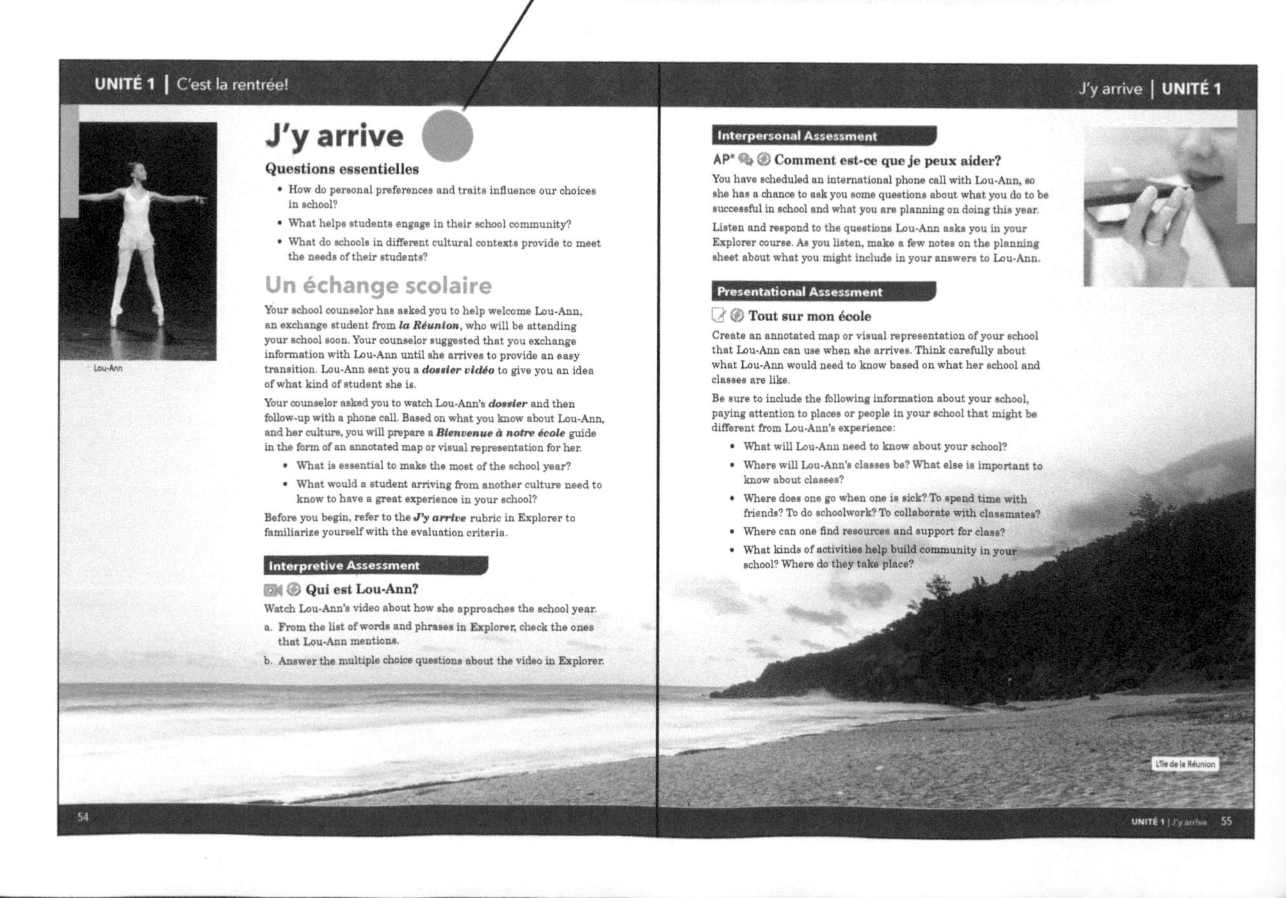

Lou-Ann

J'y arrive

Questions essentielles

- How do personal preferences and traits influence our choices in school?
- What helps students engage in their school community?
- What do schools in different cultural contexts provide to meet the needs of their students?

Un échange scolaire

Your school counselor has asked you to help welcome Lou-Ann, an exchange student from ***la Réunion***, who will be attending your school soon. Your counselor suggested that you exchange information with Lou-Ann until she arrives to provide an easy transition. Lou-Ann sent you a ***dossier vidéo*** to give you an idea of what kind of student she is.

Your counselor asked you to watch Lou-Ann's ***dossier*** and then follow-up with a phone call. Based on what you know about Lou-Ann, and her culture, you will prepare a ***Bienvenue à notre école*** guide in the form of an annotated map or visual representation for her.

- What is essential to make the most of the school year?
- What would a student arriving from another culture need to know to have a great experience in your school?

Before you begin, refer to the ***J'y arrive*** rubric in Explorer to familiarize yourself with the evaluation criteria.

Interpretive Assessment

Qui est Lou-Ann?

Watch Lou-Ann's video about how she approaches the school year.

a. From the list of words and phrases in Explorer, check the ones that Lou-Ann mentions.

b. Answer the multiple choice questions about the video in Explorer.

Interpersonal Assessment

AP® **Comment est-ce que je peux aider?**

You have scheduled an international phone call with Lou-Ann, so she has a chance to ask you some questions about what you do to be successful in school and what you are planning on doing this year.

Listen and respond to the questions Lou-Ann asks you in your Explorer course. As you listen, make a few notes on the planning sheet about what you might include in your answers to Lou-Ann.

Presentational Assessment

Tout sur mon école

Create an annotated map or visual representation of your school that Lou-Ann can use when she arrives. Think carefully about what Lou-Ann would need to know based on what her school and classes are like.

Be sure to include the following information about your school, paying attention to places or people in your school that might be different from Lou-Ann's experience:

- What will Lou-Ann need to know about your school?
- Where will Lou-Ann's classes be? What else is important to know about classes?
- Where does one go when one is sick? To spend time with friends? To do schoolwork? To collaborate with classmates?
- Where can one find resources and support for class?
- What kinds of activities help build community in your school? Where do they take place?

L'île de la Réunion

Explorer®

The online Explorer is the other half of the textbook, connecting students with language learning resources that inspire continued exploration.

Whether learning about Reunion Island through Lou-Ann's video blogs, studying grammar through flipped classroom videos, or updating language learning portfolios with new achievements, students can practice all modes of communication at their own pace and within their own comfort zone.

FlexText®

FlexText® is Wayside's unique e-textbook platform. Built in HTML5, our digital textbook technology automatically adjusts the book pages to whatever screen you are using for optimal viewing.

Your FlexText® can be accessed across all of your devices. And page by page, just like the printed textbook, FlexText® allows students and teachers to use ***EntreCultures*** on the go.

Icons Legend

The icons in this program:

- Indicate the mode of communication;
- Reference the five goal areas as listed in the *World-Readiness Standards for Learning Languages*;
- Provide a signpost where Explorer offers more support; and,
- Prepare teachers and learners for the type of each task/activity.

Linguistic or cultural comparisons

Connections

Communities

Cultures

Interpretive Print

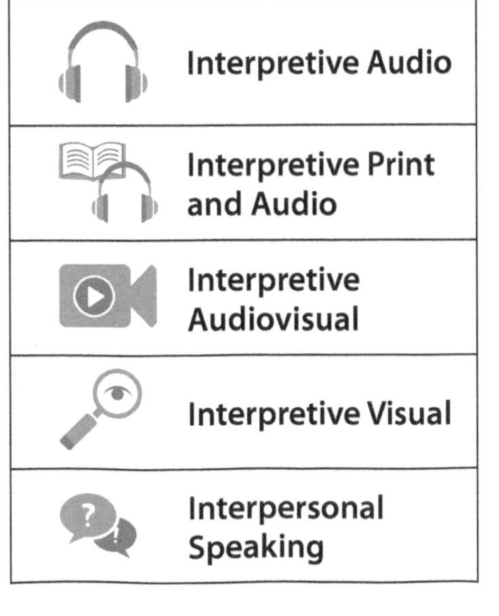

Scavenger Hunt

This scavenger hunt is designed to give you an opportunity to explore the different helpful and interesting features of your ***EntreCultures 2*** text and online Explorer.

What animal is featured on the cover? Investigate the animal's natural habitat.	Identify the focus of the first ***Zoom culture*** in Unit 5.	Find the ***Expressions utiles*** in Unit 5, ***Comment dit-on? 1***. Try your best to pronounce the expressions in French. Write down your favorite one.	What country is the focus of the ***Rencontre interculturelle*** in Unit 2?
Using the table of contents, identify on which page you can find the ***Comment dit-on? 1*** section of Unit 3.	From what country is the video blogger from Unit 6?	What do the icons before Activité 23 in Unit 3 indicate to you? Where did you find your answer?	Find three famous places in Paris from Unit 4.
In Explorer, find the forum for the ***Réflexion interculturelle*** in Unit 2 ***Comment dit-on? 1*** and list a Belgian dish.	Identify a ***Mon progrès communicatif*** in Unit 5. To what activity does it correspond?	In which unit will you learn to communicate how to stay healthy?	How many ***Découvrons*** are there in each unit?
Find an image in the book that you like and research to learn something new about the person or location pictured.	Who is the video blogger for Unit 1? Find and watch the video in Explorer.	In Explorer, find the Découvrons 1 video for Unit 4. What is the topic?	Find the ***Stratégies*** sidebar in Unit 5. What is the title? Head to Explorer to watch the video.

Unité 1: C'est la rentrée!

Objectifs de l'unité

Exchange information about academic and extracurricular offerings at your school and schools in Francophone cultures.

Read, view, and listen to information about a variety of schools in Francophone cultures to draw comparisons with your own.

Present your school to a visiting student from a Francophone culture while giving advice on how to be successful in your school.

Investigate how schools in a Francophone culture promote learning and student involvement.

Questions essentielles

How do personal preferences and traits influence our choices in school?

What helps students engage in their school community?

What do schools in different cultural contexts provide to meet the needs of their students?

Objectifs de l'unité

Exchange information about traditional dishes from Francophone cultures and share memories related to food.

Read, view, and listen to recipes, menus, videos, and invitations related to food in Francophone cultures.

Invite others to events and special meals.

Investigate how food plays an integral part in family, traditions, and celebrations in Francophone cultures.

Questions essentielles

Which culinary traditions of the past are still important today?

How are our memories with the important people in our lives connected to food?

How does food bring people together?

Unité 2: À table!

SUMMATIVE ASSESSMENT

Unité 3: Au boulot, les bénévoles!

Objectifs de l'unité

Read, view, and listen to informational texts such as announcements, videos, and personal stories about household tasks and working as a volunteer.

Negotiate with others to decide on household tasks and a volunteer opportunity.

Provide information about yourself in order to apply to a volunteer organization.

Investigate how and why people in Francophone cultures contribute to their communities through volunteerism.

Questions essentielles

How do my personal responsibilities and routines shape my daily life?

How can community members work together to improve the quality of life for themselves and others?

What kinds of volunteer opportunities exist in the Francophone world? What motivates people from different cultures to volunteer?

Objectifs de l'unité

Read, view, and listen to a variety of sources like brochures, schedules, and online reviews to access information to make plans.

Exchange preferences about places to go for fun in a Francophone city or town.

Describe past events and activities.

Investigate how and where teens in Francophone cultures and in your community enjoy a metropolitan area.

Questions essentielles

What experiences are available to young people in a city or town?

How can I access information to make plans?

How does culture influence where I go and what I do in a Francophone city or town?

Unité 4: Une ville qui bouge

SUMMATIVE ASSESSMENT

Unité 5: Des conseils pour une vie saine

Objectifs de l'unité

Read, view, and listen to informational texts such as websites, infographics, and personal stories about healthy habits.

Discuss with others the ways in which they and others stay healthy.

Research health information in order to make a presentation on adolescent health.

Investigate how people in Francophone cultures maintain their physical as well as social and emotional health.

Questions essentielles

How do people where I live and in Francophone cultures take care of their physical health?

How do people address concerns with their health?

How do people where I live and in Francophone cultures view social and emotional health?

Objectifs de l'unité

Read, view, and listen to informational texts such as announcements, videos, and personal stories about world travel.

Participate in an interview in which you discuss your travel plans.

Provide information about yourself in order to apply for a travel scholarship.

Investigate how and why people travel around the world for more than just tourism.

Questions essentielles

What do I need to know to explore another country or culture?

What is the difference between a tourist and a traveler?

How do travel experiences shape our intercultural understanding and respect for the communities we visit?

Unité 6: Voyager autrement

Ville de Luxembourg, Luxembourg

Bienvenue!

In today's world, we all live ***entre cultures***. Through technology and face-to-face communication, we can interact with people with different cultural backgrounds every day. As you use ***EntreCultures*** you will learn to speak French and explore the cultures of the Francophone world. Everything you learn will help you interact appropriately and respectfully with people whose experiences and perspectives may differ from your own.

Manapany, la Réunion

Éloïse vient de Montréal, Québec, Canada.

Maxime vient de Floriffoux et de Mornimont, Belgique.

Mathew vient de Dijon, France.

Élisa vient de Paris, France.

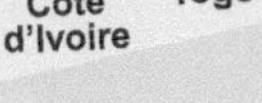

Brenda vient de Yaoundé, Cameroun.

Lou-Ann vient de Saint-Denis, la Réunion.

Meet six young people from around the Francophone world who are inviting you to join them in living ***EntreCultures***.

UNITÉ 1

C'est la rentrée!

Objectifs de l'unité

Exchange information about academic and extracurricular offerings at your school and schools in Francophone cultures.

Read, view, and listen to information about a variety of schools in Francophone cultures to draw comparisons with your own.

Present your school to a visiting student from a Francophone culture while giving advice on how to be successful in your school.

Investigate how schools in a Francophone culture promote learning and student involvement.

Questions essentielles

How do personal preferences and traits influence our choices in school?

What helps students engage in their school community?

What do schools in different cultural contexts provide to meet the needs of their students?

When you meet young people who speak French, you will want to talk about the classes and activities you do at school. In this unit, Lou-Ann will share her school experiences in ***la Réunion*** through her video blogs. Learning about schools and education in other cultures will help you welcome new students to your school and community.

Rencontre interculturelle

L'île de la Réunion

La Réunion est une ancienne colonie française qui est devenue un département et une région d'outre-mer (DROM) en 1946. C'est petit. En un jour, on peut faire le tour de cette île volcanique, et on peut aller nager dans l'océan et escalader la montagne toute l'année!

Nom: Lou-Ann

Langues parlées: français, espagnol, anglais

Origine: la Réunion

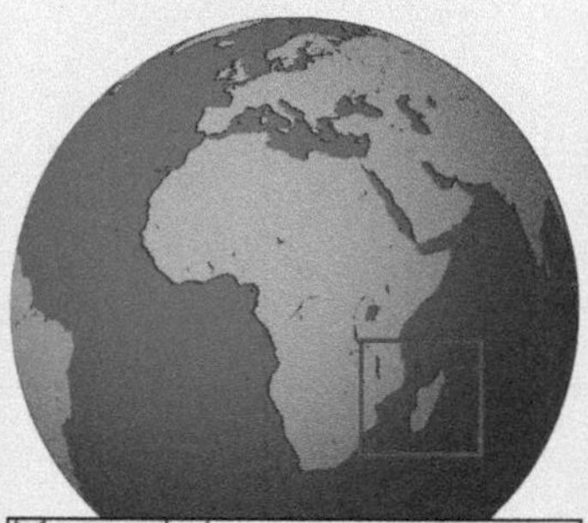

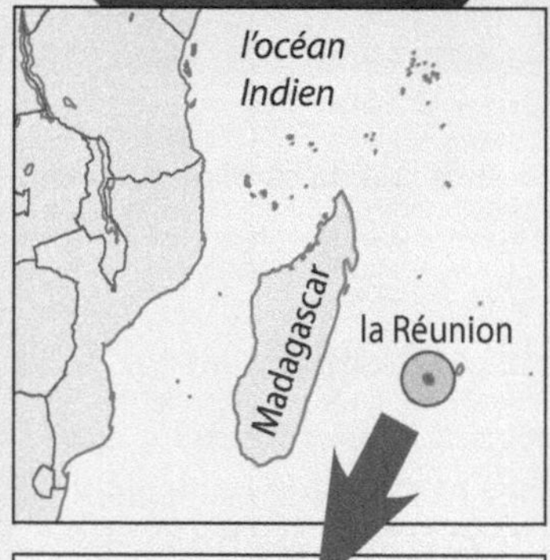

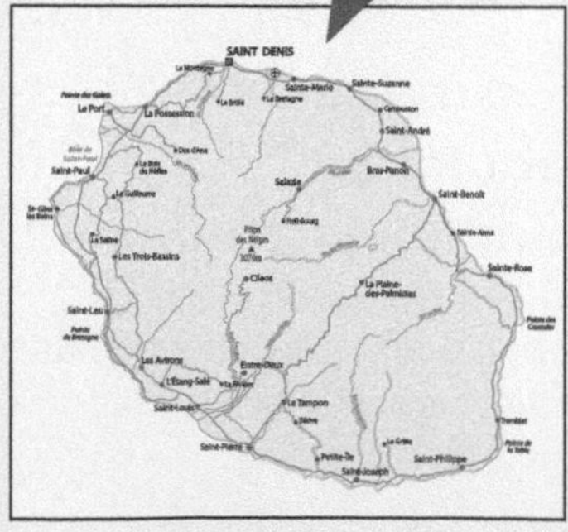

L'île de la Réunion – Département et région d'outre mer

Les Réunionnais ont un passeport de l'Union européenne et les élèves réunionnais suivent le programme de l'Éducation nationale de France; ils doivent passer le diplôme national du brevet (DNB) et le baccalauréat comme les élèves en France.

La plage de l'Hermitage

Le Piton de la Fournaise, le célèbre volcan de la Réunion

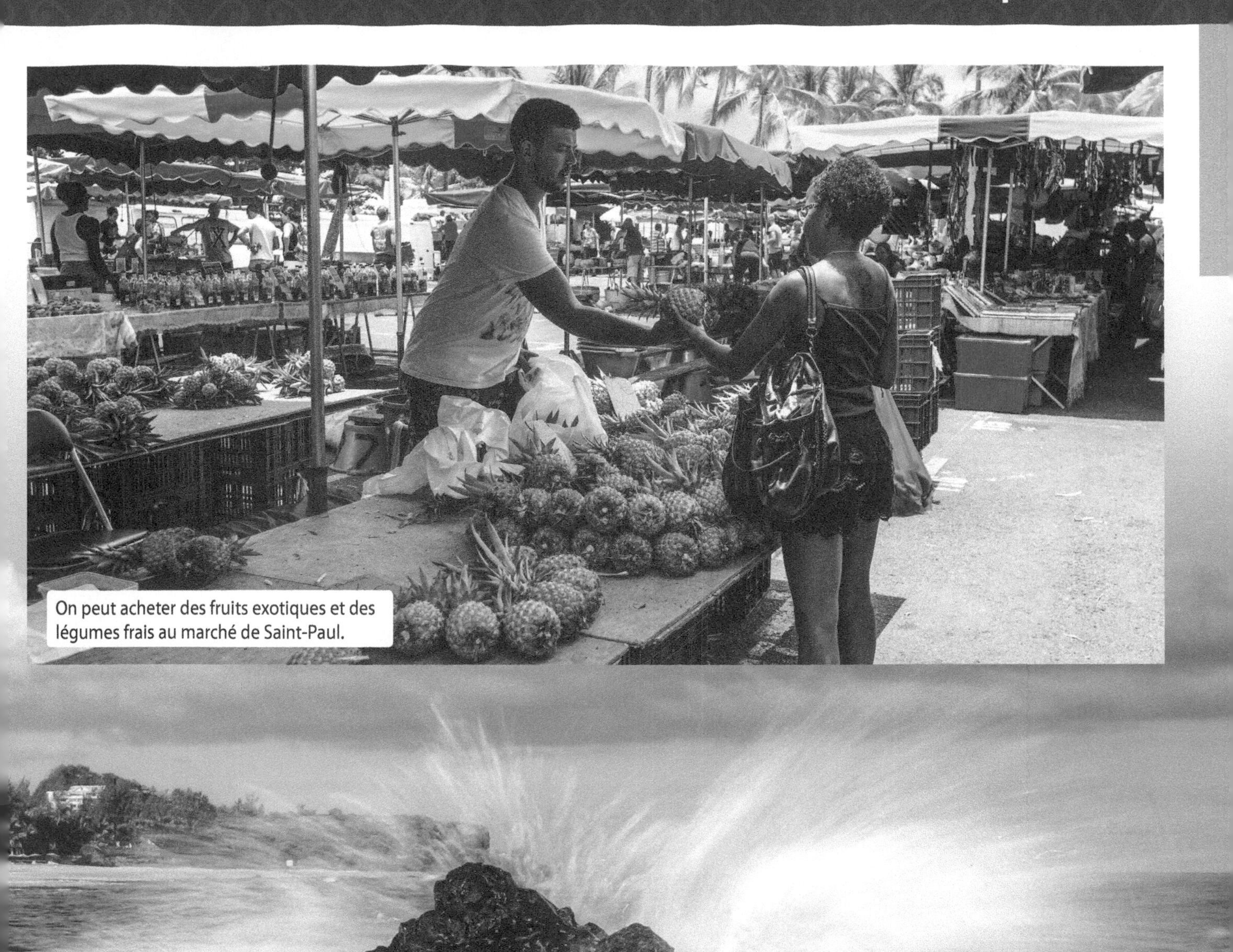

On peut acheter des fruits exotiques et des légumes frais au marché de Saint-Paul.

Je m'appelle Lou-Ann.

J'adore étudier les mathématiques.

Je vis sur l'île de la Réunion.

J'aime beaucoup parler anglais.

Lou-Ann a 13 ans et elle habite la Réunion, une île à l'est de Madagascar, au large du continent africain dans l'océan Indien. Elle vit avec ses parents Karine et Geoffray et sa sœur aînée Léa qui a 15 ans. Elle a aussi un petit chien très mignon qui s'appelle Halia. Lou-Ann est très créative. Elle aime jouer de la guitare et adore l'art, surtout la danse et le théâtre.

Lou-Ann est en 3e (troisième) au collège de La Montagne. Elle a 7 heures de cours par jour, de 8h00 à 16h30. Elle participe aux activités extrascolaires après l'école. Elle a onze professeurs différents! Les matières préférées de Lou-Ann sont l'anglais, les maths et les sciences.

France		USA	
Collège	6e (Sixième)	6th Grade	Middle School
	5e (Cinquième)	7th Grade	
	4e (Quatrième)	8th Grade	
	3e (Troisième)	9th Grade (freshman year)	High School
Lycée	2de (Seconde)	10th Grade (sophomore year)	
	1re (Première)	11th Grade (junior year)	
	Terminale	12th Grade (senior year)	
Faculté / École / Université		University / College	

On peut aussi dire

premier (1er) / première (1re)
first

deuxième (2e)
second

second(e) (2$^{d(e)}$)
second (of two)

troisième (3e)
third

quatrième (4e)
fourth

cinquième (5e)
fifth

sixième (6e)
sixth

septième (7e)
seventh

huitième (8e)
eighth

neuvième (9e)
ninth

dixième (10e)
tenth

onzième (11e)
eleventh

dernier/dernière
last

terminal(e)
last

Activité 1

Bonjour, Lou-Ann!

 **Étape 1: Préparer**

Regardez la photo de Lou-Ann et ce qu'elle dit dans les bulles *(speech bubbles)*. Comprenez-vous ces quatre phrases?

Pour chacune des phrases, indiquez si elle parle de ses préférences, de ses origines ou de son nom. Cochez (✔) la case qui correspond à la catégorie appropriée.

phrases de Lou-Ann	préférences	origines	nom
Je m'appelle Lou-Ann.			
Je vis sur l'île de la Réunion.			
J'adore étudier les mathématiques.			
J'aime beaucoup parler anglais.			
Information supplémentaire:			

La côte de Saint-Paul à l'île de la Réunion

Étape 2: Écouter

Écoutez la vidéo de Lou-Ann. Levez la main quand Lou-Ann dit les quatre phrases de l'**Étape 1**.

Étape 3: Écrire

Écoutez et regardez la vidéo encore une fois. Puis, écrivez deux phrases avec des informations supplémentaires sur la vie scolaire de Lou-Ann qui ne sont pas mentionnées dans les **Étapes 1** et **2**.

Étape 4: Parler et comparer

Avez-vous les mêmes préférences que Lou-Ann? Formez un groupe avec trois ou quatre élèves.

a. Comparez les similarités et les différences entre vos opinions sur les cours.

b. Partagez vos réponses avec la classe.

Modèle

Lou-Ann vit sur l'île de la Réunion. Je ne vis pas à la Réunion.

Lou-Ann adore étudier les mathématiques. Moi aussi, j'adore étudier les maths!

Le cirque de Mafate, île de la Réunion

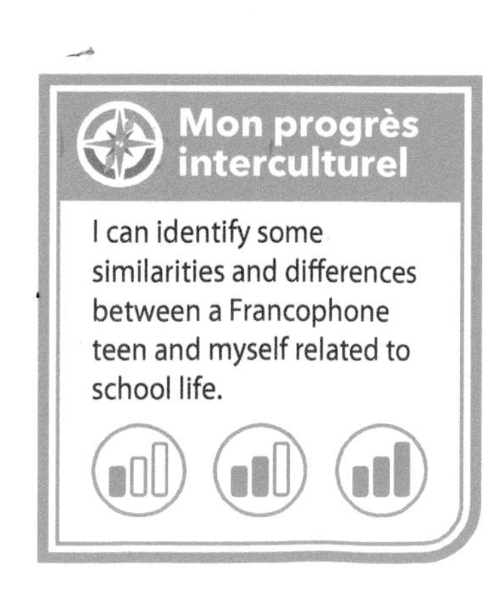

Réflexion interculturelle

What did you notice in the video about Lou-Ann's preferences at school? Are her preferences similar to or different from yours? Which aspects of her school life in ***la Réunion*** (e.g., schedules, classes, and activities) are similar to your school life? Which aspects are different? Answer the questions in the discussion forum in Explorer.

Rappelle-toi

Activité 2

Qu'est-ce qu'il te faut pour la rentrée?

Lou-Ann regarde le site web d'un magasin pour choisir ses fournitures scolaires pour la rentrée. Associez chaque photo à la lettre de la fourniture sur la liste de Lou-Ann.

Liste des fournitures scolaires:

a. un agenda scolaire

b. une trousse

c. des crayons

d. des ciseaux

e. un dictionnaire français-anglais

f. un ordinateur

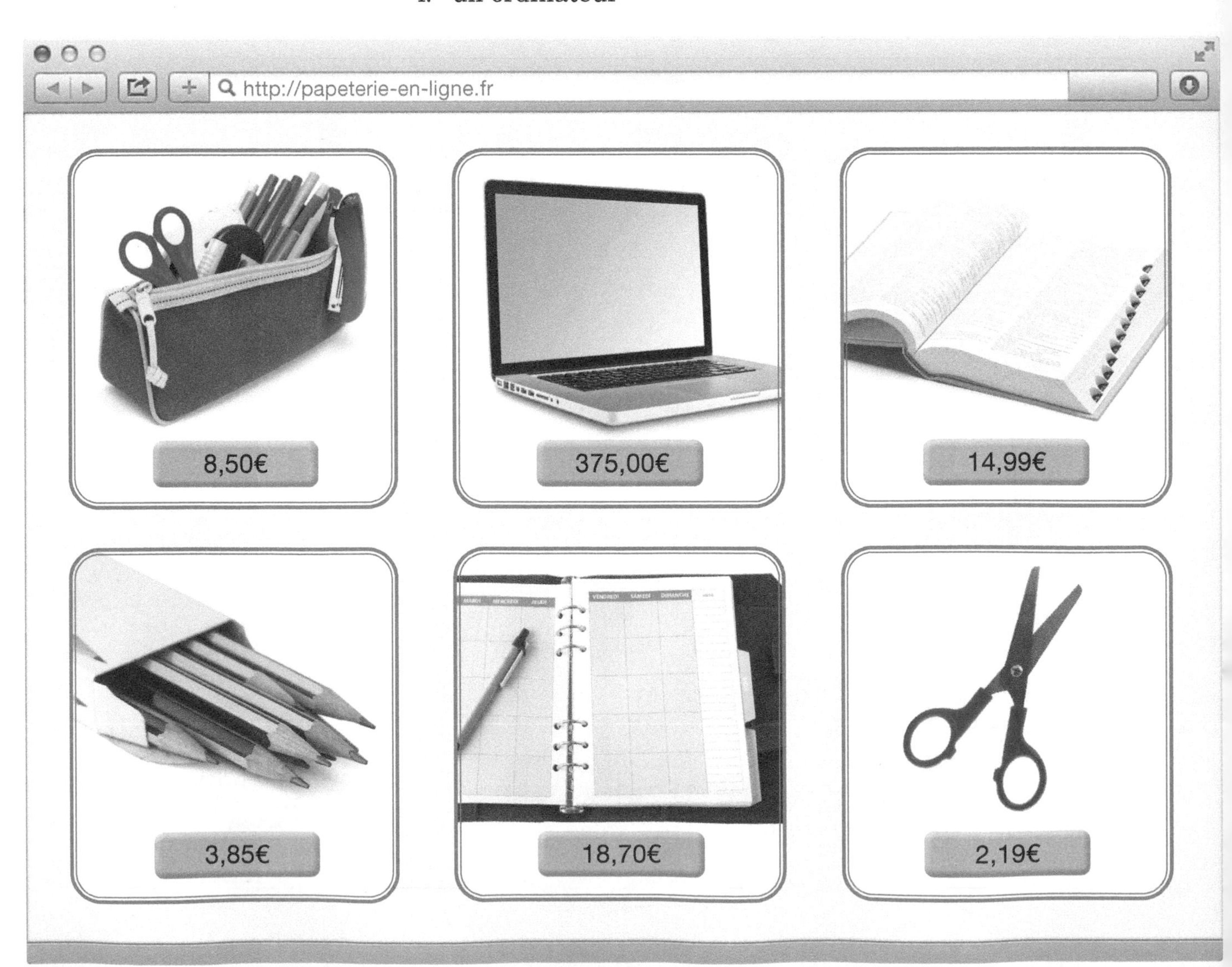

Activité 3

Qu'avez-vous dans votre sac à dos?

Étape 1: Dessiner et présenter

a. Dessinez cinq fournitures scolaires que vous avez dans votre sac à dos.

b. Présentez les cinq fournitures scolaires à votre partenaire.

Modèle

J'ai un crayon, etc.

Étape 2: Écouter et indiquer

a. Regardez la vidéo de Maxime, un élève de Belgique qui va présenter ses fournitures scolaires pour la rentrée.

b. Cochez (✔) les fournitures scolaires qu'il a dans son sac à dos.

____ une trousse
____ des ciseaux
____ un stylo
____ un crayon
____ un portable
____ une calculatrice

____ un dictionnaire
____ des feuilles
____ des cahiers
____ un journal de classe
____ un ordinateur
____ une tablette

Rappel

Les besoins

There are several ways to say what you need or what you need to do:

Je dois étudier.
= **J'ai besoin d'**étudier.
= **Il me faut** étudier.

J'ai besoin d'un stylo.
= **Il me faut** un stylo.

Rappel

Le genre des noms, les articles définis et indéfinis

Remember that nouns in French have a grammatical gender (***masculin*** or ***féminin***). Another aspect of nouns that is important to note is whether they are singular or plural.

	masculin singulier	*féminin singulier*	*pluriel*
a/an/ some	*un*	*une*	*des*
the	*le/l'*	*la/l'*	*les*

Activité 4

Il faut acheter les fournitures scolaires dans un magasin ou sur internet?

Maxime doit acheter d'autres fournitures scolaires pour la rentrée.

Regardez le graphique qui compare le prix des fournitures scolaires dans un magasin et sur internet.

a. Lisez la liste d'achats de Maxime.

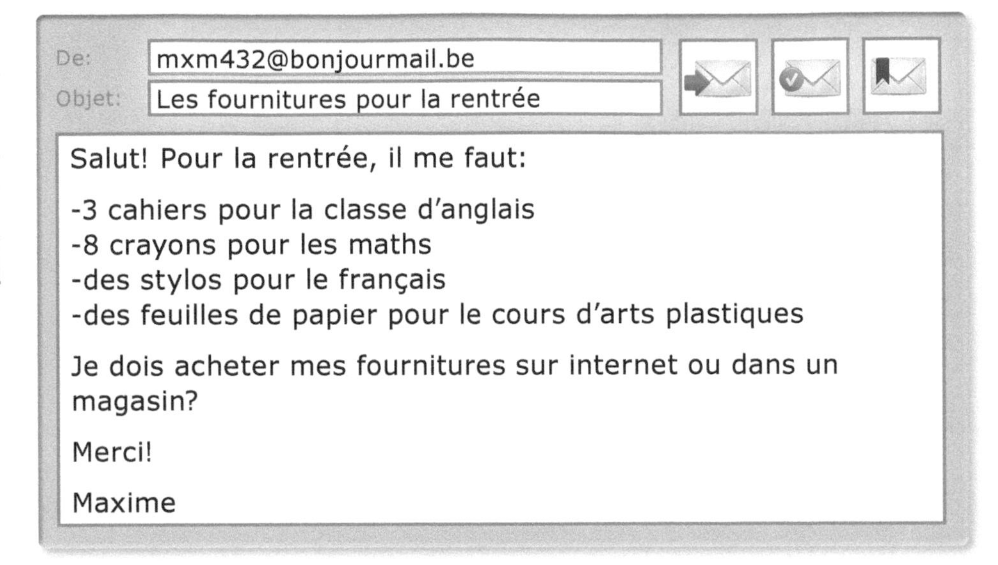

De: mxm432@bonjourmail.be
Objet: Les fournitures pour la rentrée

Salut! Pour la rentrée, il me faut:

-3 cahiers pour la classe d'anglais
-8 crayons pour les maths
-des stylos pour le français
-des feuilles de papier pour le cours d'arts plastiques

Je dois acheter mes fournitures sur internet ou dans un magasin?

Merci!

Maxime

b. Écrivez un e-mail à Maxime. Donnez des suggestions pour les fournitures sur sa liste. Il faut acheter quelles fournitures dans un magasin ou sur internet?

c. Calculez le prix total des fournitures.

Modèle

Salut Maxime,

Pour la rentrée, il faut acheter...sur internet et...dans un magasin.

Cela coûte...

Le prix des fournitures cette rentrée scolaire

paire de ciseaux

1,53€

0,80€

paquet de 12 stylos

1,90€

2,10€

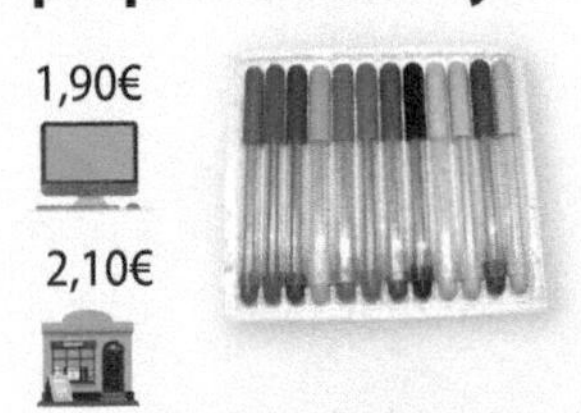

2 crayons

0,25€

0,40€

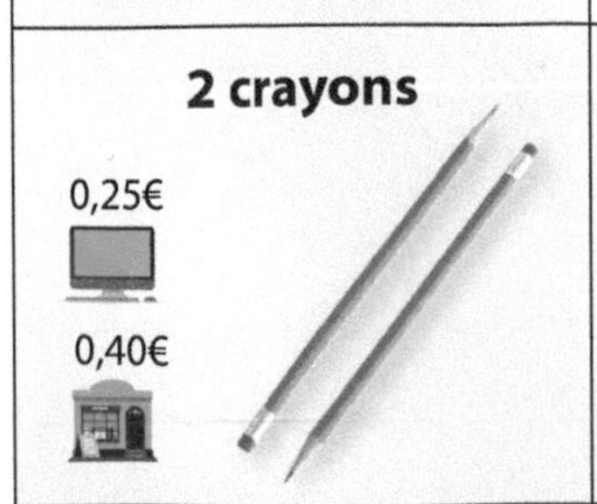

3 cahiers 120 pages

3,75€

3,20€

2 bâtons de colle

1,19€

1,27€

500 feuilles

5,30€

3,90€

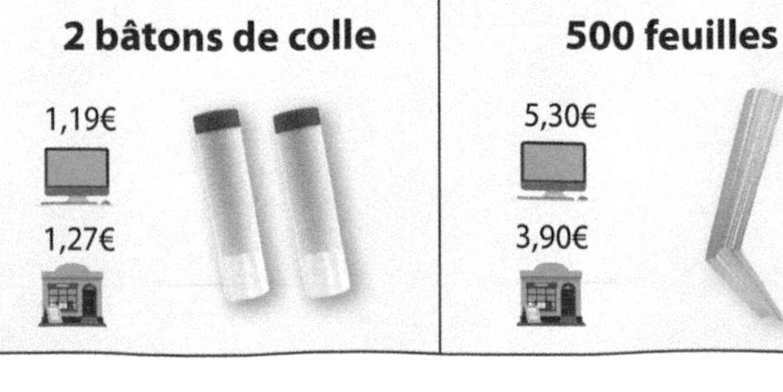

Activité 5

À quelle heure as-tu cours?

Regardez l'emploi du temps des élèves au collège Léopold Sédar Senghor à Ifs en France. Travaillez avec votre partenaire pour répondre aux questions.

<table>
<tr><th></th><th>LUNDI</th><th>MARDI</th><th>MERCREDI</th><th>JEUDI</th><th>VENDREDI</th></tr>
<tr><td>8h20 - 9h15</td><td>Anglais</td><td rowspan="2">Semaine A: SVT
Semaine B: Arts plastiques</td><td>Maths</td><td rowspan="2">Physique</td><td rowspan="2">EPS</td></tr>
<tr><td>9h20 - 10h15</td><td>Français</td><td>Anglais</td></tr>
<tr><td></td><td colspan="5">RÉCRÉATION</td></tr>
<tr><td>10h30 - 11h30</td><td>Français</td><td>Musique</td><td>Semaine A: Vie de classe
Semaine B: SVT</td><td>Histoire-Géo</td><td>Anglais</td></tr>
<tr><td>11h30 - 12h30</td><td>Repas</td><td>Repas</td><td>Maths</td><td>Espagnol</td><td>Espagnol</td></tr>
<tr><td>12h45 - 13h45</td><td rowspan="2">Histoire-Géo</td><td rowspan="2">Semaine A: Histoire ou Français
Semaine B: EPS</td><td></td><td>Repas</td><td>Repas</td></tr>
<tr><td>13h45 - 14h45</td><td></td><td></td><td>Maths</td></tr>
<tr><td></td><td colspan="2">RÉCRÉATION</td><td></td><td colspan="2">RÉCRÉATION</td></tr>
<tr><td>15h00 - 16h00</td><td rowspan="2">Technologie</td><td>Espagnol</td><td></td><td rowspan="2">Espagnol</td><td>Maths</td></tr>
<tr><td>16h00 - 17h00</td><td>Français</td><td></td><td>Français</td></tr>
</table>

fr.slideshare.net/phmorin/prsentation-du-collge-senghor-ifs.

1. Ils ont quel cours le vendredi à 8h20?
2. Ils ont quel cours le mardi et le jeudi à 15h?
3. Ils ont musique à quelle heure?
4. Ils ont maths à quelle heure?
5. Les élèves étudient combien de langues?
6. Les élèves mangent à quelle heure?

Rappelle-toi

Les fournitures scolaires
l'agenda (m.) scolaire
le cahier
la calculatrice
les ciseaux (m. pl.)
le classeur
le crayon
le dictionnaire
la feuille de papier
le livre
l'ordinateur (m.)
le portable
le sac à dos
le stylo
la tablette
la trousse

Encore des matières (mots apparentés)
l'algèbre (f.)
l'arabe (m.)
les arts plastiques (m. pl.)
la biologie
la chorale
le laboratoire (labo)
le latin
la musique
l'orchestre (m.)
la psychologie
les sciences (f. pl.)

Les matières
l'anglais (m.)
le cours
l'emploi (m.) du temps
l'espagnol (m.)
le français
la géographie (géo)
l'histoire (f.)
l'informatique (f.)
les langues vivantes (LV) (f. pl.)
la littérature
les mathématiques (maths) (f. pl.)
la musique
la physique
les sciences (f. pl.) de la vie et de la terre (SVT)
les sciences sociales (f. pl.)
le sport, l'éducation (f.) physique et sportive (EPS)

L'heure
À quelle heure?
Le cours commence à...
Le cours se termine à...
Quelle heure est-il?

Les activités à l'école

aider
déjeuner
le déjeuner
enseigner
faire attention
faire les devoirs
organiser
participer
la récréation (récré)
utiliser

Les personnes et les endroits de l'école

la cantine
le casier
le collège
l'école (f.)
le gymnase
le lycée
la médiathèque
le principal/la principale
le/la professeur (prof)
la salle de classe
les toilettes (f. pl.)

Expressions utiles

parce que/qu'
la semaine
le week-end

Comment dit-on?

 **Le calendrier scolaire**

l'année scolaire
le calendrier scolaire
les vacances
un jour férié
la rentrée

Rappel

Pour parler du calendrier

Pour dire la date:
le + # + mois
Modèle: L'examen, c'est **le quinze octobre.**
La rentrée, c'est **le premier septembre.**

Pour parler des mois:
en octobre
au mois d'octobre

Pour parler de la saison:
en automne
en hiver
au printemps
en été

Communiquons

Comment dit-on? 1

L'organisation de l'école

Le calendrier scolaire

Infos pratiques | Matières enseignées | les profs | CDI
Calendrier | Accueil | Contact

La rentrée des classes: 2 septembre

Les vacances d'hiver: 1er - 16 février

Les vacances de la Toussaint: 19 octobre - 3 novembre

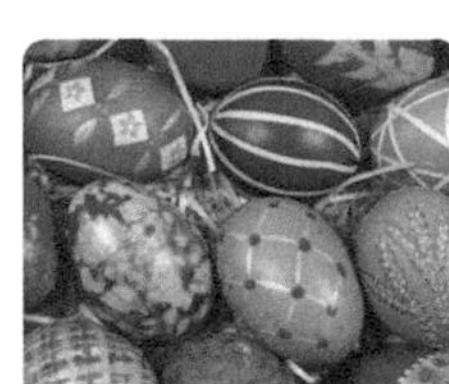

Jour férié: Lundi de Pâques - 13 avril

Jour férié: Armistice de 1918 - 11 novembre

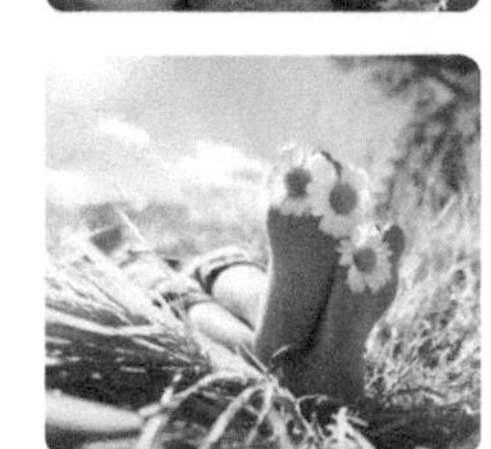

Les vacances de printemps: 4 - 19 avril

Les vacances de Noël: 21 décembre - 5 janvier

Jour férié: Lundi de Pentecôte - le 1er juin

Jour férié: Jour de l'An - le 1er janvier

Les vacances d'été: 4 juillet - 30 août

Activité 6

Comment est fait le calendrier scolaire?

Le calendrier scolaire 2019-2020 de la Réunion

rentrée
jour férié
vacances

	août	septembre	octobre	novembre	décembre	janvier	février	mars	avril	mai	juin	juillet
1	J	D	M	V	D	M	S	D	M	V	L	M
2	V	L	M	S	L	J	D	L	J	S	M	J
3	S	M	J	D	M	V	L	M	V	D	M	V
4	D	M	V	L	M	S	M	M	S	L	J	S
5	L	J	S	M	J	D	M	J	D	M	V	D
6	M	V	D	M	V	L	J	V	L	M	S	L
7	M	S	L	J	S	M	V	S	M	J	D	M
8	J	D	M	V	D	M	S	D	M	V	L	M
9	V	L	M	S	L	J	D	L	J	S	M	J
10	S	M	J	D	M	V	L	M	V	D	M	V
11	D	M	V	L	M	S	M	M	S	L	J	S
12	L	J	S	M	J	D	M	J	D	M	V	D
13	M	V	D	M	V	L	J	V	L	M	S	L
14	M	S	L	J	S	M	V	S	M	J	D	M
15	J	D	M	V	D	M	S	D	M	V	L	M
16	V	L	M	S	L	J	D	L	J	S	M	J
17	S	M	J	D	M	V	L	M	V	D	M	V
18	D	M	V	L	M	S	M	M	S	L	J	S
19	L	J	S	M	J	D	M	J	D	M	V	D
20	M	V	D	M	V	L	J	V	L	M	S	L
21	M	S	L	J	S	M	V	S	M	J	D	M
22	J	D	M	V	D	M	S	D	M	V	L	M
23	V	L	M	S	L	J	D	L	J	S	M	J
24	S	M	J	D	M	V	L	M	V	D	M	V
25	D	M	V	L	M	S	M	M	S	L	J	S
26	L	J	S	M	J	D	M	J	D	M	V	D
27	M	V	D	M	V	L	J	V	L	M	S	L
28	M	S	L	J	S	M	V	S	M	J	D	M
29	J	D	M	V	D	M	S	D	M	V	L	M
30	V	L	M	S	L	J		L	J	S	M	J
31	S		J		M	V		M		D		V

Étape 1: Observer

Regardez les premiers mois du calendrier scolaire de la Réunion où habite Lou-Ann. Que signifient les mots et les abréviations sur le calendrier? Écrivez en français ou en anglais.

1. férié
2. vacances
3. L
4. M
5. M
6. J
7. V
8. S
9. D

Étape 2: Identifier

a. Complétez la représentation schématique sur Explorer pour la Réunion.

b. Regardez le calendrier scolaire de votre école. Avec un(e) partenaire, complétez la deuxième partie de la représentation schématique.

pays/école	date de la rentrée des classes	dates des vacances	jours fériés
la Réunion			
votre école			

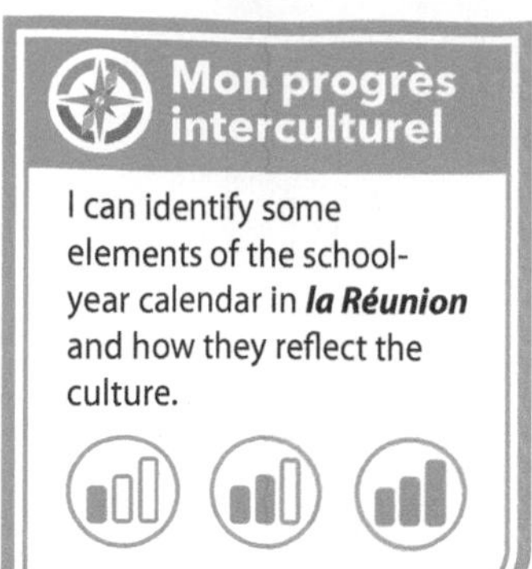

Détail linguistique

Permanence vs. *temps libre*

Students in France and the ***départements et régions d'outre-mer*** refer to their study hall time as ***permanence*** (or ***perm***, for short). If you have a free period in your school day but are assigned to a quiet room intended for study, the best word for that is ***permanence***. If you do not have a specific place to be, use ***temps libre***.

Détail grammatical

Suivre un cours

Even though you may hear some French speakers say ***Je prends un cours*** on occasion, the best way to say that you are taking a class is to use the verb ***suivre*** (to follow): ***Je suis un cours de géométrie***.

The verb ***suivre*** looks like this:

je suis	**nous suivons**
tu suis	**vous suivez**
il/elle/on suit	**ils/elles suivent**

Réflexion interculturelle

What similarities do you see between the school calendar in ***la Réunion*** and your school calendar? What differences do you notice between the academic calendars? Investigate why they have holidays when you do not and vice versa. Answer the questions in the discussion forum in Explorer.

Les matières

Cette année scolaire, je vais suivre un cours de/d'...

économie

physique-chimie

histoire-géo

allemand

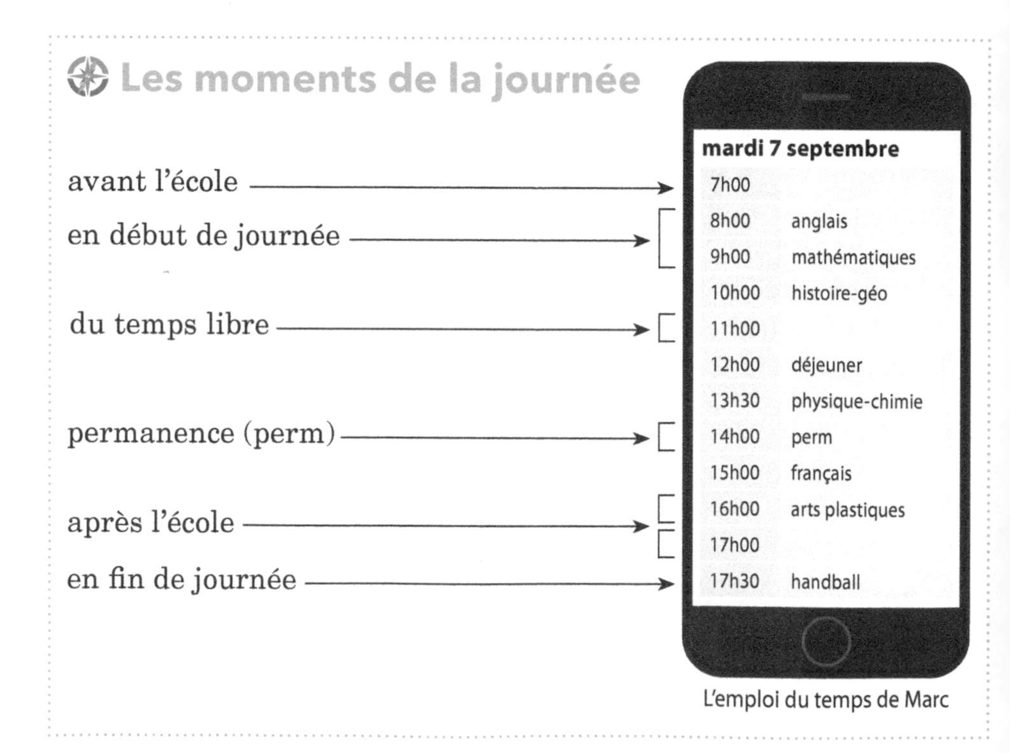

L'emploi du temps de Marc

Activité 7

Que fais-tu à différents moments de la journée?

Étape 1: Regarder et parler

Regardez l'emploi du temps sur le portable de Marc, qui va à l'école à Plouzané en France. Répondez aux questions suivantes à l'oral avec un(e) partenaire.

1. Que signifient *le début* et *la fin de la journée*? Considérez des mots apparentés en anglais.
2. Que veut dire le mot *libre*? Ce mot ressemble-t-il à un mot que vous connaissez en anglais?
3. Qu'est-ce que Marc fait *avant* (7h00) ou *après* (17h30) l'école? Est-ce qu'il a des activités extrascolaires, de la musique ou du sport, par exemple?

Étape 2: Écouter et écrire

Écoutez cette conversation entre Marc et son amie Lola.

a. Écrivez les cours et les activités de Lola dans la représentation schématique.
b. Après, regardez l'emploi du temps sur le téléphone de Marc et notez ses cours et ses activités.

les moments de la journée	Lola	Marc
en début de journée		• l'anglais • les maths
en fin de journée		
après l'école		

Étape 3: Parler

Décidez avec un(e) partenaire: Est-ce que les emplois du temps de Lola et de Marc sont faciles ou difficiles? Expliquez.

Modèle

L'emploi du temps de Marc est facile/difficile parce qu'il a mathématiques en début de journée!

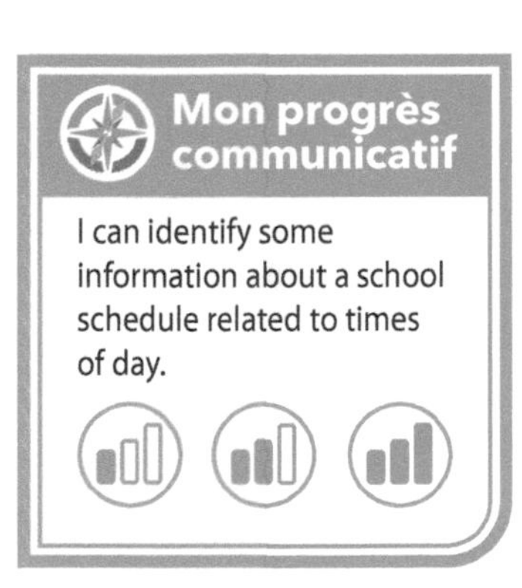

Rappel

Quand?

To give a general or relative idea of when things take place, here are a few phrases you have seen before:

le matin
(in the) morning

l'après-midi
(in the) afternoon

le soir
(in the) evening

la nuit
(at) night

avant
before

après
after

pendant
during

Activité 8

Quelles matières étudient-ils?

Lou-Ann et Diego vous invitent à leur école, mais vous n'avez pas le temps de visiter les deux. Choisissez la visite que vous préférez en écoutant les emplois du temps de Lou-Ann et de Diego.

Étape 1: Écouter

Cochez (✔) les cours mentionnés par chaque élève.

	les cours	Lou-Ann	Diego
a.	le français		
b.	l'EPS		
c.	la physique-chimie/ la chimie		
d.	l'histoire-géo/l'histoire		
e.	les maths		
f.	les sciences		
g.	l'espagnol		
h.	la biologie		
i.	l'anglais		

Étape 2: Écrire et comparer

Avec un(e) partenaire, écrivez des similarités et des différences entre:

les cours de Lou-Ann les cours de Diego

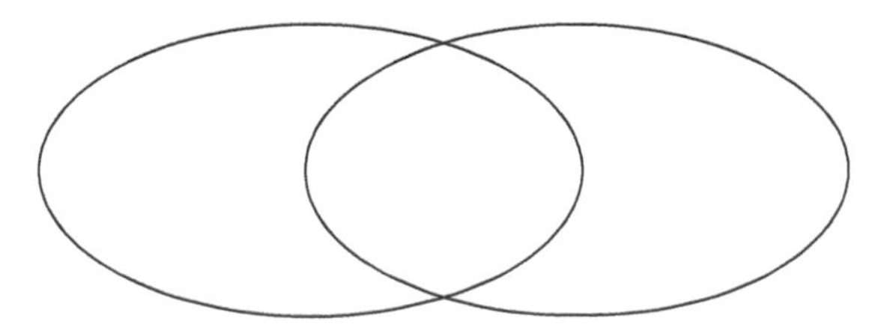

Étape 3: Parler

Quel emploi du temps préférez-vous? Et pour quelles raisons? Présentez votre préférence à votre partenaire.

Modèle

Lou-Ann a physique-chimie comme science, mais Diego a biologie. Je préfère l'emploi du temps de Lou-Ann.

Activité 9

Que va faire Lou-Ann au lycée?

Lou-Ann rentre en 3e cette année au collège de La Montagne. L'année prochaine, elle va aller au lycée Bellepierre pendant trois ans.

Étape 1: Lire et identifier

Regardez la fiche d'inscription du lycée Bellepierre à l'île de la Réunion. Lou-Ann a complété la fiche pour l'année prochaine avec les cours qu'elle voudrait suivre.

Choix des **Langues Vivantes Étrangères** en enseignement commun (cocher 1 seule case pour chaque LVE) :

LV1 : ⊠✓ANGLAIS LV1 : ⊠ CHINOIS (5h)
LV2 : ⊠ ALLEMAND LV2 : ⊠✓ESPAGNOL

Section européenne : ⊠✓ANGLAIS ⊠ ESPAGNOL

⊠✓ Dispositif EIP (élèves à haut potentiel)

<table>
<tr><th>ENSEIGNEMENTS Obligatoires</th><th>ENSEIGNEMENTS d'exploration (1 seul)</th><th>ENSEIGNEMENTS FACULTATIFS (2 maxi)</th></tr>
<tr>
<td>
<table>
<tr><th>Matières</th><th>Horaire Elève</th></tr>
<tr><td>Français</td><td>4,00</td></tr>
<tr><td>Histoire Géographie</td><td>3,00</td></tr>
<tr><td>LV1 (Anglais et Chinois)</td><td>3h/5h</td></tr>
<tr><td>LV2 (Espagnol ou Allemand)</td><td>2,50</td></tr>
<tr><td>Mathématiques</td><td>4,00</td></tr>
<tr><td>Physique Chimie</td><td>3,00</td></tr>
<tr><td>SVT</td><td>1,50</td></tr>
<tr><td>EPS</td><td>2,00</td></tr>
<tr><td>EMC</td><td>0,50</td></tr>
<tr><td>Accompagnement personnalisé</td><td>2,00</td></tr>
<tr><td>Enseignements d'exploration : 2 enseignements</td><td>3,00</td></tr>
</table>
</td>
<td>
⊠✓ Création Activités Artistiques option « Arts du spectacle »
⊠ Informatique et Création Numérique (ICN)
⊠ Littérature et Société (LS)
⊠ Méthodes et Pratiques Scientifiques (MPS)
⊠ Santé & Social (S.S)
⊠✓ Sciences de l'Ingénieur (SI)
⊠ Informatique et création numérique (ICN)
(Merci de faire 2 vœux en cas d'impossibilité de vous donner satisfaction sur le vœu 1)
⊠ Sciences Économiques et Sociales (SES) (Obligatoire)
</td>
<td>
⊠ LV3 : Espagnol (3h) (débutant)
⊠ LV3 : Chinois (3h) (débutant)
⊠✓LCA : Latin (3h)
⊠ LCA : Grec (3h)
⊠ Arts plastiques (3h)
⊠✓Danse contemporaine : (3h)
⊠ Atelier Sciences Po (2h)
⊠ Dispositif POLLEN (sur profil à la rentrée)
</td>
</tr>
</table>

EMC: *Enseignement moral et civique*

EPS: *Éducation physique et sportive*

SVT: *Sciences de la vie et de la terre*

Stratégies

Interpretive Reading

Here are a few ideas to help you become a more skillful reader in French.

1. *Scan the text to see what you notice.*
2. *Notice headlines, titles, or text in bold.*
3. *Find keywords you already know.*
4. *Identify the main idea.*

Watch the Interpretive Reading video in Explorer to hear more about tips for reading comprehension.

a. Divisez-vous en groupes. Dans la fiche d'inscription, trouvez l'équivalent en français des mots dans la liste suivante:

Groupe 1	Groupe 2	Groupe 3
• Literature and society • World languages/ modern languages • Chinese • Computer and digital design	• Scientific methods and practices • Engineering sciences • Modern dance • Moral and civic education	• Creation of artistic activities with a "performing arts" option • Health and Social [Well-being] • Economics and social sciences • Life and earth sciences

b. **Vrai** ou **faux**?

1. Lou-Ann est créative.
2. Lou-Ann préfère étudier les sciences.
3. Lou-Ann n'aime pas le sport.
4. Lou-Ann va étudier deux langues vivantes au lycée.
5. Lou-Ann va avoir trois cours de sciences au lycée.

Étape 2: Observer et comparer

Imaginez que vous allez entrer au lycée Bellepierre à la Réunion.

a. Complétez la fiche d'inscription selon vos préférences et vos besoins académiques.

b. Comparez vos réponses aux réponses de Lou-Ann. Notez trois cours qui représentent des différences culturelles.

c. Parlez de vos réponses avec un(e) partenaire.

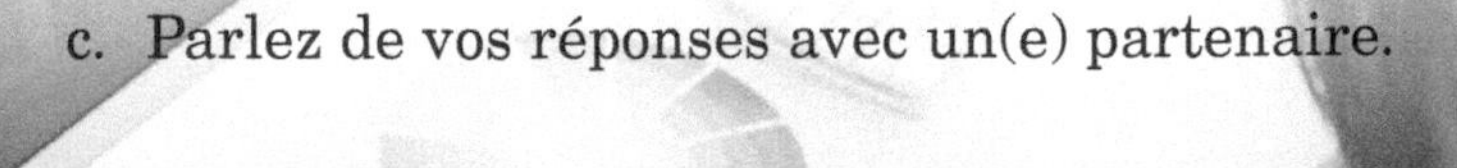

Zoom culture

Pratique culturelle: La filière scolaire

  **Connexion**

How do you choose which classes you will take each year? Which classes are already decided for you?

In France and the ***DROMs***, prior to their final two years, students' courses are mostly decided for them by the ***Ministère de l'éducation nationale***. During ***1re*** and ***terminale***, all students must take ***français, philosophie, histoire-géo, enseignement moral et civique,*** two ***langues vivantes, EPS,*** and ***humanités scientifiques et numériques***. However, students in these last two years of ***lycée*** get to choose from among ten ***disciplines de spécialité***.

The two ***spécialités*** a student chooses dictate parts of the ***baccalauréat***, which is the exit exam that determines if and where students can enroll in higher education. ***Les bacheliers*** are also required to pass tests in ***français, philosophie,*** and an oral exam. (***Le brevet*** is a comparable exam between ***collège*** and ***lycée***).

 **Réflexion**

How do students' goals after high school determine the academic choices they make?

http://www.education.gouv.fr/cid126438/baccalaureat-2021-un-tremplin-pour-la-reussite.html

Réflexion interculturelle

  Les cours obligatoires

Does your school offer the same classes as other schools in your area? What are your graduation requirements? Are they the same or different from other schools in your area? Search online to find the answers to these questions about your own culture.

Answer the questions in the discussion forum in Explorer.

 **Mon progrès interculturel**

I can identify some of the school course offerings that students take in a Francophone culture and why these courses are selected for them.

Découvrons 1

Expressing Preferences and What You Are Going to Do

Découvertes

Reflect on what you read and respond to the following questions in the graphic organizer in Explorer.

1. What do you notice about the words in bold used to talk about what Lou Ann likes to do? Do you see any patterns to what Lou-Ann says?
2. What do you notice about how Lou-Ann refers to what will occur in the near future? Do you see any similarities with how she expresses what she likes to do?
3. Share your observations with a partner. What else do you notice together or what else can you add to your observations?

View the ***Découvrons 1*** resources for this unit in Explorer and check the ***Synthèse de grammaire*** at the end of this unit.

Activité 10

La rentrée scolaire et le choix des cours

Pauvres Océane et Félix! Ils ne savent pas quels cours suivre! Choisissez des cours qu'Océane et Félix vont aimer.

 **Étape 1: Écouter**

Écoutez les préférences d'Océane et de Félix et les cours qui correspondent à leurs préférences. Écrivez les préférences et les cours dans la représentation schématique sur Explorer.

Modèle

préférences d'Océane ou de Félix	cours qui correspond(ent)
J'aime calculer et jouer avec les nombres.	l'économie/les maths

 **Étape 2: Parler**

Qu'est-ce que vous aimez faire? Quels cours correspondent à vos intérêts?

a. Préparez vos idées à l'écrit dans la représentation schématique.

b. Enregistrez *(record)* deux ou trois choses que vous aimez faire et les cours que vous choisissez selon vos préférences.

Modèle

J'aime chanter et jouer de la guitare. C'est pourquoi je choisis le cours de musique.

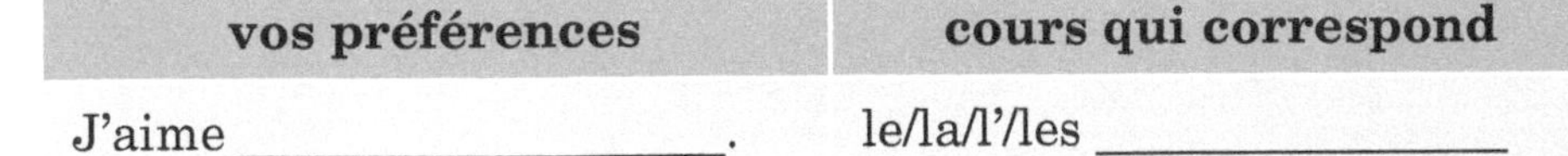

vos préférences	cours qui correspond
J'aime ________________.	le/la/l'/les ______________

Stratégies

Interpretive Listening

Here are some tips to help you focus and understand better when listening to something in French.

1. *Determine the context.*
2. *Think about what you already know about this topic.*
3. *Identify the keywords that will help you understand.*
4. *Listen again or ask someone to repeat.*
5. *Pay attention to body language and other visual cues.*

Watch the listening strategies video in Explorer to hear more about tips for listening comprehension.

Mon progrès communicatif

I can share information about what I am going to do this school year.

Activité 11

Qu'est-ce que tu vas faire pour réussir cette année scolaire?

Léa, une amie de Lou-Ann, doit faire une présentation sur son année scolaire.

Étape 1: Écouter

Aidez Léa à organiser sa présentation. Écoutez sa présentation et indiquez où elle doit placer le texte.

1

2

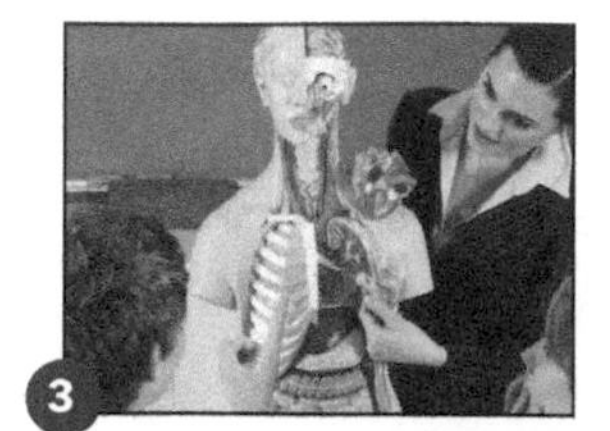
3

4

5

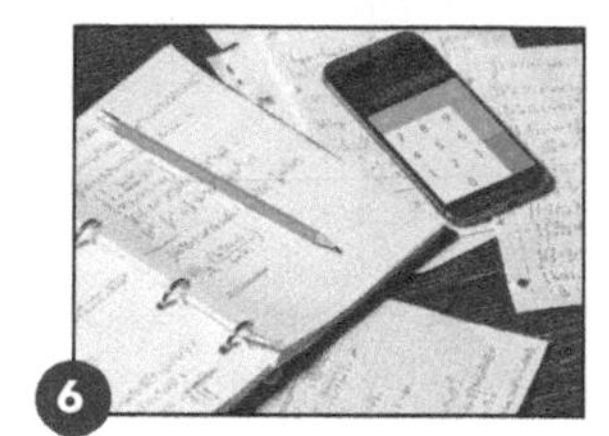
6

a) pendant mon temps libre

b) pendant mon cours d'économie

c) à la rentrée

d) pendant les vacances

e) après le déjeuner

f) en début de journée

Étape 2: Parler

Est-ce que tout le monde va faire comme Léa cette année scolaire? Interviewez 3 ou 4 personnes différentes. Utilisez des images de l'Étape 1.

Modèle

Tu vas étudier l'économie?

-Oui, je vais étudier l'économie avec monsieur Dubois.

-Non, je vais suivre la physique-chimie.

J'avance 1

Le calendrier scolaire idéal

L'île de la Réunion

You are participating in a program between your school and ***le lycée Martin***, a school in ***la Réunion***. Your two classes are working together to figure out the ideal school schedule for students. You received a podcast with recordings of three students from ***la Réunion*** talking about their day.

Étape 1: Écouter et noter

Listen to the podcasts of the students from ***la Réunion*** talking about their class schedules. Complete the chart in your Explorer course with the information about the three students: Their age, what happens during a typical school day, and what they like about school.

Modèle

élève réunionnais	âge	matière(s) préférée(s)	quand?
Manon			
Timéo			
Raphaël			

AP® Étape 2: Parler

Timéo needs to research what an American school day is like. Answer Timéo's interview questions in Explorer about your schedule.

Étape 3: Sélectionner

To finalize the research project, each student in your class and each student in the class from ***la Réunion*** will write a description of the ideal school calendar so that you can vote on the best one. Write your proposal in Explorer by answering the following questions.

Dans le calendrier scolaire idéal…

- Quand est la rentrée des classes?
- Combien de jours fériés avez-vous? Quand?
- Combien de jours (ou de périodes) de vacances avez-vous? Quand?

All of the materials for ***J'avance 1*** can be found in Explorer.

Détail linguistique

Les synonymes

Have you ever heard alternative names for a school library, such as "media center" or "resource center"?

In French, a synonym for ***la médiathèque*** is ***le CDI (Centre de documentation et d'information).*** You may hear either word used.

Comment dit-on? 2

Les ressources dans mon école

Qu'y a-t-il dans ton école?

Il y a **le bureau central**.

le parking

un terrain de sport

une salle d'informatique

Ça, c'est **le couloir**.

Nous avons **un accueil**.

Ici, dans **le foyer**, on peut passer du temps avec des amis.

Voici… **le laboratoire**.

Je peux aller à **l'infirmerie** pour chercher des médicaments quand je suis malade.

On a aussi… **un complexe sportif**.

Rappel

Le pronom "on"

Recall that the word ***on*** has several meanings. In English, "one," "people in general," and even "we" are all acceptable translations of ***on***.

With ***on***, use the same form of the verb that you use with ***il*** or ***elle***:

On mange à la cantine.
On peut étudier.

Take a hint from native speakers: ***On*** is much easier than ***nous*** or ***ils/elles***!

Activité 12

Elle est comment, ton école?

Écoutez Thomas décrire les activités qu'il fait à l'école. Associez les cinq descriptions aux cinq endroits dans l'école.

Activité 13

Tu as les mêmes endroits dans ton école?

Regardez le plan du lycée Sainte-Marie à la Réunion. Sur votre copie du plan de l'école sur Explorer:

a. Entourez les endroits dans cette école que vous avez dans votre école (les similarités).

b. Mettez une étoile (*) à côté des endroits que vous n'avez pas dans votre école.

c. Réfléchissez et écrivez une liste: Quels sont les endroits que vous avez dans votre école que vous ne voyez pas *(don't see)* sur le plan du lycée Sainte-Marie?

Mon progrès communicatif

I can understand descriptions of places in school buildings and compare them to my school.

Expressions utiles

Pour parler de l'école

Il y a...
Voici...
Ça, c'est...
Ici, on peut...
passer du temps
chercher (quelque chose)

Parking

Entrée principale du lycée

Restaurant scolaire

Terrain de sport

Salles de classe

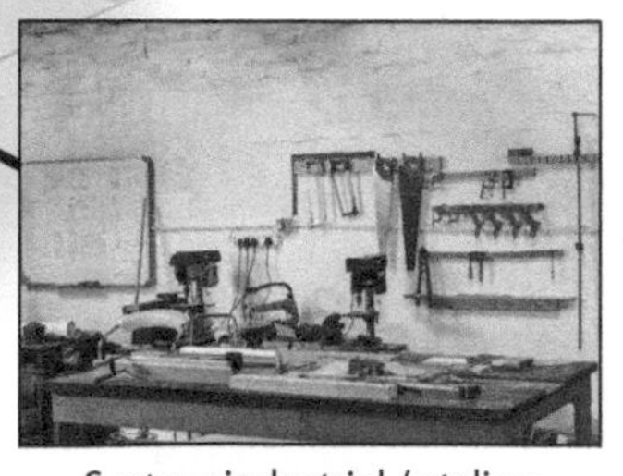

Secteur industriel / ateliers

Gymnase

Foyer

CDI

Rappel

Les contractions avec "à"

When talking about the places in a school, you may want to say you are going *to* a place or meeting someone *at* a place. In each case, you could use the word ***à*** in French.

The word ***à*** contracts with ***le*** and ***les*** as follows:

à + le restaurant scolaire = **au** restaurant scolaire

à + les salles de classe= **aux** salles de classe

There is no contraction with *la* and *l'*:

à l'infirmerie

à la salle d'informatique

Activité 14

 **Où va-t-on pour...?**

Où est-ce qu'on fait ces activités? Écrivez un ou deux endroits à l'école pour faire chaque activité.

Modèle

Je vais au CDI pour faire mes devoirs.

1. étudier pour un examen
2. utiliser un ordinateur
3. parler avec un prof
4. manger avec les amis
5. faire du sport
6. téléphoner à mes parents
7. organiser un club
8. répéter une chanson
9. prendre la voiture
10. chercher une fiche *(form)* importante

Expressions utiles

À l'école, on peut...

aller voir...
to go see...

demander conseil à...
to ask for advice from...

Zoom culture

Pratique culturelle: Le foyer des élèves

 **Connexion**

Where do you go at school to relax and spend time with friends?

A place to relax with friends or to learn something new, ***le foyer*** is an area of the French high school managed by and for the students. A group of elected students usually meet at the beginning of the school year to brainstorm ideas for ***le foyer***. These ideas can be as simple as working to get music, a TV, a video game console, books and comfortable seating, to bigger projects, such as buying indoor games like a foosball or pool table, or organizing workshops, presentations or tournaments. It is a place where students are encouraged to pick up a guitar, a paintbrush, a deck of cards, or a game controller, and enjoy themselves!

 **Réflexion**

Search the Internet for ***la charte du foyer*** and skim the documents you find. What do they tell you about how students use these spaces? What kinds of rules do students set for themselves?

Activité 15

Qu'est-ce qu'il y a dans mon école?

Étape 1: Regarder et écouter

Écoutez Léo, qui présente son lycée en France.

a. Écrivez une liste des endroits qu'il mentionne.

b. Écoutez une deuxième fois et notez **combien** il y a de chaque endroit.

Étape 2: Mentir ou dire la vérité

Préparez deux phrases vraies à propos du lycée de Léo. Préparez une phrase fausse à propos de son lycée. Lisez vos phrases à votre partenaire. Est-ce que votre partenaire peut trouver la phrase fausse?

Modèle

Au lycée de Léo, il y a un foyer mais il n'y a pas de terrain de tennis.

Étape 3: Présenter

Votre proviseur vous demande, à vous et à votre partenaire, de présenter un endroit de votre école à un groupe de nouveaux élèves.

a. Choisissez un endroit. (e.g., la salle de classe, le restaurant scolaire, le foyer, le bureau, etc.)

b. Que font les élèves dans cet endroit? (deux choses) Qu'est-ce qu'ils n'y font pas? (une chose)

c. Qu'est-ce qu'on utilise dans cet endroit? (e.g., fournitures scolaires, vêtements, etc.)

d. Avec votre partenaire, préparez une petite présentation vidéo et enregistrez-la sur Explorer.

Rappel

Le personnel de l'école

Remember the people in the school that you already know and a few words to describe them:

le/la prof

le/la principal(e)

amusant(e)

créatif/créative

génial(e)

gentil/gentille

impatient(e)

inspirant(e)

patient(e)

strict(e)

Mon progrès communicatif

I can describe some places in a school, the people who work there, and what students do in those places.

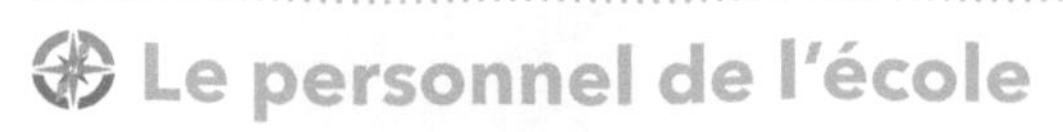

Le personnel de l'école

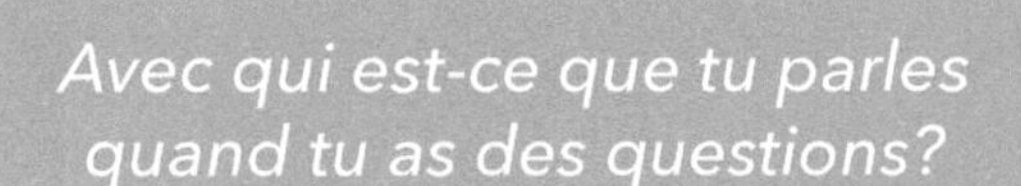

*Je **demande** à madame Robert, **la conseillère d'orientation**. Elle est **énergique** et **dynamique**. Monsieur Rivière, c'est qui?*

*C'est **l'infirmier. C'est quelqu'un** de très **positif**. On peut **aller voir** l'infirmier quand on a un problème médical. Comment est **le proviseur-adjoint**?*

*Il est assez **strict**. Il travaille avec **la proviseure**.*

Activité 16

Qui peut m'aider?

Écoutez ces élèves parler de leurs besoins et de leurs problèmes. Associez chaque problème à la bonne personne.

A. le conseiller d'orientation

B. l'entraîneur

C. la documentaliste

D. le professeur

E. la secrétaire

F. le surveillant

Mon progrès communicatif

I can understand simple descriptions of people who work at a school.

Activité 17

Où est-on?

Étape 1: Écrire

Sans montrer à votre partenaire (c'est un secret!), écrivez où se trouvent ces personnes dans votre école maintenant, en ce moment. Vous pouvez être logique ou absurde.

- l'entraîneur de foot
- le proviseur-adjoint
- la conseillère d'orientation
- l'infirmier
- le surveillant
- le prof de biologie

Modèle

Le prof de biologie est au terrain de foot.

Étape 2: Parler

Posez des questions à votre partenaire pour savoir où se trouve le personnel de l'école.

Modèle

Élève A: Je dois poser une question au prof de biologie. Où est-il?

Élève B: Il est au terrain de foot.

D'autres questions possibles:

-J'ai besoin d'aller voir ______ . Où est-il/elle?

-Je voudrais parler avec ______. Où est-il/elle?

-Je veux demander conseil à ______. Où est-il/elle?

On peut aussi dire

le surveillant/la surveillante
hall monitor, cafeteria monitor

A slang word for ***le surveillant*** is ***le pion***.

dévoué/dévouée
dedicated

exigeant/exigeante
demanding, challenging

Rappel

Comment parler à un prof?

Remember that French has two different words for you: ***tu*** and ***vous***. Students in middle school, high school, and above usually ***vouvoient*** their teachers. You can still use ***tu*** when talking to a friend or family member.

When addressing a teacher or talking about a teacher, remember that ***Monsieur*** or ***Madame*** is also appropriate.

Découvrons 2

Describing a Person's Job and Personality

"Voici notre provis**eur**. Il s'appelle monsieur Bernard. Il est très positi**f**, mais il est aussi sér**ieux**. Il est très patie**nt** et il est assez **sympa**."

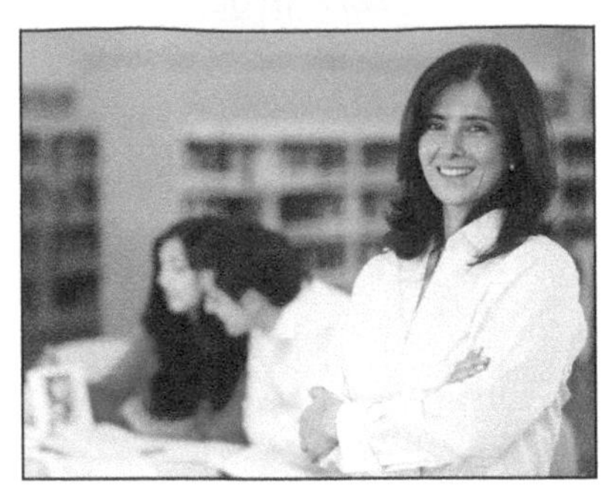

"Tu vois la femme sur la photo? C'est notre surveillante, madame Sautron. Elle est positi**ve** et travaille**use**. Elle est vraiment patient**e** et très **sympa**!"

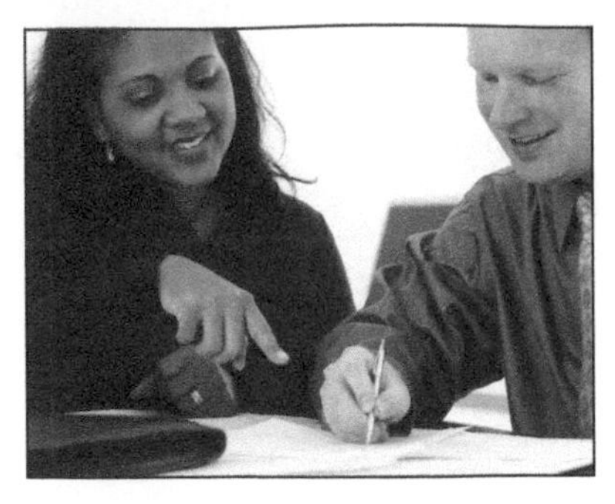

"Voici madame Robert, la conseill**ère** d'orientation. Elle est créati**ve**. Monsieur Dupont, l'autre conseill**er** d'orientation, n'est pas créati**f**."

Découvertes

Reflect on what you read, then respond to the following questions in the graphic organizer in Explorer.

1. What do you notice about the endings of the words presented in ***Découvrons 2***? You may remember some patterns, but try to look for something new as well.
2. Look at the descriptions and the words for people's jobs in ***Comment dit-on? 2***? What can you add to the chart?
3. Share your observations with a partner. What else do you notice together or what else can you add to your observations?

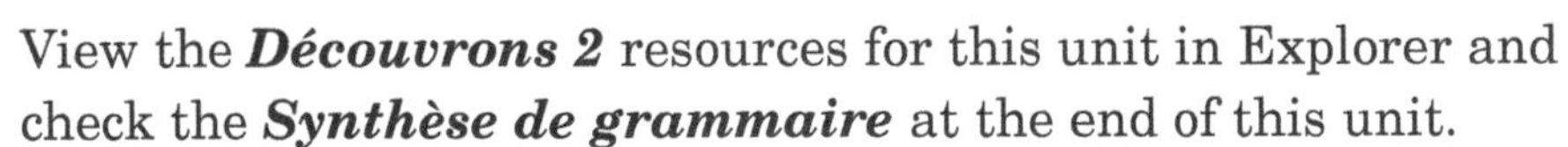

View the ***Découvrons 2*** resources for this unit in Explorer and check the ***Synthèse de grammaire*** at the end of this unit.

	for men/boys	for anyone	for women/ girls
words that describe a person's job or role			
words that describe a person's personality			

Activité 18

Qui est-ce?

Écoutez Félix et Océane parler du personnel de l'école. Pour chaque personne qu'Océane décrit, indiquez:

a. Si la personne est un homme, une femme, ou s'il est impossible de savoir (?); et

b. La profession de la personne.

homme, femme ou impossible de savoir?				profession
Modèle	homme	(femme)	?	surveillante
1.	homme	femme	?	
2.	homme	femme	?	
3.	homme	femme	?	
4.	homme	femme	?	
5.	homme	femme	?	

Activité 19

Comment sont les personnes qui travaillent à votre école?

Étape 1: Écrire une biographie

Pour le journal scolaire, il faut écrire une mini-biographie de trois adultes qui travaillent dans votre école. Pour chaque personne, expliquez son travail et donnez quelques mots pour décrire la personne.

Étape 2: Parler et deviner

Décrivez une personne qui travaille à votre école à un(e) partenaire. Votre partenaire va essayer de savoir de qui vous parlez. Est-ce que vous pouvez deviner *(guess)* de qui votre partenaire parle?

Activité 20

À la recherche de tuteurs

Étape 1: Trouver des tuteurs

Vous allez travailler avec un tuteur cette année pour préparer vos examens. Vous utilisez une appli sur votre portable pour choisir un tuteur.

a. Lisez les descriptions des tuteurs.

b. Écrivez les cours, les qualités et les heures libres des tuteurs dans la représentation schématique sur Explorer.

Trouvez le tuteur idéal! *Élèves:*

"Salut! Je suis Damien. Je suis dynamique et j'adore faire du sport. Mes cours préférés sont l'EPS et l'allemand. Je n'étudie pas le week-end. Comme tuteur, je suis exigeant. Je suis libre du lundi au vendredi en fin de journée."

"Salut! Moi, c'est Sylvie. Je suis super énergique! J'adore encourager mes amis. Je ne suis jamais impatiente. Je suis forte en histoire-géo et en art. Je suis libre le samedi après-midi entre 13h et 16h."

"Bonjour! Je m'appelle Farid. J'adore explorer de nouvelles idées dans mon cours d'économie. Je suis créatif et j'aime travailler avec les autres. Je suis très patient. Je suis libre le lundi avant l'école ou le mercredi soir."

"Salut! Je m'appelle Djamila. Mes cours préférés sont les sciences. J'adore surtout la physique-chimie et les SVT. Comme tutrice, je suis très positive et sympa, mais je suis sérieuse quand j'étudie. Je suis libre le mardi et le vendredi après l'école."

"Salut, les élèves! Je m'appelle Guillaume. Je n'aime pas commencer en retard. Mes amis pensent que je suis un peu strict! Je suis fort en anglais et en musique. Je suis libre le mardi ou le mercredi en début de journée."

Étape 2: Écrire un texto.

Maintenant, réfléchissez: Pour vous, quelles qualités sont importantes chez un tuteur? Choisissez un des tuteurs de l'**Étape 1**. Écrivez un texto à la personne avec qui vous voulez travailler.

a. Présentez-vous. (*Je m'appelle…*)

b. Décrivez où vous préférez étudier. (*Je préfère étudier à…*)

c. Vous voulez étudier pour quel cours avec l'aide du tuteur? (*Je voudrais étudier…*)

d. Quand êtes-vous libre? (*Je suis libre…*)

J'avance 2

Saint-Leu, la Réunion vue du ciel

Voici notre école!

You are preparing for a school exchange with students at ***le lycée Martin*** in ***la Réunion***.

Étape 1: Lire et associer

The students have sent a photo presentation of their favorite places in school. Go to Explorer to read about them.

Étape 2: Corriger

Using what you learned about the students' school, you will rewrite in Explorer some descriptions of their school to make the descriptions more accurate.

Mon progrès communicatif

I can understand descriptions of some places in a school, who works there, and what students do in those places.

Étape 3: Écrire

The students from ***le lycée Martin*** who described their school are eager to learn more about one of your favorite places in your school. Go to Explorer to write an email to describe a place in your school where you like to study, socialize, or participate in school or extracurricular activities. Include the following information:

- Identify the place and describe one or two activities that you can do there.
- Identify a staff member with whom you might interact in your favorite place.

Mon progrès communicatif

I can describe some places in a school, the people who work there, and what students do in those places.

Étape 4: Parler

Your classmate and you are nominating school staff members to serve on a welcoming committee for a group of students from ***le lycée Martin*** who will be visiting your school this year. You and your partner should each recommend two staff members before selecting one staff member to nominate. Record your conversation in Explorer. When recommending a staff member, be sure to:

- Identify their role in the school (e.g., teacher, counselor, coach, etc.).
- Describe one or more of their personal qualities.

All of the materials for ***J'avance 2*** can be found in Explorer.

Mon progrès communicatif

I can exchange information about school staff related to their roles and personal qualities.

Comment dit-on? 3

Comment réussir à l'école?

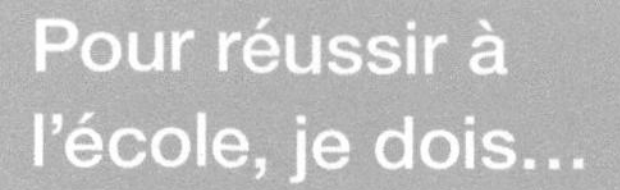

Pour réussir à l'école, je dois...

prendre des notes

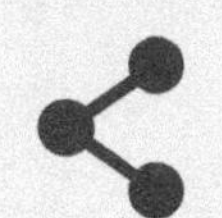
partager des ressources en ligne

accéder à la plate-forme de la classe

faire une/des pause(s)

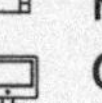

participer à des activités périscolaires

étudier des fiches de révision

Je ne dois pas...

regarder mon portable au lieu de dormir

attendre le dernier moment (pour)

utiliser mon portable en classe

dormir tard

Exact	jamais			(une) fois par semaine	tous les jours
Général	0	rarement	parfois / de temps en temps	souvent	tout le temps

Activité 21

 **Bonne idée ou mauvaise idée?**

Lisez les textos de votre ami Véronique sur ses habitudes scolaires. Puis écrivez une réponse. C'est une bonne idée ou une mauvaise idée? Expliquez pourquoi.

Modèle

Le soir, je ne regarde jamais mon portable.

Bonne idée! Au lieu de regarder ton portable, tu dois dormir.

1. **Je prends des notes en histoire-géo de temps en temps.**
2. **Je parle avec mes copains et je fais mes devoirs en même temps.**
3. **Je fais des pauses toutes les cinq minutes quand je fais mes devoirs.**
4. **Je partage des ressources en ligne avec les autres élèves tout le temps.**
5. **Je regarde souvent la télé quand j'étudie des fiches de révision.**

Prononciation

  **Les fins de mots**

When do we pronounce final consonants or not?

In ***EntreCultures 2***, you will use what you already know about the sounds of the French language to make predictions and then check those predictions by listening to a recording.

In the following transcription of Lou-Ann talking about her schedule, which underlined ends of words will be pronounced? Which ones will be silent? Is there an overall trend? Listen to the recording and complete the pronunciation activity in Explorer.

> Hey, aujourd'hui, je reviens pour vous parler du collège. J'ai environ sept heures de cours par jour, de huit heures à seize heures trente, ce qui me laisse le temps de pouvoir faire des activités extrascolaires après l'école. J'ai onze professeurs qui m'enseignent différentes matières comme par exemple, le français, l'histoire, la physique-chimie, les sciences, les maths et encore plein d'autres.

Rappel

Les activités à l'école

Remember that you already know several expressions to talk about what you do at school:

aider
faire les devoirs
organiser
passer un examen
travailler en équipe

Détail grammatical

Le verbe devoir

Devoir means "to have to," but it may be more helpful to think of it as "must":

je dois
tu dois
il/elle/on doit

Détail linguistique

Les notes **has three meanings:**

les notes = what you write in your ***cahier*** during the lesson

une note / les notes = the grade(s) that you earn in a class (100%, B+, etc.)

les notes = musical notations

To talk about what kind of grade you have or want, you might say:

*J'ai **une mauvaise note** en EPS.*

*Je vais étudier pour **avoir une bonne note** en histoire-géo.*

Activité 22

Qu'est-ce que je dois faire?

Votre ami et vous parlez de vos problèmes à l'école.

a. Écoutez les problèmes de votre partenaire.

b. Donnez des suggestions pour aider votre partenaire.

Modèle

Simon: Je ne comprends pas la géométrie.

Isabelle: **Tu dois** faire des exercices de géométrie. **Tu ne dois** pas parler quand le prof parle.

partenaire A:	**partenaire B:**
1. Je suis très fatigué(e) en classe.	1. Je veux rencontrer d'autres amis à l'école.
2. J'ai une mauvaise note en anglais.	2. Je n'écoute pas le prof d'histoire-géo.
3. Je veux mémoriser le vocabulaire en espagnol, mais c'est difficile.	3. J'ai un grand projet pour la classe d'arts plastiques.

c. À vous, maintenant! Pensez à d'autres problèmes que les élèves ont à l'école.

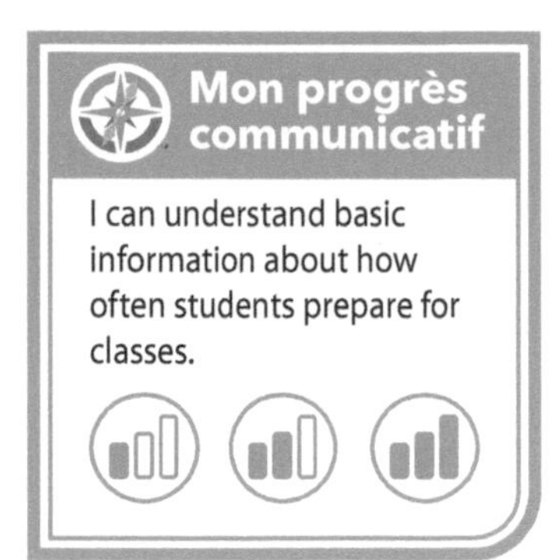

Activité 23

Qui va réussir à l'examen?

Étape 1: Écouter et noter

Les élèves du collège Beauséjour à la Réunion ont un grand examen vendredi et ils ont enregistré *(recorded)* des commentaires dans un podcast pour avoir des conseils. Écoutez Eric, Inès, Quentin, Lucie et Enzo.

a. Écoutez et notez ce qu'ils font.

b. Écoutez et notez la fréquence de ce qu'ils font (e.g., souvent, jamais, etc.). Si on ne dit pas la fréquence, écrivez un point d'interrogation (?).

Utilisez Explorer pour écrire vos réponses.

Étape 2: Discuter

Votre partenaire et vous devez préparer une conclusion pour cet épisode du podcast.

a. Parlez à votre partenaire et décidez quels élèves d'**Étape 1** vont réussir à leurs examens.

b. Expliquez vos conclusions.

c. Enregistrez votre conversation sur Explorer.

Modèle

Inès **va réussir à l'examen parce qu'**elle...

Eric **ne va pas réussir à l'examen parce qu'**il...

Détail grammatical

Ne...jamais

You're already familiar with the structure ***ne...pas*** to make sentences negative:

*Je **ne** vais **pas** faire mes devoirs.*

Ne...jamais has a different meaning, but it fits around the first verb in the same way that ***ne...pas*** does:

*Je **ne** vais **jamais** faire mes devoirs!*

Activité 24

Comment doit-on préparer un examen?

ORGANISER son TEMPS D'ÉTUDE

Il vaut mieux étudier pendant plusieurs périodes courtes qu'une trop longue. Avant un examen, réviser 8 fois 30 minutes sera plus efficace que de le faire pendant 4 heures de suite! Il faut aussi faire des pauses, aller dehors et s'aérer, ton cerveau sera plus performant en espaçant tes périodes d'étude. Tu apprendras mieux et plus vite.

Commence à étudier la veille

Dors bien

Varie tes sujets d'étude

Étudie moins longtemps mais plus souvent

Prévois un calendrier de tes périodes d'étude

On peut aussi dire

efficace	*efficient*
réviser	*to review*
ton cerveau	*your brain*
la veille	*the day before*

Étape 1: Trouver les mots

Écrivez une liste de tout le vocabulaire que vous pouvez trouver dans l'infographie selon ces deux catégories:

a. Verbes/actions relatifs aux bonnes habitudes scolaires; et

b. Des mots relatifs au temps et à la fréquence.

les bonnes habitudes scolaires	le temps et la fréquence

On peut aussi dire

Les loisirs

composer (un poème, une chanson, etc.)

créer un robot

jouer **au** basket (**au** volley, etc.)

jouer **de la** guitare (**du** piano, etc.)

regarder des films

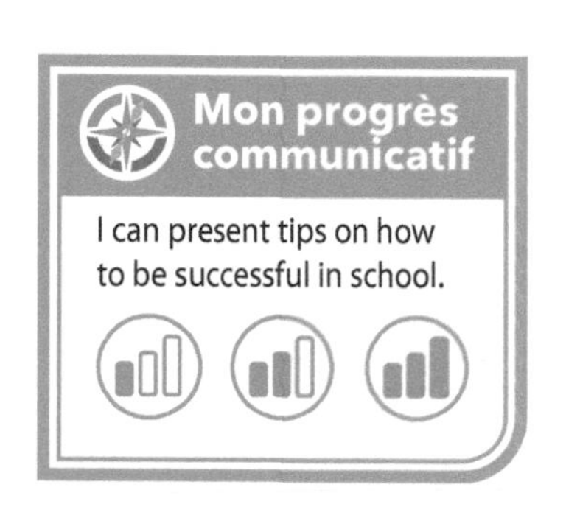

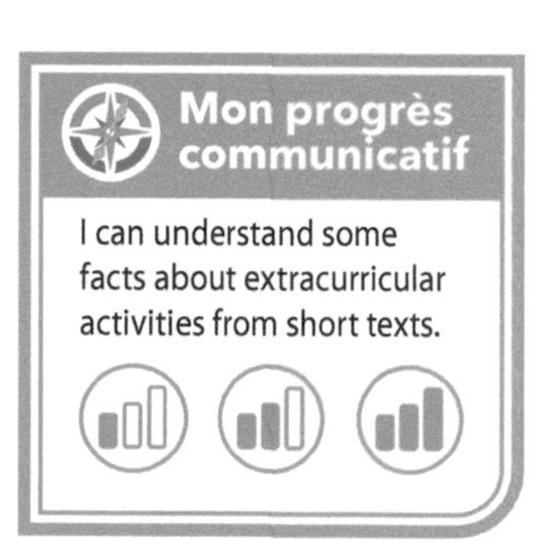

Détail grammatical

Les verbes lire, écrire, et apprendre

Here are a few helpful verbs you may want to use to talk about what you do in your ***activités périscolaires***:

lire *(to read)*
je lis / on lit / nous lisons

écrire *(to write)*
j'écris / on écrit / nous écrivons

apprendre *(to learn)*
j'apprends / on apprend

Étape 2: Comprendre le texte

Choisissez la phrase avec laquelle l'auteur de cette infographie est probablement d'accord. Expliquez pourquoi.

a. En général, on doit préparer un calendrier avec des périodes d'étude de six heures ou plus par jour.

b. Il faut beaucoup étudier le jour d'un examen.

c. Ton cerveau s'active plus quand tu étudies souvent mais pas longtemps.

Étape 3: Réfléchir

Vous voulez faire une auto-évaluation *(self-assessment)* selon cette infographie. Répondez à ces questions personnellement en phrases complètes.

1. Avant un examen, est-ce que tu étudies plus souvent mais moins longtemps?
2. Est-ce que tu prépares un calendrier de tes périodes d'étude?
3. Est-ce que tu dors bien la veille d'un examen?
4. Quand tu as un examen le vendredi, combien de fois durant la semaine est-ce que tu étudies?
5. Combien de minutes est-ce que tu révises dans une période d'étude?

Les activités périscolaires

une équipe de (foot, volley, basket, etc.)

le club théâtre, le club cinéma, le club de, etc.

Activité 25

Que choisir comme activité périscolaire?

Les collégiens parlent de leurs préférences pour les activités périscolaires.

a. Lisez les annonces pour les activités offertes aux lycéens.

b. Discutez avec votre partenaire: Quelle est la bonne activité pour chaque personne? Pourquoi?

c. *Et vous?* Quelle activité périscolaire vous intéresse? Écrivez une phrase pour expliquer votre choix.

Modèle

Le club de technologie est bien parce que...

Le ciné-club

Aimez-vous regarder des films?

Adorez-vous parler des acteurs avec vos amis?

Venez nombreux au ciné-club! On regarde des films et on discute de leurs thèmes et de leurs personnages. C'est super amusant!

Tous les mercredis après l'école au CDI

Le club de technologie

Êtes-vous passionnés par les ordinateurs? Il faut être membre du club de technologie! On peut apprendre à accéder aux plates-formes sur internet et créer des sites web. Il ne faut pas avoir un ordinateur personnel pour participer.

Deux fois par semaine avant l'école à la salle d'informatique

L'équipe de futsal

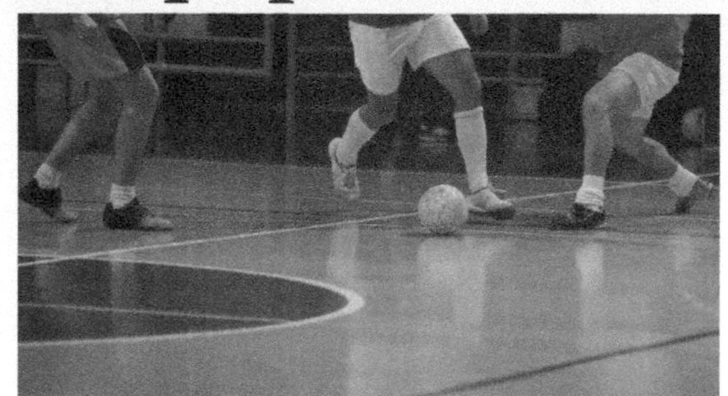

Tous les sportifs, participez aux compétitions de l'équipe de futsal! Si vous aimez courir rapidement et être membre d'une équipe dynamique, vous êtes les bienvenus! Nous nous rencontrons avec l'entraîneur une fois par semaine.

Tous les vendredis à 16h au gymnase

Jean

À l'école, je préfère mes cours de littérature et de cinéma. Après l'école, j'adore regarder des films comiques et lire des magazines sur les acteurs célèbres.

Simon

Moi, j'adore les jeux vidéos. Je joue aux jeux vidéos tous les jours après l'école. J'aime partager des idées et des ressources sur les jeux vidéos en ligne.

Leïla

Souvent, je reste après l'école pour travailler dans la salle d'informatique. Je travaille pour gagner de l'argent pour acheter un ordinateur. Je voudrais étudier la programmation.

Isabelle

Je suis très sportive. Mon cours préféré, c'est l'EPS parce que j'adore faire du sport avec mes amis.

Activité 26

Qu'est-ce qui t'intéresse comme activité?

Texte A

Qu'est-ce que vous allez faire cette année?

GÉNÉRATION DÉCOUVERTE

Inscrivez-vous!

Poterie, anglais, théâtre, échecs et beaucoup d'autres activités artistiques et sportives... que vont choisir vos enfants cette année?

Notre ville organise des activités périscolaires éducatives et amusantes pour les collégiens et les lycéens, il est temps d'inscrire vos enfants!

Pour plus d'informations, contactez-nous au Centre de la jeunesse et des sports (8 rue du Coufran, 01 36 21 42 00)

À la rentrée, nous proposons aussi des cours de danse latine, de langue des signes et d'arts martiaux (judo et taekwondo) via l'Institut de la culture et des activités sportives!

Pendant les vacances scolaires, nous proposons des ateliers robotiques et de cuisine chinoise, profitez-en!

Pour pouvoir participer, votre enfant doit être scolarisé en 6e à la rentrée 2019! Informations et tarifs: 01 36 21 42 01

Texte B

©Ministère de l'Education nationale, de l'Enseignement supérieur et de la Recherche (2016), "Activités spécifiques organisées pendant les TAP", Récupérée de https://tinyurl.com/yc47flyb.

Étape 1: Identifier les points clés

Trouvez les réponses aux questions suivantes dans le Texte A (*Qu'est-ce que vous allez faire cette année?*).

1. Quel est l'**objectif** de ce texte?
   a. faire de la publicité b. amuser c. expliquer des étapes
2. **Qui** propose de nouvelles activités à la rentrée?
3. **À qui** sont proposées ces activités?
4. **Où** est-ce qu'on peut trouver plus d'information et s'inscrire *(sign up)*?

Étape 2: Identifier les activités

a. Dans la colonne “activité,” travaillez avec un(e) partenaire pour écrire une liste de toutes les activités spécifiques mentionnées dans Texte A.

b. Après cela, dans la colonne “catégorie,” décidez dans quelle catégorie de Texte B peuvent être classées les activités.

activité (texte A)	catégorie (texte B)

Zoom culture

Pratique culturelle: Qu’est-ce qu’on propose comme activités périscolaires?

Connexion

What part do extracurricular activities play at your school and in your life?

In France and the ***DROMs***, like ***la Réunion***, students can participate in a variety of activities, including sports, visual arts, performing arts, and games on Wednesdays and Saturdays. In many communities, these activities have no connection with the school. They are offered at community centers [like ***les Maisons des jeunes et de la culture (MJC)***] or by ***la mairie*** (city hall). Students who come from these communities to the U.S. are often surprised by the emphasis on sports and “school spirit.” Extracurricular offerings vary greatly across Francophone countries. For example, ***Québec*** is fairly similar to the U.S. with regard to competitive high school sports, which you can learn about through ***le Réseau du sport étudiant au Québec***.

Réflexion

What are the advantages and challenges of extracurricular activities? Does considering cultural attitudes about extracurricular activities change your perspective?

Réflexion interculturelle

Do an Internet search for some examples of ***activités périscolaires*** at specific Francophone schools. Which sports and activities are the most popular? How many are also offered in your community? Are there any activities that are usually not available in your community? If so, why do you think that is?

Mon progrès interculturel

I can identify some extracurricular activities and the role they play in Francophone cultures.

Activité 27

Qu’est-ce que vous allez faire comme activité périscolaire?

Vous rencontrez une nouvelle élève de votre classe de français. Répondez à ses questions à propos d’une activité périscolaire que vous allez faire cette année. Enregistrez (*record*) vos réponses sur Explorer.

Découvrons 3

Comparing How Much or How Often

Découvertes

Reflect on what you observe. Find examples and draw conclusions using the graphic organizer in Explorer.

1. Do you understand the word ***plus***? Find examples in the preceding sentences.
2. Examine the sentences again. When do Félix and Mariame add the word ***que***?
3. Examine the sentences again. When do Félix and Mariame add the word ***de***?
4. Share your observations with a partner. Do you both agree on your conclusions?

View the ***Découvrons 3*** resources for this unit in Explorer and check the ***Synthèse de grammaire*** at the end of this unit.

Activité 28

Combien de fois par semaine?

 **Étape 1: Observer et noter**

Heures	Lundi	Mardi	Mercredi	Jeudi	Vendredi
8h à 9h	Étude	Espagnol	Anglais	Français	EPS
9h à 10h	Français	Musique	Musique	Français	Latin
10h à 11h	Histoire	Maths	Espagnol	Maths	Maths
11h à 12h	Géographie	Maths	Histoire	SVT	Géographie
12h à 13h	Déjeuner	Déjeuner	Déjeuner	Déjeuner	Déjeuner
13h à 14h	EPS	Français		CDI	Français
14h à 15h	EPS	Physique-Chimie		Physique-Chimie	Anglais
15h à 16h	SVT			Histoire	
16h à 17h	Anglais				
17h à 17h40	Guitare	Guitare		Guitare	Guitare

Avec un(e) partenaire, regardez l'emploi du temps d'Inès. Faites un X dans la colonne qui convient pour déterminer la fréquence de ses activités ou de ses cours au collège.

matières / activités	jamais	une fois par semaine	deux fois par semaine	trois fois par semaine	souvent	tous les jours
latin		X				

  **Étape 2: Comparer et écrire**

Inès veut comparer son emploi du temps avec votre emploi du temps. Travaillez avec un(e) partenaire.

a. Une personne va jouer le rôle d'Inès et une personne va être l'élève américain.

b. Échangez des textos pour comparer les emplois du temps.

Modèle

Inès, tu as histoire **plus** souvent **que** moi.

Tu as **plus de** classes le mercredi **que** moi.

J'ai **plus de** cours de sciences **que** toi.

Activité 29

Quel est mon profil scolaire?

Étape 1: Réfléchir

Écrivez vos activités scolaires sur le graphique pour indiquer avec quelle fréquence vous les faites.

Étape 2: Discuter et trouver

Prenez *(take)* votre copie du diagramme et un crayon/stylo.

a. Choisissez une activité.

b. Posez la question aux autres élèves.

c. Écrivez les noms des élèves sur le diagramme et indiquez la fréquence qui correspond à la réponse.

Modèle

Moi: **Est-ce que tu** participes **souvent** aux activités du club d'échecs?

Corinne: Je vais au club d'échecs **tous les jours**.

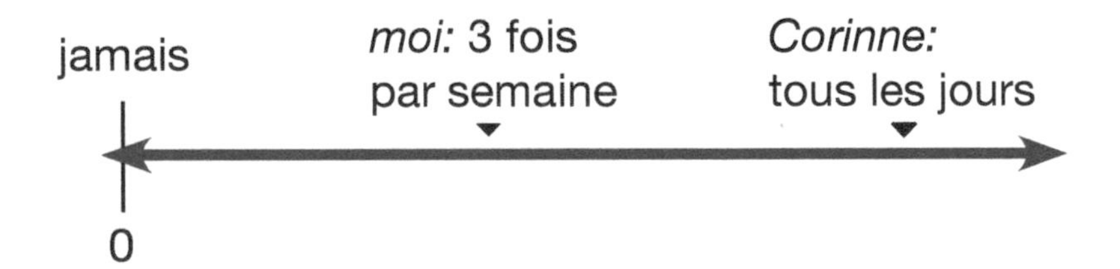

Étape 3: Écrire et comparer

a. Qui fait l'activité plus souvent que vous?

b. Vous faites l'activité plus souvent que quels élèves de la classe?

c. Écrivez une ou deux phrases où vous comparez vos habitudes scolaires avec les habitudes scolaires des autres élèves de la classe.

Modèle

J'étudie **plus que** Marc, mais il utilise son portable en classe **plus que** moi.

J'avance 3

Un échange d'idées

Diego and his friends from ***la Réunion*** are participating in an online competition to give the most effective study tips for their classes. The winners will have their tips recorded in a video to be shown to students all over the Francophone world.

 Étape 1: Écouter

Listen to what Diego and his friends say about how they prepare for their classes. Use the graphic organizer in Explorer to collect the requested information.

For each activity the students mention:

- Place a check (✔) in the box of the activities they do.
- If they do not mention the activity, leave the box blank.

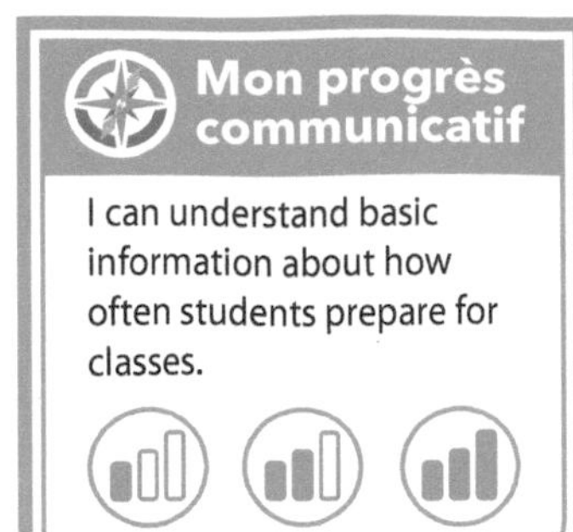

 Étape 2: Commenter

The student contestants are eager for feedback on their recordings and would like to hear some of your ideas. They have invited you to participate in an online discussion forum. Go to Explorer to add your comments and responses.

 Étape 3: Parler

Inspired by the online competition, your school principal has decided to start a similar project in your school. Each student will submit a recording of study tips to be shared with next year's new students. Choose one of your classes and submit a short recording describing what you think a student taking the class needs to do or not do to experience success. Go to Explorer to record your tips.

All of the materials for ***J'avance 3*** can be found in Explorer.

Synthèse de grammaire

1. Expressing Preferences and What You are Going to Do: *préférer/aimer + l'infinitif et le futur proche*

When expressing that you like or prefer something, you will use verbs like ***aimer*** or ***préférer***, frequently followed by another verb. In that case, it is essential to remember that the first verb is conjugated according to the subject of the sentence and the second verb remains in its infinitive form, meaning that keeps its ***-er***, ***-ir***, or ***-re*** ending.

J' **aime** (1) **parler** (2) français.

Tu **préfères** (1) **lire** (2) ou **jouer** (2) de la guitare?

It is similar when you are expressing that something is going to happen soon, in the near future. The verb ***aller*** changes according to the subject to convey the idea that the action is "going to" happen, but the second verb does not change, no matter the subject.

Le futur proche du verbe "étudier"

je **vais étudier**	nous **allons étudier**
tu **vas étudier**	vous **allez étudier**
il **va étudier** elle **va étudier** on **va étudier**	ils **vont étudier** elles **vont étudier**

If you need to make your sentence negative, your **ne...pas** will go around the first verb:

Je **n'**aime **pas** lire. Je **ne** vais **pas** étudier.

2. Describing a Person's Job and Personality: *le genre des noms et l'accord des adjectifs*

In French, all nouns have a grammatical gender (masculine or feminine). When we use adjectives to describe nouns, we generally have to make sure the adjective endings match up with the noun they are describing. In the case of people in a school, the descriptive words you might use to describe people in a school are professions and adjectives of personality.

a. Professions: Many words for a person's job have a masculine form and a feminine form. In some cases, the same word will be used regardless of the person's gender.

masculin	*féminin*	*masculin ou féminin*
principal	**principale**	entraîneur documentaliste
surveillant	**surveillante**	
infirmier	**infirmière**	

Note: Do not forget to choose appropriately between ***un/une*** and ***le/la/l'*** when working with words for someone's profession.

b. Adjectives of personality: The same idea will be true for adjectives that describe someone's personality. There are common patterns of changes based on the endings of the words. This almost always changes the pronunciation of the word.

masculin	*féminin*	*masculin ou féminin*
dévoué	**dévouée**	dynamique énergique sympa
créatif	**créative**	
travailleur	**travailleuse**	

3. Comparing How Much or How Often: *le comparatif des noms, des verbes et des adverbes*

When you want to compare how much you do something or how often something happens, you can use comparative structures:

plus *more*
plus...que *more...than*
plus de...que *more (of something) than*

J'étudie **plus** au lycée. *I study more in high school.*

Although it is possible to use ***plus*** on its own, your meaning is clearer if you add more information to your sentence.

J'étudie **plus que** mon frère. *I study more than my brother.*
J'étudie **plus** souvent **que** mon frère. *I study more often than my brother.*

Notice that the structure follows this pattern:

Item A + **PLUS** + (Expression of frequency) + **QUE** + Item B

If you are comparing how many of something (e.g. ***examens, notes, activités***), you will need to add the word ***de*** before the nouns in the comparison:

J'étudie **plus de** jeux vidéo **que de** livres pour l'école!
I study more video games than school books!

Vocabulaire

Comment dit-on? 1: I can talk about the school year, the school day, and subjects I study.

Le calendrier scolaire	*School calendar*
l'année (f.) scolaire	*school year*
un jour férié	*holiday*
la rentrée	*back-to-school*
les vacances (f. pl.)	*vacation*

Les matières	*School subjects*
Je vais suivre un cours de/d' ____ .	*I'm going to take a/an ____ class.*
l'allemand (m.)	*German*
l'économie (f.)	*economics*
l'histoire-géo (f.)	*history-geography*
la physique-chimie	*physics-chemistry*

Les moments de la journée	*Times of the day*
en début de journée	*at the beginning of the day*
avant l'école	*before school*
en fin de journée	*at the end of the day*
après l'école	*after school*
du temps libre	*free, unscheduled time*
une permanence ("perm")	*study hall*

Comment dit-on? 2: I can talk about places and people in my school.

Les endroits de l'école	*Places at school*
l'accueil (m.)	*reception area*
le bureau central	*main office*
le complexe sportif	*sports complex*
le couloir	*hallway*
le foyer	*student lounge*
l'infirmerie (f.)	*nurse's office*
le laboratoire	*laboratory*
le parking	*parking lot*
la salle d'informatique	*computer room*
le terrain de sport	*sports field*

Expressions utiles	
aller voir...	*to go see...*
Ça, c'est...	*This is...*
chercher quelque chose	*to look for something, to go get something*
demander conseil à...	*to ask for advice from...*
Ici, on peut...	*Here, you can...*
Il y a...	*There is/are...*
passer du temps	*to spend time*
Voici...	*Here is...*

Le personnel de l'école	School staff
le conseiller/la conseillère d'orientation	school counselor
le/la documentaliste	library media specialist
l'entraîneur	coach/trainer
l'infirmier (m.)/ l'infirmière (f.)	nurse
le proviseur/la proviseure	high school principal
le proviseur-adjoint/la proviseure-adjointe	assistant principal
le/la secrétaire	secretary

Pour décrire quelqu'un	Describing someone
C'est quelqu'un de/d'____	He/She's a ____ person.
dynamique	dynamic
énergique	energetic
positif/positive	positive

Comment dit-on? 3: I can talk about what I do at school.

De bonnes habitudes	Good habits
accéder à la plate-forme de la classe	to access the class learning platform
prendre des notes	to take notes
étudier des fiches de révision	to study notecards
faire une/des pause(s)	to take a break, to take breaks
partager des ressources en ligne	to share online resources
participer à des activités périscolaires/extrascolaires	to participate in extracurricular activities

De mauvaises habitudes	Bad habits
attendre le dernier moment (pour)	to wait until the last minute (to)
dormir tard	to sleep late
regarder mon portable au lieu de dormir	to look at my phone instead of sleeping
utiliser mon portable en classe	to use my phone in class

Les expressions de fréquence	Expressions of frequency
de temps en temps	from time to time
jamais	never
parfois	sometimes
rarement	rarely
souvent	often
tous les jours	everyday
tout le temps	all the time
(une) fois par semaine	(one) time per week

Les activités périscolaires	Extracurricular activities
le club théâtre, le club cinéma, le club de____	theater club, film club, ____ club
une équipe de (foot, volley, basket, etc.)	a (soccer, volleyball, basketball, etc.) team

Expressions utiles	
Je ne dois pas...	I must not...
Pour réussir à l'école, je dois...	To be successful at school, I must...

Lou-Ann

J'y arrive

Questions essentielles

- How do personal preferences and traits influence our choices in school?
- What helps students engage in their school community?
- What do schools in different cultural contexts provide to meet the needs of their students?

Un échange scolaire

Your school counselor has asked you to help welcome Lou-Ann, an exchange student from ***la Réunion***, who will be attending your school soon. Your counselor suggested that you exchange information with Lou-Ann until she arrives to provide an easy transition. Lou-Ann sent you a ***dossier vidéo*** to give you an idea of what kind of student she is.

Your counselor asked you to watch Lou-Ann's ***dossier*** and then follow-up with a phone call. Based on what you know about Lou-Ann, and her culture, you will prepare a ***Bienvenue à notre école*** guide in the form of an annotated map or visual representation for her.

- What is essential to make the most of the school year?
- What would a student arriving from another culture need to know to have a great experience in your school?

Before you begin, refer to the ***J'y arrive*** rubric in Explorer to familiarize yourself with the evaluation criteria.

Interpretive Assessment

Qui est Lou-Ann?

Watch Lou-Ann's video about how she approaches the school year.

a. From the list of words and phrases in Explorer, check the ones that Lou-Ann mentions.

b. Answer the multiple choice questions about the video in Explorer.

Interpersonal Assessment

AP® Comment est-ce que je peux aider?

You have scheduled an international phone call with Lou-Ann, so she has a chance to ask you some questions about what you do to be successful in school and what you are planning on doing this year.

Listen and respond to the questions Lou-Ann asks you in your Explorer course. As you listen, make a few notes on the planning sheet about what you might include in your answers to Lou-Ann.

Presentational Assessment

Tout sur mon école

Create an annotated map or visual representation of your school that Lou-Ann can use when she arrives. Think carefully about what Lou-Ann would need to know based on what her school and classes are like.

Be sure to include the following information about your school, paying attention to places or people in your school that might be different from Lou-Ann's experience:

- What will Lou-Ann need to know about your school?
- Where will Lou-Ann's classes be? What else is important to know about classes?
- Where does one go when one is sick? To spend time with friends? To do schoolwork? To collaborate with classmates?
- Where can one find resources and support for class?
- What kinds of activities help build community in your school? Where do they take place?

L'île de la Réunion

UNITÉ 2
À table!

Objectifs de l'unité

Exchange information about traditional dishes from Francophone cultures and share memories related to food.

Read, view, and listen to recipes, menus, videos, and invitations related to food in Francophone cultures.

Invite others to events and special meals.

Investigate how food plays an integral part in family, traditions, and celebrations in Francophone cultures.

Questions essentielles

Which culinary traditions of the past are still important today?

How are our memories with the important people in our lives connected to food?

How does food bring people together?

Food plays an important role in our lives. It is a part of our daily activities, but it is also a focal point of many traditions and memories. In this unit, Maxime and his family will share their memories of what they used to eat and how they enjoyed cooking and eating together.

Rencontre interculturelle

La Belgique

Nom: Maxime

Langues parlées: français, néerlandais, anglais

Origine: Floriffoux et Mornimont, Belgique

La Belgique a trois langues officielles: le néerlandais, le français et l'allemand. La plupart du pays est divisée en une région francophone (la Wallonie) et une région flamande (la Flandre ou Vlaanderen en néerlandais). La Belgique est aussi un des six pays fondateurs de l'Union européenne. Bruxelles, la capitale de la Belgique, est une ville importante dans l'Union européenne. On y trouve le Conseil européen et la Commission européenne.

La Belgique est un pays riche en traditions. On peut voir de l'architecture médiévale dans beaucoup de villes et il y a des festivals traditionnels comme le carnaval de Binche (qui ressemble un peu au Mardi Gras de la Louisiane aux États-Unis). Les gaufres sont une spécialité culinaire belge qui date du Moyen Âge. On fait du chocolat en Belgique depuis le dix-septième (17e) siècle.

La citadelle de Namur et la rivière Sambre

Les "Gilles", un costume traditionnel du carnaval de Binche

Les drapeaux de l'Union européenne devant la Commission européenne à Bruxelles

Voici Philippe, le roi des Belges, et la reine Mathilde. La Belgique est une monarchie constitutionnelle où il y a un roi mais également un gouvernement parlementaire.

Voilà comment on faisait des gaufres dans le passé!

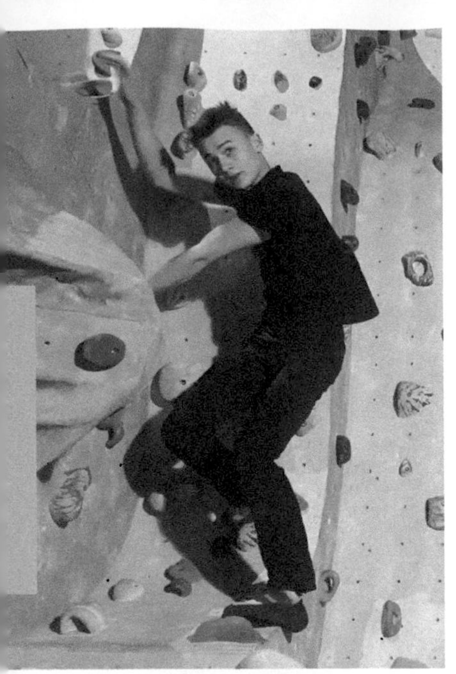

Maxime fait du VTT et de l'escalade.

Maxime a 15 ans et il vit en Wallonie, la partie francophone de la Belgique. Il vit avec son père, sa belle-mère et sa belle-sœur dans le village de Floriffoux. Il vit aussi avec sa mère, son beau-père, sa demi-sœur et sa belle-sœur dans le village de Mornimont.

Maxime est en quatrième (4e) à l'institut Saint-Louis dans la ville de Namur. Il parle français, mais il apprend aussi le néerlandais et l'anglais. Maxime est sportif. Pendant son temps libre, il aime faire du jogging, de l'escalade et du VTT (vélo tout terrain). Il en fait assez souvent.

Maxime étudie le néerlandais, une des trois langues officielles de la Belgique.

Activité 1

Bonjour, Maxime!

Étape 1: Préparer

Regardez la photo de Maxime, son introduction et ce qu'il dit dans les bulles. Utilisez la représentation schématique sur Explorer pour noter quelques détails sur:

a. sa famille;

b. ses préférences;

c. où il vit; et

d. sa région et son pays.

Étape 2: Écouter

a. Regardez la vidéo où Maxime se présente. Dans quel ordre dit-il les détails suivants?

____ Il parle des sports qu'il aime faire.

____ Il parle deux langues en plus du français.

____ Il explique le rôle de la Belgique dans l'Union européenne.

____ Il dit avec qui il habite.

____ Il explique comment écrire son prénom.

b. Maintenant, regardez de nouveau et écrivez les détails qu'il dit dans votre représentation schématique.

Étape 3: Écrire

Complétez la colonne "moi" de votre représentation schématique.

a. Comment est votre famille?

b. Quelles sont vos préférences?

c. Où vivez-vous?

d. Dans quel pays vivez-vous? Dans quelle région?

Bruxelles, Belgique

Étape 4: Comparer

Demandez à votre partenaire de comparer ses réponses avec les informations de Maxime.

Modèle

Quelles similarités/différences est-ce qu'il y a entre tes préférences et les préférences de Maxime?

Réflexion interculturelle

In his introduction video, Maxime shared some important facts about his region and country. Why do you suppose he thought these were important to share with you? If you were introducing yourself, what do you think you would include about the place where you live? Answer the questions in the discussion forum in Explorer.

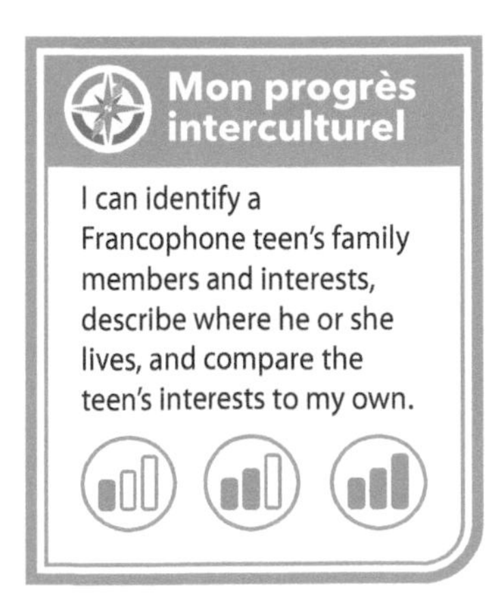

Cafés à Bruxelles

Rappelle-toi

Activité 2

Que prenez-vous au café?

Étape 1: Regarder et écouter

Maxime a un copain, Lucien, qui habite à Bruxelles. Il vous explique ce que les membres de sa famille prennent dans ce café.

a. Regardez la carte du Café bruxellois et les photos du repas.

b. Écrivez les lettres qui correspondent à ce que Lucien et les membres de sa famille mangent au Café bruxellois.

1. Lucien ________
2. son frère, Hugo ________
3. ses sœurs ________
4. leur mère ________

a. un croque-monsieur
b. une omelette
c. une quiche du jour
d. un sandwich jambon-fromage
e. un poulet rôti
f. un steak-frites
g. une salade
h. un chocolat chaud
i. de l'eau plate (carafe)
j. de l'eau gazeuse (bouteille)
k. un jus d'orange
l. un thé
m. un café
n. des frites

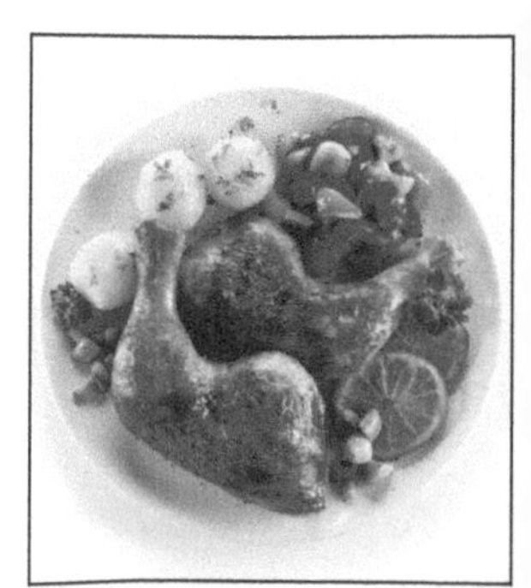

Étape 2: Parler

Imaginez que vous allez manger dans ce café. Dans un groupe de trois ou quatre personnes, parlez de ce que vous préférez commander.

Modèle

Je prends un croque-monsieur avec des frites et un café comme boisson.

Je voudrais un croissant et un thé sans sucre, s'il vous plaît.

Café bruxellois

Menu petit déjeuner		Déjeuner	
croissant + boisson = 7 €		Croque-monsieur	10 €
		Omelette	9 €
Boissons		Quiche du jour	11 €
chocolat chaud	4 €	Sandwich jambon-fromage	8 €
eau plate/gazeuse	4 €	Poulet rôti	13 €
thé	3 €	Steak-frites	13 €
café	3 €	+salade/frites	2 €

Activité 3

Quelles sont leurs préférences?

Étape 1: Lire

Lucien vous envoie une photo de sa famille. Ils arrivent la semaine prochaine pour rendre visite à Lucien et viennent dîner chez vous. Ils vous disent ce qu'ils préfèrent manger. Faites une liste des préférences de la famille dans la représentation schématique dans l'**Étape 2**.

Rappel

Chez

Tu vas rentrer **chez** toi après l'école?

Non, je vais manger **chez** ma grand-mère après l'école.

Rappel

La possession

Quand Maxime parle, il utilise ***mon, ma, mes***:
mon *pays* (m.)
ma *tante* (f.)
mes *parents* (pl.)

Quand on parle de Maxime, on utilise ***son, sa, ses***:
son *pays* (m.)
sa *tante* (f.)
ses *parents* (pl.)

Quand on parle à une autre personne, on utilise ***ton, ta, tes*** ou ***votre, vos***:
ton *pays* (m.)
ta *tante* (f.)
tes *parents* (pl.)
votre *pays* (m.)
votre *tante* (f.)
vos *parents* (pl.)

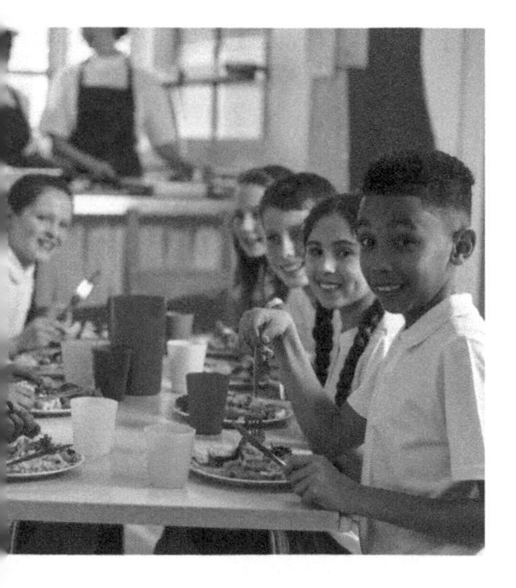

Étape 2: Écrire

Vous planifiez le dîner pour la famille de Lucien. Proposez un ou deux plats avec des ingrédients que tout le monde peut manger.

membre de la famille	préférences	possibilités pour le repas
Modèle: sa grand-mère	pas salé	salade de légumes, salade de fruits

Étape 3: Écrire

Écrivez une liste de ce qu'il faut acheter au supermarché, avec les quantités nécessaires.

Modèle

trois tomates

des carottes

trois baguettes

de la glace

Activité 4

Vous mangez quoi à l'école?

Lou-Ann et Maxime vous ont envoyé les menus de leurs restaurants scolaires parce que vous avez demandé ce qu'ils mangent à l'école.

a. Quel repas préférez-vous et pourquoi? Donnez plusieurs raisons selon vos préférences.

b. Enregistrez votre réponse sur Explorer.

Modèle

Je voudrais le repas de mardi de la Réunion parce que j'adore le fromage et les tomates. J'aime les desserts de fruits et la pastèque est bien sucrée. C'est délicieux!

Restaurant scolaire - la Réunion

lundi
Salade bicolore (betterave/carotte)
Cuisse de poulet rôti
Riz, pois et citrouille
Yaourt aromatisé
Ananas frais

mardi
Salade de tomate
Omelette fromagère
Riz, pois du cap
Fromage, pastèque

mercredi
Salade verte
Filet de poisson pané
Pâte à la tomate
Crème dessert chocolat

jeudi
Salade de concombre
Cari de porc au massalé
Riz, lentilles
Fromage, poire

vendredi
Salade de chou
Pâtes à la bolognaise
Fromage, mangue

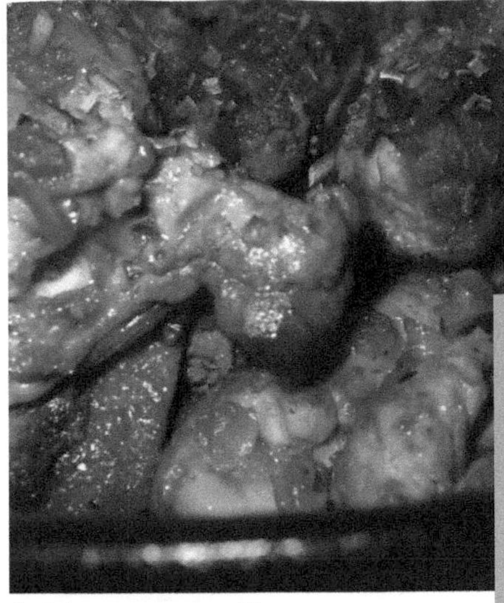

Cari de porc au massalé

Cantine scolaire - la Belgique

lundi	Soupe à l'oignon Brochette de porc, sauce provençale Purée de pommes de terre Yaourt
mardi	Soupe de tomates Steak, sauce moutarde Ratatouille, riz Mousse au chocolat
mercredi	Soupe aux carottes Rôti de poulet Pommes de terre à la vapeur Compote de pommes
jeudi	Crème de tomates Poisson aux petits légumes Poire chaude
vendredi	Soupe aux quatre légumes Spaghettis sauce bolognaise Tartelette aux fruits

Brochette de porc et purée de pommes de terre

Rappelle-toi

Les repas et la nourriture

le déjeuner
le dîner
le petit déjeuner
le repas

la baguette
la banane
les boissons (f. pl.)
le dessert
le fromage
les fruits (m. pl.)
le gâteau
la glace
le jus d'orange/de pomme
le lait
les légumes (m. pl.)
la mangue
l'œuf (m.)
le pain
les pâtes (f. pl.)
le poisson
les pommes de terre (f. pl.)
le poulet
le riz
la salade verte
la soupe
le steak
la tarte
la viande

Expressions utiles

délicieux/délicieuse
épicé/épicée
léger/légère
riche
salé/salée
sucré/sucrée

Au café/au restaurant

le café
la carte
le chocolat chaud
la crêpe beurre-sucre
le croissant
le croque-monsieur
l'eau (f.) plate/gazeuse/minérale
le menu
l'omelette (f.)
le poulet rôti
la quiche
le sandwich jambon-fromage
le steak-frites
le thé

La famille

le cousin/la cousine
l'enfant (m. ou f.)
la fille
le fils
le frère
la grand-mère
le grand-père
les grands-parents (m. pl.)
la mère
l'oncle (m.)
les parents (m. pl.)
le père
la sœur
la tante

Expressions utiles

C'était...
cuit(e)(s) avec...
fait(e)(s) avec...
Il y avait...
nature
servi(e)(s) avec...

Communiquons

Comment dit-on? 1

Les traditions et la nourriture

Les plats traditionnels belges

Dans ma famille, c'était toujours un plaisir de partager un repas et il y avait toujours beaucoup de personnes à la maison pour les repas. Je vais vous parler de trois de mes plats préférés.

Le **waterzooï** est un plat de viande (poulet) ou de poisson cuit avec des légumes et de la **crème** fraîche et servi avec des pommes de terre.

Les moules-**frites** sont très populaires. Les **moules** sont des **fruits de mer** cuits avec des **oignons** et du **céleri**. Elles sont servies nature ou en sauce avec des frites.

Les **gaufres** de Bruxelles sont faites avec de la **farine**, des œufs, du sucre, du beurre, et du lait. Au carnaval de Binche, Maxime mangeait des gaufres avec de la **crème** fouettée et des **fraises**.

Activité 5

Quels sont les ingrédients?

 **Étape 1: Chercher**

Regardez les plats de la page précédente.

Est-ce que vous pouvez identifier...

... une viande?

... deux légumes?

... un produit de la mer?

... un produit laitier *(dairy product)*?

Étape 2: Identifier

Le 21 juillet, c'est la fête nationale belge et la ville de Floriffoux organise un dîner. Pour cette occasion, vous préparez un waterzooï au poulet avec Maxime.

a. Regardez la recette et les ingrédients que vous avez déjà.

b. Qu'est-ce que vous devez acheter pour faire ce plat?

Modèle

Pour faire un waterzooï, on doit acheter quatre pommes de terre...

On peut aussi dire

l'ail (m.)
garlic

un bouquet garni
bundle of herbs for flavoring soups or sauces

des épices (f. pl.)
spices

un poireau
leek

Waterzooï de poulet

Ingrédients pour 4 personnes

- 1 poulet de 1,5 kg
- 4 pommes de terre
- 4 carottes
- 4 petits poireaux
- 3 branches de céleri
- 4 navets *(turnips)*
- 1 oignon
- 1 bouquet garni
- 20 cl de vin blanc *(white wine)*
- 15 cl de crème fraîche
- beurre
- sel/poivre

Vous avez déjà...

Rappel

Questions avec "est-ce que"

Remember that adding ***est-ce que*** to the beginning of a statement is an easy way to form a yes/no question.

Est-ce que nous avons du sel?

You can also place the **est-ce que** after a question word to form an informational question.

*Où **est-ce que** tu vas acheter les moules?*

*Quand **est-ce que** nous allons manger?*

Mon progrès communicatif

I can exchange information about ingredients in a traditional dish.

Rappel

Pour parler de la cuisine

Remember that you already know a few verbs related to cooking and eating.

cuisiner
déguster
être gourmand/gourmande

Étape 3: Écrire

Maxime est déjà au supermarché et il vous demande par texto la liste des ingrédients à acheter. Regardez la liste et répondez à Maxime via texto avec les ingrédients à acheter.

Modèle:

Salut, c'est Maxime! Je suis au supermarché.

Salut Maxime! Tu dois acheter quelques ingrédients pour le waterzooï.

Est-ce que je dois acheter de la viande? 

Ok. Qu'est-ce qu'il faut acheter comme légumes? ...

D'accord. Et est-ce qu'il faut des produits laitiers? 

Bien. Est-ce qu'il faut des épices? ...

Ok, est-ce qu'il faut autre chose? 

D'accord. À plus tard! 

Activité 6

Quelles gaufres goûter?

Étape 1: Identifier

Pour le 21 juillet, Maxime organise une fête de la gaufre et il fait un menu. Regardez les images et complétez les descriptions des gaufres avec les ingrédients ci-dessous:

banane - fraises - chocolat - caramel -
crème fouettée - glace à la vanille

Gaufre nature

Gaufre aux ______ et à la ____________.

Gaufre au ______ et à la ____________.

Gaufre à la ______ et au ____________.

Gaufre au ______ salé.

Étape 2: Écouter

Aïcha, Florent et Chloé appellent Maxime pour dire ce qu'ils vont apporter *(bring)*. Écoutez les descriptions et identifiez les images de l'**Étape 1** qui correspondent aux gaufres mentionnées.

1. Aïcha
2. Florent
3. Chloé

Étape 3: Discuter

Quelles gaufres les élèves de la classe veulent-ils goûter *(taste)*? Pourquoi ou pourquoi pas? Posez la question à trois élèves de la classe.

Modèle

Élève 1: Quelle gaufre est-ce que tu veux goûter et pourquoi?

Élève 2: Je veux goûter la gaufre nature parce que je n'aime pas beaucoup le sucre. Et toi?

Rappel

Le verbe vouloir

The verb ***vouloir*** is a useful way to express what people want.

Je **veux** goûter le poulet moamba parce que j'aime les plats épicés.

Mon ami **veut** goûter la tarte au riz parce qu'il aime les plats sucrés.

Quels plats est-ce que vous **voulez** goûter?

Mon progrès communicatif

I can exchange information about foods I would like to try, providing reasons and simple details.

Activité 7

Quel plat choisir?

Café Tchantchès

Nos spécialités belges

La salade liégeoise (pommes de terre, haricots verts, et lardons)	14,85€
Notre stoemp du jour (purée de pommes de terre et de carottes) et ses saucisses	15,85€
Vol au vent (avec une salade verte)	14,85€
Carbonnade flamande (+ frites)	16,85€
Notre waterzooï au poulet (avec une salade verte)	15,85€
Nos moules (servies avec des frites)	
Moules nature	20,90€
Moules marinières (à l'ail et au vin blanc)	22,90€
Moules aux tomates	21,90€

On peut aussi dire

la carbonnade flamande
Belgian beef stew

la carotte
carrot

les lardons (m. pl.)
cubed ham, bacon pieces

la purée
mashed (potatoes)

la saucisse
sausage

Un vol au vent est une pâtisserie salée avec de la crème, du poulet, des boulettes de viande et des champignons *(mushrooms)*.

Étape 1: Identifier

Vous déjeunez au Café Tchantchès à Liège avec votre groupe scolaire. Lisez le menu des spécialités belges.

Combien de plats ont...

... des frites?

... du poisson?

... des fruits de mer?

... de la salade?

Étape 2: Écouter

Élodie et Gabriel sont au restaurant avec vous et ils ne savent pas quoi prendre. Écoutez leurs préférences et suggérez-leur deux plats dans la représentation schématique sur Explorer.

vos suggestions	plat 1	plat 2
Élodie		
Gabriel		

Étape 3: Parler

Vous partagez sur un forum: Qu'est-ce que vous voulez prendre? Pourquoi? Qu'est-ce que vous ne voulez pas prendre? Pourquoi?

a. Préparez vos idées dans la représentation schématique.

b. Enregistrez vos réponses dans le forum sur Explorer.

Modèle

Je veux prendre les moules marinières parce que j'adore les fruits de mer et l'ail. Je ne veux pas prendre le vol au vent parce que c'est trop riche.

	quel plat?	pourquoi?
Je veux prendre ...		
Je ne veux pas prendre ...		

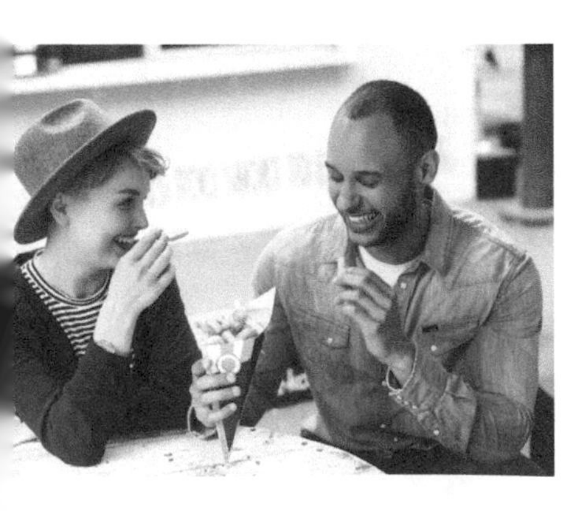

Réflexion interculturelle

Take a look at some of the Belgian dishes you have already seen in ***Unité 2***. How do these dishes compare to those that people in your community make to celebrate a holiday in your country? Answer the question in the discussion forum in Explorer.

Mon progrès interculturel

I can compare traditional dishes from my community to traditional dishes in Belgium.

Encore des plats traditionnels

Dans ma famille, on mangeait des plats belges et des plats congolais parce que ma tante est de la République démocratique du Congo. Tous les plats étaient délicieux! Dans chaque plat, il y avait un goût différent.

Le drapeau de Belgique

Le drapeau de la République démocratique du Congo

La tarte au riz est sucrée.

Les beignets congolais sont croustillants.

Le filet américain est salé.

Le poulet moamba est épicé.

Rappel

Quelques expressions

À table!

Bon appétit!

Je voudrais…

Je prends…

avec

comme

sans

On peut aussi dire

croustillant/croustillante
crispy, crunchy

le goût
taste (n.)

goûter
to taste

Activité 8

Quel plat voulez-vous goûter?

Étape 1: Parlez

Regardez les plats traditionnels belges et congolais. Avec un(e) partenaire, décidez quelles sont les recettes que vous voulez goûter des deux pays et expliquez pourquoi.

Modèle

Élève A: Quel plat congolais est-ce que tu veux goûter?

Élève B: Je veux goûter les beignets congolais.

Élève A: Pourquoi est-ce que tu veux goûter les beignets congolais?

Élève B: Parce que j'aime les beignets pour le petit déjeuner.

Étape 2: Écrivez et comparez

Partagez quelques-unes de vos préférences sur Explorer.

Stratégies

Word Families

Word families are groups of words that share a common root. Look at the similarities between these words, both in spelling and meaning. As you study French, you will become familiar with word families and be able to power up your vocabulary!

1. Find the root of the word.
2. Consider how the words are used in context.
3. Look at the words to determine if they are nouns, verbs, or adjectives.

Découvrons 1

Describing the Past

Une fête quand j'étais petite

C'**était** le 2 février, la fête de la Chandeleur.

Il y **avait** des œufs, du lait, du sucre et de la farine et ... il y **avait** beaucoup de crêpes!

Je **mangeais** des crêpes avec toute ma famille. Elles **étaient** sucrées et délicieuses.

Découvertes

Reflect on what you observe and respond to the following questions in the graphic organizer in Explorer.

1. What do you notice about the words **in bold**? Do you see any patterns?
2. What do you observe about how these words are used in the descriptions of the holiday tradition when Océane was little? Can you figure out when to use ***était*** and ***étaient***? How about ***il y avait*** and ***je mangeais***?
3. Share your observations with a ***partenaire*** or with your teacher. What else do you notice together? Can you add to your observations?

View the ***Découvrons 1*** resources for this unit in Explorer and check the ***Synthèse de grammaire*** at the end of this unit.

Activité 9

Quelle est l'origine des frites?

Étape 1: Lire

Lisez le texte. Est-ce que vous pouvez associer les mots en **caractère gras** avec une image?

Que savez-vous de l'origine des frites? Sont-elles vraiment françaises?

Accueil
Portails thématiques
Article au hasard
Contact

Non, en fait, les frites sont probablement **belges**, de la ville de Namur, près de Bruxelles. Un plat populaire de Namur était de servir des petits poissons **frits**. Au 17e siècle (1 siècle=100 ans), **la rivière gelait** souvent et il n'était pas possible de **pêcher**. Les habitants de Namur avaient beaucoup de pommes de terre. C'était logique de remplacer les poissons par ces pommes de terre. Ils les coupaient en forme de petits poissons et les faisaient **frire**. Deux siècles plus tard, les pommes de terre étaient **coupées en forme de bâton**. Et voilà, l'origine des pommes **frites**! On estime que 350 kilogrammes de frites sont consommés chaque seconde dans **le monde**!

la rivière [de Namur] - frire / frits / frites - le monde
coupées en forme de bâton - gelait - belges - pêcher

A

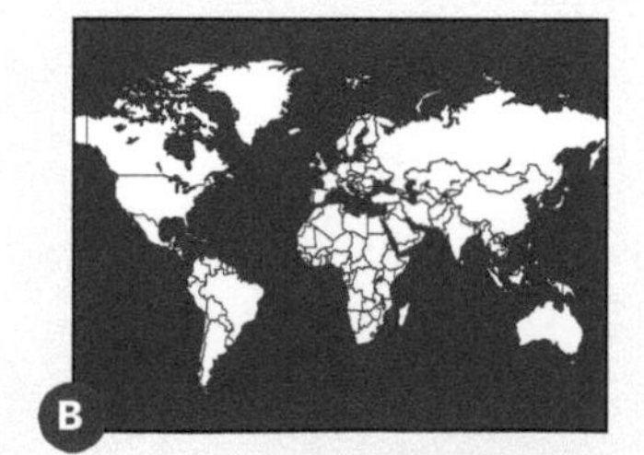
B

C

D

E

F

G

Étape 2: Parler

Maintenant, répondez aux questions oralement avec un(e) partenaire.

Modèle

Élève 1: Est-ce que les frites étaient en premier des poissons?

Élève 2: Oui, c'**étaient** des petits poissons frits.

1. Est-ce que la population de Namur aimait manger des poissons?
2. Comment est-ce qu'on préparait les petits poissons?
3. Est-ce qu'il était toujours possible de pêcher à Namur?
4. Quand on ne pouvait pas pêcher, on remplaçait les poissons par quoi?

Activité 10

Qu'est-ce qu'on mangeait?

Étape 1: Regarder et comparer

Regardez les statistiques concernant la consommation de la nourriture en 1970 et en 2008. Écrivez trois phrases pour comparer la consommation entre les deux années.

Modèle

On mangeait plus de légumes et de fruits en 2008.

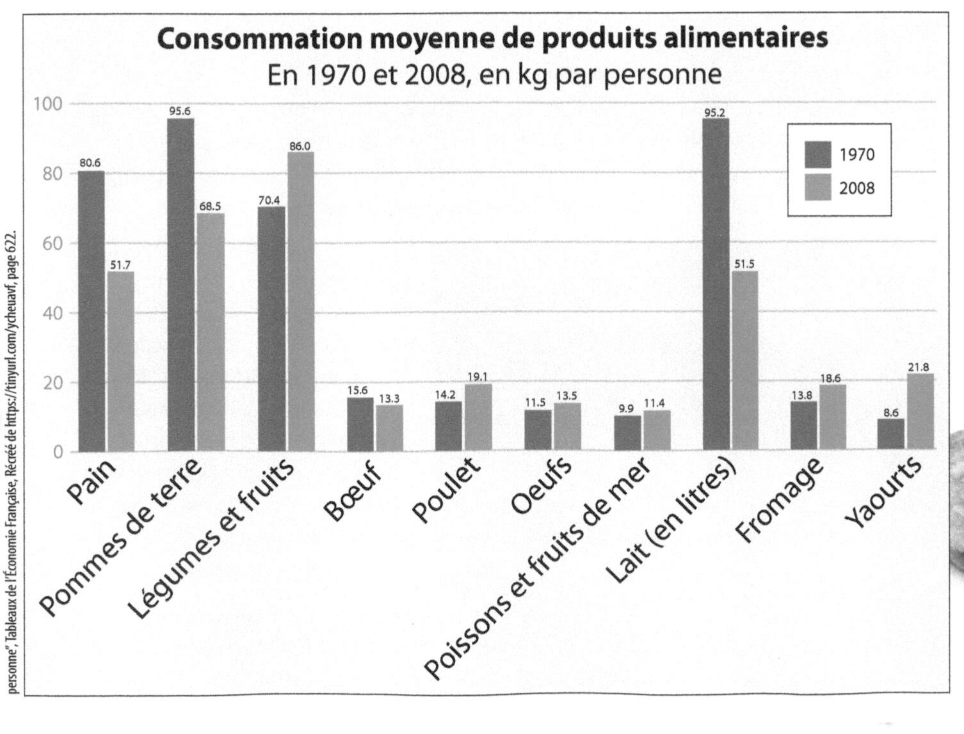

personne", Tableaux de l'Économie Française, Recréé de https://tinyurl.com/ycheuavf, page 622.

Rappel

Les comparaisons

Remember that you made comparisons about quantities using ***plus de... que:***

J'ai **plus de** cours de sciences **que** toi.

Il a **plus de** jeux vidéo **que** de livres!

Now you'll be able to transfer this knowledge to talk about quantities of various foods you used to eat in the past and eat now.

On mangeait **plus de** fromage **que** de yaourt en 1970.

Rappel

L'article partitif

Remember that using the partitive article is a good way to express "some" of something, which is useful in describing amounts of food.

du sucre	(masculin)
de la crème	(féminin)
de l'ail	(devant une voyelle; masculin singulier)
de l'eau	(devant une voyelle; féminin singulier)
des œufs	(pluriel)

Je mangeais toujours **des** crêpes avec **du** beurre et **du** sucre quand j'étais petit(e).

Étape 2: Écrire

Indiquez ce que vous mangez de ces produits alimentaires (dans le graphique à la page précédente) et comparez vos réponses à quand vous étiez petit(e).

Modèle

maintenant	dans le passé
Je mange du bœuf maintenant.	Quand j'étais petit(e), je ne mangeais pas de bœuf. Je mangeais du poulet.

Étape 3: Parlez

Comparez vos réponses à celles des autres élèves de votre classe à l'oral.

Zoom culture

Produit culturel: La baraque à frites

 Connexions

Which kinds of street food do you like to eat?

La baraque à frites a la patate en Belgique! As you may know and as the Belgian superstar Stromae said at the start of each concert on his American tour, French fries aren't really French – they're Belgian!

"Monsieur Fritz" (Jean Frédéric Krieger-Zacharidès) and his brother Georges are believed to have started the first ***baraque à frites***. They were traveling entertainers who decided to sell fries at the fair in Liège in 1835. It was a total success! In 1838, they started a business in a traveling trailer. They adopted the name "Fritz," recalling both the frying and their German origin. The ***baraque à frites*** was born.

Today, the ***baraques à frites*** and the ***frites*** they sell are an integral part of Belgian identity. In Belgium, almost every neighborhood has one! Mostly small family businesses, there are nearly 5,000 ***baraques à frites*** across 589 municipalities. Some are permanent structures like a typical carry-out restaurant, but many are true ***baraques*** *(shacks)*. As a means of increasing their popularity, the ***baraques à frites*** will offer a large variety of signature sauces.

 Réflexion

How often are fries served for meals that you eat? Why might different cultures want to take credit for inventing fries? What other foods do you eat today that come from food traditions of the past? Answer the questions in the discussion forum in Explorer.

Activité 11

Il mangeait comment?

Étape 1: Écouter et écrire

Regardez la vidéo de Diego où il décrit ce qu'il mangeait pendant les vacances. Puis cochez (✔) les descriptions qui correspondent à celles de Diego:

____ Diego mangeait des croissants croustillants à Paris.

____ Il était chez sa grand-mère au château de Passavant.

____ Il y avait beaucoup de fruits pour la confiture à Passavant.

____ Il était à la Rochelle avec ses cousins.

____ Il mangeait des crêpes aux fraises et à la crème fouettée avec ses cousins.

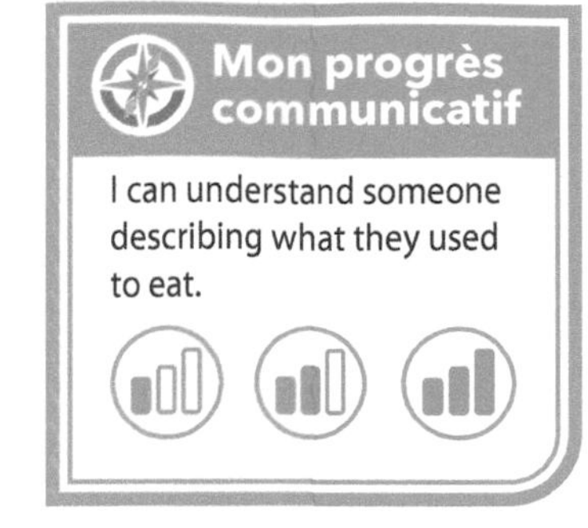

Étape 2: Filmer et parler

À vous de décrire ce que vous mangiez dans le passé. Créez un film comme celui de Diego avec des descriptions.

a. Trouvez quelques photos sur votre téléphone ou sur internet.

b. Utilisez les phrases suivantes pour commencer vos phrases: Il y avait, C'était, Je mangeais.

c. Postez votre vidéo sur Explorer.

Modèle

C'était le week-end dernier. **Je mangeais** un gâteau très sucré pour mon anniversaire. **Il y avait** mes amis Zoé et Corentin.

J'avance 1

C'était comment?

Étape 1: Regarder

Watch the video from Maxime's aunt, Ndona, where she describes what she used to eat. Then, check the descriptions that match what Ndona says.

Étape 2: Écouter et répondre

Based on the meals that Ndona described in her video, ask a classmate about which dish he or she may prefer to taste and why. Then switch roles. Record your conversation in Explorer.

Étape 3: Écrire

You have heard Maxime's aunt Ndona share what she used to eat. Now you will write an email to Maxime to share some foods that you used to eat. Use a special occasion from your past, like a weekly tradition of making and eating a certain food or a holiday meal, as inspiration.

All of the materials for ***J'avance 1*** can be found in Explorer.

Comment dit-on? 2

Comment préparait-on le repas?

Souvenirs de la ferme

Mon album de famille

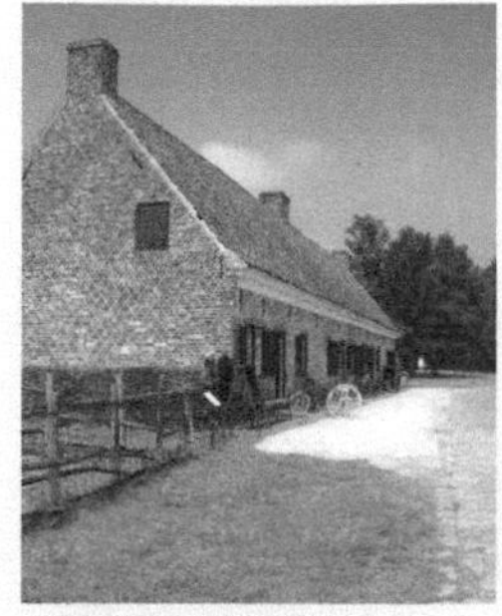
Quand j'étais petit, je passais l 'été à **la ferme** de mon oncle et ma tante.

Le matin, il fallait chercher des **framboises** et des fraises.

Le dimanche, ma tante faisait de **la confiture** aux framboises.

Pour le souper, c'était toujours moi qui mettais la table avec des **fourchettes**, des **assiettes**, des **couteaux**, et des **cuillères**.

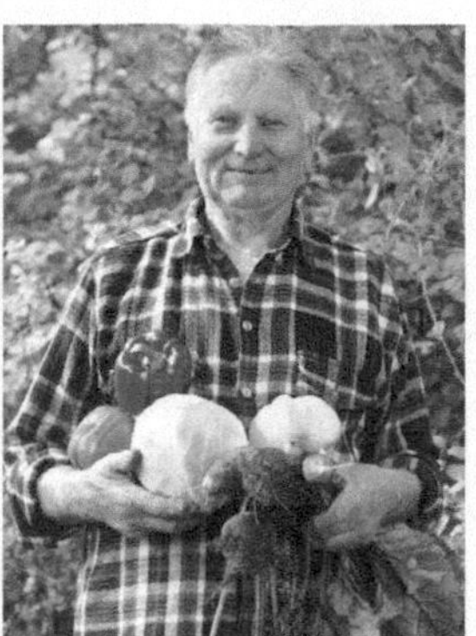
Mon oncle allait chercher des légumes comme des **choux**, des poivrons, et des betteraves.

Activité 12

Quelles activités faisait-on à la ferme?

Diego va faire une présentation à l'école au sujet de sa grand-mère avec une vidéo qu'elle lui a envoyée.

Étape 1: Écouter

Oups! Diego a préparé ces cartes pour sa présentation, mais il y a quelques erreurs.

a. Regardez la vidéo de sa grand-mère.

b. Corrigez les erreurs qui sont soulignées en les remplaçant par d'autres mots.

la ferme - des cerises - des compotes - des framboises
des gâteaux - des mûres - des poires - des pommes - des tartes
des haricots - des mûres - des œufs - des petits pois

1. Quand elle était petite, ma grand-mère passait ses vacances à Paris.
2. Elle allait chercher des tomates et des oignons.
3. Les fruits à la ferme étaient des bananes, des oranges et des mangues.
4. Comme dessert, la famille mangeait souvent de la glace.

Expressions utiles

Il fallait

Quand j'étais petit/petite

Détail grammatical

Le pluriel en "x"

La plupart des noms en français se mettent au pluriel avec la lettre -s, mais, pour certain mots, la terminaison est différente:

un animal → des anim**aux**

un chou → des chou**x**

un gâteau → des gâteau**x**

Étape 2: Comparer

Est-ce que la famille de Maxime est similaire à la famille de Diego?

a. Regardez l'album de photos de Maxime et la vidéo de Mylène (la grand-mère de Diego).

b. Écrivez des phrases qui comparent les deux familles.

Modèle

Mylène passait les vacances chez sa grand-mère, mais Maxime passait les vacances chez son oncle et sa tante.

Activité 13

Que pouvait-on cueillir?

Mangez local et de saison!	printemps			été			automne			hiver		
	mars	avril	mai	juin	juil	août	sept	oct	nov	déc	janv	fév
betterave rouge												
céleri vert												
chou de Bruxelles												
chou rouge												
endive												
fraise												
framboise												
oignon												
poire												
pomme												
tomate												

Étape 1: Lire

La grand-mère de Maxime consulte ce calendrier belge de fruits et légumes pour savoir ce qu'elle peut préparer quand Maxime vient pour une visite. Avec votre partenaire, répondez aux questions dans des phrases complètes.

Modèle

On pouvait faire un gâteau.

1. L'automne dernier, que pouvait-on cueillir pour faire une tarte?
2. Que pouvait-on faire avec des légumes de printemps?
3. L'automne dernier, que pouvait-on cueillir pour faire de la confiture?
4. L'hiver dernier, que pouvait-on chercher pour faire une soupe?
5. Que pouvait-on faire avec des fruits d'été?

Étape 2: Parler

a. Choisissez cinq fruits ou légumes du calendrier.

b. Posez des questions pour savoir si les autres élèves mangeaient ce fruit ou ce légume quand ils ou elles étaient petit(e)s.

Modèle

Tu mangeais des framboises quand tu étais petit(e)?

	personne 1	personne 2	personne 3
fruit			
légume			

On peut aussi dire

les betteraves (f. pl.)
beets

le canard
duck

les cerises (f. pl.)
cherries

la compote
applesauce (or other fruit compote)

cueillir (les fruits, les fleurs)
to pick (fruit, flowers)

les haricots (verts) (m. pl.)
(green) beans

le lapin
rabbit

les mûres (f. pl.)
blackberries

les petits pois (m. pl.)
peas

les poires (f. pl.)
pears

les poivrons (m. pl.)
peppers

les pommes (f. pl.)
apples

la serviette
napkin

Réflexion interculturelle

Take another look at the ***Mangez local et de saison!*** chart. What do you notice about local produce in Belgium? Do you know which kinds of foods grow well near where you live? Do you know when you can buy them in season? Why do you think people care about buying local, seasonal produce? Answer the questions in the discussion forum in Explorer.

On peut aussi dire

le four
oven

le moule
baking mold or pan

presser
to press

verser
to pour

Détail linguistique

Une moule ou un moule

C'est la fête! On va manger des moules et une tarte aux fruits! Mon frère veut goûter **une** moule. Je vais préparer la tarte dans **un** moule.

Dans la cuisine

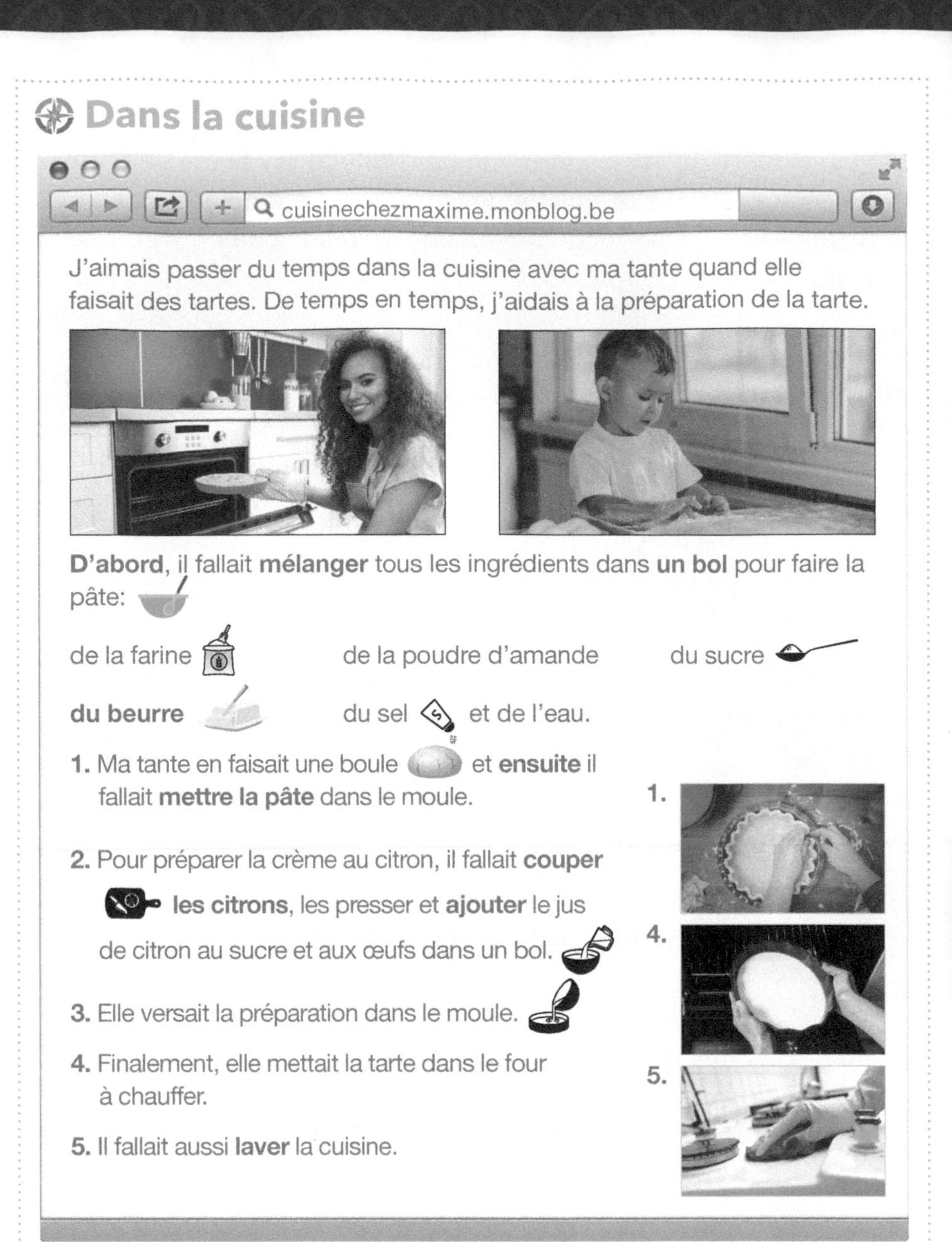

cuisinechezmaxime.monblog.be

J'aimais passer du temps dans la cuisine avec ma tante quand elle faisait des tartes. De temps en temps, j'aidais à la préparation de la tarte.

D'abord, il fallait **mélanger** tous les ingrédients dans **un bol** pour faire la pâte:

de la farine — de la poudre d'amande — du sucre

du beurre — du sel — et de l'eau.

1. Ma tante en faisait une boule et **ensuite** il fallait **mettre la pâte** dans le moule.
2. Pour préparer la crème au citron, il fallait **couper** **les citrons**, les presser et **ajouter** le jus de citron au sucre et aux œufs dans un bol.
3. Elle versait la préparation dans le moule.
4. Finalement, elle mettait la tarte dans le four à chauffer.
5. Il fallait aussi **laver** la cuisine.

Activité 14

Comment Diego va-t-il préparer la tarte?

Étape 1: Écouter et regarder

Diego lit le blog cuisine de Maxime. Il va préparer la tarte au citron comme le faisaient Maxime et sa tante.

Mettez en ordre ce que fait Diego.

_____ Il coupe les citrons avec un couteau.

_____ Il met du sucre et trois œufs dans un bol.

_____ Il mélange la farine, le sucre et le beurre dans un bol.

_____ Il ajoute le jus de citron au bol.

Étape 2: Laisser un message

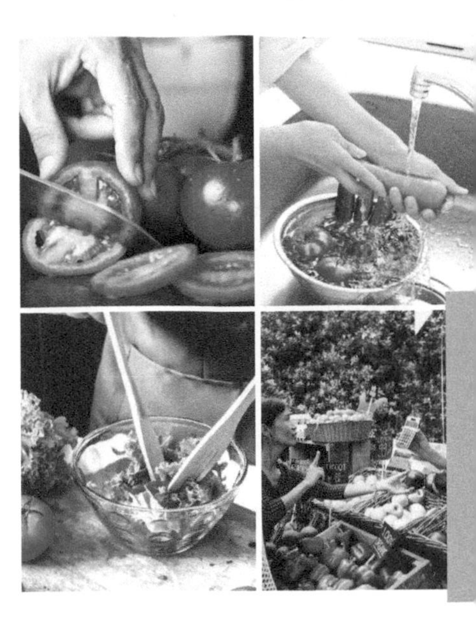

Le chef, c'est vous! Diego aime faire la cuisine et cherche des idées de recettes. Vous expliquez à Diego une recette simple de salade que vous faisiez quand vous étiez plus jeune.

a. Regardez les images et les débuts de phrase.
   Je coupais.../Je lavais.../Je mélangeais.../Je cherchais...
b. Expliquez comment vous faisiez la salade quand vous étiez plus jeune.
c. Utilisez les mots connecteurs pour expliquer le bon ordre (d'abord, ensuite, après, finalement).
d. Enregistrez votre message sur Explorer.

Modèle

Je préparais une salade quand j'étais plus jeune. D'abord...

Activité 15

Que prenait la grand-mère de Diego le matin?

Étape 1: Écouter et regarder

Diego parle sur internet avec sa grand-mère, Mylène. Diego voudrait savoir ce que prenait sa grand-mère pour le petit déjeuner. Diego va préparer un collage de l'assiette du petit déjeuner pour son blog.

Écoutez leur conversation. Écrivez les lettres des images que Diego doit inclure dans le collage.

Détail linguistique

Variations régionales pour parler des repas

Pour les trois repas principaux, en France, on dit:
le petit déjeuner
le déjeuner
le dîner

Mais en Suisse, en Belgique, et au Canada, on dit:
le déjeuner
le dîner
le souper

Étape 2: Écrire

Diego cherche des idées. Il veut écrire une légende *(caption)* pour l'image du petit déjeuner de sa grand-mère. Écrivez une description de l'image de l'assiette de sa grand-mère que Diego peut mettre sur son blog.

Modèle

Mamie Mylène mangeait... Elle ne mangeait pas de...

Zoom culture

Pratique culturelle: On va au marché?

Connexion

Where do people you know buy their food? How often do people you know go shopping for food?

Like many countries, ***la Belgique*** faces the challenge of maintaining its traditions while adapting to an ever-changing world. The traditional image of the Belgian consumer involves regular visits to the open-air food market (***le marché***) and stops at ***la boulangerie-pâtisserie, la charcuterie*** and ***la boucherie*** to buy bread and pastries, pork products, and beef.

However, consumer trends are changing in Belgium. Just under half of Belgians still buy their ***pain français*** in ***une boulangerie. Les supermarchés*** continue to be more popular, with people making just one stop to buy what they need. In 2016, there was a 50% increase in online ordering, including delivery and ***le foodbox***. Even so, 92% of Belgians prefer grocery shopping in a real store.

Not all trends pose a threat to tradition! For example, Belgians continue to experiment with cuisine from around the world, but traditional dishes are still more popular than ever. Belgians are also adapting their food production and purchasing to help their health and the environment; efforts like organic farming (***bio*** or ***biologique***), eating local, and reducing waste continue to gain popularity. One Belgian grocery store chain has even begun growing vegetables on the roofs of its own stores!

Réflexion

Why do you think people are changing the way they buy and eat food? Why are some people keeping up their traditional way of buying and eating food? Answer the questions in the discussion forum in Explorer.

Découvrons 2

Talking About What You Used to Do

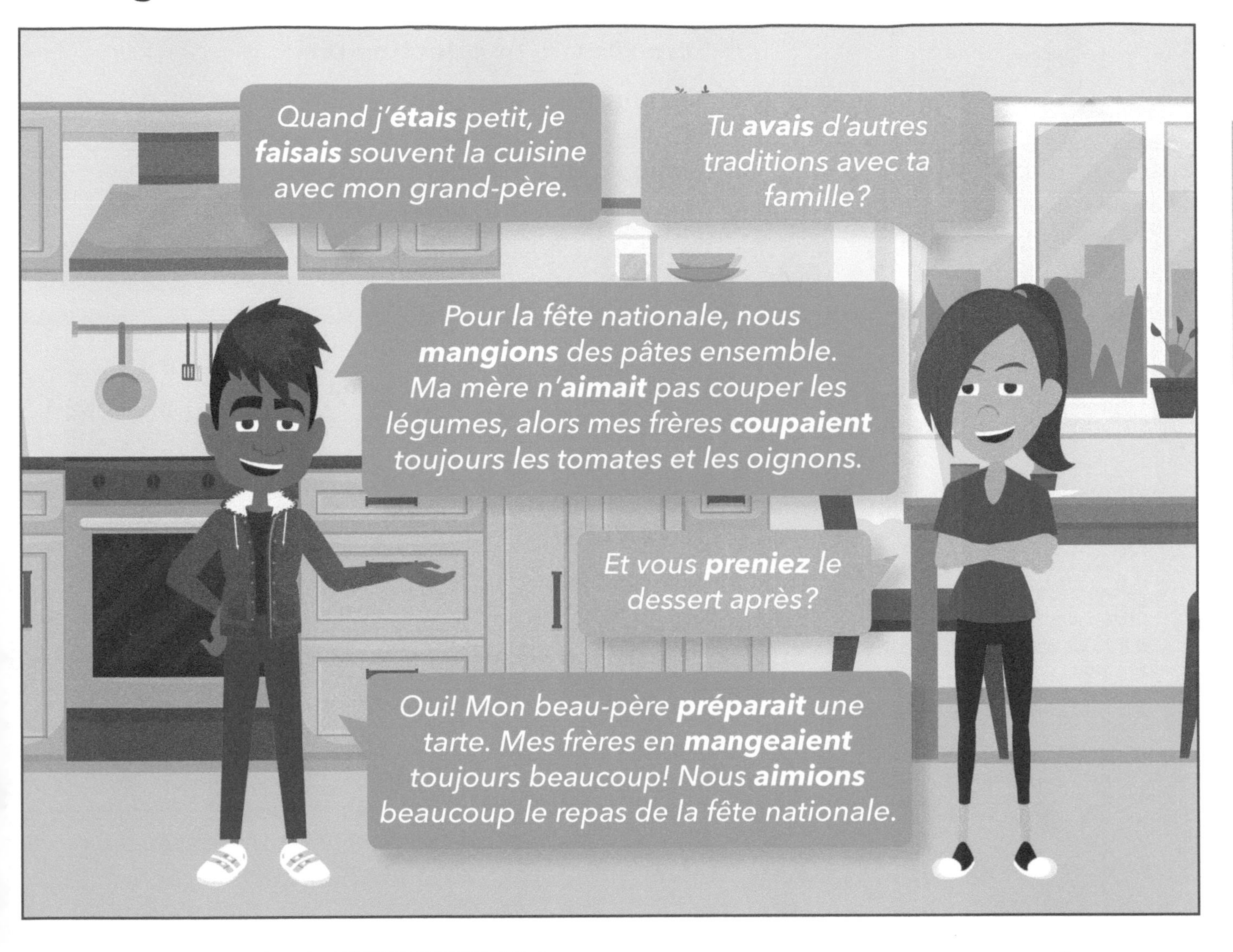

Découvertes

Reflect on what you observe and respond to the following questions in the graphic organizer in Explorer.

1. Look at the words in bold in ***Découvrons 2***. Can you identify which verb each one is? For example, did you recognize that ***tu avais*** is a form of the verb ***avoir***?
2. List the different verb endings that you notice.
3. What do you notice about the stems of the verbs?
4. Do you see any verbs that do not follow the patterns of the others? What is different about those verbs?

Discuss your observations with a ***partenaire***. View the ***Découvrons 2*** resources for this unit in Explorer and check the ***Synthèse de grammaire*** at the end of this unit.

Activité 16

Qu'est-ce que je faisais quand j'étais plus jeune?

Étape 1: Lire et sélectionner

Lisez les phrases suivantes. Cochez (✔) les phrases qui décrivent votre vie quand vous étiez plus jeune.

____ Je passais du temps chez mon oncle et ma tante.

____ Je mangeais souvent de la viande.

____ Je participais à la préparation des fêtes.

____ Ma famille mangeait beaucoup de légumes.

____ Il y avait de la salade au restaurant scolaire.

____ Mon prof avait du chocolat dans son bureau.

____ C'était sympa de faire la cuisine.

____ Il fallait chercher du lait au supermarché.

Étape 2: Parler

a. Maintenant, parlez avec les autres élèves de votre classe.

b. Demandez si les phrases **(Étape 1)** décrivent leur vie quand ils ou elles étaient petit(e)s.

c. Si l'élève répond, "oui," écrivez son nom à côté de l'activité correspondante.

Modèle

Est-ce qu'il y avait de la salade au restaurant scolaire quand tu étais petit(e)?

-Non, il n'y avait pas de salade au restaurant scolaire.

Est-ce que tu participais à la préparation des fêtes quand tu étais plus jeune?

-Oui, je faisais souvent des gâteaux pour les fêtes d'anniversaire.

Activité 17

Que mettre comme légende?

Maxime a trouvé ces photos de son enfance chez son oncle et sa tante. Comme il était adorable! Aidez Maxime à écrire la légende parfaite.

a. Écrivez trois légendes possibles. (N'oubliez pas les hashtags!)

b. Échangez avec un(e) partenaire.

c. Choisissez la meilleure légende de votre partenaire.

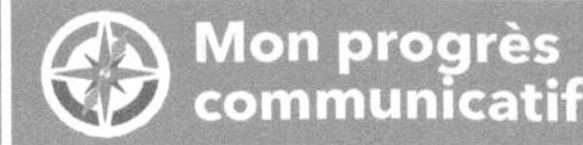

I can write descriptions for photo captions about what people used to do, cook, or eat in the past.

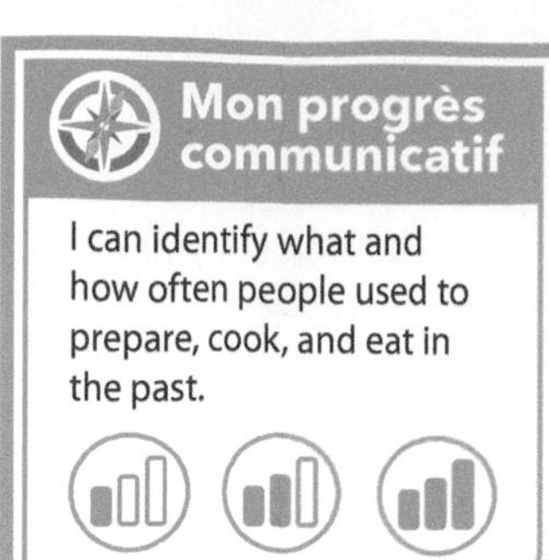

Activité 18

Que mangeaient nos grands-parents?

Étape 1: Chercher la bonne réponse

Mamie Joëlle envoie des textos à ses petits-enfants.

Regardez les textos des petits-enfants de Mamie Joëlle. Comment est-ce qu'elle répond à chacun?

Vous mangez des fruits et des légumes?

J'adore les tomates et les oignons. J'en mange souvent dans les salades et sur la pizza.

Jérôme

Je prends un pain au chocolat tous les matins au café.

Gabrielle

Je fais des tartes aux framboises tous les week-ends.

Sébastian

Mon père prépare du poisson de temps en temps, mais je n'aime pas le poisson.

Sandrine

a. Tu manges beaucoup de sucre! Il faut manger plus de légumes. Je mangeais rarement du chocolat quand j'étais jeune, mais mes sœurs et moi, nous chauffions du lait pour en faire un chocolat chaud tous les samedis.

b. Quand j'étais jeune, le poisson coûtait très cher parce qu'on ne vivait pas près de l'eau. On mangeait du poisson le vendredi soir. Mais, c'est délicieux, le poisson! Il faut goûter le poisson avec du poivre et des légumes. Courage!

c. C'est génial! Quand j'étais petite, on mangeait beaucoup de légumes parce qu'on vivait près de la campagne et nos amis cueillaient des choux. Je mangeais une salade tous les jours.

d. Moi, j'allais chercher des fruits tous les matins en été quand j'étais petite. Je mangeais des fraises tous les jours. Mais, il y a beaucoup de sucre dans les tartes aux fruits! Si tu aimes les fruits, prends des fraises.

 Étape 2: Classer

Les petits-enfants de Mamie Joëlle veulent écrire une biographie sur son enfance. Vous aidez ses petits-enfants à organiser leurs idées.

a. Lisez les textos de Mamie Joëlle dans l'**Étape 1**.

b. Décidez si elle faisait chaque activité a) une fois par semaine ou b) tous les jours.

1. Mamie Joëlle mangeait des légumes.
2. Elle prenait du chocolat.
3. En été, Mamie Joëlle allait chercher les fruits.
4. La famille de Mamie Joëlle mangeait du poisson.
5. Mamie Joëlle mangeait des fraises.

Activité 19

Qu'aimais-tu manger?

Savez-vous comment les autres élèves de votre classe mangeait quand ils ou elles étaient petit(e)s?

a. Préparez vos réponses aux questions.

b. Circulez dans la salle de classe et posez ces questions aux autres élèves.

	Qu'est-ce que tu ne voulais jamais manger au dîner?	Qu'est-ce que tu cherchais au supermarché?	Qui faisait la cuisine chez toi?
moi			
personne 1			

Détail grammatical

Le verbe mettre

mettre = *to put, set, or put on*

Pour parler au présent:

Est-ce que ta grand-mère **met** du sucre dans son café?

Non, mais moi, je **mets** du lait dans mon café.

Pour parler au passé:

Quand tu étais petit, tu **mettais** du ketchup sur tes frites?

Oui! Et mon frère, il **mettait** de la mayonnaise sur ses frites.

Activité 20

Que mettiez-vous sur les frites?

Étape 1: Écrire

Que mettiez-vous dans vos sandwichs? Et sur les frites?

a. Dans la représentation schématique sur Explorer, écrivez une liste de vos plats préférés.

b. Indiquez ce que vous mettiez avec ou sur des plats différents.

Modèle

des céréales: Quand j'étais petit(e), je mettais de la banane dans mes céréales.

Étape 2: Discuter

Demandez à votre partenaire comment il ou elle mangeait ces mêmes plats dans le passé.

Modèle

–Qu'est-ce que tu mettais dans tes céréales quand tu étais petit(e)?

–Je mettais beaucoup de sucre dans mes céréales.

Activité 21

Quelles étaient mes traditions?

Étape 1: Écrire

Regardez le tableau *Nzombo le soir* de l'artiste congolais, Jean Paul Mika. Imaginez que vous étiez présent(e) à ce marché. Écrivez une description de la soirée. Considérez:

1. Qui était là?
2. Qu'est-ce qu'on achetait?
3. Qu'est-ce qu'on voulait préparer?
4. Qui faisait la cuisine? C'était pour une fête spéciale?
5. Qu'est-ce que vous mangiez? C'était comment? Il y avait quelque chose de spécial?

Étape 2: Parler

Posez des questions à votre partenaire et répondez à ses questions pour comparer vos descriptions.

Modèle

Élève A: La grand-mère préparait des légumes?

Élève B: Oui, et l'oncle achetait des poissons.

J'avance 2

Les souvenirs du passé

After finding an old family postcard, Maxime has invited you to join him in participating in an international youth movement to document memories from the past for future generations. Students from all over the world are working to interview their older relatives and preserve old family documents as well as to document their own childhood memories.

Étape 1: Lire et noter

Maxime has been helping his aunt and uncle clean out the farmhouse and he just found an old postcard that his uncle received as a child. Read the postcard and tell whether the images represent something that a) took place every day or b) took place once a week.

AP® Étape 2: Parler

Looking at the postcard made Maxime curious about your experience as a child and what you liked to eat when you were little. Answer Maxime's questions over the phone about your childhood experiences with cooking and food preferences.

Étape 3: Présenter

As part of the international memory documentation project, you are submitting a scrapbook page about the role that food played in celebrations in the past. Include some images and write a short description about what people used to do, cook, or eat in the past. You can write about yourself or someone else.

All of the materials for ***J'avance 2*** can be found in Explorer.

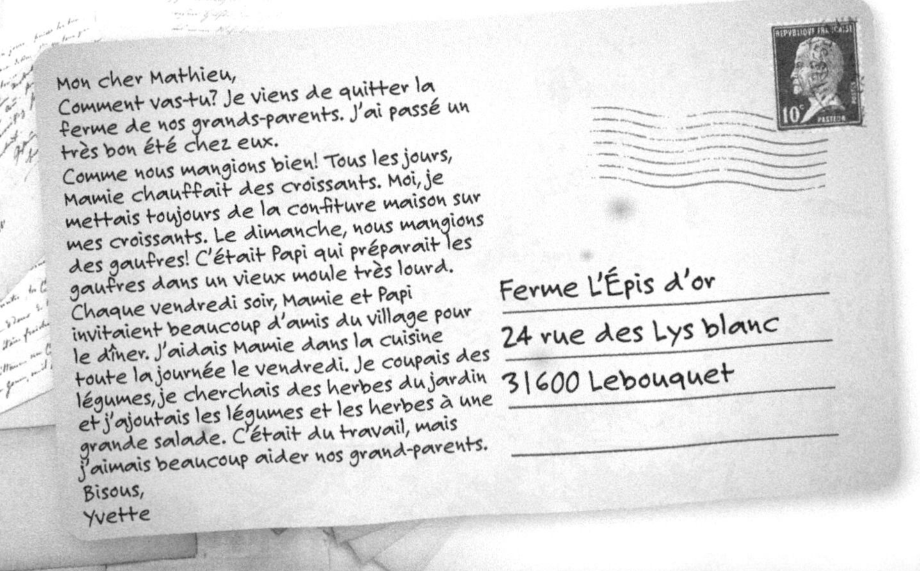

Mon cher Mathieu,
Comment vas-tu? Je viens de quitter la ferme de nos grands-parents. J'ai passé un très bon été chez eux.
Comme nous mangions bien! Tous les jours, Mamie chauffait des croissants. Moi, je mettais toujours de la confiture maison sur mes croissants. Le dimanche, nous mangions des gaufres! C'était Papi qui préparait les gaufres dans un vieux moule très lourd.
Chaque vendredi soir, Mamie et Papi invitaient beaucoup d'amis du village pour le dîner. J'aidais Mamie dans la cuisine toute la journée le vendredi. Je coupais des légumes, je cherchais des herbes du jardin et j'ajoutais les légumes et les herbes à une grande salade. C'était du travail, mais j'aimais beaucoup aider nos grand-parents.
Bisous,
Yvette

Ferme L'Épis d'or
24 rue des Lys blanc
31600 Lebouquet

Comment dit-on? 3

Venez nombreux!

Une invitation à un repas

1. 
Public
Soyez les bienvenus aux **soirées** gourmandes de Namur la semaine du 13 au 18 avril. Le meilleur chef de la région vous invite à goûter ses spécialités au dîner de gala. On va se régaler! Réservez sur notre site: www.festival-culinaire.be.

2. 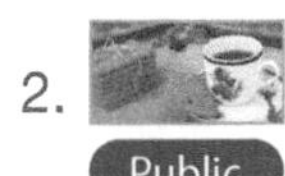
Public
Ça vous dit de venir à la fête de la rentrée le 9 septembre? Le déjeuner commence à 7h30 au restaurant scolaire. 2€ = 1 café/chocolat chaud & 2 spéculoos. Parlez-en à vos amis!

3. 
Public
Avez-vous des enfants? **Venez nombreux à un événement** spécial au lac de Bambois ce week-end entre 12h et 15h. Le Centre de la jeunesse va **servir** des frites, des barbes à papa, et plein d'autres délices des pique-niques. Gratuit pour les moins de 12 ans.

4. 
Privé
Salut les amis! **Je vous invite** chez moi pour **un repas** convivial et chaleureux le 14 mai vers 18h. Je vous propose un menu avec mes plats belges préférés. N'hésitez pas à me contacter si vous avez des questions!

Expressions utiles

gratuit/gratuite
On va se régaler!
Parlez-en à vos amis!
réservez

On peut aussi dire

Describing a culinary event

chaleureux/chaleureuse
warm, welcoming

convivial/conviviale
friendly, lively

Activité 22

Tu viens à la fête?

 **Étape 1: Lire**

Avec deux ou trois autres élèves, regardez les annonces des événements et complétez la représentation schématique.

	Quelle sorte d'événement?	Pour quel public?	Où?	Autres détails (prix, date, heure, etc.)

Étape 2: Écouter

Oh là là! Vous avez reçu ces messages téléphoniques par accident! Aidez les hôtes *(hosts)* en associant chaque message à un événement.

1. Martin
2. Amandine
3. Pauline Renard
4. Arnaud Nguyen
5. Xavier

Étape 3: Parler

Avec un(e) partenaire, décidez à quel événement vous préférez aller ensemble. Enregistrez votre conversation sur Explorer.

Modèle

–Tu veux aller à la fête de la rentrée?

–Non, je préfère les soirées gourmandes parce que j'adore goûter des spécialités belges.

Activité 23

C'était comment, l'événement?

Étape 1: Regarder

Regardez la vidéo et notez l'ordre dans lequel Maxime parle des aspects du souper congolais.

____ la musique

____ l'atmosphère générale

____ les plats

____ la réservation

Étape 2: Écrire des questions

Vous avez écouté ce que pense Maxime. Maintenant, écrivez des questions que vous pouvez poser aux autres participants pour les interviewer.

1. ______________________________?
   C'était vraiment convivial! Tout le monde était content!
2. ______________________________?
   Il y avait de la musique super! C'était sympa de danser avec mes amis dynamiques.
3. ______________________________?
   Non, il n'y avait pas de gaufres, mais il y avait des bananes plantain et d'autres spécialités congolaises.
4. ______________________________?
   Mais oui! Il fallait faire une réservation avant le 1er septembre.

Rappel

Quelques expressions

Je voudrais…

J'ai envie de…

J'ai faim!

J'ai soif!

Expressions utiles

Comment répondre à une invitation

Avec plaisir!

Oui, je veux bien.

Désolé/Désolée, mais je ne peux pas.

Activité 24

Que proposez-vous comme événement?

Étape 1: Créer

Votre classe veut célébrer la cuisine du monde. Écrivez une invitation où vous proposez un événement basé sur les spécialités de la Belgique ou d'un autre pays francophone. N'oubliez pas:

- le nom ou le thème de l'événement (Quoi?)
- la date et l'heure (Quand?)
- le lieu (Où?)
- les plats que vous allez servir (Quoi?)

Étape 2: Inviter

a. Regardez les invitations des autres élèves dans votre classe.

b. Choisissez une invitation.

c. Parlez à deux ou trois personnes. Invitez-les à l'événement que vous avez choisi.

Zoom culture

Produit culturel: Le chocolat, une tradition belge à savourer!

 Connexion

Which desserts do you associate with special events or holidays?

What is ***la crème de la crème*** of festive treats for family gatherings and most other celebrations? ***Oui, c'est le chocolat!*** Going back to the XVIth century when Belgium was still under Spanish rule, cocoa beans were shipped to Belgium from Central America. In the XIXth century, cocoa beans produced in the Congo were tastier than those from America. Today, ***la praline*** (a chocolate shell with creamy chocolate filling) is the most famous variety of chocolates from Belgium. It was invented by Jean Neuhaus, a Swiss pharmacist who opened a store in Brussels: He covered his medicine in delicious chocolate to make it more palatable. His grandson turned the pharmacy into a ***chocolaterie***!

Congolese cocoa farmers use traditional methods of fermentation with banana leaves that are environmental friendly to produce high quality organic chocolate. While ***Côte d'Ivoire*** is currently the world's largest cocoa bean producer, perhaps Congolese cocoa production will lead tomorrow's market?

Réflexion

On average, a Belgian consumes over 10 kg of chocolate every year and considers this luscious food as a "national heritage." Is chocolate an important component of your holiday gatherings? Answer the question in the discussion forum in Explorer.

On peut aussi dire

Pour être plus spécifique, on peut dire:

un événement spécial

une fête d'anniversaire

une fête religieuse

un mariage civil

un repas familial (=avec la famille)

une soirée chez des amis

Détail grammatical

Le verbe venir

Use the verb ***venir*** to invite:

Venez nombreux!

Ask if people are coming to your event:

Tu viens à la fête? ***Vous venez*** à la fête?

Or tell them that you are coming to the event:

Oui, ***je viens!***

Détail grammatical

Je t'invite OU je vous invite?

When inviting just one friend, remember to change the ***vous*** to ***te/t'*** in the following expressions:

Ça vous dit *d'aller à fête?* → ***Ça te dit*** *d'aller à la fête?*

Je vous invite *chez moi.* → ***Je t'invite*** *chez moi.*

Détail linguistique

Quelques expressions idiomatiques

Since food is such an important part of our daily lives, it's also a rich area of creativity with language. Here are a few fun idioms.

J'ai la dalle! or ***J'ai une faim de loup!*** *(J'ai très très faim!)*

Je dois manger sur le pouce! *(Je dois manger vite!)*

Activité 25

Ça vous dit de venir souper?

Pendant votre visite en Belgique, vous rencontrez Aïcha, la cousine de Maxime. Ensemble, vous regardez cette invitation près de son école.

Étape 1: Lire et répondre

Lisez l'invitation au souper aux moules. Aïcha veut venir au souper, mais elle a des questions. Répondez à ses textos.

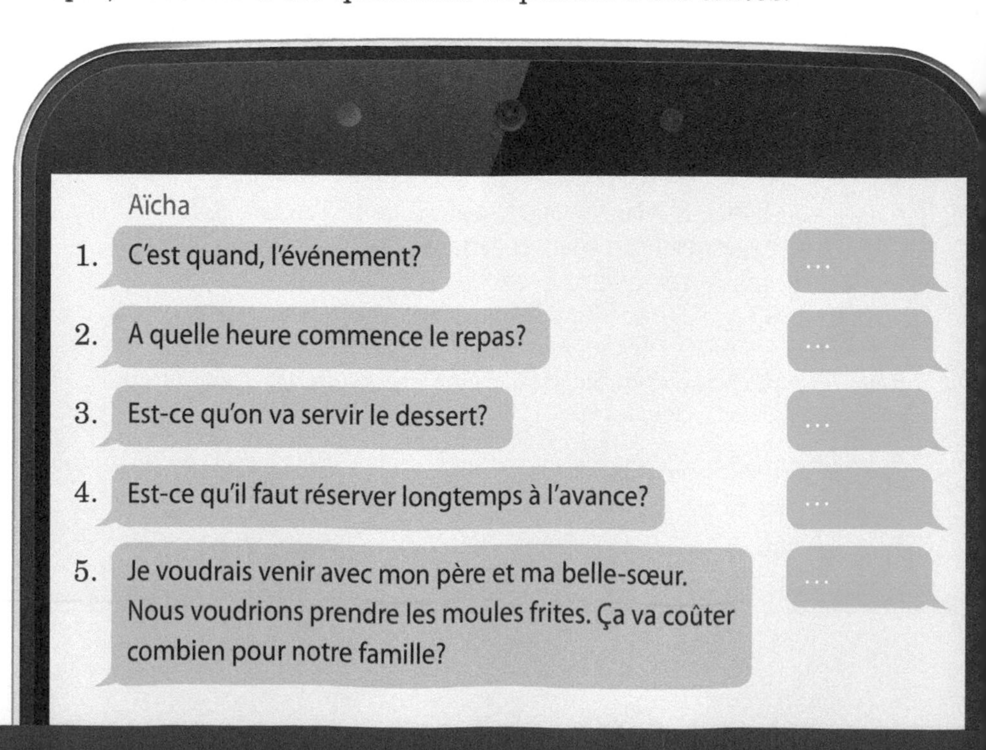

 Étape 2: Écouter

Pendant votre visite en Belgique, il y a aussi une soirée de culture belge le même soir que le souper aux moules.

a. Écoutez l'annonce radio et notez les similarités et les différences entre les événements.

b. Comparez vos réponses avec un(e) partenaire.

	souper aux moules	soirée culture belge
réservation nécessaire?		
plat(s) servi(s)		
activités		
prix pour 1 personne		

 Étape 3: Laisser un message

Téléphonez à Aïcha et laissez un message pour l'inviter à un des événements. Considérez les préférences d'Aïcha et vos préférences aussi.

Modèle

Salut, Aïcha! Ça te dit d'assister à...?

AïchaLaGourmande  

AïchaLaGourmande

Salut! Je préfère les plats salés. J'adore la musique. Je suis spontanée et je n'aime pas faire les réservations.

Mon progrès interculturel

I can identify why community members organize an event, that includes food, to benefit a cause in Francophone cultures and in my community.

Réflexion interculturelle

The ***Souper aux moules*** was organized to help fund a community event for children for ***la fête de Saint-Nicolas (le 6 décembre)***. What are some examples of events you have heard of or participated in where members of the community organized the event to benefit a cause? Why do you think community members might organize or attend an event that benefits a cause? Why do you think organizers might choose to include food as part of the event? Answer the questions in the discussion forum in Explorer.

Prononciation

L'accent tonique

What is the rhythm of French?

You already know that the emphasis or accent in most French words falls on the last syllable, but what about where the emphasis falls in a phrase or sentence? Make predictions and then check them by listening to a recording.

In the following transcription of a party announcement, choose the word or syllable in each grouping that you think is emphasized. Listen to the recording and complete the pronunciation activity in Explorer.

Salut les amis!/À la fin du mois, /je vais avoir/18 ans./À cette occasion, /j'organise une fête chez moi à Liège,/ et je vous invite tous!/Pour cet événement spécial,/je vous propose/une soirée dansante/avec un buffet./ Je pensais servir/du poulet épicé,/du riz,/une variété de salades/et beaucoup de desserts./Mon frère veut faire le gâteau/et c'est un excellent pâtissier./Venez nombreux,/on va se régaler!

Découvrons 3

Avoiding Repetition Using "*en*"

Michel va inviter sa grand-mère à un repas samedi après-midi. Il va préparer une salade de fruits. Il est au supermarché. Il envoie des textos à sa sœur Lina pour demander quels ingrédients ils ont à la maison et quels ingrédients il faut acheter.

Michel

Salut, Lina! Nous avons des pommes à la maison?

Lina

Oui, nous **en** avons quatre!

Super! Il nous faut des bananes aussi. Nous **en** avons? ¯_(ツ)_/¯

Non, nous n'**en** avons pas. 

D'accord. Je vais **en** acheter. Est-ce qu'il y a des framboises à la maison?

Non, il n'y **en** a pas.

Merci. Et des citrons? Nous **en** avons?

Oui, nous **en** avons beaucoup!  

Découvertes

Reflect on what you observe and respond to the following questions in the graphic organizer in Explorer.

1. What did you notice about when the word ***en*** was used?
2. What did you notice about the word order? Where was ***en*** used in relation to the verb?
3. What differences did you notice between the sentences that include ***en*** and the sentences that do not?

Share your observations with a ***partenaire***. View the ***Découvrons 3*** resources for this unit in Explorer and check the ***Synthèse de grammaire*** at the end of this unit.

Activité 26

Et des tomates, nous en avons?

Étape 1: Mettre en ordre

Votre amie Bernadette et vous préparez un repas pour votre club. Bernadette est au supermarché. Elle envoie des textos pour vous demander quels ingrédients il faut acheter.

a. Regardez dans votre cuisine.

b. Mettez les mots en ordre pour répondre aux textos de Bernadette.

Vous avez déjà...

Modèle

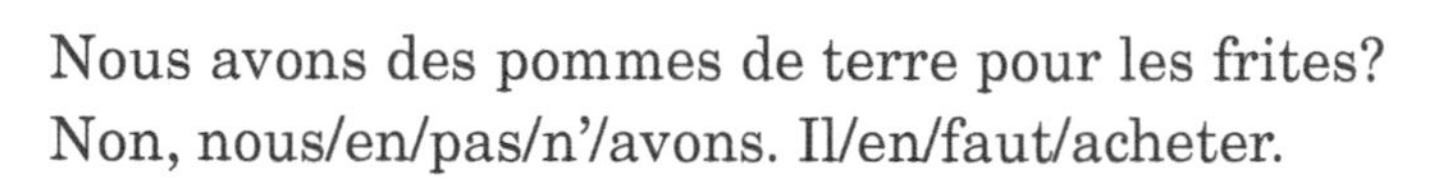

Nous avons des pommes de terre pour les frites?
Non, nous/en/pas/n'/avons. Il/en/faut/acheter.

Non, nous n'en avons pas. Il faut en acheter.

1. Il faut préparer la salade! Nous avons des tomates?
   Oui,/nous/trois/avons/en. C'est assez?
2. Oui. Et est-ce qu'il y a de la farine pour la tarte?
   Oui,/y/il/un/dans/en/sac/a.
3. Bon. Il faut couper des citrons pour la tarte. Nous en avons?
   Non,/nous/en/pas/n'/avons. Tu/acheter/en/peux/s'il/te/plaît?
4. Alors, pour finir, il nous faut des fourchettes?
   Oui,/nous/beaucoup/en/avons. Tu besoin/n'as/d'en/pas/acheter.

Étape 2: Répondre

Bernadette a une bonne idée! Elle voudrait préparer des gaufres pour le dessert. Elle vous envoie encore des textos du supermarché pour demander si vous avez les ingrédients nécessaires.

a. Regardez les ingrédients dans votre cuisine.

b. Répondez aux questions de Bernadette.

Modèle

Tu as des fraises? — Oui, j'en ai.

Tu as des citrons? — Non, je n'en ai pas.

1. Tu as de la crème fouettée?
2. Tu as du sucre?
3. Tu as des framboises?
4. Tu as du beurre?
5. Tu as de la glace?

Activité 27

On a tout ce qu'il faut pour la recette?

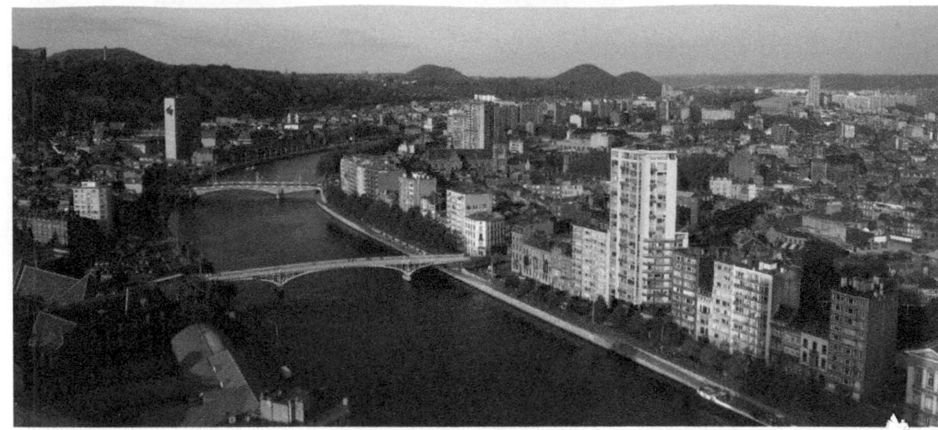

Vous allez préparer un plat belge, les boulets à la liégeoise, pour votre classe avec un(e) partenaire.

a. Cochez (✔) les ingrédients que vous avez déjà.

b. Demandez à votre partenaire s'il ou si elle a les autres ingrédients.

c. Entourez les ingrédients qu'il faut acheter.

Modèle

Tu as du porc? Oui, j'en ai.

Tu as du pain? Non, je n'en ai pas. (Moi non plus!)

Recette: Les boulets à la liégeoise

Ingrédients:

____ 700 g de porc et bœuf

____ 100 g de pain de mie

____ 15 cl de lait

____ 2 œufs

____ sel

____ poivre

____ 2 gros oignons

____ 50 g de beurre

____ 1 cuillère à soupe de farine

Partenaire A:

Partenaire B:

J'avance 3

Bon appétit!

The ***Souper Moules*** committee in Tiège needs your help! They have planned the event, but they need a young person to help them manage their social media account and promote the event with local teenagers.

Étape 1: Lire et choisir la réponse

Read the flyer for the event. Then, read the questions that interested community members have posted on the message board and choose the appropriate response to send back to them.

Étape 2: Répondre aux messages

Maxime's friend Clément attended a ***Souper Moules*** event last month. Text him to ask how it was so you have more content for your promotional material.

Étape 3: Presenter

Create a promotional video that the ***Souper Moules*** committee can share on their social media account using the information from the flyer and from Clément's review. The committee would like you to encourage people to attend.

You might want to include:

- An invitation that is welcoming and encouraging.
- The date and time the event will take place.
- What will be served at the event.
- What people can do at the event.

All of the materials for ***J'avance 3*** can be found in Explorer.

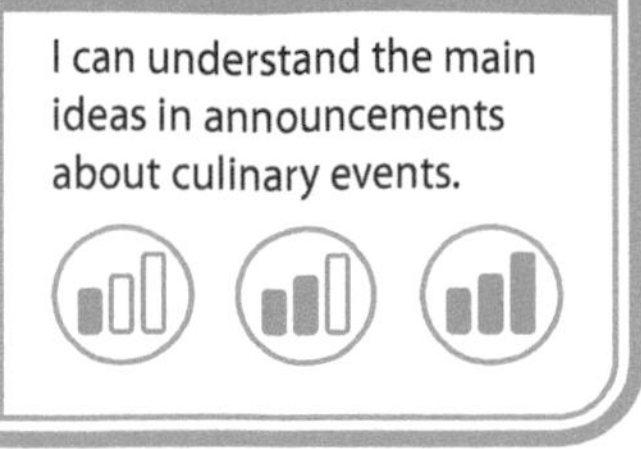

Mon progrès communicatif

I can understand the main ideas in announcements about culinary events.

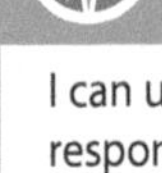

Mon progrès communicatif

I can understand and respond to text messages about an event.

Mon progrès communicatif

I can create and present a simple advertisement to persuade others to attend a community event.

Synthèse de grammaire

1. Describing the Past: *l'imparfait*

When talking about things that happened in the past, especially events that happened on a regular basis, or general descriptions about the way things were and what there was in a given place, use the ***imparfait***:

C'était génial!
It was great!

Il y avait des framboises et des fraises.
There were raspberries and strawberries.

Les fruits étaient délicieux.
The fruits were delicious.

You can usually recognize the ***imparfait*** by its endings: ***-ais, -ait, -aient*** and others. ***C'était*** is the ***imparfait*** of ***c'est; il y avait*** is the ***imparfait*** of ***il y a***. You can describe many things that happened in the past just by knowing these two expressions.

Contrast this new verb tense, the ***imparfait***, with the tenses you already know:

Le présent: Je mange des gaufres. *I eat / I am eating waffles.*

Le futur proche: Je **vais** mang**er** des gaufres. *I am going to eat waffles.*

L'imparfait: Je mange**ais** des gaufres. *I ate / I used to eat / I was eating waffles.*

Note: In the same way that the ***-ent*** ending of a present tense verb is silent, the ***-aient*** ending should sound the same as ***-ais*** and ***-ait***.

2. Talking About What You Used to Do: *la formation de l'imparfait*

a. To figure out the beginning/stem of your ***imparfait*** verb, think of the ***nous*** form of that verb in the present tense. E.g., ***nous faisons, nous aimons, nous voulons***. Then, remove the ***-ons*** ending. E.g., ***fais-, aim-, voul-***. This is the beginning of your ***imparfait*** verb for all subject pronouns.

b. There is one verb that does not follow this pattern: the verb ***être***. All forms of ***être*** in the ***imparfait*** begin with ***ét-***. E.g., ***j'étais, c'était***

c. Once you know how your verb begins, just add the appropriate ending:

je	**faisais**	nous	**faisions**
tu	**faisais**	vous	**faisiez**
il/elle/on	**faisait**	ils/elles	**faisaient**

The verb ***manger*** and others like it have a special spelling rule. The ***je, tu, il/elle/on,*** and ***ils/elles*** forms of the verb will have an extra letter ***e***, but the ***nous*** and ***vous*** forms will not. Why? It's all in the sound. The combination ***ge*** in ***mangeais*** needs to have the same "soft g" sound as the ***gi*** in ***mangions***.

je	**mangeais**	nous	**mangions**
tu	**mangeais**	vous	**mangiez**
il/elle/on	**mangeait**	ils/elles	**mangeaient**

3. Avoiding Repetition Using *le pronom "en"*

The function of any pronoun is to refer back to something already mentioned in a conversation or text without repeating the exact words. In French, the pronoun ***en*** takes the place of a specific set of phrases.

A: Tu as besoin **de pommes** pour la tarte?
*Do you need **(some/any) apples** for the pie?*

B: Oui, j'**en** ai besoin!
*Yes, I need **some (of them)**.*

A: Et **des poires**?
*And **(some/any) pears**?*

B: Non, je n'**en** ai pas besoin.
*No, I don't need **any (of them)**.*

The key points to know when using ***en*** are:

- ***En*** takes the place of a specific noun/phrase. E.g., In the conversation above, Speaker B does not repeat the words ***pommes*** and ***poires*** when answering.
- Even though the original, specific noun came after the verb, the pronoun ***en*** usually goes before the verb.
- The pronoun ***en*** is specifically used to take the place of noun phrases beginning with ***de, d', des (des pommes), du (du fromage), de la (de la soupe), de l' (de l'oignon)*** or other quantities, including numbers and ***un/une***. When using quantities and numbers, you can usually keep the specific amount while using ***en*** to replace the noun.
E.g., Tu as beaucoup **de pommes**? → Oui, j'**en** ai beaucoup.
Tu **en** as combien? → J'**en** ai cinq.

Vocabulaire

Comment dit-on? 1: I can describe traditional dishes from Francophone countries.

Les plats belges et congolais	*Belgian & Congolese dishes*
les beignets congolais (m. pl.)	*Congolese donuts*
le filet américain	*steak tartare (raw, seasoned beef)*
la gaufre	*waffle*
les moules-frites (f. pl.)	*mussels served with fries*
le poulet moamba	*chicken cooked in palm oil with vegetables*
la tarte au riz	*rice pie*
le waterzooï	*meat or fish stew with a cream sauce*

Expressions utiles	
C'était...	*It was...*
Il y avait...	*There was..., There were...*
cuit(e)(s) avec	*cooked with*
fait(e)(s) avec	*made with*
nature	*plain (referring to food)*
servi(e)(s) avec	*served with*

Les aliments (m. pl.)	*Foods*
le céleri	*celery*
la crème	*cream*
la farine	*flour*
la fraise	*strawberry*
les fruits de mer (m. pl.)	*seafood*
la moule	*mussel*
l'oignon (m.)	*onion*

Comment dit-on? 2: I can talk about foods I used to make and eat.

Les connecteurs	*Transition words*
d'abord	*first (of all)*
ensuite	*next, then*
finalement	*finally, lastly*

Les aliments de la ferme	*Foods from the farm*
le beurre	*butter*
le chou	*cabbage*
le citron	*lemon*
la confiture	*jam, jelly*
la framboise	*raspberry*

Mettre la table	Setting the table
l'assiette (f.)	*plate*
le couteau	*knife*
la cuillère	*spoon*
la fourchette	*fork*

Expressions utiles	
Il fallait...	*It was necessary (to)...*
Quand j'étais petit(e)...	*When I was little...*

Pour faire la cuisine	Cooking
ajouter	*to add*
le bol	*bowl*
chauffer	*to heat, to warm*
couper	*to cut*
laver	*to wash*
mélanger	*to mix*
mettre	*to put or place*
la pâte	*dough*

Comment dit-on? 3: I can invite others to a special meal or event.

Pour inviter	To invite
Ça vous dit (de...)?	*Are you interested (in...)?*
Je vous invite (à...)	*I'm inviting you (to...)*
Je vous propose (...)	*I'm suggesting to you (...)*
servir	*to serve*
Soyez les bienvenu(e)s (à...)	*You are welcome to come (to...)*
Venez nombreux (à...)	*Come one and all (to...)*

Expressions utiles	
Avec plaisir!	*With pleasure!, Gladly!*
Désolé/Désolée, mais je ne peux pas.	*Sorry, but I can't.*
gratuit/gratuite	*free, no cost*
On va se régaler!	*We're really going to savor this!*
Oui, je veux bien.	*Yes, I'd really like to.*
Parlez-en à vos amis!	*Tell your friends about it!*
réserver	*to reserve*

Quand on mange ensemble	When people eat together
l'événement (m.)	*event*
la fête	*party, holiday*
le repas	*meal*
la soirée	*party, gathering in the evening*

J'y arrive

Questions essentielles

- Which culinary traditions of the past are still important today?
- How are our memories with the important people in our lives connected to food?
- How does food bring people together?

Un goût de chez vous

Quelle bonne nouvelle! Maxime and some of his family members will be traveling near where you live. To celebrate their arrival, you and some of your classmates have decided to plan a traditional Belgian meal. You already have some ideas for most of the meal, but you have asked Maxime to email you a few recipes from online food blogs.

You will need to read and select which side dish you will include in the meal. Then, you will be able to share with your classmates to see how food is an important factor in other people's childhood memories.

Once you select which dishes you would like to include, prepare a video invitation to the meal to send to Maxime's family.

Before you begin, refer to the ***J'y arrive*** rubric in Explorer to familiarize yourself with the evaluation criteria.

Interpretive Assessment

 **Quel plat choisir?**

Read two food blog recipes that Maxime sent to you.

a. Decide whether the statements in Explorer apply to ***Texte A, Texte B,*** or both.

b. Select the ingredients that you would need for each dish. Check the boxes in the table in Explorer.

Interpersonal Assessment

Souvenirs de nos repas

As you are getting ready to prepare the meal for Maxime's family, you have decided to brainstorm with your classmates about the memories you have surrounding food so as to think about what might be important to include in your special meal. Talk to each other about:

- What you remember eating when you were younger.
- What you remember about who did the cooking.
- Which foods went with which special occasions.

Presentational Assessment

Je vous invite

Create a video invitation to send to Maxime and his family. Be sure to include the following:

- An appropriate greeting or introduction.
- A description of the traditional dishes you will serve.
- An explanation of your choice of the side dish that references the memories that the food bloggers shared with their recipes.
- Time and place of the meal.
- An appropriate sign-off or conclusion.

UNITÉ 3

Au boulot, les bénévoles!

Objectifs de l'unité

Read, view, and listen to informational texts such as announcements, videos, and personal stories about household tasks and working as a volunteer.

Negotiate with others to decide on household tasks and a volunteer opportunity.

Provide information about yourself in order to apply to a volunteer organization.

Investigate how and why people in Francophone cultures contribute to their communities through volunteerism.

Questions essentielles

How do my personal responsibilities and routines shape my daily life?

How can community members work together to improve the quality of life for themselves and others?

What kinds of volunteer opportunities exist in the Francophone world? What motivates people from different cultures to volunteer?

Helping others is essential to a functional community. It helps us develop as individuals and makes a real difference in the world. In this unit, Éloïse and Yngara will share information about what they do to be helpful.

Rencontre interculturelle

Le Québec

Nom: Éloïse

Langues parlées: français, anglais

Origine: Montréal, Québec, Canada

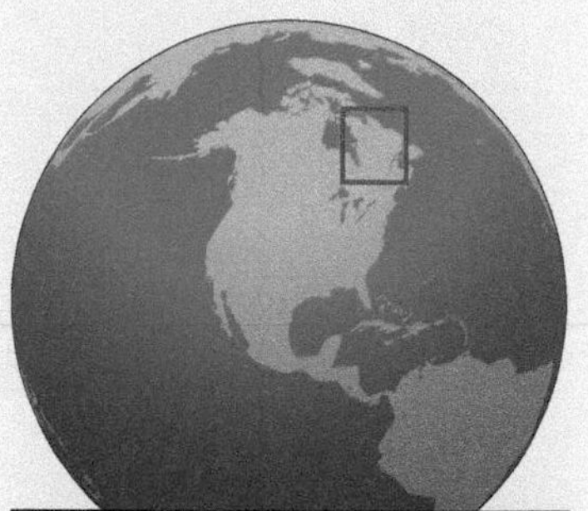

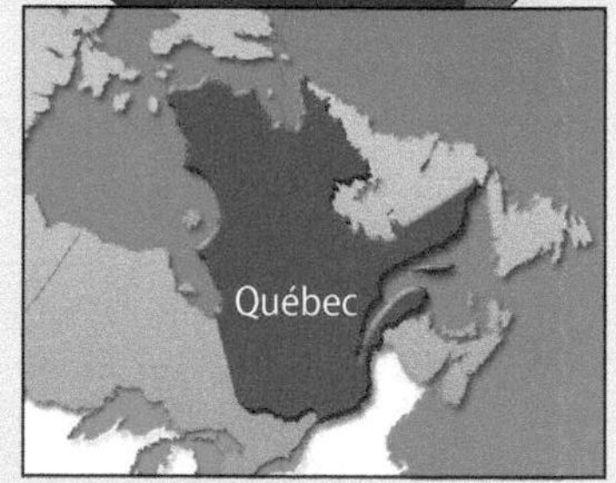

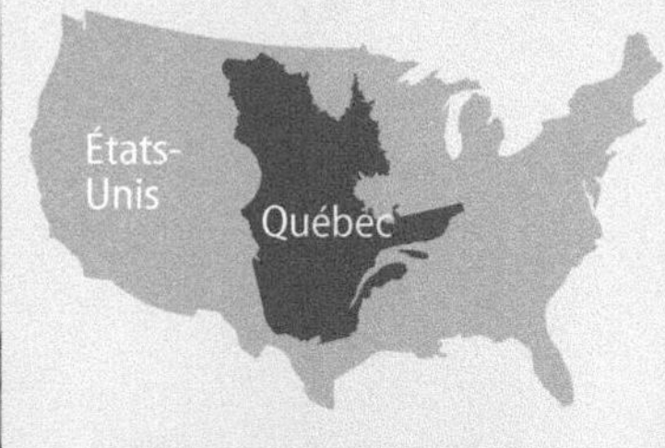

Le Québec est vaste! Regardez sa superficie comparée à celle des États-Unis.

Le Québec est la plus grande province du Canada. C'est une des deux provinces canadiennes qui ont le français comme langue officielle. La langue française est considérée comme un élément essentiel de l'héritage culturel québécois. Le drapeau du Québec s'appelle le fleurdelisé parce qu'il a quatre fleurs de lys!

La ville de Québec, la capitale de la province du Québec, a été fondée *(founded)* en 1608 par l'explorateur Samuel de Champlain. Cette province, comme le reste du Canada, utilise le système métrique et le dollar canadien, et elle offre un système de santé *(health)* accessible à tous.

Il y a beaucoup de choses à faire et à voir au Québec. La nature est très belle, avec de vastes forêts et une multitude d'animaux.

La ville de Québec et le Château Frontenac

Activité 1

Un tour au Québec

Étape 1: Lire

Vous voulez organiser un voyage au Québec. Lisez les informations sur la province du Québec et trouvez les mots pour finir chaque phrase.

1. La plus grande province canadienne est...
2. Le drapeau du Québec s'appelle...
3. Un explorateur important pour la ville de Québec s'appelle...
4. Le plus grand animal du fleuve ou de l'océan s'appelle...
5. Une activité amusante avec des chiens est de...

On peut faire du kayak et admirer une baleine *(whale)* sur le fleuve (grande rivière) Saint-Laurent. On peut observer beaucoup d'animaux!

On peut faire du traîneau *(sled)* à chiens sur la neige et voir des aurores boréales! On peut aussi aller à des festivals en été comme en hiver!

Étape 2: Discuter

Sélectionnez quelques activités au Québec que vous trouvez intéressantes. Comparez vos choix avec deux ou trois élèves de la classe.

Modèle

Moi, je veux voir une aurore boréale parce que c'est unique et beau. Et toi?

Éloïse a 16 ans et elle habite à Montréal dans une maison près de l'université Concordia avec ses parents et ses deux frères, Maxence et Médéric. Elle est en terminale à l'École internationale de Montréal. Elle parle français et anglais mais elle apprend aussi l'espagnol. Éloïse aime beaucoup la lecture et l'écriture. Elle apprécie la nature et le sport. Quand il y a de la neige, donc du mois de novembre au mois d'avril, elle est monitrice *(instructor)* de ski!

Activité 2

Salut, Éloïse!

Étape 1: Lire et décider

Avec un(e) partenaire, regardez la photo d'Éloïse et lisez son introduction et ce qu'elle dit dans les bulles. Est-ce que les déclarations suivantes sont vraies ou fausses?

1. Éloïse aime rester chez elle.
2. Éloïse aime passer du temps avec les livres.
3. Il y a cinq membres dans la famille d'Éloïse.
4. Elle habite à la campagne.
5. Elle est sportive.

Michaëlle Jean était la 27e gouverneure générale du Canada et la troisième secrétaire générale de l'Organisation internationale de la Francophonie.

Étape 2: Regarder

Regardez la vidéo d'Éloïse. Discutez avec un(e) partenaire pour décider dans quel ordre elle mentionne les informations suivantes, et écrivez les numéros qui correspondent aux lettres:

____ a. Elle aime beaucoup le frisbee et le volley-ball.

____ b. Elle habite à Montréal.

____ c. Elle aime beaucoup la lecture et l'écriture.

____ d. Elle va à l'École internationale de Montréal.

____ e. Son prénom est Éloïse.

____ f. L'an prochain, elle va aller au Cégep Saint-Laurent.

____ g. Elle est monitrice de ski.

____ h. Elle a deux frères qui s'appellent Médéric et Maxence.

Réflexion interculturelle

In her introduction video, Éloïse shared information about herself and some things she does in her free time. What is the connection between where Éloïse lives and the things she is able to do for fun? Are there any activities you do that are especially available where you live? Answer the questions in the discussion forum in Explorer.

Le centre-ville de Montréal vu du fleuve Saint-Laurent

Rappelle-toi

Activité 3

Quelle chambre pour chacun?

Vous allez passer un séjour d'immersion au Québec pendant l'été et vous habitez en famille d'accueil *(host family)* avec quelques autres élèves internationaux.

Étape 1: Écouter

Écoutez vos hôtes et les trois autres élèves se présenter dans le bulletin électronique du programme. Notez les réponses aux questions suivantes.

Association séjour en famille - ASF

BULLETIN D'AUTOMNE – Faites la connaissance de votre famille d'accueil et d'autres élèves! Trouvez les réponses à ces questions et BEAUCOUP PLUS en cliquant sur les liens.

Madame et monsieur Singh	Manuela	Caleb	Ayoub

Combien d'enfants ont-ils? **Pourquoi** ont-ils de la place pour vous et d'autres élèves?	**Comment** est-elle? **Qu'est-ce qu'elle** fait généralement le matin?	**D'où** vient-il: de Chicoutimi ou de Trois-Rivières? **Quand** est-ce qu'il fait du sport?	**Que** fait-il comme activités? **Où** sont les animaux qu'il mentionne?
cliquer ici pour les écouter	cliquer ici pour l'écouter	cliquer ici pour l'écouter	cliquer ici pour l'écouter

Étape 2: Lire

Lisez l'e-mail que madame Singh vous a envoyé.

a. Écrivez une liste des quatres options possibles où les autres élèves et vous pouvez dormir.

b. Pour chaque option, notez les caractéristiques importantes à considérer dans la représentation schématique.

À: manuela32@mail.ca; kleb@mail.ca, ayub
De: r.singh@mail.ca
Objet: Chez nous

Bonjour:

Je voudrais expliquer un peu plus la maison. Notre chambre est au premier étage, et les deux autres chambres sont au rez-de-chaussée avec le salon, la salle de bain, la cuisine et le bureau de mon mari, Raj.

Moi, je fais le petit déjeuner assez tôt le matin et j'ai quelques élèves de piano, donc pour les personnes qui ont besoin de silence le matin, je recommande la chambre à côté du bureau. Cette chambre est aussi un peu plus grande que l'autre.

Dans l'autre chambre, il y a beaucoup de soleil mais la connexion wifi n'est pas très bonne. Les deux chambres ont des lits pour deux personnes.

À part les deux chambres, il y a un sofa convertible dans le bureau de Raj. Nous en avons un dans le salon aussi, mais il n'y a pas de porte à fermer, bien entendu!

Avez-vous des suggestions? Qui doit dormir dans chaque endroit?

À bientôt,

Madame Singh

possibilités	détails	personne(s)
la chambre à côté du bureau de M. Singh		

Étape 3: Parler

Discutez avec d'autres élèves: Quelle personne doit dormir dans quelle partie de la maison?

Modèle

Manuela doit dormir dans la chambre à côté du bureau parce qu'elle…

Expressions utiles

Les prépositions de lieu

à côté de

dans

sur

Étape 4: Écrire

Répondez à l'e-mail de madame Singh. Où peut dormir chaque élève international? N'oubliez pas de dire où vous allez dormir!

Modèle

Bonjour Madame:

J'ai quelques idées. Moi, je peux dormir dans…

Bien cordialement,

PSEUDO:
ZackarySim

MA BIOGRAPHIE EN 3 MOTS:
courageux, canadien, blond

JE ME SENS: fatigué

PSEUDO:
SimuMégane

MA BIOGRAPHIE EN 3 MOTS:
canadienne, active, cuisinière

JE ME SENS: affamée

PSEUDO:
JaydenLeMeilleur

MA BIOGRAPHIE EN 3 MOTS:
jeune, créatif, sportif

JE ME SENS:
pas motivé

PSEUDO:
CharlotteChampionne

MA BIOGRAPHIE EN 3 MOTS: musicienne, québécoise, ambitieuse

JE ME SENS:
relaxée

Activité 4

Où sont-ils?

Vous jouez à un jeu de simulation qui a lieu *(takes place)* dans une grande maison virtuelle, mais vous n'êtes pas certain(e) où sont vos amis. Vous regardez leurs profils pour savoir.

a. Avec un(e) partenaire, posez une question pour vérifier où sont les amis dans la maison simulée.

b. Posez une autre question inspirée par l'icône qu'ils ont choisie.

Modèle

Tu joues dans le garage? Pourquoi est-ce que tu vas prendre la voiture?

Activité 5

À qui penses-tu?

Étape 1: Écrire

Votre classe célèbre les héros de votre communauté. Complétez l'infographie en décrivant trois personnes que vous connaissez qui sont de bons exemples originaires de votre école ou de votre maison, de votre ville et du monde.

Les héros des communautés où je vis

le monde

ma ville

mon école ou ma maison

Étape 2: Présenter

Présentez les trois personnes à un groupe d'autres élèves.

Rappelle-toi

Chez moi

l'appartement (m.)
la chambre (à coucher)
le jardin
la maison
la salle à manger
la salle de bains
le salon
les toilettes (f. pl.)
la ville

Mots interrogatifs

Combien?
Comment?
Où?/D'où?
Pourquoi?
Quand?
Que?/Qu'?
Qui?

Les adjectifs

actif/active
âgé/âgée
ambitieux/ambitieuse
canadien/canadienne
courageux/courageuse
créatif/créative
dynamique
énergique
généreux/généreuse
gentil/gentille
intelligent/intelligente
jeune
patient/patiente
positif/positive
québécois/québécoise
sportif/sportive

Expressions utiles

à côté de
dans
sur

Expressions utiles

donner à manger
to feed

donner un coup de main
to lend a helping hand

faire le lit
to make the bed

Communiquons

Comment dit-on? 1

Une semaine typique

Mes responsabilités chez moi

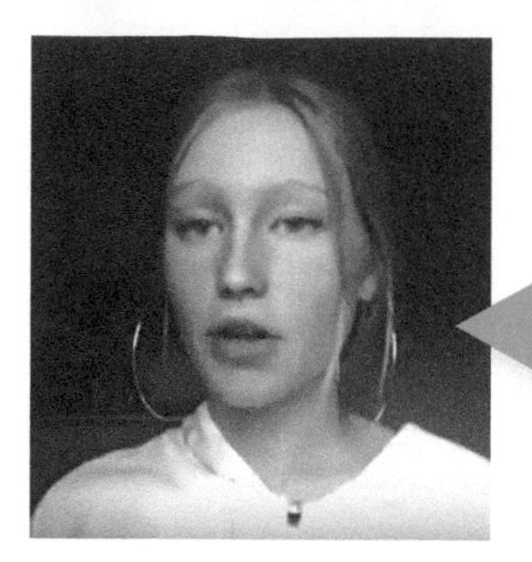

*Dans ma famille, je donne un coup de main et je participe aux **tâches ménagères**. Je vais vous parler de mes tâches **quotidiennes, hebdomadaires** et **mensuelles**.*

Mes tâches quotidiennes

Tous les jours, je dois faire le lit. Dans la cuisine, je dois **mettre le couvert**, **débarrasser le lave-vaisselle**, et donner à manger au chien.

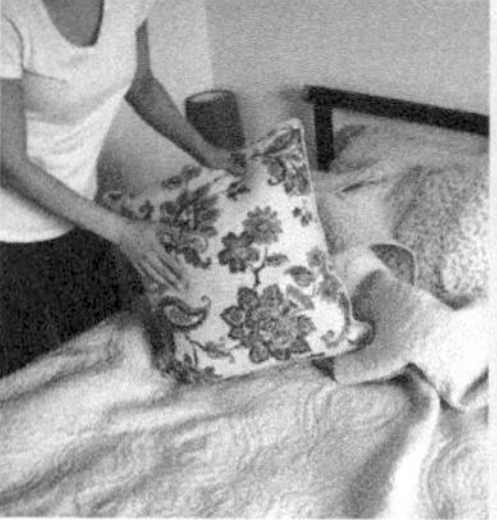

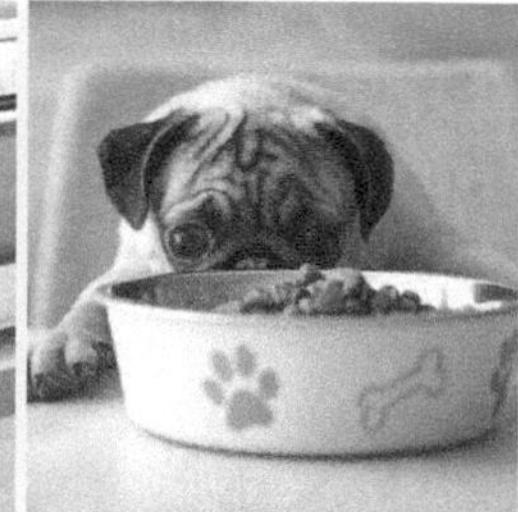

Mes tâches hebdomadaires

Une fois par semaine, je dois **laver et plier mon linge**, **ranger** ma chambre, **passer l'aspirateur** et **garder** mon petit frère.

Mes tâches mensuelles

Une fois par mois, je dois **arroser** les cactus sur mon bureau et **ramasser les déchets** dans le jardin. En plus, je **fais du jardinage** avec ma mère.

Activité 6

Éloïse fait-elle ses tâches ménagères?

Étape 1: Chercher

Regardez les informations à propos des tâches ménagères d'Éloïse. Quelles tâches fait-elle dans les endroits suivants?

Dans sa chambre:

Dans la cuisine:

Dans la maison en général:

À l'extérieur de la maison:

Étape 2: Identifier

Chez elle, Éloïse a des tâches ménagères et elle décide d'utiliser un aide-mémoire pour marquer les tâches accomplies. Avec votre partenaire, regardez l'aide-mémoire d'Éloïse du mois dernier et décidez quelles semaines ses parents font les déclarations suivantes.

tâches quotidiennes

Semaine 1	lun	mar	mer	jeu	ven	sam	dim
mettre le couvert		✔			✔		
débarrasser le lave-vaisselle	✔	✔	✔	✔	✔	✔	✔
donner à manger au chien	✔	✔	✔	✔	✔	✔	✔

Semaine 2	lun	mar	mer	jeu	ven	sam	dim
mettre le couvert	✔	✔	✔	✔	✔	✔	✔
débarrasser le lave-vaisselle	✔	✔	✔	✔	✔	✔	✔
donner à manger au chien	✔	✔	✔	✔	✔	✔	✔

Semaine 3	lun	mar	mer	jeu	ven	sam	dim
mettre le couvert	✔				✔		✔
débarrasser le lave-vaisselle	✔	✔	✔		✔	✔	✔
donner à manger au chien	✔	✔	✔	✔	✔	✔	✔

Semaine 4	lun	mar	mer	jeu	ven	sam	dim
mettre le couvert		✔			✔		
débarrasser le lave-vaisselle	✔	✔	✔		✔		
donner à manger au chien	✔	✔	✔	✔	✔		

tâches hebdomadaires

	sem 1	sem 2	sem 3	sem 4
laver et plier mon linge	✔	✔	✔	
garder mon frère après l'école	✔	✔	✔	✔
passer l'aspirateur dans ma chambre	✔	✔		✔

tâches mensuelles

laver le chien	✔
arroser mon cactus	✔
faire du jardinage	✔

Modèle

Éloïse, tu dois mettre le couvert plus régulièrement!
Réponse: Semaine 1, 3 et 4

1. Bravo Éloïse, toutes tes tâches ménagères sont faites!
2. Éloïse, pourquoi tu ne débarrasses pas le lave-vaisselle le jeudi?
3. Éloïse, comment était ton week-end de camping?
4. Éloïse, tu dois laver et plier ton linge!
5. Éloïse, pourquoi tu ne passes pas l'aspirateur dans ta chambre?

Étape 3: Écrire

Éloïse veut comparer ses tâches ménagères avec les vôtres *(yours)*. Elle vous demande par texto si vous avez aussi des responsabilités chez vous. Répondez à Éloïse via texto.

Modèle

Salut, c'est Éloïse! J'ai beaucoup de tâches ménagères à faire. Est-ce que tu en as, toi?

Salut Éloïse! Oui, je dois participer et aider aux tâches ménagères chez moi.

1. Est-ce que tu aides ta famille dans la cuisine chez toi?
2. Et est-ce que tu dois faire quelque chose dans ta chambre?
3. D'accord. Et dans le reste de la maison?
4. Je vois. Et est-ce que tu as des tâches mensuelles?
5. D'accord, c'est très intéressant. Merci pour toutes tes réponses et à plus tard!

Activité 7

Quelles sont leurs responsabilités?

Étape 1: Regarder

Regardez la vidéo d'Éloïse. Est-ce que vous pouvez compléter ce que dit Éloïse avec les mots ci-dessous?

linge - chambre - tâches - ménagères toilettes - semaines - aspirateur

Chez moi, comme _________ _________, je passe l'_________ une fois par semaine, je fais ma __________, je fais mon lavage* et je plie mon __________, et finalement, je lave les __________ environ une fois par deux __________.

*je fais mon lavage = je lave

Étape 2: Regarder et organiser

Regardez la vidéo d'Yngara. Avec un(e) partenaire et à l'oral, remettez ce qu'elle dit en ordre. Ensuite, écrivez les phrases ordonnées dans votre cahier.

1. (je suis en terminale.) (j'ai 17 ans et) (je m'appelle Yngara.) (Bonjour,) (Je suis centrafricaine,)
2. (que j'ai à la maison.) (je vais vous parler de quelques) (Aujourd'hui,) (responsabilités)
3. (si j'en ai besoin.) (Après, je fais du linge) (D'habitude, je fais) (marcher mon chien.)
4. (si j'ai besoin de la faire,) (je range ma chambre.) (Et aussi,)

Étape 3: Comparer

Regardez les deux vidéos d'Éloïse et de son amie Yngara.

a. Est-ce que c'est Yngara ou Éloïse qui dit les phrases suivantes?
   1. Moi, je suis centrafricaine.
   2. Je passe l'aspirateur.
   3. J'ai un chien adorable!
   4. Je dois laver les toilettes.
   5. Je plie mon linge.

b. Les deux tâches ménagères qu'Yngara et Éloïse ont en commun sont:

   ranger la chambre — donner à manger au chien
   passer l'aspirateur — faire le linge

Activité 8

Comment organiser les tâches?

Étape 1: Écouter

Pendant les vacances d'hiver, Charlotte et Binta, les amies d'Éloïse, travaillent à la station de ski du Mont Orford près de Montréal. Elles partagent un appartement et doivent décider au téléphone qui va faire les tâches ménagères.

a. Écoutez leur conversation.

b. Avec un(e) partenaire, décidez quelle image va avec quelle amie.

Binta **Charlotte**

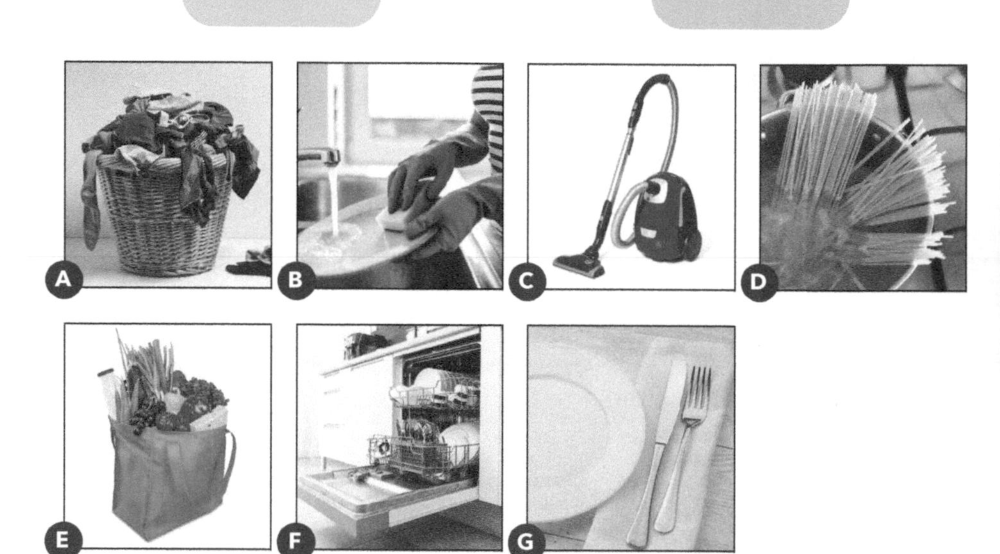

Étape 2: Discuter

Qu'est-ce que vous faites chez vous?

a. Choisissez quatre tâches ménagères.

b. Posez des questions pour savoir si les autres élèves ont des responsabilités similaires chez eux.

Modèle

Est-ce que tu fais ton lit chez toi?

mes responsabilités	élève 1	élève 2	élève 3

Activité 9

Peut-on ranger sa chambre en 10 minutes?

Avant de lire, discutez avec votre partenaire: Quelles tâches ménagères sont importantes pour vous quand vous rangez votre chambre? Quelles tâches ne sont pas importantes pour vous? Pourquoi?

On peut aussi dire

une éponge	*sponge*
par terre	*on the floor*
sortir	*to take out*

Ranger sa chambre en 10 minutes

Sortez tout ce qu'il faut pour ranger (des sacs poubelle, une éponge et l'aspirateur) ***(2 minutes)***

Identifiez les priorités ***(30 secondes)*** – Les chaussettes sales par terre? Les papiers et les livres? Le lit défait?

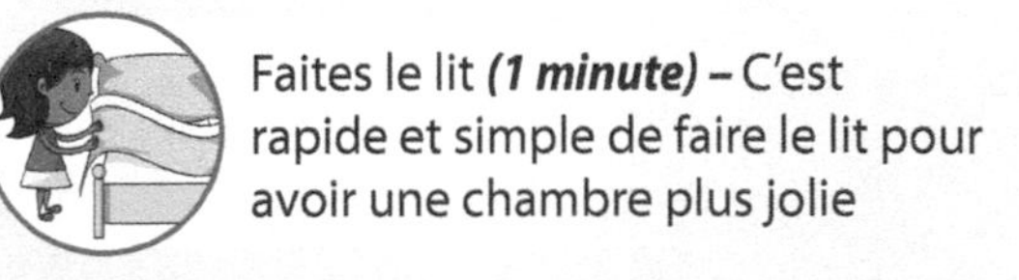

Faites le lit ***(1 minute)*** – C'est rapide et simple de faire le lit pour avoir une chambre plus jolie

Sortez la poubelle et le recyclage ***(2 minutes)***

Mettez les vêtements sales dans le panier à linge ***(30 secondes)***

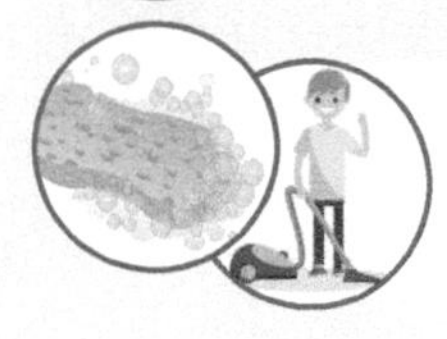

C'est bientôt fini! Passez un coup d'éponge rapide sur le bureau et la table de nuit. Puis, passez l'aspirateur. ***(4 minutes)***

Étape 1: Lire et répondre

a. Lisez l'infographie.

b. Le petit frère d'Éloïse lit l'infographie rapidement et ne comprend pas très bien. Avec votre partenaire, corrigez les phrases du frère d'Éloïse.

1. L'auteur pense que pour ranger rapidement, il faut tout d'abord passer l'aspirateur.
2. L'auteur pense qu'il faut laver et plier le linge.
3. L'auteur pense qu'il faut passer deux minutes à arroser les plantes.

Mon progrès communicatif

I can understand an infographic about chores in the home.

Étape 2: Écrire un texto

Lisez le texto d'Éloïse. Elle doit ranger sa chambre rapidement. (Elle a seulement 5 minutes!) À votre avis, quelles sont les trois priorités pour Éloïse?

> Tu peux m'aider? Mes parents rentrent à la maison dans cinq minutes et ma chambre n'est pas rangée! Qu'est-ce que je peux faire en **cinq minutes**?

Modèle

Éloïse, tu dois…

Activité 10

Que font les filles et les garçons comme tâches ménagères?

Lisez l'infographie sur les tâches ménagères faites par les filles et les garçons francophones (selon un sondage de leurs parents). Quelle sont les tâches décrites dans chaque phrase?

cuisiner	repasser	laver la voiture	faire du baby-sitting

1. Beaucoup de filles font ces tâches.
2. Plus de garçons que de filles font cette tâche.
3. Très peu de garçons font ces tâches.
4. 21% des filles font cette tâche.
5. Cette tâche est la plus populaire pour les filles et les garçons.

On peut aussi dire

les ados (m. pl.)	*teens*
repasser	*to iron*

Les ados et la parité:

Les filles repassent et les garçons lavent la voiture.

+ de 50% des jeunes filles cuisinent	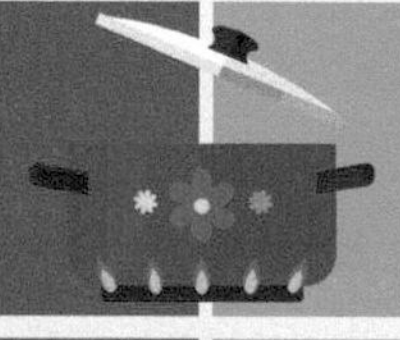	**1/3** des jeunes garçons cuisinent
21% des jeunes filles repassent		**5%** des jeunes garçons repassent
11% des jeunes filles lavent la voiture		**24%** des jeunes garçons lavent la voiture
14% des jeunes filles de 13/14 ans font du baby-sitting		**2%** des jeunes garçons de 13/14 ans font du baby-sitting
42% des jeunes filles de 16/18 ans font du baby-sitting		**13%** des jeunes garçons de 16/18 ans font du baby-sitting

Terrafemina

Zoom culture

Pratique culturelle: Les tâches ménagères au Canada

 **Connexions**

Which types of chores do you do at home? Are the chores that you are expected to do similar to or different from the chores that you prefer? Are your chores similar to or different from those of your friends of similar and different genders?

The sharing of household tasks by men and women is more equal in Canada than in many other countries. Over the last 40 years, the sharing of household tasks has become more equal, but women, on average, continue to do more unpaid household work than men. Today, in households shared by a man and a woman, men do about 39% of the chores, while women do 61% of the chores. Compared to 1986, when women did, on average, 75% of the chores, Canadian men now have a sizable increased responsibility for household chores.

 **Réflexion**

Why do you think men and women might complete different types or amounts of chores? Why might individuals or societies have a goal of equal participation in chores between men and women? How does more evenly distributed participation in chores impact the daily lives of men and women? What are the advantages and disadvantages of sharing chores equally in a home? And in a society?

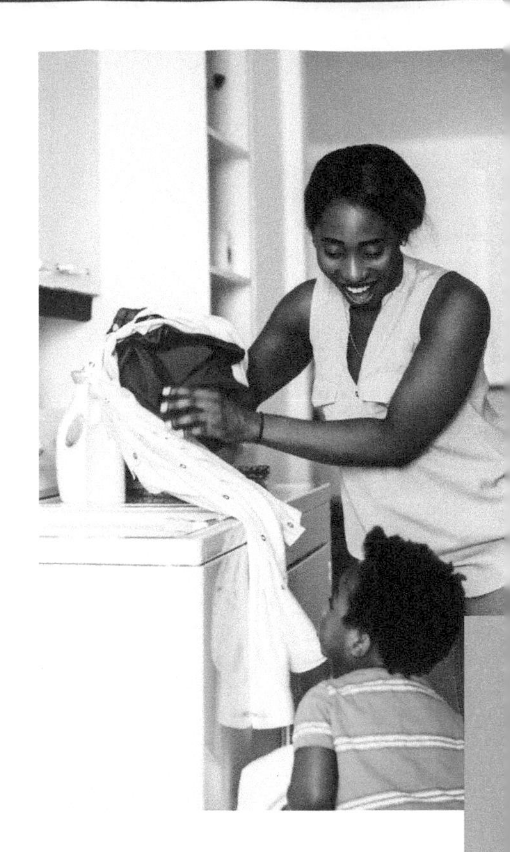

Réflexion interculturelle

What role do you think culture, gender, and age play in influencing the types of chores that people choose to do or are expected to do? What are your considerations (or your parents' considerations) when you are choosing or being assigned chores at home? Answer the questions in the discussion forum in Explorer.

 **Mon progrès interculturel**

I can identify some ways that culture, gender, and age affect the types of chores people do.

Activité 11

Que faut-il faire?

Quel désastre! La famille d'Yngara va inviter des amis à la maison, mais la maison est en désordre. Yngara poste des mèmes sur internet.

a. Regardez chaque photo.

b. Répondez aux mèmes d'Yngara avec des suggestions. Que faut-il faire pour ranger la maison? Enregistrez vos réponses sur Explorer.

Modèle

Il faut ramasser les déchets! Et tu dois passer l'aspirateur.

Découvrons 1

Describing What People Can and Want to Do

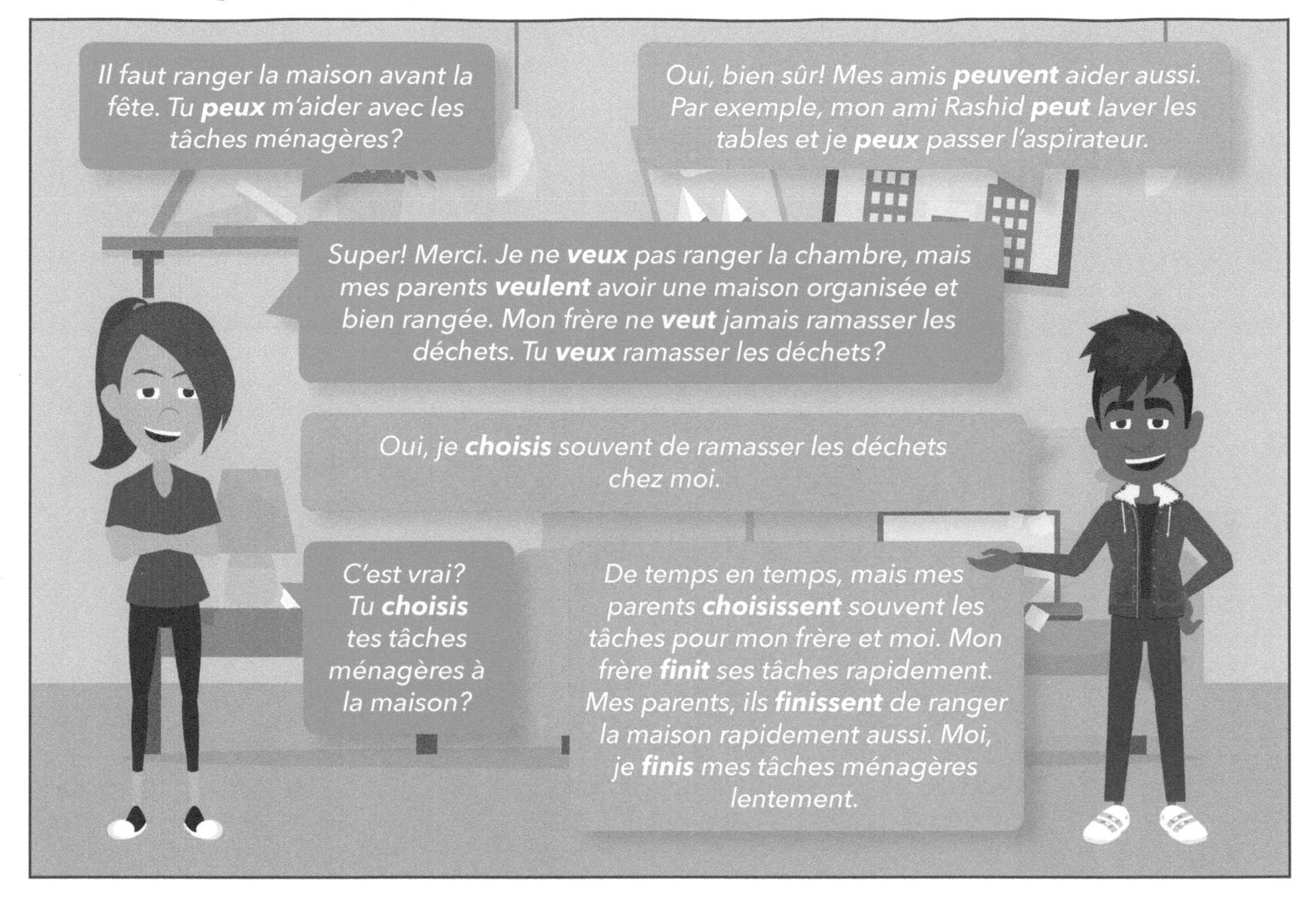

Découvertes

Reflect on what you observe and respond to the following questions in the graphic organizer in Explorer.

1. Look at all of the words in bold in the conversation above. Sort the words in bold into categories that make sense to you.
2. Explain to a partner how you decided to group the words in bold.
3. What do you observe about the ***je*** and ***tu*** forms of the verbs?
4. What do you observe about the ***il/elle/on*** form of the verb? How is it similar to or different from the ***je*** and ***tu*** forms?
5. Share your observations with a ***partenaire*** or with your teacher. What else do you notice together? Can you add to your observations?

View the ***Découvrons 1*** resources for this unit in Explorer and check the ***Synthèse de grammaire*** at the end of this unit.

Activité 12

Ils peuvent nous aider?

Votre prof organise un projet de service dans le parc à côté de l'école.

a. Lisez la liste de tâches que le prof a écrite dans un message.

b. Suggérez des tâches pour les autres personnes sur la liste du prof.

> Tu veux participer avec les amis au projet de service dans le parc? Je choisis des tâches pour tout le monde. Les secrétaires peuvent organiser l'horaire des tâches. Le documentaliste finit les invitations au projet. Tu peux suggérer des volontaires pour les autres tâches, s'il te plaît?

Modèle

Salut! Je peux planter des arbres. Mon ami José choisit de laver les tables....

je	choisir (de)	arroser les fleurs
le proviseur	finir (de)	faire du jardinage
mon ami	pouvoir	inviter les amis
mes amis	vouloir	laver les tables
les élèves travailleurs		planter des arbres
		ramasser les déchets

Activité 13

Tu peux passer l'aspirateur?

Étape 1: Selectionner

Votre classe de français va participer à un projet bénévole *(volunteer)*. Votre prof veut savoir quelles tâches vous pouvez faire pour organiser la première réunion *(meeting)*.

a. Indiquez vos préférences sur le formulaire.

b. Écrivez une autre tâche importante pour la réunion de bénévoles.

Réunion d'organisation: Projet bénévole jeudi à 4h dans le CDI	
Nom:	
Choisissez trois tâches que vous préférez faire. Écrivez "MOI" à côté des trois tâches que vous voulez faire dans la colonne "Qui?"	
	Qui?
Je peux passer l'aspirateur dans le CDI.	
Je veux ranger les livres dans le CDI.	
Je peux inviter le proviseur.	
Je peux ramasser les déchets après la réunion.	
Je finis les invitations pour les élèves.	
Je finis d'organiser les documents pour la réunion.	
Je veux laver les tables dans le CDI.	
Je choisis les boissons pour la réunion.	
Autre tâche: ________________	

Étape 2: Parler

Trouvez des élèves pour faire les autres tâches que vous n'aimez pas beaucoup.

a. Posez des questions aux autres élèves.

b. Écrivez leurs noms sur le formulaire.

Modèle

Tu peux inviter le proviseur?

-Non, je ne peux pas inviter le proviseur. Mais, je veux ranger les livres dans le CDI.

Étape 3: Écrire un e-mail

Écrivez un e-mail à votre professeur. Expliquez qui va faire chaque tâche pour préparer la réunion.

Modèle

Cher/Chère prof,

Avant la réunion, je peux ranger les livres dans le CDI. Corinne et David veulent laver les tables. Moi, je choisis les boissons, et Paul finit les invitations.

AP® Étape 4: Répondre aux questions

Avant la réunion dans le CDI, le documentaliste pose des questions sur les tâches que les élèves vont faire. Répondez à ses questions.

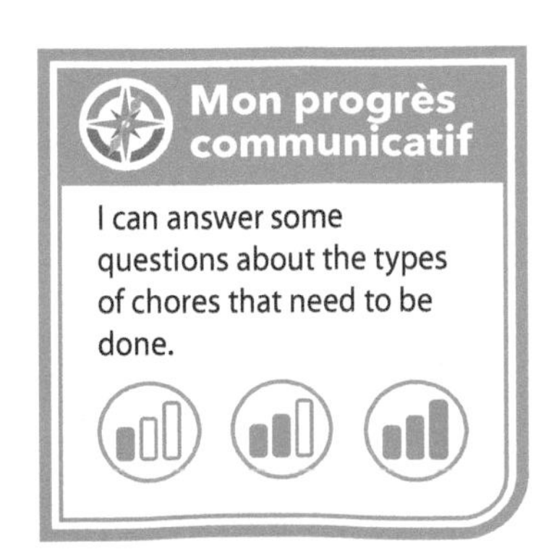

J'avance 1

Comment s'organiser pour habiter ensemble?

You are planning to participate in a volunteer summer camp with students from all over the world who are interested in volunteering in Montreal. You will be sharing a common area (kitchen, living room, and dining room) with Olivier and Amina for two months at the camp. You would all like to keep your living area clean, so your roommates have asked you to create a chore chart to organize which roommate will do which chores.

Étape 1: Écouter

Listen to Olivier and Amina as they describe the ways they help at home.

a. In the graphic organizer in Explorer, check off the chores that each student does at home.

b. Then, check off the chores that you do at home.

Étape 2: Écrire un e-mail

Using the chore chart you have created, write an email to Olivier and Amina explaining the chores that you have assigned to each person for the time that you are staying at the volunteer summer camp.

AP® Étape 3: Écouter et répondre

Amina has received your email and would like to discuss the chores with you. She has some questions about the chores that you have assigned to her.

All of the materials for ***J'avance 1*** can be found in Explorer.

Comment dit-on? 2

Je me prépare à être bénévole

Je fais ma part

Quiz: Quel rôle est fait pour toi?

Quel rôle occupes-tu dans ton groupe d'amis ou quand tu **réalises** un projet scolaire? Choisis les cinq options qui te semblent *(seem)* les plus intéressantes.

Rappel

L'accord des adjectifs

N'oubliez pas de changer la fin d'un adjectif pour l'accorder à son nom:

Il est patient.
Elle est patient**e**.

Il est travaill**eur**.
Elle est travaill**euse**.

Ils sont compréhen**sifs**.
Elle sont compréhen**sives**.

Aimes-tu...

❑ **...servir** des repas?

❑ **...aider** les autres à travailler?

❑ **...contribuer à** des projets?

Total (A) _____

❑ **...conseiller** des amis?

❑ **...accueillir** de nouveaux élèves à ton école?

❑ **...réconforter** quelqu'un qui est triste?

Total (B) _____

❑ **...gérer** des projets

❑ **...organiser** ton emploi du temps?

❑ **...lancer** de nouvelles idées?

Total (C) _____

Résultats:

- Majorité colonne A: Comme tu es **travailleur**! On aime travailler avec toi parce que tu bosses beaucoup et tu fonctionnes bien en équipe.
- Majorité colonne B: Tu es **compréhensif** et un ami **fidèle**. Tu écoutes bien les autres et tu as de l'intelligence émotionnelle.
- Majorité colonne C: C'est toi, le **chef** du groupe! Tu es quelqu'un d'**organisé** et **motivé**!

Détail linguistique

Les anglicismes

En français moderne, on dit souvent certains mots en anglais. Ces mots s'appellent des **anglicismes**.

Il est un bon leader.
C'est moi le boss!

Il est impossible d'arrêter le mélange des langues, surtout avec internet, mais on fait un grand effort dans le monde francophone pour encourager l'usage de la langue française.

Rappel

Pour faire des suggestions

Ça te dit de…

Tu peux…

Activité 14

Quel est ton rôle?

Étape 1: Répondre

a. Répondez aux questions du quiz de personnalité.

b. Comptez vos réponses pour arriver à votre résultat.

Étape 2: Partager

Parlez avec d'autres élèves de la classe. Comparez vos résultats du quiz et posez des questions.

Modèle

Le quiz dit que je suis travailleuse. Quels sont tes résultats?

Activité 15

Quelle offre t'intéresse?

Étape 1: Choisir

Lisez ces deux annonces qui proposent des offres de bénévolat aux jeunes à Montréal.

a. Avec un(e) partenaire, choisissez l'offre que vous trouvez la plus intéressante.

b. Notez trois raisons pour expliquer votre préférence.

Opération Bibliothèque de bienvenue

Nous cherchons quelqu'un de compréhensif, patient et motivé pour accueillir nos clients. Cette personne va aider des enfants réfugiés à trouver et lire des livres de notre collection. Cette personne va aussi gérer la collection. Veuillez contacter monsieur Rachid Ahmed (r.ahmed@bibliobienvenue.asso.ca)

L'école du leadership

Tu as entre 13 et 17 ans? Tu as des capacités de chef? Inscris-toi avant le 19 janvier pour notre 11e cours du leadership chaque fin de semaine du mois de février 2020. Nous allons t'enseigner à lancer des projets, gérer une équipe et conseiller les autres chefs pour réussir. Contacte-nous +1 418 657 4321

AP® Étape 2: Partager

William, un ami d'Éloïse, veut faire une de ces activités mais il ne sait pas comment choisir. Répondez à ses questions pour l'aider. Enregistrez votre conversation sur Explorer.

Activité 16

Qui est fait pour ce rôle?

Étape 1: Écouter

Ces adolescents se présentent comme candidats pour être président d'une organisation à votre école. Regardez leurs qualités et leurs dons *(talents)* et choisissez les phrases qui décrivent chaque personne.

1. Gaby
2. Emmanuel
3. Phara

A. accueille de nouveaux élèves
B. est un(e) ami(e) fidèle
C. contribue aux projets des autres
D. donne un coup de main
E. gère des projets
F. lance de nouvelles idées
G. est motivé(e)
H. est organisé(e)
I. organise des groupes
J. est travailleur(euse)

Détail grammatical

La formation des verbes servir et accueillir

Voici quelques exemples de ces verbes en contexte:

J'**accueille** le nouvel élève à mon école.

Tu **accueilles** aussi des parents qui visitent l'école?

Je **sers** des repas aux personnes qui en ont besoin.

Elle **sert** des goûters aux enfants après l'école.

Étape 2: Écrire

Dans un post du réseau social *(social network)*, recommandez une personne pour être président de l'organisation. Expliquez pourquoi vous recommandez cette personne.

Modèle

Je recommande __________ comme président(e) de l'organisation parce qu'il/elle...

Expressions utiles

construire des maisons
planter des arbres
répondre au téléphone
sortir le recyclage et la poubelle
trier et distribuer le courrier

On peut aussi dire

engagé/engagée
actively involved

expérimenté/expérimentée
experienced

Comment fonctionne une association de bénévoles?

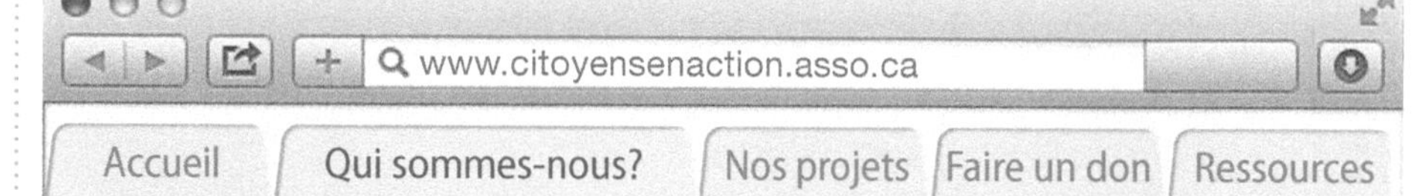

Citoyens en action

Citoyens en action est un groupe de jeunes **bénévoles** qui aident la communauté. Chaque semaine, nous avons **une réunion** pour parler de nos objectifs. Nous travaillons ensemble et chaque personne a son propre rôle.

Vous voulez nous aider au bureau? Nous avons besoin de bénévoles qui peuvent:

- trier et distribuer le courrier

- répondre au téléphone

- sortir le recyclage et la poubelle

Nous avons toutes sortes de projets hors du bureau:

- Il y a des bénévoles qui plantent des arbres dans les espaces publiques et font du jardinage chez des personnes âgées.

- Il y a des bénévoles qui construisent des maisons.

Prononciation

 **Une combinaison de lettres à deux sons**

How do we pronounce the double "L" in French?

You already know that the double "L" in French words can be pronounced either as an "L" sound as in ***elle***, or a "Y" sound, as in ***travailler***. How do we know which sound it is when we see a word with a double "L"? Make predictions and then check them by listening to a recording.

In the following transcription of a radio announcement for a volunteer opportunity, see if you can identify which double "L" sound is the right one. Listen to the recording and complete the pronunciation activity in Explorer.

> On recherche des bénévoles travailleurs et patients, pour soutenir le programme d'été de notre belle école pour les petits enfants au mois de juillet. Le travail consiste à accueillir les familles dans la salle principale, les aider à compléter les feuilles d'inscription, conseiller les enfants et aller à la piscine une fois par semaine. Si cela vous intéresse, téléphonez aux directrices. Elles peuvent répondre à vos questions.

Activité 17

Comment placer ces bénévoles potentiels?

 **Étape 1: Associer**

Écoutez ces messages des personnes qui ont téléphoné à l'association *Citoyens en action*. Décidez si chaque personne est faite pour a) travailler comme chef de l'équipe, b) aider au bureau, ou c) travailler hors du bureau.

1. Isaac 2. Jade 3. Maeva

 **Étape 2: Répondre aux textos**

Maintenant, répondez aux textos d'Isaac, de Jade et de Maeva avec des recommandations plus exactes.

Modèle

Ça vous dit de répondre aux téléphones? / Préférez-vous … ou …? / Vous pouvez… / Vous voulez…?

Isaac

Bonjour. Vous avez des suggestions pour moi?

Jade

Est-ce que vous avez des nouvelles?

Maeva

Bonjour. Avez-vous reçu mon message?

Activité 18

Quel est le projet bénévole d'Édrige Oris?

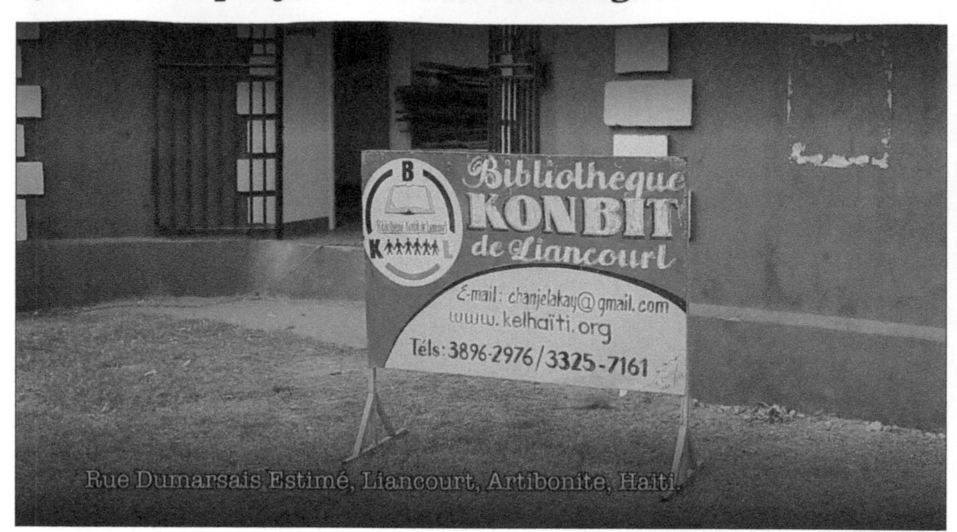

Étape 1: Regarder

Vous cherchez un bon exemple de jeune bénévole pour inspirer votre classe.

a. Regardez la vidéo d'Édrige Oris et associez ces termes pour identifier les détails importants.

1. Sa motivation
2. Un problème qui existait dans sa communauté
3. Un nouveau problème
4. Sa méthode pour lancer son projet

a. les jeunes s'intéressaient plus au rap qu'à l'école
b. le tremblement de terre de 2010
c. réunir des jeunes leaders de la communauté
d. encourager les jeunes à lire

b. Complétez la mini-biographie d'Édrige Oris en écrivant des détails de la vidéo dans la représentation schématique.

Nom:	Édrige Oris	**Nation:**	
Ville:	Liancourt	**Département:**	Artibonite
Son projet bénévole:	Il organise ________ où les ________ écrivent pour parler de leur communauté.		

Des gens achètent et vendent des objets devant un bâtiment effondré à Port-au-Prince, en Haïti.

Étape 2: Comparer

Avec un(e) partenaire, pensez à une personne que vous connaissez qui fait du bénévolat. Comparez la personne à Édrige Oris dans le diagramme de Venn.

- Comment est cette personne?
- Que fait cette personne comme bénévole?

Édrige Oris — une personne que je connais

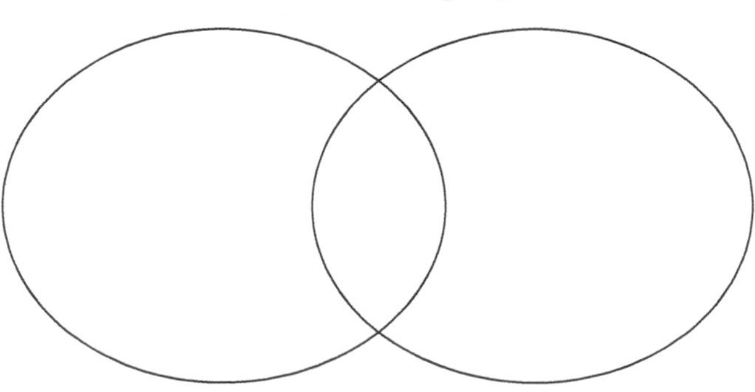
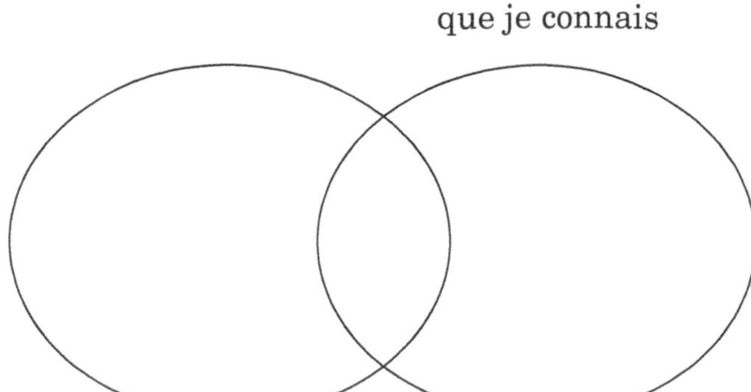

Étape 3: Partager

a. Parlez avec d'autres élèves de la classe et partagez votre diagramme de Venn.

b. Notez une similarité et une différence entre les personnes que vous avez présentées.

La plupart des bâtiments du centre-ville de Port-au-Prince restent encore affaiblis et risqués.

Réflexion interculturelle

In the video, you discovered how Édrige Oris responded to a difficult time in his country. What are some positive ways that people in your community have responded to challenges together? What life lessons can you take away from Édrige's example? Answer the questions in the discussion forum in Explorer.

Mon progrès interculturel

I can identify ways people in my community and Francophone cultures respond to challenges and give reasons why.

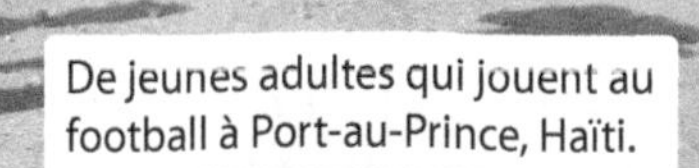

De jeunes adultes qui jouent au football à Port-au-Prince, Haïti.

Découvrons 2

Asking "Which" and "What" Questions

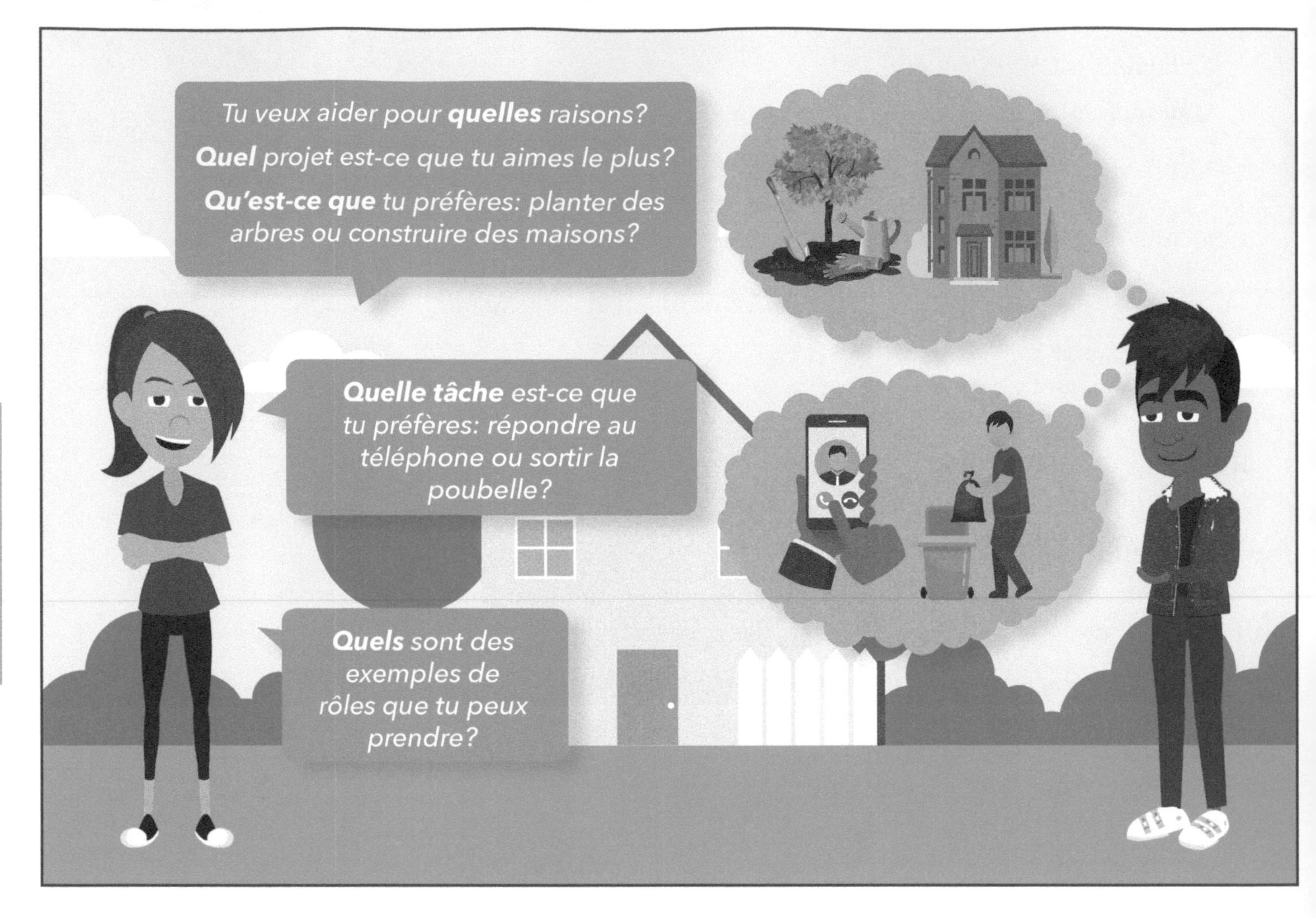

Découvertes

Reflect on what you observe and respond to the following questions in the graphic organizer in Explorer.

1. Can you identify all the forms of the word ***quel***? When is each one used?
2. Compare the use of ***quel*** and ***qu'est-ce que***. What do they have in common? When should you use one or the other?
3. If you were trying to teach another student how to put together a question using ***quel***, how would you explain it? What about questions using ***qu'est-ce que***?
4. Share your observations with a partner. What else do you notice together or what else can you add to your observations?

View the ***Découvrons 2*** resources for this unit in Explorer and check the ***Synthèse de grammaire*** at the end of this unit.

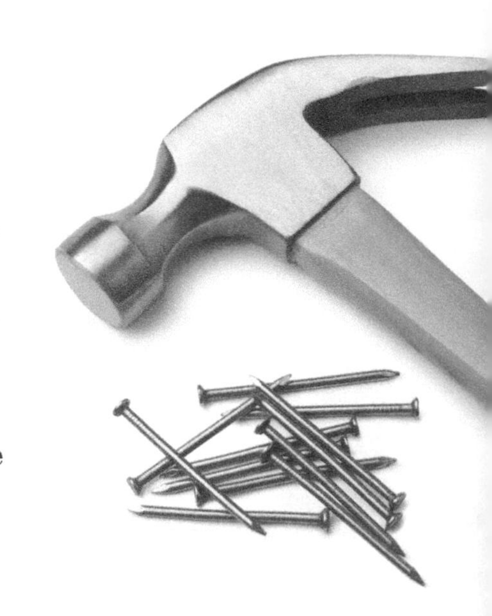

Activité 19

Quelles questions peux-tu poser?

Citoyens en action vous demande d'évaluer les autres élèves de votre classe pour savoir qui peut être bénévole.

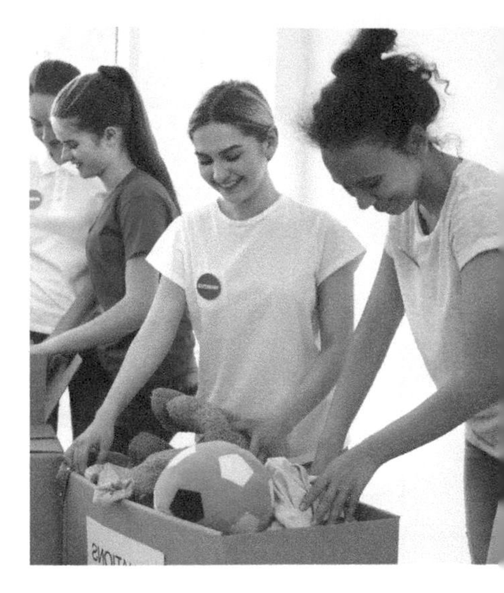

Étape 1: Préparer

Écrivez des questions que vous pouvez poser aux autres élèves. Utilisez ces débuts de phrases pour construire vos questions et ajoutez une autre question.

questions	réponses des autres élèves
Modèle: Quelles sortes de tâches est-ce que tu as à la maison?	
Quels sont tes projets pour [période de temps]?	
Qu'est-ce que tu préfères: ... ou ... ?	
[votre question]	

Étape 2: Interviewer

Interviewez un(e) partenaire et notez ses réponses dans la représentation schématique.

Étape 3: Recommander

Est-ce que vous recommandez cette personne comme bénévole ou non? Enregistrez votre recommandation sur Explorer.

Modèle

Je recommande ____ parce que... / Je ne recommande pas ____ parce que...

On peut aussi dire

à la recherche de
in search of

devenir
to become

un organisme à but non-lucratif (OBNL)
not-for-profit organization (NPO)

Activité 20

Tu voudrais devenir bénévole?

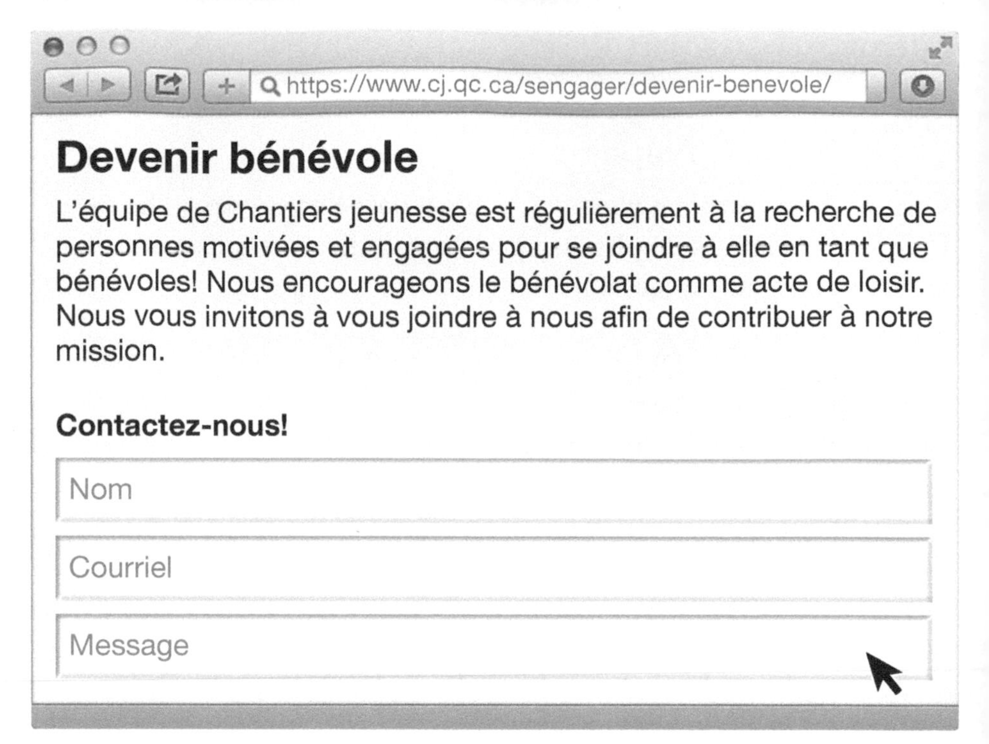

https://www.cj.qc.ca/sengager/devenir-benevole/

Devenir bénévole

L'équipe de Chantiers jeunesse est régulièrement à la recherche de personnes motivées et engagées pour se joindre à elle en tant que bénévoles! Nous encourageons le bénévolat comme acte de loisir. Nous vous invitons à vous joindre à nous afin de contribuer à notre mission.

Contactez-nous!

Nom

Courriel

Message

Étape 1: Comprendre

Travaillez avec un(e) partenaire pour comprendre ce site en répondant aux questions.

1. Qu'est-ce que c'est, Chantiers jeunesse?
2. Quelle sorte de personnes est-ce que cette association cherche?

Étape 2: Poser des questions

Complétez le formulaire en ligne du site Chantiers jeunesse.

a. Expliquez pourquoi vous voulez devenir bénévole.

b. Expliquez pourquoi vous êtes un(e) bon(ne) candidat(e).

c. Posez des questions pour en savoir plus.

Modèle

Je voudrais devenir bénévole parce que… / Quel(le) est votre…? / Quel(le)s sont vos…?

Zoom culture

Pratique culturelle: La jeunesse engagée au Canada

  **Connexions**

Do you or people you know volunteer in your community? What kinds of things do people do as volunteers?

On the whole, Canada has a strong tradition of community involvement and volunteerism. This includes more than 2.2 million ***Québécoises*** and ***Québécois***. ***Les bénévoles*** accounted for 268 million work hours in 2013 alone! The estimated dollar amount (if organizations had to hire employees instead of having volunteers) adds up to $7,000,000*. It is also important to note that 15- to 24-year-olds in Canada are more likely than any other age group to be involved in ***le bénévolat***.

This enormous positive impact is helped by the variety of volunteer opportunities available to Canadians. From restoring historic buildings and public spaces to fundraising to provide help directly to specific populations such as senior citizens, refugees, or children, whatever your interest, you will find a volunteer opportunity ***au Canada!***

*en dollars canadiens

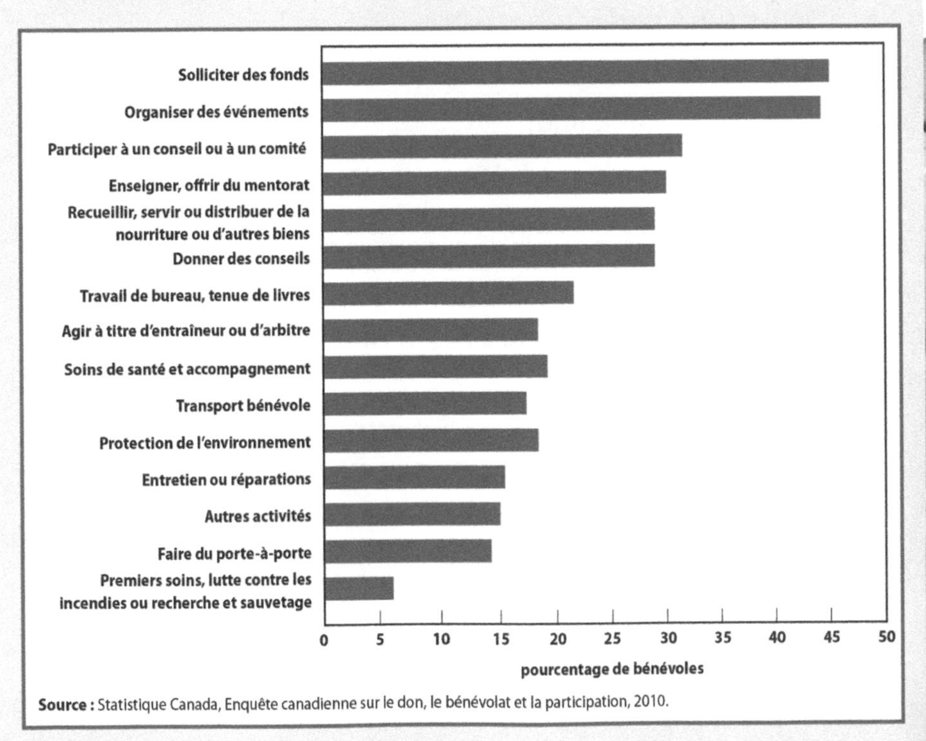

  **Réflexion**

Take a look at the graph from ***Statistique Canada*** to see some volunteer efforts in which Canadians get involved. How many can you identify?

J'avance 2

Choisissez le citoyen du mois!

Citoyens en action is sponsoring a prize for volunteerism and leadership in the community. Watch their video announcement of the prize and then make your recommendation for the best candidate.

Étape 1: Écouter

Watch the video and check the traits you hear in the graphic organizer in Explorer so you know what kind of nominee ***Citoyens en action*** is looking for.

Étape 2: Proposer

Fill out the online form to nominate someone you know as ***citoyen*** or ***citoyenne de l'année***. Be sure to include:

- The person's name;
- How you know the person;
- Personality traits; and,
- Volunteer activities or roles.

Étape 3: Choisir

Read two of your classmates' nominations and with a partner, decide which one of the nominations is the best choice. Record your conversation in Explorer.

- Ask each other questions and give reasons for your choices.
- Make sure it is clear at the end of your conversation whom you are recommending.

All of the materials for ***J'avance 2*** can be found in Explorer.

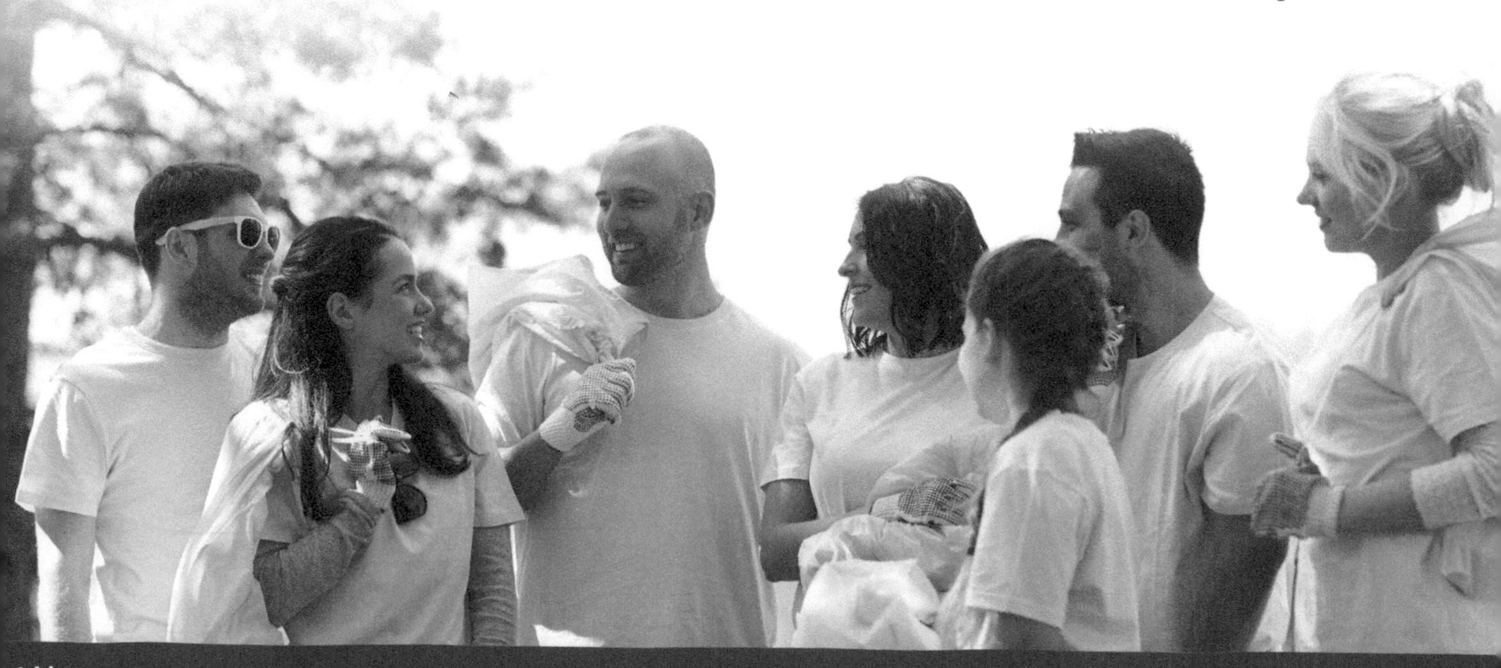

Comment dit-on? 3

Allons faire du bénévolat!

Où peut-on faire du bénévolat?

Bénévol@

un refuge pour sans-abri

une banque alimentaire

un refuge pour animaux

un jardin communautaire

une garderie

une fondation

un foyer de soins

un hôpital

On peut aussi dire

un abri
shelter

un chantier
work site

une collecte
drive (as in blood drive, food drive, etc.)

donner du sang
to give blood

des dons (m. pl.)
donations

des fonds (m. pl.)
funds

un réseau
network

Réflexion interculturelle

Take a look at the volunteer sites shown in the ***Bénévol@*** app. How many of them are in your community as well? Choose at least three of the places from the app and see if you can find an example online of one in Montreal where Éloïse lives. Answer the questions in the discussion forum in Explorer.

Mon progrès interculturel

I can identify and locate volunteer sites in my community and in a Francophone community.

Expressions utiles

Discuter et argumenter

Bonne idée!
Good idea!

Je ne suis pas d'accord (avec toi).
I disagree (with you).

Je suis d'accord (avec toi).
I agree (with you).

Activité 21

Quel bénévole pour quel projet?

L'organisme *Citoyens en action* a beaucoup de nouveaux bénévoles, mais il faut mettre chaque personne avec le projet où il ou elle peut bien travailler.

Étape 1: Lire

Lisez les profils des bénévoles potentiels. Puis, associez un projet de l'appli *Bénévol@* à chaque personne.

1. **Nicolas:** Moi, j'ai deux chiens et un chat à la maison. Je leur donne à manger tous les jours!

2. **Mia:** Je suis un vrai chef. J'aime gérer des groupes de personnes et organiser des projets. Je préfère être active (pas assise devant un ordinateur!)

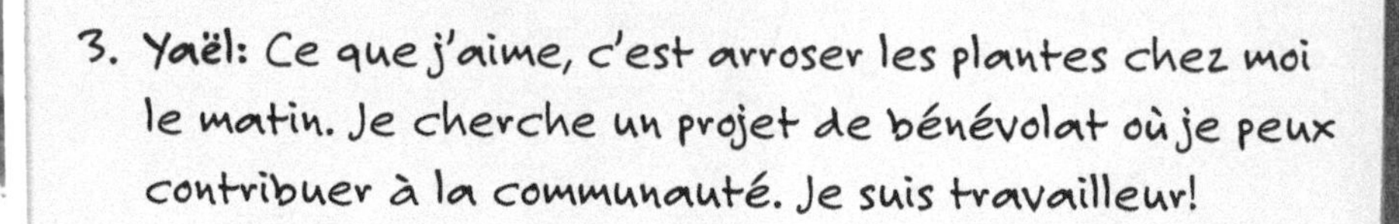

3. **Yaël:** Ce que j'aime, c'est arroser les plantes chez moi le matin. Je cherche un projet de bénévolat où je peux contribuer à la communauté. Je suis travailleur!

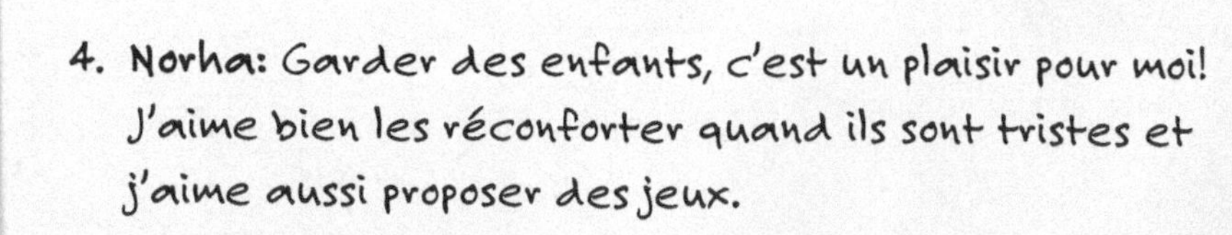

4. **Norha:** Garder des enfants, c'est un plaisir pour moi! J'aime bien les réconforter quand ils sont tristes et j'aime aussi proposer des jeux.

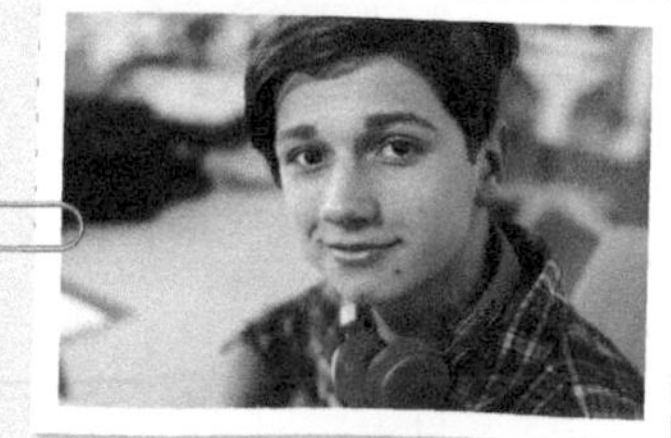

5. **Zachary:** Je voudrais être bénévole, mais j'ai beaucoup d'allergies (aux animaux, aux plantes...à beaucoup de choses!). Je suis un peu timide aussi, alors je cherche un projet de bénévolat où je peux être calme et accueillir quelqu'un qui a besoin d'aide.

Étape 2: Discuter

a. Expliquez aux autres élèves pourquoi vous mettez ces personnes avec certains projets bénévoles.

b. Si les autres élèves ont des réponses différentes, posez des questions pour arriver à un consensus.

Modèle

–Je pense que Zachary va mieux avec un refuge pour animaux.

–Mais non! Je ne suis pas d'accord avec ça. Il a des allergies!

Activité 22

Comment peut-on participer à cet événement spécial?

Le bénévolat est si important qu'il y a parfois des événements pour fêter et encourager les bénévoles.

Étape 1: Regarder

a. Regardez la première partie de la vidéo (12 secondes) et répondez aux questions pour comprendre cette occasion spéciale.

1. Comment s'appelle l'événement?
2. Quand se passe cet événement?
3. Combien de bénévoles est-ce qu'il y a au Canada (selon cette vidéo)?

b. Regardez le reste de la vidéo et écrivez une liste de tous les (groupes de) mots que vous comprenez.

Stratégies

Arriving at a Decision

Some conversations have a desired outcome, like arriving at a decision. When discussing choices with another person, here are a few things to keep your conversation clear and focused.

1. Decide what the goal of the conversation is and present the topic of the conversation to your listener.
2. Ask questions if you need to know more information or need clarification.
3. Discuss the pros and cons of the different possibilities.
4. Acknowledge the decision out loud to be sure that you and your partner agree.

Expressions utiles

C'est important de...
It's important to...

un monde meilleur
a better world

Détail grammatical

Nouveau

You may have noticed that, in the phrase ***nouveaux amis***, the word ***nouveaux*** comes before ***amis***.

Generally, most adjectives in French appear after the noun: une fille **intelligente**.

Nouveau is an exception to this pattern.

Nouveau has five forms:

un **nouveau** projet (m. s.)

un **nouvel** ordinateur (m. s. starting with a vowel sound)

de **nouveaux** amis (m. pl.)

une **nouvelle** tâche (f. s.)

de **nouvelles** idées (f. pl.)

Étape 2: Créer

Avec un(e) partenaire, créez une publicité pour un site où l'on peut faire du bénévolat (e.g., refuge, hôpital, etc.) pour cette occasion spéciale. N'oubliez pas d'y mettre:

- Le nom du site;
- La ville (et peut-être l'adresse);
- La date et l'heure; et
- Les tâches ou les rôles que les bénévoles peuvent faire.

Pourquoi suis-je bénévole?

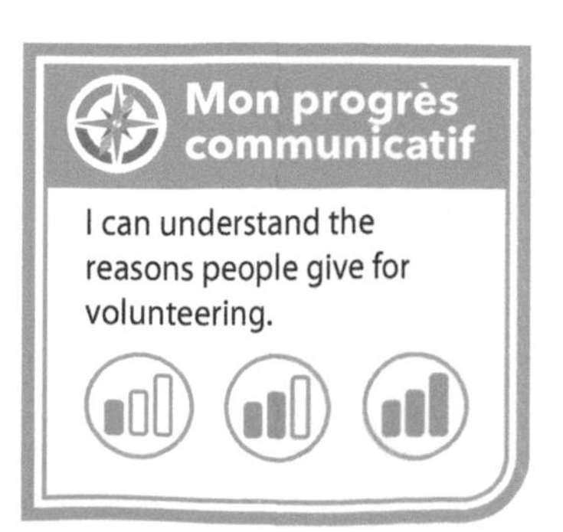

Activité 23

Quelles sont nos motivations pour faire du bénévolat?

Écoutez les amis qui parlent de leurs motivations pour faire du bénévolat. Décidez si les motivations sont a) personnelles, b) professionnelles (pour le travail), ou c) communautaires (pour les autres).

Activité 24

Où faire du bénévolat?

 Étape 1: Lire et indiquer

Vous travaillez avec une organisation de bénévoles à Montréal.

a. Lisez la lettre de motivation d'Éloïse. Elle veut faire du bénévolat, mais elle ne sait pas quelle offre choisir.

b. Lisez les annonces de deux offres de bénévolat.

c. Indiquez sur la représentation schématique si les motivations d'Éloïse vont avec ces offres.

Madame, Monsieur,

Je voudrais travailler comme bénévole à Montréal. J'ai 16 ans et je veux essayer quelque chose de nouveau. J'aimerais apprendre à travailler avec les autres et rencontrer de nouveaux amis. Je suis sportive et j'aime passer du temps dans les jardins et les parcs. Je suis bilingue (français/anglais), patiente et travailleuse. J'adore travailler avec les jeunes enfants. Je ne parle pas souvent avec les personnes âgées.

Bien cordialement,

Éloïse

Association récréative Milton-Parc

Entraîneurs adjoints pour le programme de soccer récréatif et les ligues de maison. Les tâches incluent: réunion des entraîneurs avant la pratique; accueillir les enfants (de 2 à 7 ans) et les parents et encourager les joueurs; aider les personnes moins confiantes, encourager les enfants à rester en ligne et écouter. Les compétences requises incluent: bilinguisme, patience, enthousiasme. | Lieu de travail: Parc Jeanne-Mance - terrain de soccer | Bénévoles requis: 6; 2h, 2 à 3 fois par semaine.

Contact: Helen Angelopoulos, Coordinator sport & leisure 514.843.7000
helen.angelopoulos@miltonpark.org
http://cabm.net/v/30811

Hôpital Gloire des Neiges

Le CHSLD (centres d'hébergement et de soins de longue durée) de l'hôpital Gloire des Neiges recherche des **bénévoles**. Les résidents du CHSLD sont des personnes âgées et nous voulons trouver des bénévoles pour leur rendre visite. Les tâches consistent à faire diverses activités avec nos résidents. Par exemple, le ou la bénévole peut organiser des jeux, des activités manuelles, des discussions ou des promenades dans le parc avec nos résidents. Vous aimez le contact avec les personnes âgées? Vous pouvez faire une visite hebdomadaire de deux heures? Vous êtes bilingue (français-anglais), dynamique, patient, et compréhensif? Alors, cette offre est pour vous!

Contact: Florent Lajeunesse, responsable des ressources humaines bénévoles / florent.lajeunesse@hopitalgloiredesneiges.ca

	association récréative	hôpital
travailler avec les enfants		
passer du temps dans le parc		
rencontrer de nouveaux amis		
faire du sport		
essayer quelque chose de nouveau		

 Étape 2: Laisser un message

Téléphonez à Éloïse et laissez un message pour lui proposer une offre de faire du bénévolat. Expliquez-lui pourquoi c'est une bonne offre pour elle.

Modèle

Bonjour, Éloïse. Vous pouvez être bénévole à... Vous voulez...? Vous pouvez...

Détail linguistique

Des expressions idiomatiques

Avez-vous le cœur sur la main?

(Êtes-vous généreux/généreuse?)

In French, idiomatic expressions like this often use interesting imagery or figurative language to express ideas. Consider some other examples of idiomatic expressions associated with ***la main***:

avoir la main verte (réussir son jardinage)

mettre la main à la pâte (aider à la tâche)

Can you think of any similar idiomatic expressions in English or other languages?

Zoom culture

Pratique culturelle: Le bénévolat comme intégration

 Connexions

What are the reasons people get involved in volunteerism in your community? Have you ever formed a friendship through volunteering?

In Canada, volunteering is a popular activity for people from a variety of backgrounds. Immigrants and refugees are two groups of people in Canada who can benefit in a special way by becoming volunteers. Through volunteering, immigrants may find opportunities to learn about the culture of the country where they live, experience the work culture of the country, and make connections with friends and future colleagues. ***Le bénévolat*** is a way for people of any background to have a sense of accomplishment and belonging in their community.

Le réseautage *(networking)* is an important skill that can be developed by becoming a ***bénévole***. Forming connections with other volunteers, community leaders, and business people can lead to more job opportunities for those who have just arrived in Canada, but it's certainly a good idea for anyone. Apart from looking for work, ***le bénévolat*** can help people find others who have similar interests and motivations.

 Réflexion

Other than job opportunities, can you think of reasons why people who are new to a community might need to establish connections?

Découvrons 3

Connecting Phrases with "qui," "que," and "où"

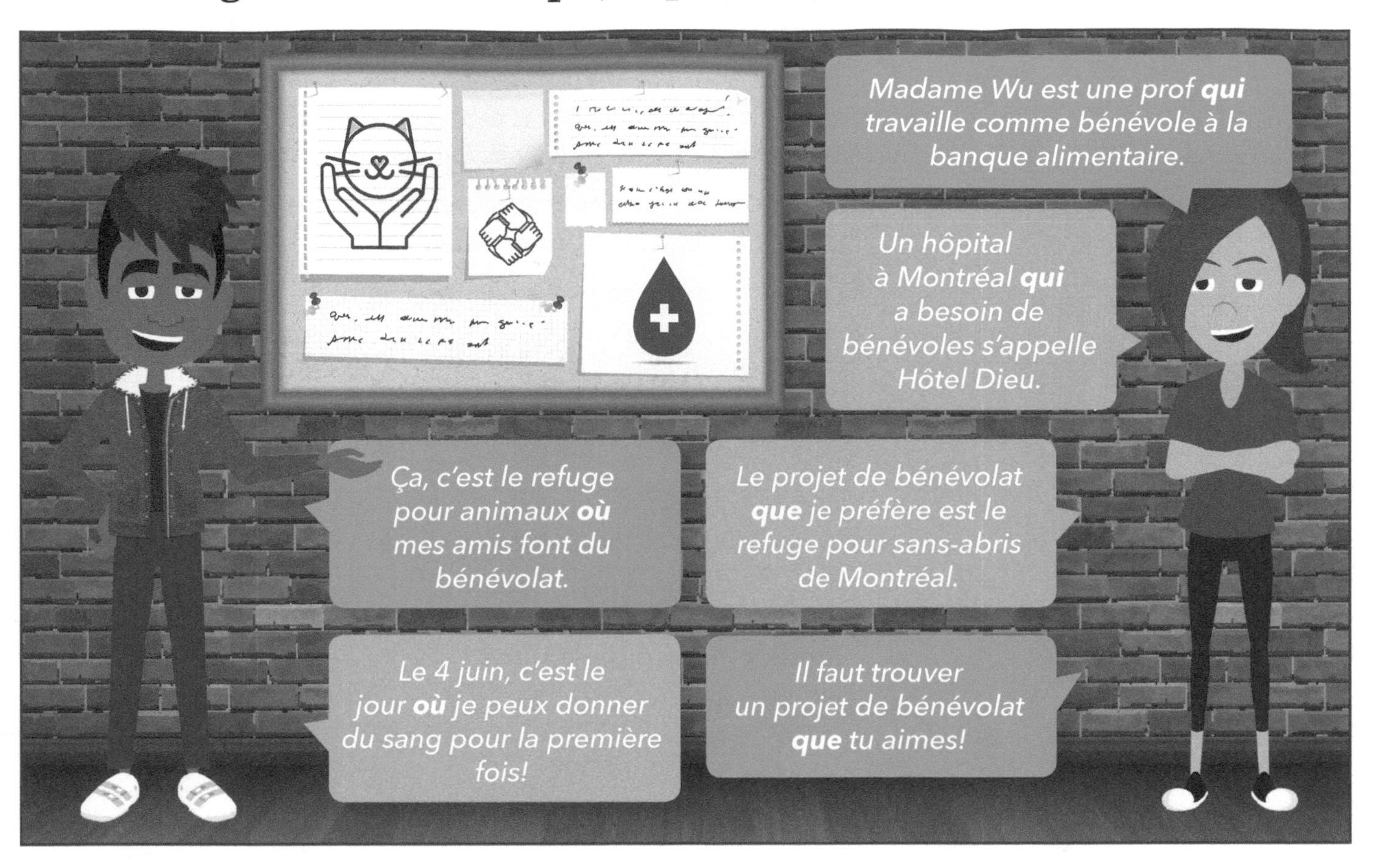

Découvertes

Reflect on what you observe and respond to the following questions in the graphic organizer in Explorer.

1. What is the purpose of ***où, qui*** and ***que*** in these examples? Why use them at all?
2. Notice which phrases or which kinds of words come before and after the words ***où, qui***, and ***que***. When is each one used?
3. Share your observations with a partner. What else do you notice together or what else can you add to your observations?
4. Test your theory! Which word would you use in the blank in each of the following examples?
   a. C'est ma mère ____ encourage ma sœur et moi à devenir bénévoles.
   b. C'est le moment ____ je suis devenu bénévole.
   c. Il y a une affiche ____ je vois tous les jours à mon école. C'est pourquoi je suis bénévole!

On peut aussi dire

gratter	*to scrape*
(re)peindre	*to (re)paint*

Activité 25

Qu'est-ce qu'il y a comme possibilités de bénévolat?

Les refuges pour animaux, les hôpitaux, les refuges pour sans-abris...ce n'est pas tout! Il y a beaucoup de possibilités variées où on peut faire du bénévolat. Voici un exemple.

a. Regardez le reportage et complétez le résumé de la vidéo en écrivant les mots ***qui, que,*** ou ***où*** dans les blancs.

   Dans cette vidéo, on voit de jeunes bénévoles (a)____ restaurent *(are restoring)* une maison (b)____ est importante pour l'héritage culturel du Québec. Le jour (c)____ on filmait, il y avait du soleil et il faisait beau. La maison (d)____ ils dorment, c'est une autre maison à côté de la maison (e) ____ les bénévoles restaurent.

b. Dans la représentation schématique, notez les activités faites par les bénévoles dans la vidéo et leurs motivations probables.

activités	motivations
Modèle: Ils repeignent une maison.	Pour...

Activité 26

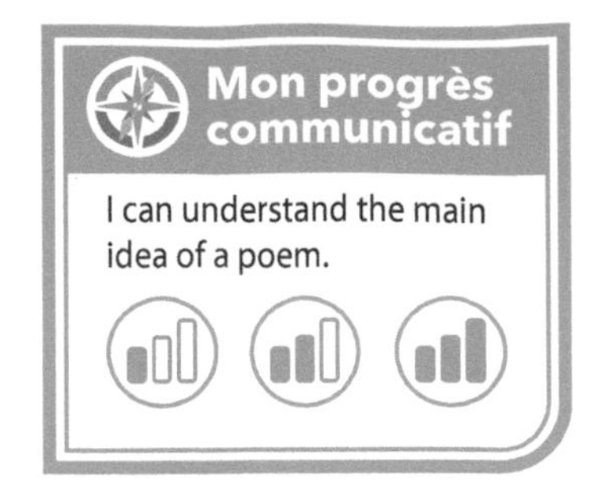

Pouvez-vous le définir pour moi?

Avec d'autres bénévoles, vous voulez mettre un texte créatif sur le site de votre organisme.

Étape 1: Lire

Lisez ce poème et décidez où mettre les images pour l'illustrer. Indiquez l'image qui va le mieux avec chaque strophe *(stanza)* du poème.

DÉFINITIONS DU BÉNÉVOLAT

Le bénévolat,
c'est l'art de la gratuité du coeur,
du geste et du temps.

Le bénévolat
ne connaît d'autres lois
que le besoin de l'autre,
percevoir avec lui et trouver ensemble les solutions nécessaires.

L'engagement bénévole,
ne serait-ce pas là une façon d'humaniser
une société qui s'individualise de plus en plus?

Le bénévolat,
c'est une fleur que l'on s'offre.

Le bénévolat,
c'est un cheminement personnel:
c'est une fenêtre ouverte sur le monde.

Le bénévolat
a tellement de valeur
qu'il n'a pas de prix.

(AUTEUR INCONNU)

Étape 2: Improviser

a. Avec un groupe d'autres élèves, utilisez ces débuts de phrases (ou autres) pour improviser un poème à l'oral qui définit un mot relatif au bénévolat.

- Le bénévolat, c'est quelque chose que je fais pour...
- Un refuge pour animaux, c'est un endroit où...
- Un bénévole, c'est une personne qui...

b. Partagez vos meilleures strophes avec la classe.

Activité 27

Pourquoi fais-tu du bénévolat?

Une fondation à Montréal veut être partenaire de votre école et cherche de jeunes bénévoles.

Étape 1: Préparer

Complétez le formulaire pour exprimer votre intérêt.

Nom: ______________________________

Prénom(s): ______________________________

Date de naissance: ______________________________

Compétences particulières: ______________________________

Langues: ______________________________

À quel site voulez-vous travailler comme bénévole?

____

____

Pourquoi voulez-vous devenir bénévole dans notre organisme?

____

____

Étape 2: Écrire

Cet organisme a aussi demandé une interview. Comme préparation avec votre partenaire, vous participez à un tchat pour anticiper les questions de l'interview. Envoyez vos messages sur Explorer.

N'oubliez pas de poser des questions au sujet de:

- vos intérêts et vos compétences;
- votre site ou projet préféré; et
- vos motivations.

Modèle

Élève A: Où voulez-vous travailler comme bénévole?

Élève B: Je préfère être bénévole à l'hôpital.

J'avance 3

Notre projet de bénévolat

Your French Club would like to participate in a service project on your class trip to ***Montréal*** next summer, but there are so many options! Read a few testimonials of Canadian students who already volunteer in a variety of ways. Then, discuss those options with your class in an online forum. Finally, create a video to announce the service project you prefer.

Étape 1: Lire

Read the testimonials ***(témoignages)*** of volunteers from ***Montréal***. In the graphic organizer in Explorer, identify a) where they volunteer, b) what they do there, and c) why they do it.

Étape 2: Discuter en ligne

a. Post your opinion of which volunteer opportunity you think is best for your club's service project in your Explorer discussion forum. Be sure to include reasons why your choice is a good one.

b. Then, respond to your classmates' posts and give reasons why you would not choose one of the different options proposed by other club members.

Prepare a video announcement to be shown at your school to announce your class's preferred volunteer organization. Include information about the types of activities available there and share some reasons for volunteering there.

All of the materials for ***J'avance 3*** can be found in Explorer.

Haute vue de la fresque québécoise

Synthèse de grammaire

1. Describing What People Can and Want to Do: *les verbes vouloir, pouvoir, choisir et finir*

When talking about volunteering, you will want to express what you want to do ***(vouloir)***, can do ***(pouvoir)***, choose to do ***(choisir)***, as well as the work you are finishing ***(finir)***. Here are the present tense forms of these four verbs:

je **veux**	nous v**ou**lons	je **peux**	nous **pou**vons
tu **veux**	vous v**ou**lez	tu **peux**	vous **pou**vez
il/elle/on v**eut**	ils/elles v**eu**lent	il/elle/on p**eut**	ils/elles p**eu**vent

je choisis	nous choisissons	je finis	nous finissons
tu choisis	vous choisissez	tu finis	vous finissez
il/elle/on choisit	ils/elles choisissent	il/elle/on finit	ils/elles finissent

Although ***vouloir, pouvoir, choisir*** and ***finir*** have different endings from the ***-er*** verbs you might be used to, they still have a few recognizable patterns that you should notice:

1. The ***je*** and ***tu*** forms of each verb are identical to each other, but the ***il/elle/on*** form is different. It is also common that verbs that end in ***-x*** or ***-s*** in the ***je*** and ***tu*** forms will change to a ***-t*** ending in the ***il/elle/on*** form.
2. There are two variations of the beginnings of the verbs ***vouloir*** and ***pouvoir***: ***eu*** vs. ***ou***.
3. ***Choisir*** and ***finir*** have longer endings in common than just ***-ons, -ez, -ent***.

2. Asking "What" and "Which" Questions: *les mots interrogatifs "qu'est-ce que" et "quel"*

When asking an open-ended *what* question, use ***qu'est-ce que***:

Qu'est-ce que tu préfères?

Qu'est-ce que nous faisons après l'école?

When asking a "what/which" question, where the answer you are looking for is a specific kind of noun, use a form of the word ***quel*** with the specific noun:

	masculin	féminin
singulier	**Quel** projet est-ce que tu choisis?	**Quelle** tâche est-ce que tu préfères?
pluriel	**Quels** bénévoles vont au refuge?	**Quelles** idées est-ce que tu vas lancer?

3. Connecting Phrases with *Qui, Que,* and *Où: quelques pronoms relatifs*

The words ***qui***, ***que***, and ***où*** are connectors you can use to create sentences that are longer and more sophisticated. They allow you to give more information about a person, place or thing mentioned earlier in the same sentence. You may recognize the words ***qui*** and ***où*** as question words, but, when used in the middle of a sentence to connect ideas, their meanings are less important than the role that they serve.

Use ***où*** when you want to give more information about **a place** or **a time** in the same sentence:

C'est **l'hôpital *où*** je fais du bénévolat.

C'est **l'heure *où*** nous commençons à travailler.

Notice that ***où*** in the second example does not mean *where* but *when*.

Use ***qui*** when the word that comes next is a **verb**:

C'est un bénévole ***qui* est** compréhensif.

C'est un organisme ***qui* aide** les personnes âgées.

Notice that ***qui*** in the second example does not really mean *who*.

Use ***que*** when the word that comes next is a **subject**:

C'est une tâche ***que* monsieur Gassama** fait bien.

C'est un projet ***qu'*elles** lancent au mois de décembre.

Notice that ***que*** becomes ***qu'*** before a vowel sound.

Vocabulaire

Comment dit-on? 1: I can describe my responsibilities at home.

Les tâches ménagères	*Household tasks*
arroser	*to water*
débarrasser	*to clear, to empty*
garder	*to keep, look after, babysit*
le jardinage	*gardening*
laver et plier le linge	*to wash and fold laundry*
le lave-vaisselle	*dishwasher*
mettre le couvert/la table	*to set the table*
passer l'aspirateur	*to vacuum*
ramasser les déchets	*to pick up the trash*
ranger	*to tidy up, put away*

quotidien/quotidienne	*daily*
hebdomadaire	*weekly*
mensuel/mensuelle	*monthly*

Expressions utiles	
donner à manger	*to feed*
donner un coup de main	*to lend a helping hand*
faire le lit	*to make the bed*

Comment dit-on? 2: I can describe what being a good volunteer means to me.

Les compétences d'un bénévole	*Abilities of a volunteer*
accueillir	*to welcome*
aider	*to help*
conseiller	*to give advice to*
contribuer à	*to contribute to*
gérer	*to manage*
lancer de nouvelles idées	*to introduce, to initiate new ideas*
organiser son emploi du temps	*to organize one's schedule*
réaliser	*to make something a reality*
réconforter (quelqu'un)	*to comfort (someone)*
servir	*to serve*

Les qualités d'un bénévole	*Traits of a volunteer*
le/la chef	*leader*
compréhensif/ compréhensive	*understanding*
fidèle	*loyal*
motivé/motivée	*motivated*
organisé/ organisée	*organized*
travailleur/ travailleuse	*hard-working*

Les activités d'une association	*Activities in an organization*
le/la bénévole	*volunteer*
le citoyen/la citoyenne	*citizen*
le projet	*project, plan*
la réunion	*meeting*

Expressions utiles	
construire des maisons	*to build houses*
planifier	*to plan*
planter des arbres	*to plant trees*
répondre au téléphone	*to answer the telephone*
trier et distribuer le courrier	*to sort and hand out, distribute the mail*

Comment dit-on? 3: I can talk about where and why I volunteer.

Où faire du bénévolat	*Where to volunteer*
faire du bénévolat	*to volunteer, to do volunteer work*
la banque alimentaire	*food bank*
la fondation	*foundation*
le foyer de soins	*nursing home*
la garderie	*daycare facility*
l'hôpital (m.)	*hospital*
le jardin communautaire	*community garden*
le refuge pour animaux	*animal shelter*
le refuge pour sans-abris	*homeless shelter*

Pourquoi faire du bénévolat?	Why volunteer?
améliorer	*to improve*
apprendre	*to learn*
l'avenir (m.)	*the future*
créer	*to create*
essayer quelque chose de nouveau	*to try something new*
rencontrer de nouveaux amis	*to meet new friends*
soutenir	*to support*

Expressions utiles	
Bonne idée!	*Good idea!*
C'est important de...	*It's important to...*
Je ne suis pas d'accord (avec toi).	*I disagree (with you).*
Je suis d'accord (avec toi).	*I agree (with you).*
un monde meilleur	*a better world*

J'y arrive

Questions essentielles

- How do my personal responsibilities and routine shape my daily life?
- How can community members work together to improve the quality of life for themselves and others?
- What kinds of volunteer opportunities exist in the Francophone world? What motivates people from different cultures to volunteer?

Être bénévole à Montréal

Your French teacher is organizing a class trip to ***Montréal***. Your class has decided that since volunteerism is so important to the ***Québécois*** that the trip will include community service. After seeing some of the sites of the city, you will pair up with another classmate to spend part of your trip serving the communities of ***Montréal***. Because of timing and other limitations of your itinerary, your travel company has narrowed down your options for you.

First, you will need to read and understand the two volunteer postings from a website. Then, you and your classmate will agree upon which one of the postings you would both like to do.

Once you have decided, you will each need to complete the ***formulaire pour devenir bénévole.***

Before you begin, refer to the ***J'y arrive*** rubric in Explorer to familiarize yourself with the evaluation criteria.

Interpretive Assessment

 Choisir l'offre bénévole idéale

Read postings about two volunteer opportunities in Montréal. Look at images in Explorer and decide which volunteer opportunity each of the images depicts. Then, from a list in Explorer, classify words from the postings based on whether they describe a place *(un endroit)*, a task, or a personal quality.

Interpersonal Assessment

On va faire du bénévolat, mais où?

You and a classmate are planning to participate together in one of the two volunteer opportunities. Discuss which opportunity to choose, giving reasons for your preference. Be sure to arrive at a conclusion before you end your conversation.

Presentational Assessment

Je commence tout de suite!

Now that you have decided which volunteer opportunity to try, complete the volunteer application by providing some basic information and explaining a bit more about yourself.

UNITÉ 4

Une ville qui bouge

Objectifs de l'unité

Read, view, and listen to a variety of sources like brochures, schedules, and online reviews to access information to make plans.

Exchange preferences about places to go for fun in a Francophone city or town.

Describe past events and activities.

Investigate how and where teens in Francophone cultures and in your community enjoy a metropolitan area.

Questions essentielles

What experiences are available to young people in a city or town?

How can I access information to make plans?

How does culture influence where I go and what I do in a Francophone city or town?

Big cities are full of options for entertainment and transportation. It can be especially rewarding to enjoy a city the way the locals do. In this unit, Élisa will share information about where she likes to go for fun in and around Paris.

Nom: Élisa (Lili)

Langues parlées: français, espagnol, anglais

Origine: Paris, France

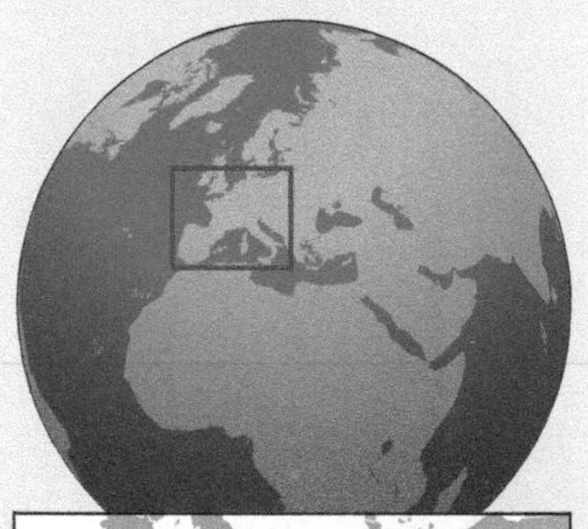

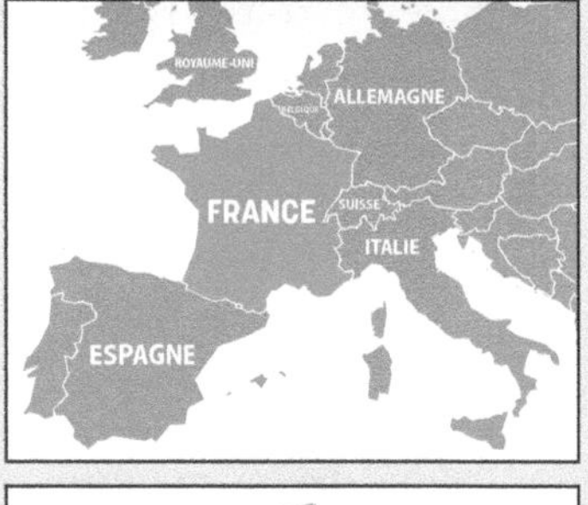

Rencontre interculturelle

La France et Paris

La France, ou depuis 1875, la République française, est un pays dans l'ouest du continent européen. Elle a aussi des territoires (comme l'île de la Réunion) sur tous les autres continents, excepté en Asie. La langue officielle de la France est le français. Sa capitale est Paris et sa monnaie est l'euro.

Quelques siècles avant J.-C., un petit village de pêcheurs *(fishermen)* s'est développé sur une île de la Seine. Cette tribu, les Parisii, a donné son nom à la ville de Paris. Au Moyen Âge, le roi des Francs, Clovis, a nommé Paris sa capitale.

Conséquemment, il y a de nombreuses structures très anciennes à Paris et beaucoup d'attractions touristiques!

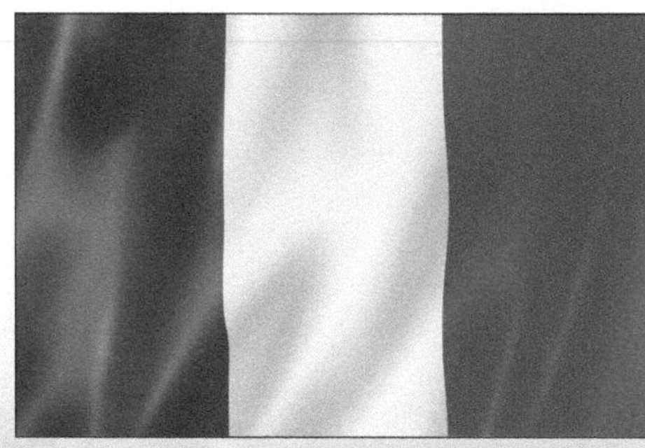

Le drapeau français qui représente la 5e République est tricolore. Le bleu et le rouge représentent la ville de Paris et le blanc représente la monarchie.

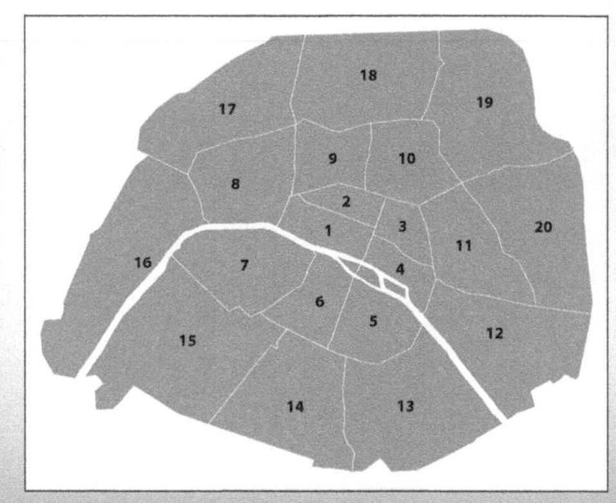

Regardez la carte de Paris. Est-ce que vous pouvez identifier la Seine et ses deux îles au centre?

Salut! Je vais vous présenter ma ville, Paris.

Pourquoi la tour Eiffel est-elle aujourd'hui le symbole le plus important de Paris? Elle n'a pas 150 ans et certains monuments parisiens existent depuis le Moyen-Âge, comme la Conciergerie sur cette photo!
Les gargouilles de Notre-Dame représentent des animaux ou des monstres. Ils servent à protéger *(protect)* la cathédrale.
Le coq est l'oiseau national. Les supporters des équipes de foot françaises ont souvent des chapeaux qui utilisent ce symbole!
Voici une pièce d'or des Parisii du 2e siècle avant J.-C.
Pour voir le centre de Paris, l'île de la Cité, l'île Saint-Louis et les jolis ponts de la Seine, il faut faire un tour en bateau-mouche!
Pourquoi le nom "bateau-mouche"?
À l'origine, les bateaux-mouches sont construits dans les années 1860 à Lyon (une autre ville de France) dans un endroit qui s'appelle le quartier de la Mouche. Les organisateurs de l'exposition universelle (*world's fair*) de 1867 en font venir 30 à Paris. Les Parisiens et les touristes les adorent!

Activité 1

Qu'est-ce que c'est?

Élisa veut voir si vous faisiez attention quand elle vous parlait de Paris. Relisez les informations pour avoir les réponses de sa chasse au trésor *(treasure hunt)*.

A. Je suis idéal pour visiter Paris sur la Seine.

B. Je suis une statue qui protège Notre-Dame.

C. Je suis la tribu gauloise à l'origine de Paris.

D. Je suis la ville à l'origine des bateaux-mouches.

E. Je suis le roi qui a choisi Paris comme capitale.

F. Je suis une île au centre de Paris à côté de l'île de la Cité.

Activité 2

Salut, Élisa!

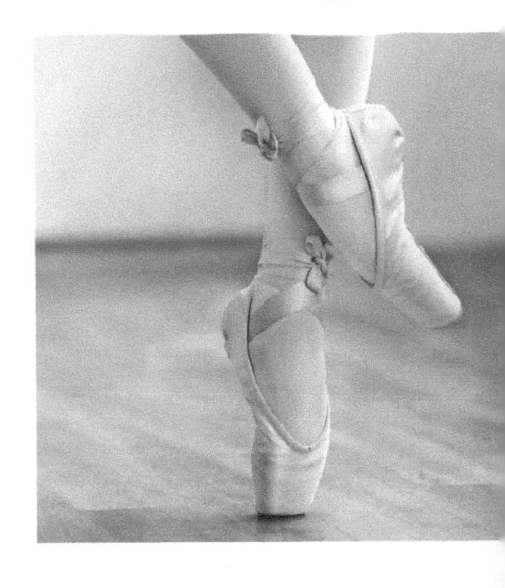

Étape 1: Regarder et lire

Regardez la vidéo d'Élisa et lisez les informations de sa maman. Avec un(e) partenaire, cochez (✔) les informations qui sont aussi mentionnées dans la vidéo.

Bonjour,

Je m'appelle Anne et je suis la maman d'Élisa. ____

Ma fille est née à Paris. ____

Aujourd'hui, elle a 17 ans. ____

Nous habitons dans une maison à Croissy-sur-Seine. ____

Avant, nous habitions dans le 13e arrondissement. ____

Élisa est élève au lycée Alain. ____

Élisa a trois sœurs. ____

Elle aime aller régulièrement au cinéma. ____

Elle fait de la danse classique depuis qu'elle est petite. ____

~Anne

Étape 2: Noter et parler

a. Notez deux ou trois choses que vous avez en commun avec Élisa sur une feuille de papier.

b. Puis, partagez vos réponses avec un(e) partenaire et écoutez les réponses de votre partenaire.

Réflexion interculturelle

Élisa shared some important things about her life near Paris. What is daily life like where you live? How is life in your town similar to or different from Élisa's? Answer the questions in the discussion forum in Explorer.

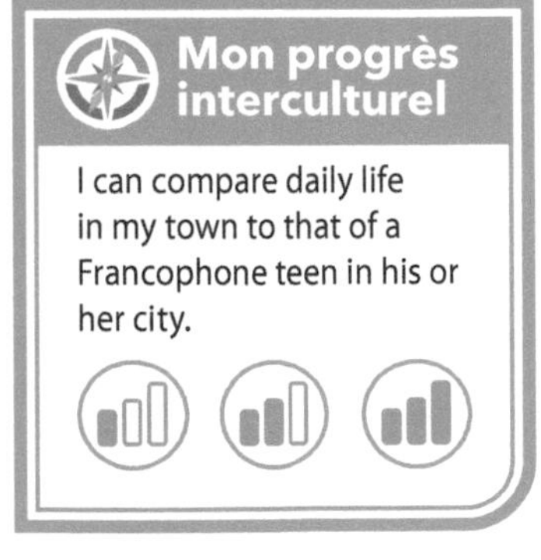

Rappelle-toi

Activité 3

Qu'est-ce qu'il faut acheter?

Vous venez d'arriver à l'hôtel en banlieue (*suburb*) parisienne pour une visite à Paris. Vous voulez acheter des affaires indispensables.

Étape 1: Regarder, écouter et noter

a. Regardez le plan de ville *(map)* que l'hôtel distribue.

b. Écoutez les messages des autres élèves et notez les aspects importants dans la représentation schématique sur Explorer.

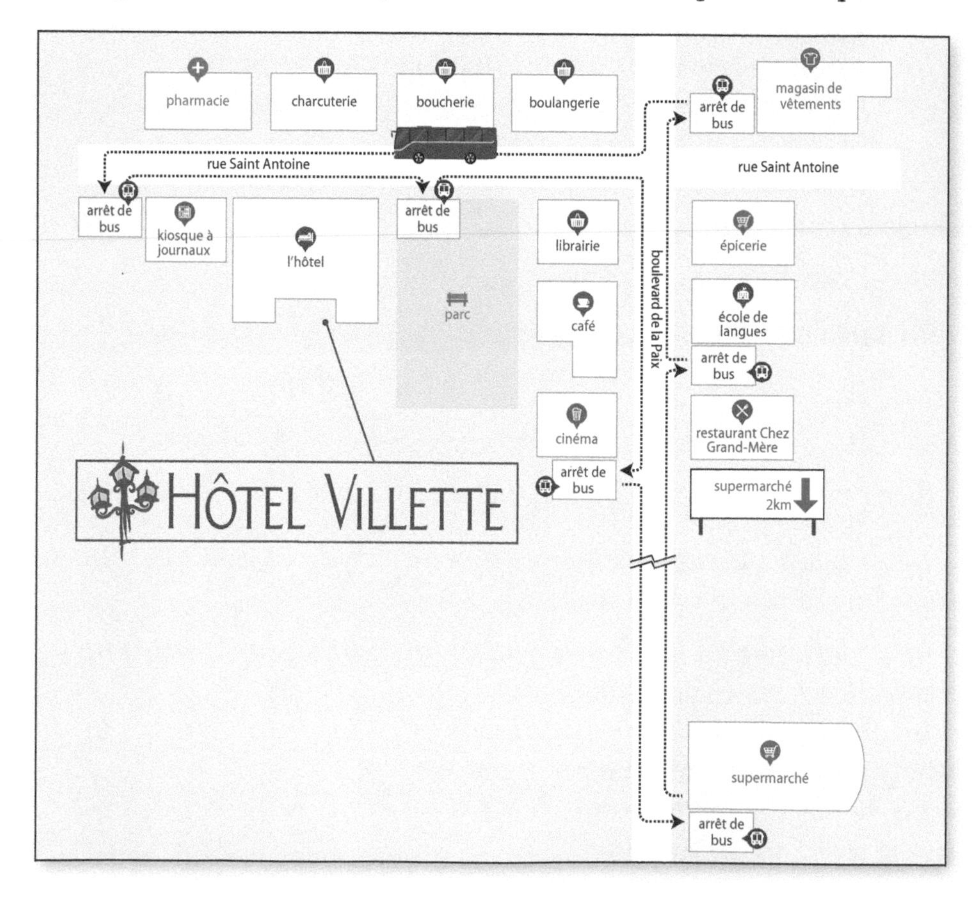

élève du groupe	endroits	transport
Quentin		
Catherine		
Marc		
Sophie		

Étape 2: Lire et écrire

Une élève du groupe a envoyé un texto.

a. Ajoutez les informations de Sophie dans la représentation schématique de l'**Étape 1**.

b. Et vous? Écrivez dans votre message à vos amis ce que *(what)* vous allez acheter et dans quel magasin.

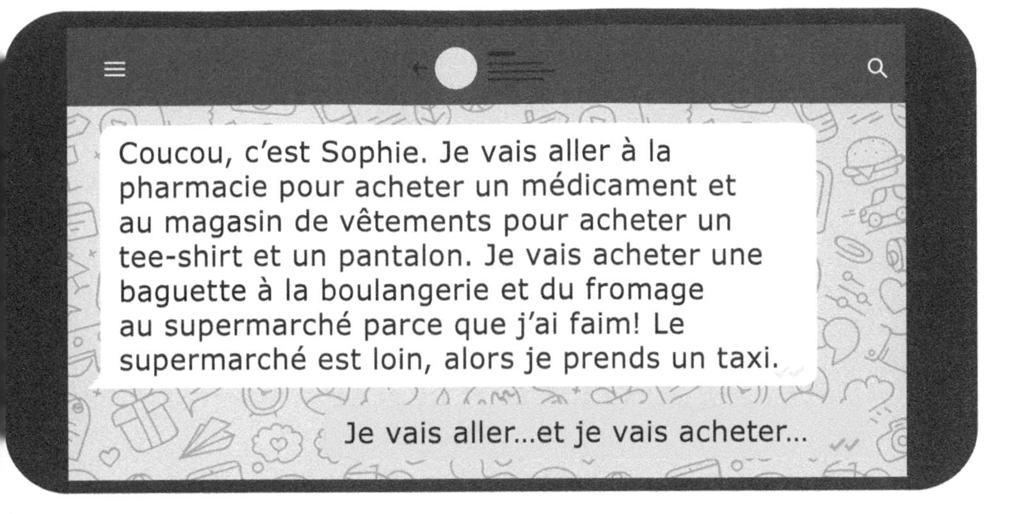

Rappel

Pour parler des achats

faire du shopping
faire les boutiques
faire les courses
faire les magasins

Activité 4

Comment est notre ville?

Cette banlieue de Paris est différente de votre ville. Parlez aux autres élèves du groupe de quelques endroits *(places)* dans votre ville, des activités que vous y faites et des moyens de transport que vous prenez en général.

Modèle

Notre ville est plus petite que Paris. Dans notre ville, il n'y a pas de boulangerie. J'achète du pain au supermarché. On n'a pas de bus dans notre ville. Nous prenons toujours la voiture.

Rappel

Pour parler des villes

à + [nom de la ville]
dans (à l'intérieur de) votre ville

Le centre-ville de Pontoise, au nord-ouest de Paris.

Expressions utiles

Les activités dans le passé

J'ai fait…

Je suis allé(e) à…

Des croissants dans une boulangerie.

Activité 5

Qu'est-ce que vous avez fait?

Vous écrivez une petite description d'un week-end magnifique dans le passé. Les autres élèves vont la lire pour deviner qui l'a écrite. Décrivez où vous êtes allé(e) et les activités que vous avez faites.

Modèle

L'été dernier, je suis allé(e) à Montréal avec ma famille. J'ai fait les boutiques et je suis allé(e) à la boulangerie pour acheter un croissant.

Des magasins à Montréal, au Québec, Canada.

Des magasins à Paris, en France.

Rappelle-toi

Pour s'amuser en ville
au café
au cinéma
au concert
au festival
au gymnase
à la maison
à la médiathèque
à la piscine
au restaurant
au stade
au terrain de ________ (sport)

Pour faire des achats
à la boucherie
à la boulangerie
à la boutique
au centre-ville
à la charcuterie
à la crèmerie
à l'épicerie (f.)
au fast-food
au magasin
à la pâtisserie
à la pharmacie
au supermarché

Le transport
à pied
l'autobus (m.), le bus
la moto
le scooter
le taxi
le vélo
la voiture

Les activités en ville
acheter
faire
regarder
visiter

Les prépositions de lieux
à côté (de)
à droite (de)
à gauche (de)
dans
devant
derrière
en face (de)
près (de)
loin (de)

Expressions utiles
J'ai fait...
Je suis allé(e) à...

Expressions utiles

un endroit
Je te conseille de/d'...
Je vais...
pour s'amuser
se trouver

Communiquons

Comment dit-on? 1

Visitons le meilleur de Paris

Mes endroits préférés en ville

*Le week-end, j'adore explorer les vingt arrondissements de ma ville. Chaque **quartier** a son caractère unique. Voici le top 5 de mes **endroits** préférés à Paris!*

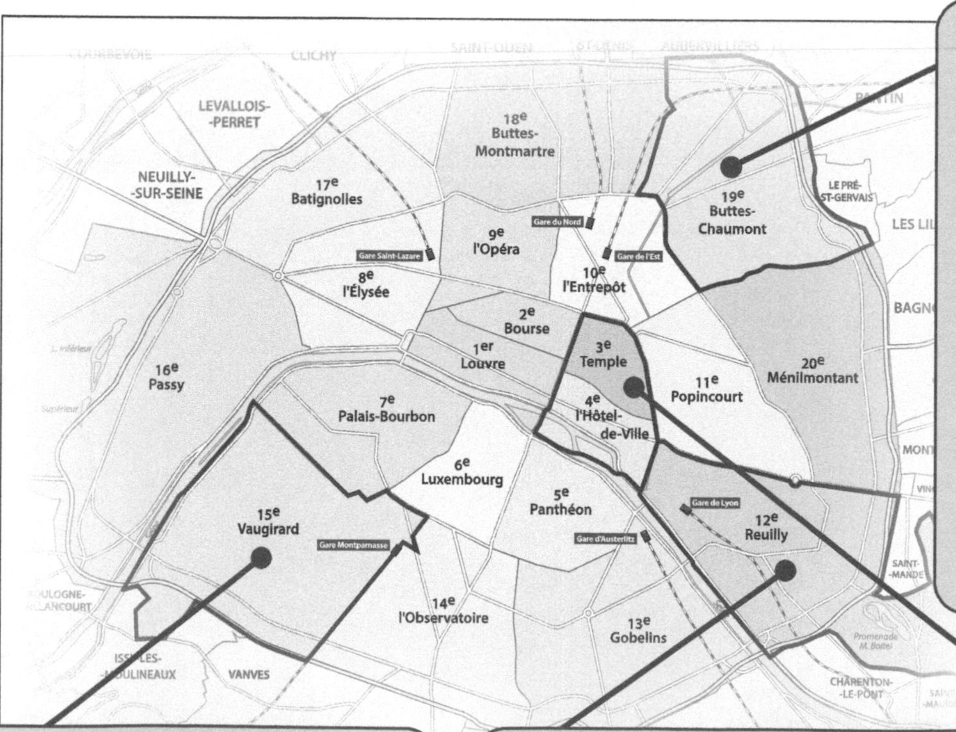

Quand je veux lire ou me relaxer, je vais au **parc.** Il y a beaucoup de jolis parcs à Paris, comme le parc des Buttes-Chaumont. Ce parc se trouve entre la **rue** Manin et la rue Botzaris dans le 19e arrondissement.

Je ne vais pas souvent au Louvre, mais il y a d'autres **musées** que j'aime, comme la Cité des sciences et de l'industrie dans le 19e arrondissement. Ce musée organise **une exposition** temporaire sur les effets spéciaux.

Si tu veux voir un **spectacle,** je te conseille d'aller au **théâtre** ou à une salle de concert, comme le Dôme de Paris dans le 15e. Moi, j'ai vu *Les Trois Mousquetaires* l'année dernière.

Dans le 12e, il y a la foire du Trône du mois de mars au mois de mai. J'adore y aller pour rencontrer des amis et faire des tours de montagnes russes. Il y a de plus grands **parcs d'attractions** à l'extérieur de Paris, comme le parc Astérix et le parc Disneyland.

Pour moi, la **place** des Vosges est le plus bel endroit de Paris. C'est un square entre le 3e et le 4e où on peut aller pour s'amuser et être au calme. Il y a aussi la maison de l'auteur Victor Hugo.

Réflexion interculturelle

When you think of Paris, what are some of the monuments and places that come to mind? ***La tour Eiffel?*** Others? Why do you think Élisa did not include those places in her top five favorite places? Are there cultural or historical monuments near where you live? How often do you visit them? Answer the questions in the discussion forum in Explorer.

Mon progrès interculturel

I can give some reasons why people choose various places to spend their free time in Francophone cities and in my own community.

Activité 6

Qu'est-ce qu'on doit visiter à Paris?

Vous voyagez à Paris avec un groupe scolaire. Voici la liste d'excursions que l'agence propose comme activités pendant le week-end.

Étape 1: Lire

Lisez les descriptions de la liste et identifiez dans quelle sorte d'endroit se passe chaque excursion.

On peut aussi dire

- l'aquarium (m.)
- l'arrondissement (m.)
- le bowling
- le concert
- les montagnes (f. pl.) russes
- l'opéra (m.)
- la salle de concert
- la visite guidée
- le zoo

VOYAGES SCOLAIRES PARISIENS

Nos excursions du week-end

Option 1: La Comédie-Française

Allez voir la nouvelle adaptation française de la pièce célèbre *Roméo et Juliette*.

Option 2: La Quille

Passez un après-midi amusant et jouez à un jeu. Boule, chaussures, et un ticket boisson offert. Il y a également des jeux de billards.

Option 3: Le Jardin d'acclimatation

Au bois de Boulogne, choisissez votre cheval et faites un tour sur le Grand Carrousel ou allez voir un film au cinéma interactif. Pour les plus courageux, essayez la montagne russe, Les Speed Rockets.

Option 4: L'Atelier des Lumières

Visitez l'exposition multimédia immersive. Des œuvres de l'artiste Gustav Klimt sont projetées dans la halle avec une musique électronique.

Option 5: Le Zénith Paris

Passez une soirée inoubliable en regardant le spectacle du rappeur-compositeur Orelsan, vainqueur de trois prix aux Victoires de la musique de 2018.

Option 6: Le palais Garnier

Venez chasser le mythique Fantôme! Participez à un jeu d'évasion en équipes de 5 personnes et visitez le palais Garnier en même temps. Résolvez des énigmes et reconstituez des puzzles. Votre mission: Aider des musiciens de *La Flûte enchantée* de Mozart!

Une plaque de rue à Paris

Modèle

un théâtre → la Comédie-Française

A. une salle de concert

B. un musée

C. un bowling

D. un opéra

E. un parc d'attractions

Étape 2: Conseiller

a. Posez des questions aux autres élèves de la classe pour savoir ce qu'ils ou elles aiment.

b. Conseillez à chaque personne un endroit à Paris. Vous pouvez parler des endroits de l'**Étape 1** ou du vocabulaire de **Comment dit-on? 1**.

Modèle

–Qu'est-ce que tu aimes?

–Moi, j'aime l'art. Où est-ce que tu me conseilles d'aller?

–Je te conseille d'aller à l'Atelier des Lumières.

partenaire	intérêt	recommandation

Activité 7

Qu'aiment faire les jeunes en ville?

Étape 1: Regarder

Brenda, une élève du Cameroun, va parler des activités qu'elle aime faire pour s'amuser dans sa ville. Écoutez ses préférences et indiquez si elle aime ou pas aller aux endroits mentionnés.

	aime	n'aime pas
aller au parc		
aller au cinéma		
aller au restaurant		
aller au musée		
aller au stade		

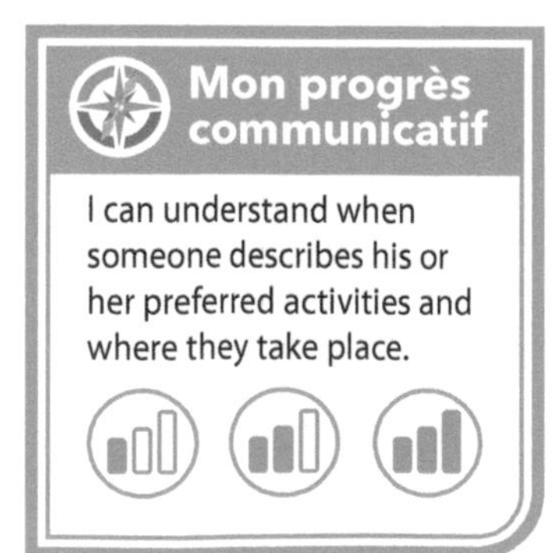

Zoom culture

Produit culturel: Les arrondissements

 **Connexions**

How is your town arranged? How do you refer to the different neighborhoods? Do they have names at all?

Depuis 1859, la ville de Paris est divisée en 20 **arrondissements** municipaux. Les arrondissements servent à organiser l'administration politique de la ville. Par exemple, on peut vite comprendre le code postal d'une adresse à Paris; si le code postal est 75017, cela veut dire que l'adresse se trouve dans le 17e arrondissement. Il y a un maire de la ville de Paris, mais chaque arrondissement élit aussi son propre maire.

On appelle chaque arrondissement par son numéro: le premier (1er) arrondissement, le vingtième (20e) arrondissement ou simplement "le premier" ou "le vingtième." Si on regarde le plan de Paris, on observe que le premier arrondissement se trouve au centre de la ville et les autres arrondissements sont organisés en forme de spirale (comme un escargot). On trouve une atmosphère unique dans chaque quartier et certains arrondissements sont bien connus sous d'autres noms. Montmartre (18e), le Marais (3e et 4e) et Saint-Germain-des-Prés (6e) sont très fréquentés par des touristes qui visitent Paris.

Réflexion

Look at the statistics in the infographic. What do you understand about the 1st, 6th, 12th, and 19th ***arrondissements***? Can you think of places around your town that fit those same descriptions?

Étape 2: Parler

Votre partenaire et vous voulez inviter Brenda à passer le week-end dans votre ville ou une autre ville que vous connaissez. Considérez les endroits dans la ville et décidez où Brenda va s'amuser le plus.

- le café
- le théâtre
- le parc
- le zoo
- le bowling
- la salle de concert

Modèle

On peut aller au café parce que Brenda aime déjeuner avec ses amis.

Étape 3: Écrire un e-mail

Écrivez un e-mail à Brenda pour l'inviter à passer le week-end dans votre ville.

Modèle

Chère Brenda,

Ça te dit de venir à ______ avec nous? On peut...

Rappel

Pour inviter

Ça te dit (de...)?
Je t'invite (à)...
Je te propose...

Activité 8

Qu'est-ce qu'il y a dans votre ville?

Avant de lire le poème, parcourez *(skim)* le texte et identifiez des mots que vous comprenez.

Étape 1: Lire

Lisez le poème de Jacques Charpentreau. Avec un(e) partenaire, associez chaque image aux strophes appropriées.

a. la ville

b. le quartier

c. la rue

d. l'école

L'école

Dans notre ville, il y a **a.**
Des tours, des maisons par milliers,
Du béton[1], des blocs, des quartiers,
Et puis mon cœur, mon cœur qui bat[2]
Tout bas.

Dans mon quartier, il y a **b.**
Des boulevards, des avenues,
Des places, des ronds-points[3], des rues,
Et puis mon cœur, mon cœur qui bat
Tout bas.[4]

Dans notre rue, il y a **c.**
Des autos, des gens qui s'affolent,
Un grand magasin, une école.
Et puis mon cœur, mon cœur qui bat
Tout bas.

Dans cette école, il y a **d.**
Des oiseaux chantant tout le jour
Dans les marronniers[5] de la cour.
Mon cœur, mon cœur, mon cœur qui bat
Est là.

— Jacques Charpentreau, 1976

Mon progrès communicatif

I can understand information about a city in a poem.

1 concrete
2 my beating heart
3 rotaries/roundabouts/traffic circles
4 softly
5 horse chestnut trees

1

2

3

4

5

Étape 2: Écrire un poème

Le journal local veut publier des poèmes au sujet de la ville. Écrivez un poème dans le style du poème de Charpentreau pour décrire votre ville. Qu'est-ce qu'il y a dans:

- votre ville?
- votre quartier?
- votre rue?
- votre école?

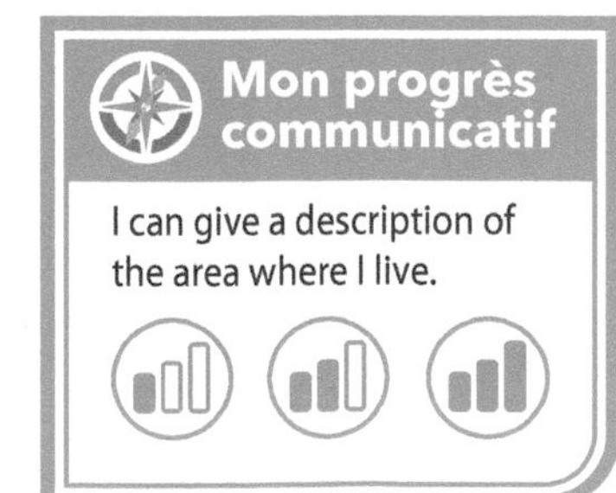

Activité 9

Qu'aiment faire les jeunes Parisiens?

Étape 1: Écouter

Écoutez ces mini-épisodes d'un podcast fait par de jeunes Parisiens. Choisissez la meilleure pochette *(album art)* pour chaque extrait.

A

B

C

D

E

I can create and present a short podcast to give reasons for visiting a favorite place.

Étape 2: Créer un podcast

Choisissez une attraction ou un endroit que vous aimez à Paris ou dans votre ville. Sur Explorer, enregistrez un mini-podcast dans lequel vous conseillez cet endroit à votre public.

Modèle

Je vous conseille d'aller (à)… C'est…

Musée du Louvre, Paris

Découvrons 1

Expressing the Most, Least, Best, and Worst

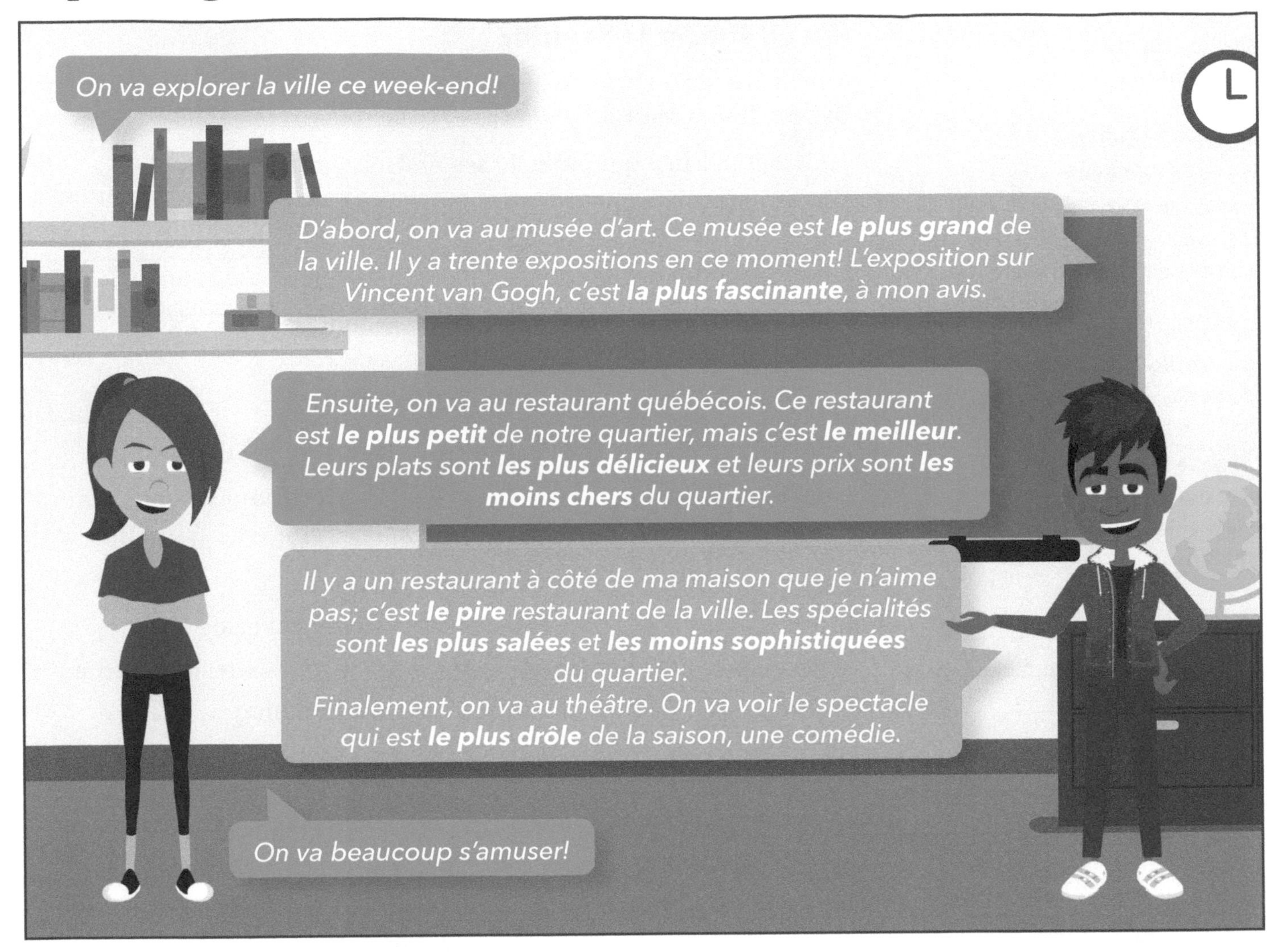

Découvertes

Reflect on what you observe and respond to the following items in the graphic organizer in Explorer.

1. What do you notice about the words in bold?
2. What do you observe before and after the words ***plus*** and ***moins***?
3. How do the words change based on what they are describing?
4. How are the words ***meilleur*** and ***pire*** used?
5. Share your observations with a partner. What else do you notice together or what else can you add to your observations?

Détail grammatical

L'ordre des mots avec des adjectifs

Most adjectives in French appear *after* the noun they describe:
un musée **intéressant**
une ville **dynamique**

There is a small group of adjectives that appear before the noun they describe. This group includes ***nouveau/nouvelle, petit/petite, grand/grande, vieux/vieille, bon/bonne***, and ***beau/belle,*** as well as their plural forms and superlatives:

une **belle** statue
un **grand** parc
mon **meilleur** ami
le **plus beau** musée

Notre-Dame de Paris

Détail linguistique

Des synonymes

Sometimes you will hear French speakers using alternatives for words like ***aussi*** and ***parce que***.

Instead of ***aussi***:
de plus
également

Instead of ***parce que:***
car

Activité 10

Quels endroits Élisa aime-t-elle visiter à Paris?

Étape 1: Écouter

Vous voyagez à Paris. Avant de voyager, vous voulez créer une liste des meilleurs endroits à Paris.

a. Écoutez Élisa qui parle de ses endroits préférés en ville.

b. Choisissez le bon mot pour compléter la description d'Élisa.

meilleur(e)(s)	cinéma	plus	musée
beau	théâtre	grand(e)	café

Salut, c'est Lili!

Aujourd'hui, je vais vous parler des __________ endroits où je suis allée. Il y a le __________ __________, le Grand Rex à Paris qui est dans le deuxième arrondissement. C'est très grand, il y a beaucoup de lumières... c'est le __________ __________ et le __________ __________. Il y a beaucoup de salles de cinéma, sept, mais également la __________ __________ salle de comédie et de __________ que j'ai vue. Il y a également un grand club et un __________.

Avec mes amis, nous aimons bien nous installer en terrasse au café. Dans ma ville, à Croissy cette fois, il y a, près du RER, un __________ qui s'appelle "Le bureau" où tous les jeunes de mon âge se retrouvent pour prendre un café ou un verre. Je trouve que c'est le __________ café de ma ville. À la prochaine!

Étape 2: Compléter

Lisez cet article sur des endroits qui battent *(break)* des records à Paris. Choisissez la meilleure expression de la banque de mots pour compléter l'article.

Banque de mots

la plus ancienne | la plus chère | la plus colorée | la plus courte | le plus vieux

a) Avec les Champs-Élysées et l'avenue Georges V, l'avenue Montaigne délimite le "triangle d'or" où on trouve des maisons des familles riches ainsi que des magasins et des hôtels de luxe. L'avenue Montaigne, c'est l'avenue ____ ________ ________ de Paris.

b) Située au 51 rue de Montmorency, la maison de Nicolas Flamel a été construite entre 1397 et 1407. C'est la maison ____ ________ ______ de Paris.

c) Zone piétonnière depuis 1993, la rue Crémieux est parfaite pour une jolie photo. Chaque façade pittoresque est peinte d'un pastel différent. C'est la rue ____ ________ ________ de Paris.

d) Avec 5,75 mètres de long, la rue des Degrés se trouve dans le 2e arrondissement. Cette rue n'est qu'un escalier de quatorze marches. C'est la rue ____ ________ ________ de Paris.

e) Malgré son âge, le Pont-Neuf garde son nom à cause de sa nouveauté à l'époque de sa construction à la fin du 16e siècle. C'est ______ ______ ______ pont de Paris.

Étape 3: Discuter

Vous allez passer un jour à Paris, donc vous avez seulement le temps de visiter trois endroits. Considérez la vidéo d'Élisa et l'article. Sur Explorer, négociez avec les autres élèves de la classe.

Modèle

Il faut voir la tour Eiffel. C'est le monument le plus haut de Paris!

I can exchange online messages to trade opinions about the best places to visit in a city or town.

On peut aussi dire

bas/basse	*low*
haut/haute	*high*
court/courte	*short*
long/longue	*long*
étroit/étroite	*narrow*
large	*wide*
ancien/ancienne	*old, ancient*
cher/chère	*expensive*
fréquenté/ fréquentée	*busy, popular (for a place)*

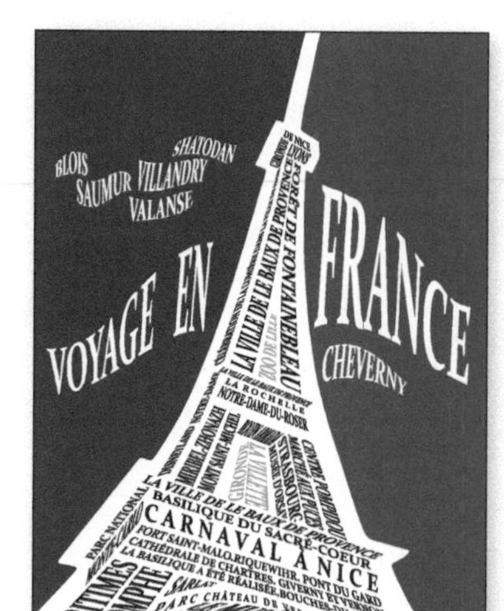

Activité 11

Quels sont les endroits uniques de Paris?

Étape 1: Créer une affiche publicitaire

Le site web Tourisme Paris Jeunesse cherche des affiches publicitaires pour présenter les endroits uniques de la ville.

a. Choisissez un endroit à Paris qui a une qualité unique.

b. Créez une affiche pour présenter cette qualité.

Modèle

Visitez le monument le plus haut, la tour Eiffel!

Étape 2: Présenter votre affiche

Présentez votre affiche aux autres élèves.

a. Montrez l'affiche aux autres élèves.

b. Expliquez la qualité unique de l'endroit choisi.

Activité 12

Quels sont les endroits les plus intéressants de votre ville?

Le journal de votre ville va publier un article sur des endroits de votre ville. Nommez des endroits que vous connaissez.

1. le meilleur restaurant
2. la plus grande salle de concert
3. l'endroit le plus calme
4. le magasin le plus fréquenté
5. le plus beau parc

Modèle

Je pense que le plus beau parc de notre ville est le parc Garfield parce que...

J'avance 1

Bienvenue dans notre ville

Amir, un ami d'Élisa, va passer du temps dans votre ville cet été avec d'autres élèves de son école. Avant leur arrivée, vous discutez en ligne avec lui.

Étape 1: Écouter

Amir parle de sa ville. Écoutez sa description et sélectionnez les endroits qu'il décrit.

AP® Étape 2: Répondre

Amir a des questions sur votre ville. Répondez à ses questions.

Étape 3: Créer une brochure

Préparez une brochure présentant trois endroits de votre ville à Amir et aux autres élèves de son école. Classez les endroits par ordre de préférence.

a. Choisissez trois endroits de votre ville.

b. Présentez des images et écrivez une description. Considérez:

—Qu'est-ce que c'est?

—Qu'est-ce qu'on peut faire dans cet endroit?

Allez sur Explorer pour trouver tous les documents nécessaires de **J'avance**.

L'Arc de Triomphe de l'Étoile, Paris

Comment dit-on? 2

Je m'organise pour sortir en ville

Je fais des recherches

Paris-Ados

Mes recommandations pour organiser votre journée à Paris

Voici ce que mes amis et moi avons fait le week-end dernier:

En premier,

...on a **fait du lèche-vitrine,**

...on est allés **aux puces,**

...et on a **fait un tour de manège** à **la fête foraine.**

Après, j'ai **fait de l'accrobranche** et **du roller** avec ma meilleure amie, c'était super!

À votre tour! Pas de YOLO, pour aller en ville, il faut être organisé! **Faites des recherches en ligne pour...**

...**vérifier les heures d'ouverture.**

...acheter un **billet d'entrée** en ligne (e-ticket).

Si ce n'est pas possible, vous pouvez aussi acheter vos billets sur place, au guichet.

Achetez vos **tickets** de RER et de métro à **la gare.**

Ensuite, téléchargez...

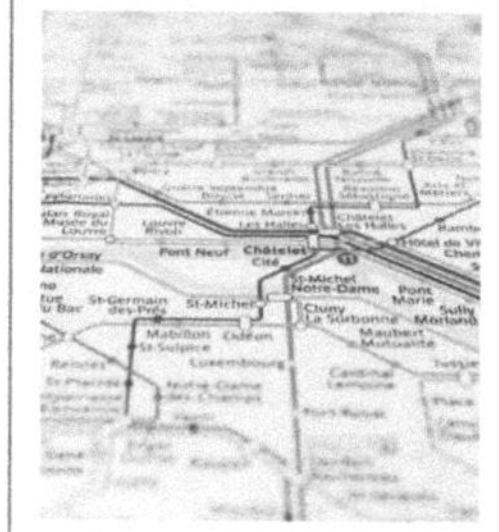

...un **plan** de la ville.

...une appli[-cation] pour le métro, le bus ou les activités proposées dans la ville.

Vous pouvez aussi consulter...

...**l'horaire** des trains ou des métros

...les menus en ligne des endroits où vous pouvez déjeuner.

Enfin, n'oubliez pas **d'inviter quelqu'un,** c'est plus amusant!

Envoyez un texto ou **téléphonez à** un ou deux amis.

Vous pouvez aussi **poster** ce que vous allez faire sur internet ou sur un réseau social.

Passez une excellente journée en ville!

Activité 13

Où est allé Cédric à Paris?

Cédric a passé une journée à Paris. Écoutez-le et associez chaque description à la photo qui convient.

A

B

C

D

E

F

Mon progrès communicatif

I can understand how someone spent a day in Paris and the places he or she visited.

On peut aussi dire

beaucoup de monde
lots of people

le guichet
ticket window, counter

le RER (Réseau Express Régional)
a commuter rail service serving Paris and its suburbs

le réseau social
social network

Pont Alexandre III, Paris

Activité 14

Quelles activités choisir?

Élisa et ses amies veulent passer une journée à Paris mais est-ce qu'elles veulent faire les mêmes activités?

Étape 1: Lire et identifier

Avec un(e) partenaire, lisez les commentaires d'Élisa et ses amies. Identifiez une ou deux activités pour chaque personne.

J'adore lire et je préfère rester tranquille. Je collectionne les vieux livres. Je veux en acheter. J'ai aussi besoin d'un nouveau sac-à-dos.

Il me faut de l'action! Je déteste faire des courses, c'est ennuyeux! Je veux aller à un endroit où il y a beaucoup de musique et de gens.

J'ai beaucoup d'énergie aujourd'hui, et les sensations fortes, j'adore ça! J'aime avoir peur et crier avec mes amis!

J'aime bien faire du sport mais je n'aime pas quand il y a beaucoup de monde. C'est amusant de faire du roller et de regarder les boutiques. Je veux passer du temps à discuter tranquillement avec les autres.

Étape 2: Discuter et grouper

Élisa et ses amies ne veulent pas faire les mêmes activités en ville. Elles ont besoin de se séparer. Discutez avec votre partenaire pour décider comment les amies vont se séparer.

Modèle

–Je pense que ______ doit aller à Paris avec ______ parce qu'elles aiment ______. Qu'est-ce que tu en penses?

–Je ne sais pas. Peut–être...

Activité 15

Quelles sont les informations importantes?

 **Étape 1: Lire et associer**

Vous êtes à Croissy dans la région parisienne et vous voulez faire une activité sportive dans un parc.

- Regardez les informations des deux parcs.
- Associez chaque déclaration suivante avec le nom du parc qui convient: parc Tarzan-Manie ou parc Bois-des-Lutins.

1. Ce parc est bien pour faire du jogging ou du roller.
2. Une activité de ce parc coûte 22€ pour les adultes.
3. Il ne faut pas payer (excepté pour le manège).
4. On peut y faire de l'accrobranche.
5. On peut voir de belles plantes exotiques dans ce parc.
6. On peut imaginer être un singe *(monkey)* dans les arbres.

On peut aussi dire

une aire de jeux
a playground

un mur d'escalade
a climbing wall

Parc Tarzan-Manie

Activités:

Conquête des arbres:

Vous cherchez à rencontrer Tarzan? Explorez nos arbres magnifiques avec des cordes et des filets!

De 7 à 11 ans (parcours à faire avec un adulte). Prix: 15€ pour 2 heures / 20€ pour 3 heures

12 ans et plus. Prix: 22€ pour 2 heures / 26€ pour 3 heures

Pas de sandales! Vous devez porter des chaussures fermées!

Adrénaline au top:

C'est une descente en tyrolienne qui fait monter l'adrénaline!

Accessible dès 12 ans. Prix: 10€ pour 1 descente

Informations pratiques:

Accès au parc:
12 allée Jungle Boy, 8300 Cergy

RER: Ligne A direction Cergy le Haut → Cergy Préfecture

En voiture: A15 → sortie numéro 9 direction Préfecture

Ouverture: Le parc Tarzan-Manie est ouvert d'avril à octobre.

→ Tous les week-ends et les jours fériés.

→ Pendant les vacances scolaires: tous les jours de 10h à 18h.

Consultez notre calendrier sur le site web pour découvrir nos nouveautés!

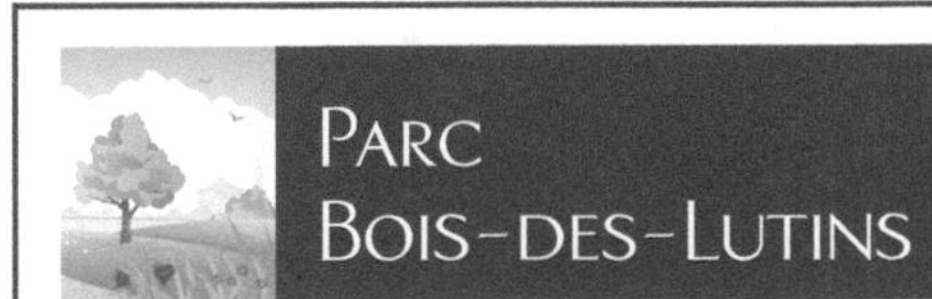

Informations générales:

L'accès au parc est gratuit. Toute l'année, vous pouvez profiter du long parcours sportif pour les joggeurs. Il y a aussi un mur d'escalade, des terrains pour les jeux de ballon, un jardin botanique, un manège payant, quelques aires de jeux, dont une de jeux d'eau, et un lac qui sert de refuge pour de nombreux oiseaux.

Horaires: Le parc est ouvert à toute heure du jour et de la nuit.

Moyens d'accès: RER ligne A, station Nanterre-préfecture /Bus lignes 159, 160, 304, 358

 Accessible aux personnes à mobilité réduite

Étape 2: Lire et corriger

Corentin est déjà allé au parc Bois-des-Lutins et il écrit un e-mail à votre groupe pour vous donner des informations sur le parc. Mais faites attention, il y a des erreurs dans son message!

a. Regardez les informations sur les parcs et lisez son message.

b. Avec un(e) partenaire, trouvez les erreurs.

c. Sur Explorer, répondez aux questions de Corentin et corrigez ses erreurs.

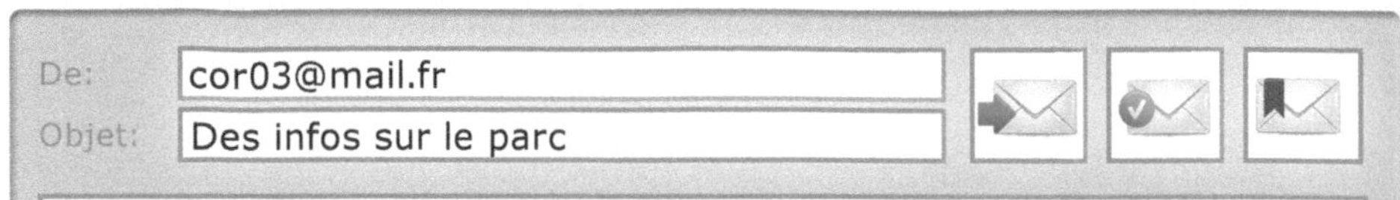

Salut à tous! Vous voulez aller au parc Bois-des-Lutins? C'est mon parc préféré et j'y vais souvent! J'ai quelques informations pour vous aider: Avant de partir, il faut prévoir 5 euros pour payer l'entrée. Ensuite, il faut prendre le RER et c'est assez rapide. Le parc ouvre à 8h et ferme à 20h. Vous pouvez y faire du jogging, du manège et de l'escalade mais il n'y a pas de terrain de foot alors gardez votre ballon à la maison. Et si vous aimez la nature, ce n'est pas un endroit pour vous car il n'y a pas beaucoup de plantes et d'animaux. Mais il y a une aire de jeux d'eau très amusante! Est-ce que vous y allez aujourd'hui? Je veux venir avec vous!

Modèle

Salut Corentin,

Oui, nous y allons aujourd'hui et tu peux venir avec nous mais tu as fait des erreurs. D'abord, ...

Étape 3: Comparer et discuter

Regardez vos réponses des **Étapes 1** et **2** et les informations des parcs. Avec deux ou trois élèves de la classe, décidez si vous allez aller au parc Bois-des-Lutins ou à Tarzan-Manie. Expliquez votre choix. Allez sur Explorer pour écrire vos réponses dans le forum.

Stratégies

Navigating Websites and Mobile Apps

Les sites web et les applications sont un excellent moyen d'élargir vos connaissances et de vous amuser en français.

1. Déterminez la fonction de l'application.
2. Lisez les titres.
3. Explorez d'autres éléments.
4. Sauvegardez le site dans vos favoris.

Découvrons 2

Describing What You Did

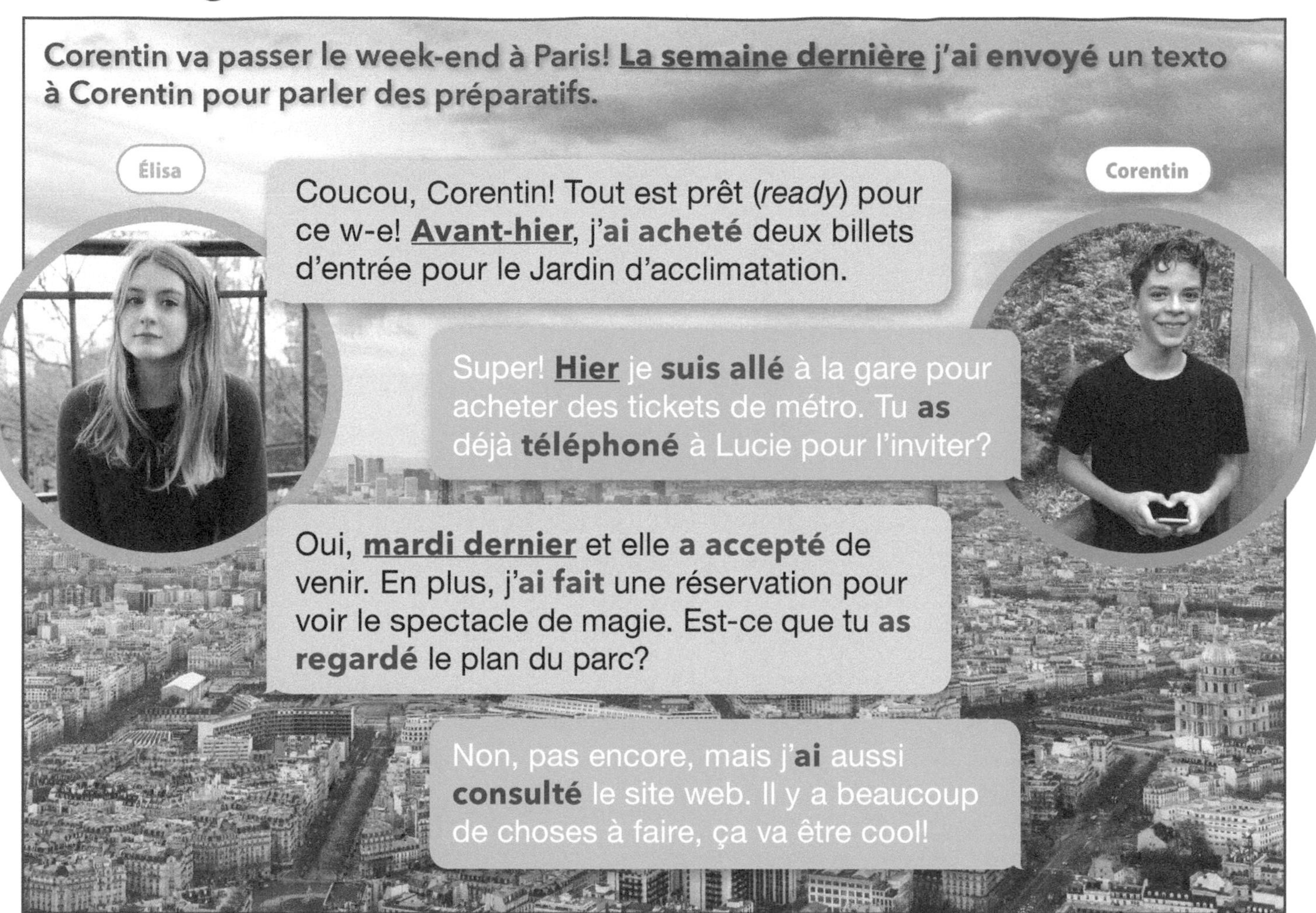

Découvertes

Read, think, and reflect on what you observe in Élisa and Corentin's conversation. Respond to the following items in the graphic organizer in Explorer.

1. What do you notice about the words presented in bold in ***Découvrons 2***?
2. What is the difference between the underlined words in bold purple and the words in bold blue? What are the roles of these groups of words?
3. Where you see the words in bold blue, how many appear together each time? How do these words compare to other forms you have seen of the same words?
4. Share your observations with a partner. What else do you notice together or what else can you add to your observations?

Activité 16

Qu'est-ce qu'on a fait le week-end dernier?

Étape 1: Lire et sélectionner

Lisez les phrases suivantes. Cochez (✔) les phrases qui décrivent vos activités du week-end dernier.

____ J'ai envoyé des textos à mes amis pour organiser mon week-end.

____ J'ai fait du lèche-vitrine et j'ai acheté des vêtements.

____ J'ai regardé un film à la télé ou au cinéma.

____ J'ai fait du sport.

____ J'ai étudié mes leçons et fait mes devoirs.

____ J'ai utilisé mon téléphone pour avoir des informations.

____ Avec ma famille, on est allés dîner chez des amis ou au restaurant.

____ Avec ma famille, on a acheté de la nourriture au supermarché.

Étape 2: Parler et noter

Est-ce que les autres ont fait les mêmes activités que vous?

- Demandez à plusieurs élèves de votre classe si ces phrases décrivent leurs activités du week-end dernier.
- Écrivez le nom des élèves qui ont fait ces activités.

Modèle

Est-ce que tu as envoyé des textos à tes amis pour organiser ton week-end?

-Non, mais j'ai envoyé des textos à mes amis pour avoir des informations sur les devoirs.

Est-ce que tu as fait du lèche-vitrine et acheté des vêtements ce week-end?

-Oui, j'ai acheté une jupe et un pull au centre commercial.

Étape 3: Écrire

Écrivez un paragraphe au sujet de votre week-end dernier. (Vous pouvez utiliser quelques activités mentionnées dans l'**Étape 1**.)

Activité 17

Qu'est-ce qu'on a fait samedi?

Étape 1: Chercher la bonne réponse

Lola était avec Élisa samedi dernier mais elle a oublié *(forgot)* certains détails de la journée. Maintenant, elles sont au café et Lola pose des questions à Élisa à propos du week-end dernier.

Lisez les questions de Lola. Est-ce que vous pouvez trouver les réponses d'Élisa?

Lola:	Qu'est-ce qu'on a fait samedi dernier en premier?
Élisa:	
Lola:	Ah oui et après, on a déjeuné. Où est-ce qu'on a déjeuné? Je ne sais plus.
Élisa:	
Lola:	C'est vrai! Et après, on a choisi de faire des courses mais où est-ce qu'on est allées?
Élisa:	
Lola:	Tu as raison. En plus, je les porte aux pieds! On a fait autre chose?
Élisa:	

Les réponses d'Élisa en désordre:

A. Oui, on a téléphoné à ta mère et elle a décidé de venir nous chercher. On était très fatiguées!

B. On a mangé un croque-monsieur à ton bistrot préféré derrière la gare.

C. Le matin, on a fait du vélo sur les quais de la Seine. C'était extra!

D. On a pris le métro et on est allées aux Halles. Tu as acheté des chaussures.

Expressions utiles

avant-hier
hier
mercredi dernier
la semaine dernière
le week-end dernier
l'année dernière
déjà
pas encore

Étape 2: Trouver

Élisa et Lola regardent des photos de samedi dernier. Avec un(e) partenaire, regardez les réponses d'Élisa de l'**Étape 1** et associez chaque réponse à une photo.

I can identify and compare where young people go to gather socially in Francophone cultures and in my community.

Zoom culture

Pratique culturelle: Allons au café!

 Connexions

Where do you go in your city or town to relax, spend time with friends, or study?

Le premier café de Paris, le Procope, ouvre ses portes en 1686. C'est le premier endroit où les Parisiens peuvent prendre un café assis et lire tranquillement et confortablement. Depuis, les cafés sont devenus (*became*) très populaires à Paris. C'est l'endroit préféré des lycéens pour se retrouver (*to meet up*), s'asseoir, discuter et regarder un match de foot. Élisa adore aller au café. Elle a commencé à y boire du café parce que c'est la boisson la moins chère. Même une boisson gazeuse est plus chère qu'un petit noir*! Elle aime le café près de son lycée à Chatou car les jeunes serveurs sont amusants et la carte propose des pizzas, des quiches, des salades composées et des crêpes pour le dessert. En plus, la décoration est élégante avec des bougies** sur les tables et une moto vintage au centre. En plus, il y a toujours de la place et on peut y aller quand un professeur est absent, c'est génial!

  Réflexion

Going to the café is part of a student's daily routine in French cities. It is a place to relax, see friends, and even do some homework after school. Is there a place that serves the same purpose where you live?

Activité 18

Que mettre comme commentaire?

Élisa a trouvé ces photos d'une journée à Paris et elle veut les poster en ligne sur un réseau social avec des commentaires. Aidez Élisa à écrire de bons commentaires.

a. Pour chaque photo, écrivez deux commentaires possibles. (N'oubliez pas les hashtags!)

b. Échangez avec un(e) partenaire.

c. Choisissez le meilleur commentaire de votre partenaire.

Activité 19

Et si on sortait en ville?

Étape 1: Parler

Vous parlez à deux ami(e)s du très bon week-end que vous avez passé en ville. Posez des questions en employant des expressions du nuage de mots. Enregistrez votre conversation sur Explorer.

allé à la fête foraine
fait du lèche-vitrine
acheté des billets sur internet
acheté des billets
vérifié l'horaire
consulté internet
consulté l'horaire
acheté des billets d'entrée
fait de l'accrobranche
fait un tour de manège
téléphoné à un ami
téléchargé un plan
allé au café
allé au parc d'attractions
allé aux puces

Modèle

Élève A: Est-ce que tu as invité un(e) ami(e)?

Élève B: Oui, j'ai invité Pauline. Tu as téléchargé le plan de métro?

Élève A: Non, mais j'ai consulté le site sur internet.

Étape 2: Écrire

Maintenant que vous savez ce que votre partenaire a déjà fait, invitez-le/la à faire une activité qu'il ou elle n'a pas encore faite. Envoyez-lui une invitation par texto avec le nom de l'activité, le jour et l'heure que vous proposez et un ou deux détails sur l'activité.

Modèle

Tu veux aller ___________?

- jour
- heure
- détails

Activité 20

Vous avez fait quoi ce week-end?

Vous rentrez du week-end à Paris avec Élisa et ses amis. Votre copain, Hugo, n'est pas allé à Paris. Vous laissez un message vocal à Hugo.

Modèle

Coucou Hugo! J'ai passé un super week-end! J'ai fait...

J'avance 2

Organisons nos activités

 Étape 1: Lire et identifier

Vous organisez une journée au Jardin d'acclimatation avec un groupe d'amis. Lisez les informations pratiques. Répondez aux questions à choix multiples.

 Étape 2: Parler

L'avez-vous déjà fait? Vous voulez savoir ce que vos amis ont déjà fait en région parisienne pendant leur séjour.

a. En groupes de trois, regardez les images des activités à Paris que vous avez sur votre fiche.

b. Demandez à vos partenaires s'ils ou si elles ont déjà fait les activités présentées sur votre fiche.

c. Répondez aux questions de vos partenaires.

d. Enregistrez la conversation de votre groupe sur Explorer.

 Étape 3: Présenter

Maintenant que vous savez *(know)* ce que vos amis ont déjà fait à Paris, vous organisez une journée où vous allez faire quelque chose de différent. Complétez une invitation sur internet pour inviter tout le monde.

Allez sur Explorer pour trouver tous les documents nécessaires de **J'avance**.

vue de Notre-Dame de Paris, Paris

Expressions utiles

arriver à l'heure
arriver en retard

J'ai passé (la journée).
J'ai pris…
Je suis rentré(e) (chez moi).
J'ai vu…

On peut aussi dire

la billetterie
ticket counter, online ticket sales

le fleuve
river

la location
rental, renting

la lumière
light

le quai
platform, paved riverbank

Comment dit-on? 3

On y va!

Je bouge en ville

***Récemment**, j'ai passé la journée en ville avec mes amis. J'ai créé une page dans mon album comme souvenir de cette journée magnifique.*

Le matin, j'ai pris **le métro** (ligne 10) pour rencontrer mes amis à la **station de métro** Porte d'Auteuil. Il y a un très beau jardin, le jardin des serres d'Auteuil juste à côté de la station.

L'entrée du métro dans le style Art nouveau par Hector Guimard

Le jardin des serres d'Auteuil

Le meilleur kebab du quartier!

Nous avons mangé dans un kebab et puis, après le déjeuner, mon ami Fabien est arrivé en bus. Il arrive toujours en retard! (Pas nous! Nous arrivons toujours à l'heure!)

Avec Fabien, nous sommes allés à pied à la billetterie du stade pour chercher nos billets. Nous avons **assisté à un match** de foot. L'équipe de Paris Saint Germain a gagné contre l'équipe de Marseille.

Parc des Princes

Après le match, nous avons **loué** des vélos pour aller voir la Seine. J'ai fait une promenade avec mes amis sur les quais du fleuve.

Notre bateau-mouche sur la Seine avant notre embarquement

Location de vélos. En ville, je roule lentement!

Après le dîner, nous avons pris **un bateau-mouche** sur la Seine. C'était tranquille d'être sur le fleuve et de **prendre des photos**. Comme ça, j'ai vu beaucoup de lumières sur les monuments! Je suis rentrée tard chez moi. Quelle journée!

J'ai pris une très belle photo de la cathédrale Notre-Dame la nuit.

Activité 21

Qu'est-ce qu'elle a fait pour son anniversaire?

Étape 1: Écouter

Regardez la vidéo qu'Élisa a postée sur l'Atelier des Lumières et notez les détails importants.

1. Élisa et son amie Lola sont allées à un ______ (où?).
2. L'Atelier des Lumières se trouve dans le ______ (quel numéro?) arrondissement.
3. Comme transport, elles ont pris le ______ (quelle sorte de transport?) et le ______ (quelle autre sorte de transport?)
4. Leur trajet était _______ (combien de temps?).
5. À l'Atelier des Lumières, elles ont vu ______ (quoi?).
6. Élisa a payé le billet de Lola parce que c'était ______________ (quel jour spécial?).

Étape 2: Lire et corriger

Après la sortie en ville avec Élisa, Lola écrit une carte postale à son cousin, David. Mais Lola a des souvenirs différents de ceux d'Élisa! Avec un(e) partenaire, lisez sa carte postale et notez les différences.

Cher David,
Aujourd'hui, j'ai passé une journée incroyable avec mon amie Lili pour mon anniversaire. Nous sommes allées à l'Atelier des Lumières, un parc dans le 5e arrondissement à Paris. De la maison de Lili, c'était un trajet de 10 minutes. Nous avons pris le bus et puis un taxi. À l'Atelier des Lumières, nous avons vu des animaux et des plantes. Élisa a payé mon billet parce que c'était la fête nationale.

Élisa dit...	mais Lola dit...

Détail grammatical

En métro et à vélo

Quand on parle des modes de transport, surtout après le verbe **aller**, on dit:
Je vais **en** voiture, **en** métro, **en** train, **en** bateau, etc.

Mais on dit:
Je vais **à** pied, **à** vélo, **à** cheval.

Après le verbe **prendre**, on peut simplement utiliser **un/une** ou **le/la**:
Je prends **le** métro tous les jours.
J'ai pris **un** vélo pour aller au Louvre.

 Étape 3: Poser des questions

Maintenant, vous n'êtes pas certain(e) si c'est Lola ou Élisa qui se souvient *(remembers)* de la journée correctement. Écrivez un e-mail à Élisa pour vérifier.

Modèle

Salut Élisa! Est-ce que tu es allée à l'Atelier des Lumières samedi ou dimanche?

Mon progrès interculturel

I can identify similarities and differences in cultural factors that affect teenage independence in Francophone cultures and in my community.

Réflexion interculturelle

Did you notice in the video that Élisa (Lili) and her friend Lola spent the day in a big city without adult supervision? This is not uncommon for French teenagers. Would you be allowed to go to a large city by yourself or with other teenagers? Why or why not? Answer the questions in the discussion forum in Explorer.

Activité 22

Quel mode de transport choisir?

 Étape 1: Interpréter et répondre

Émeric planifie une sortie en ville, dans le 18e arrondissement. Il habite le 9e. Ça fait un trajet de 2 km. Utilisez l'infographie pour répondre aux textos d'Émeric.

Rappel

Pour parler des prix

3€ = **Ça coûte** trois **euros.**

4,50$ = **C'est** quatre **dollars** cinquante (centimes).

0,35€ = **C'est** trente-cinq **centimes.**

LE TRANSPORT À PARIS

Combien de temps faut-il pour un trajet de 2 km à Paris?

Voiture	**Métro**	**Vélib'**	**À pied**	**Bus**
8-16 minutes	17 minutes	12 minutes	25 minutes	20 minutes

Combien coûte un trajet en moyenne?

Bus	**Métro**	**Vélib'**
1,90€	1,90€	3,10€ par mois (abonnement)

1. Combien coûte un trajet en bus?
2. Il faut combien de temps pour arriver en métro?
3. Et si je loue un vélo, le trajet va durer combien de temps?
4. Quel mode de transport est le moins rapide?
5. Le plus important, c'est que j'arrive à l'heure. À quelle heure dois-je partir pour mon cours qui commence à 10h?

Zoom culture

Pratique culturelle: Comment se déplacer à Paris

Connexions

How do you get places in your daily life? How many options are there for transportation where you live?

En région parisienne, il y a du transport pour tous! Pour un trajet efficace à bon prix, il y a le métro, le RER et le bus. Un ticket de métro parisien peut aussi payer un tour sur **le funiculaire** de Montmartre. Pas besoin de monter les escaliers pour visiter le Sacré-Cœur!

Pour ceux qui préfèrent rouler à deux roues, Vélib' Métropole propose la **location de vélos** mécaniques ou électriques. Si on aime se déplacer sur l'eau, il y a aussi le bateau-bus, un taxi sur la Seine, qui s'arrête à tous les monuments principaux.

Pour les touristes, Paris offre des moyens de transport plus amusants pour faire des visites guidées. Pourquoi pas visiter la ville en calèche (tirée par un cheval), en Segway® PT, ou en 2 CV ("deux chevaux", une voiture classique française)?

Réflexion

If students from a Francophone culture came to where you live, what would be the best way to show them around? What would be memorable and fun for them? What would allow them to see the important places in your town?

En France, le permis de conduire une voiture est à 18 ans et beaucoup d'ados apprécient pouvoir conduire un scooter un peu plus tôt, dès 14 ans.

Étape 2: Laisser un message

Vous avez décidé d'accompagner Émeric. Téléphonez à Émeric et laissez un message pour lui expliquer:

- comment vous y allez
- pourquoi vous avez choisi ce mode de transport

Modèle

Salut, Émeric! Je vais prendre le bus parce que...

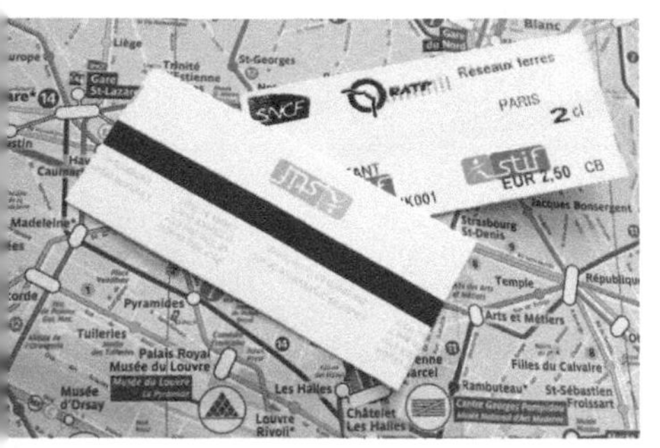
Un plan du métro et des tickets

On peut aussi dire

la monnaie *change (money)*
le trajet *route, trip*

Comment prendre le métro

Votre guide du métro parisien en sept questions

Pour acheter votre ticket:

- Plein **tarif** (1,90€) ou **tarif réduit** (0,95€)?
- Un ticket ou **un carnet** de 10 tickets à 14,50€?
- Allez-vous payer **en espèces** ou par carte bancaire?

Pour prendre le métro:

- Quelle **ligne**? (1, 2, 7, 14, etc.)
- C'est un trajet direct ou il y a **une correspondance**?
- Quelle direction? Par exemple: Boulogne Pont de Saint-Cloud ou Gare d'Austerlitz?
- À quelle station faut-il **descendre**?

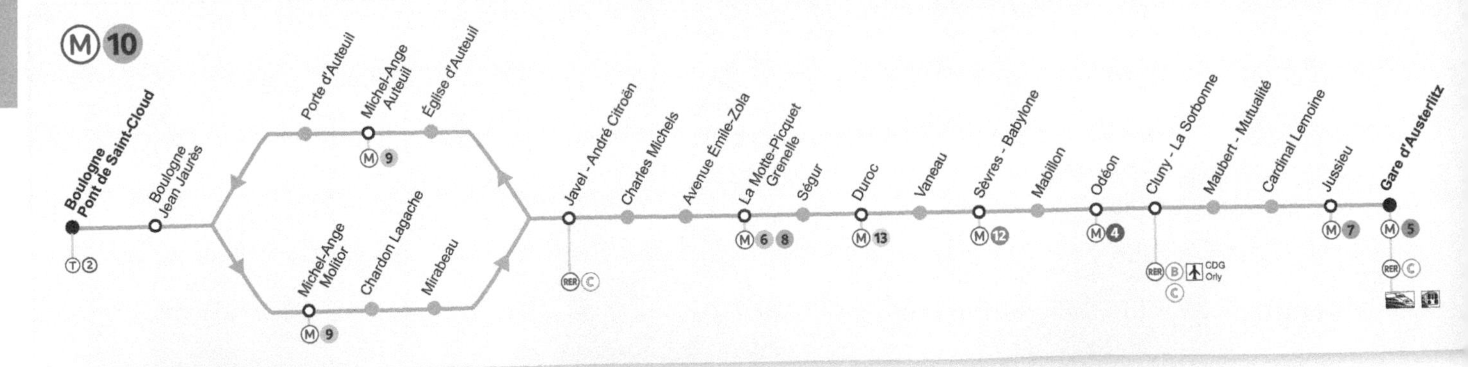

La station Odéon

Prononciation

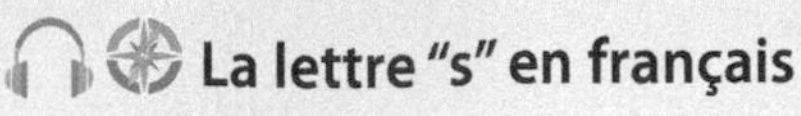

La lettre "s" en français

zzz
zzz
zzz

sss
sss
sss

The letter "s" in French is pronounced either as an ***s*** or a ***z*** sound, depending on the letters that come before and after it. How do we know which sound it is when we see a word with an "s"? Make predictions and then check them by listening to a recording.

In the following transcription of a phone message from Clémence, a student in Paris, see if you can identify whether the "s" is pronounced ***s*** or ***z***. Listen to the recording and complete the pronunciation activity in Explorer.

> Vous passez le week-end à Paris? Je vous conseille de visiter la Maison de Balzac, un musée dans le seizième arrondissement où vous pouvez assister à un spectacle ou voir une exposition. En ce moment, il y a *Une passion dans le désert*, l'histoire d'un soldat dresseur de panthère, et c'est superbe! Il faut simplement consulter les horaires en ligne. Il y a souvent des annonces sur les réseaux sociaux aussi. Choisissez une bonne pâtisserie après car vous devez goûter au Paris-Brest, ce dessert est une spécialité de la ville. Amusez-vous bien!

Activité 23

Comment est-ce que j'arrive au cinéma?

Étape 1: Mettre en ordre

Élisa et ses amis vous invitent à voir un film au Ciné Paris Panorama. Avec un(e) partenaire, mettez en ordre les étapes nécessaires pour arriver au cinéma.

_____ Descendez à Ségur.

_____ Commencez à la station Mirabeau.

_____ Payez 1,90€ en espèces.

_____ Prenez la ligne 10 direction Gare d'Austerlitz.

_____ Sélectionnez un ticket plein tarif.

AP® Étape 2: Parler

Vous êtes bien arrivé(e) au cinéma, mais vous êtes la première personne. Vous téléphonez à Lola pour savoir où est tout le monde et vous regardez votre smartphone pour lui donner des informations. Enregistrez la conversation sur Explorer.

Ciné Paris Panorama

Infos pratiques

Tarifs

Plein: 10,50€
Réduit: 7,50€ (étudiants/-26 ans/ retraités) tous les jours sauf week-ends et jours fériés
Matin (séance jusqu'à 13h00): 6,50€

Accès

Ⓜ 10 Ségur

Activité 24

Comment expliquer le métro parisien à un ami

Étape 1: Écouter

Votre ami arrive à Paris demain, mais il n'a jamais pris le métro.

a. Écoutez son message pour avoir les informations.

b. Puis, à chaque endroit, identifiez la station de métro la plus proche en regardant les plans de Paris.

	réponse	station
1. Où est son hôtel?		
2. Où veut-il vous rencontrer?		
3. Quelle autre activité veut-il faire?		

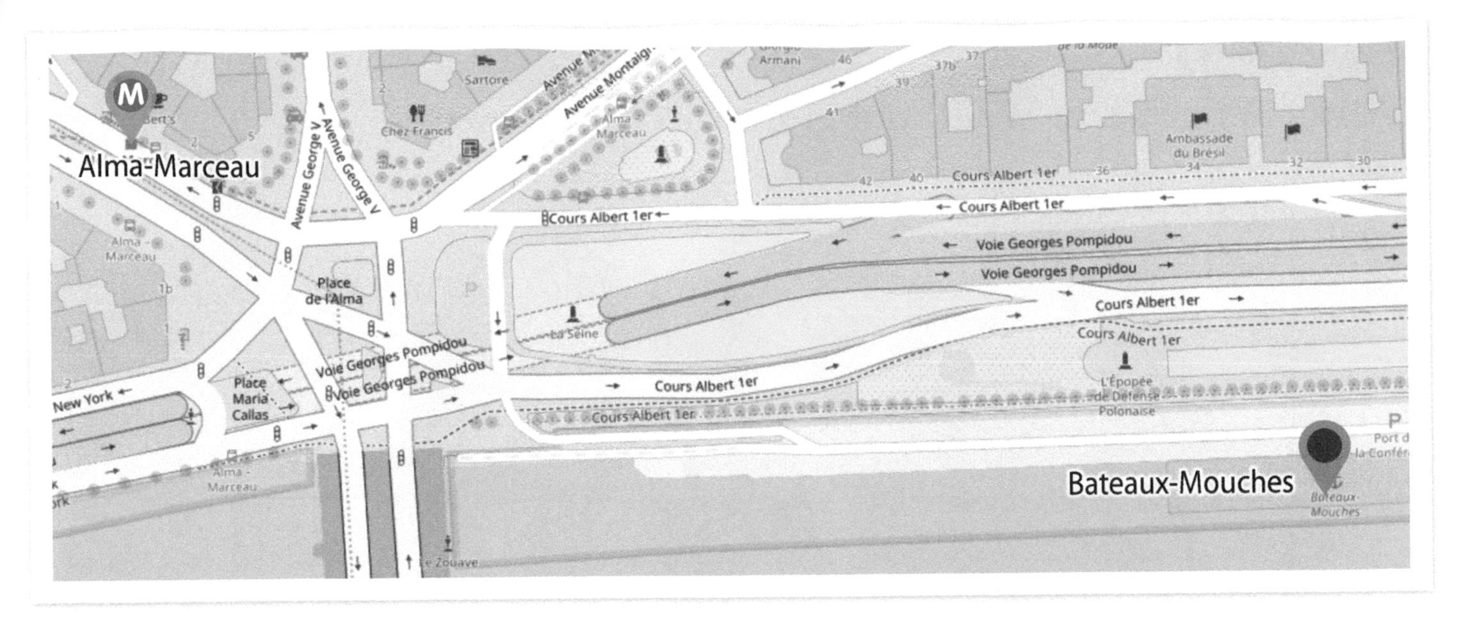

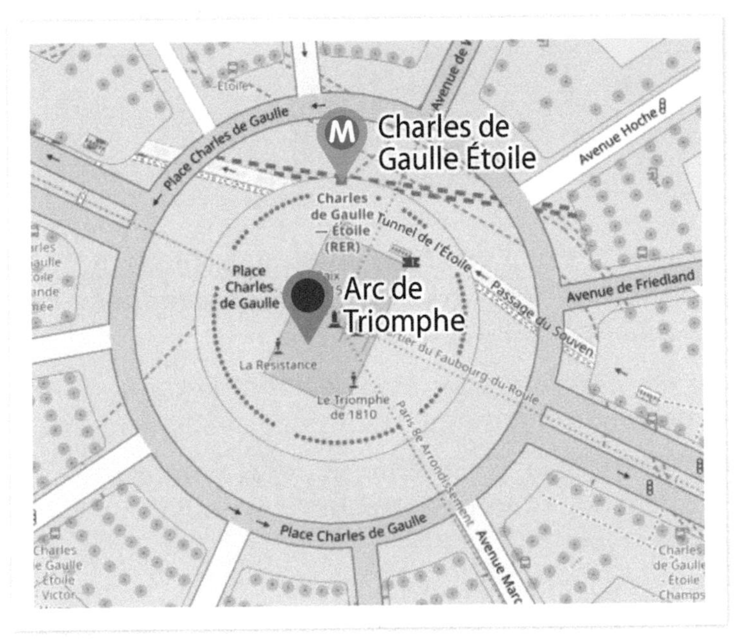

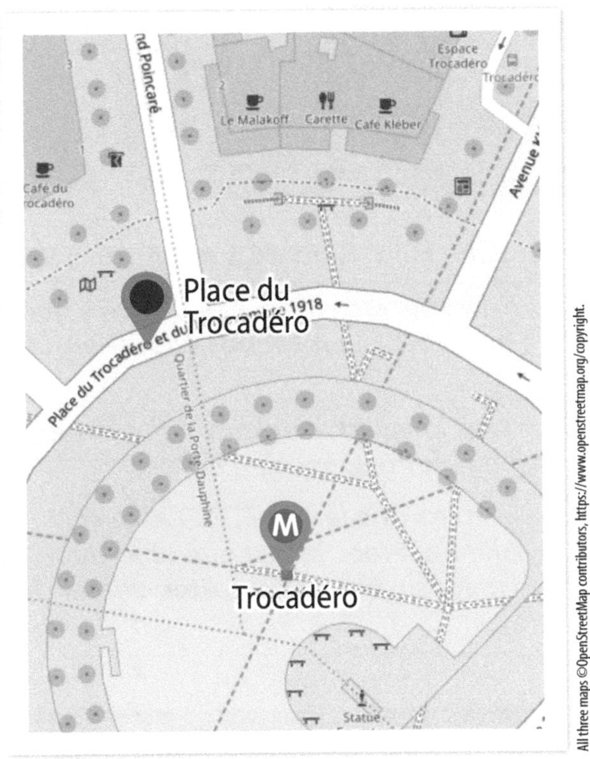

Étape 2: Répondre

Maintenant, collaborez avec un groupe sur un e-mail à votre ami pour expliquer en détail comment prendre le métro. Utilisez le plan du métro de Paris sur Explorer.

> Salut!
>
> Je suis très content(e) de pouvoir te voir bientôt. Alors, pour le métro, tout d'abord il faut commencer à la station...et prendre le métro ligne #, direction...

Découvrons 3

Telling Where You Went and How You Got There

Océane: Salut Félix. Tu **es** déjà **arrivé** au café?

Félix: Oui, j'y **suis arrivé**. Où es-tu? Est-ce que Priya est avec toi? Elle **n'est pas** encore **arrivée** non plus!

Océane: Oui, Priya est avec moi. Nous **avons pris** la ligne 7 du métro. C'est bien ça?

Félix: Vous **avez pris** la ligne 7? Oui, c'est bien ça. Alors, dis-moi, est-ce que tu **as vu** un grand magasin quand vous **êtes descendues** du métro?

Océane: Non, je n'**ai** pas **vu** de magasin. Je pense que nous ne **sommes** pas **descendues** à la bonne station de métro.

Félix: D'accord, vous **êtes** déjà **rentrées** à la station de métro?

Océane: Non, pas encore, mais j'**ai acheté** un carnet de tickets ce matin, donc j'ai tout ce qu'il nous faut.

Félix: Super. À bientôt!

Découvertes

Reflect on what you observe and respond to the following items in the graphic organizer in Explorer

1. Can you identify the verbs ***prendre, voir, arriver, rentrer*** and ***descendre***? What do they look like in this context?
2. What part of the text in bold stays the same for all subjects? What is different? What changes?
3. When Océane and Félix speak in the negative, where do they place the ***ne...pas***?
4. Share your observations with a partner. What else do you notice together or what else can you add to your observations?

Activité 25

Qui a pris le métro aujourd'hui?

Vous parcourez *(skim)* un site web de tourisme pour les jeunes. Lisez les commentaires anonymes et décidez si les commentaires ont été écrits par:

a. un garçon;

b. une fille;

c. deux garçons;

d. un garçon et une fille;

e. deux filles; ou

f. impossible de savoir.

www.majourneeaparis.fr

Qu'est-ce que vous avez fait aujourd'hui à Paris?

1. Ce soir nous sommes allées au spectacle de son et lumière sur les quais de la Seine.
2. J'ai pris le métro à la place des Vosges ce matin pour prendre des photos.
3. Je suis arrivée en retard au théâtre. Quel désastre!
4. On a assisté à un match de rugby.
5. J'ai vu une exposition au musée sur l'histoire du transport public à Paris.
6. Nous ne sommes pas descendus à la bonne station de métro pour aller au parc.

La basilique du Sacré-Cœur de Montmartre, Paris

Félix

Je suis allé au centre Pompidou et c'était facile d'y arriver. J'ai payé 1,90€ et j'avais la possibilité d'arriver à trois stations différentes.

Océane

J'habite à côté d'une station de location, et en plus, ça m'a fait faire un peu d'exercice.

Élisa

Comme j'habite loin du centre-ville, je dois faire un trajet un peu plus long en train.

Priya

Moi, je préfère voir où je suis quand je visite la ville, donc je n'ai pas pris le métro. Quand j'ai vu le musée, j'ai demandé un arrêt et je suis descendue du véhicule.

Activité 26

Quel est le meilleur mode de transport?

Étape 1: Lire et associer

Vous essayez de choisir le meilleur mode de transport pour aller à un musée d'art moderne à Paris. Lisez les textos de vos amis qui sont déjà allés au Centre Pompidou.

a. Avec un(e) partenaire, déterminez quel mode de transport chaque personne a pris.

1. Félix a pris le...	a. vélo
2. Océane est allée à...	b. RER
3. Élisa est arrivée en...	c. métro
4. Priya a pris un...	d. bus

b. Déterminez quel est le meilleur mode de transport pour vous. ("Je vais prendre... pour aller au centre Pompidou parce que...")

INFORMATIONS PRATIQUES

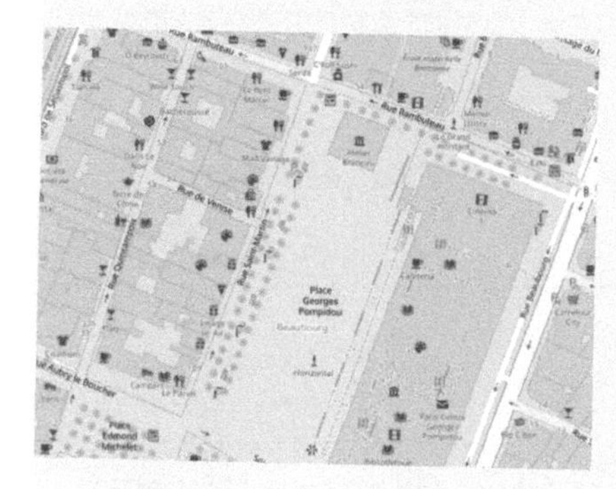

ACCÈS

Métro: Rambuteau (ligne 11), Hôtel de Ville (lignes 1 et 11), Châtelet (lignes 1, 4, 7, 11 et 14)

RER: Châtelet Les Halles (lignes A, B, D)

Bus: 29, 38, 47, 75

Vélib': station n°4020, face 27, rue Quincampoix, station n°3014, face 34, rue Grenier Saint-Lazare, station n°3010, 46, rue Beaubourg

Autolib': station 204, rue Saint-Martin, station 36, rue du Temple

Parking centre Pompidou: accès au 31, rue Beaubourg

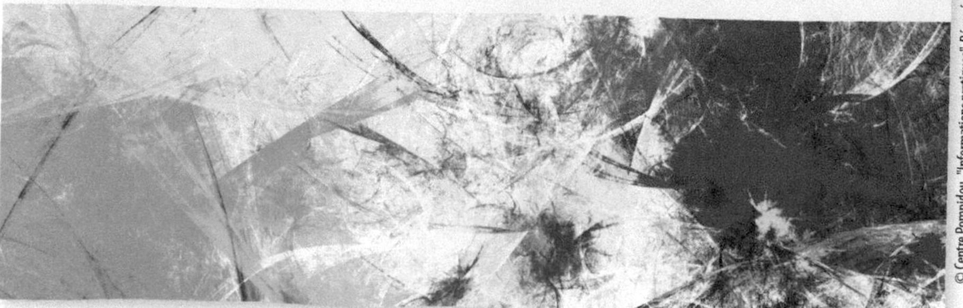

Étape 2: Répondre

Vos amis veulent savoir comment vous avez aimé le centre Pompidou. Envoyez-leur un message où vous expliquez:

- comment vous êtes arrivé(e) au musée
- ce que vous avez vu au musée
- ce que vous avez fait après le musée

La fontaine Stravinsky devant le centre Pompidou. Regardez ses sculptures!

Un portrait

Voici un tableau abstrait.

Activité 27

Pouvez-vous résoudre l'énigme?

Étape 1: Lire

Vous regardez vos papiers et les autres souvenirs de votre visite à Paris, mais votre mémoire n'est pas bonne!

a. Avec votre partenaire, examinez les indices *(clues)*.

b. Identifiez ce que représente chaque papier.

Modèle

C'est un billet de... / C'est pour...

LOCATION DE GYROPODE Segway® PT

(Place Joffre)

Découvrez la ville en louant un Segway® PT

Balades de 1 heure ou 2 heures

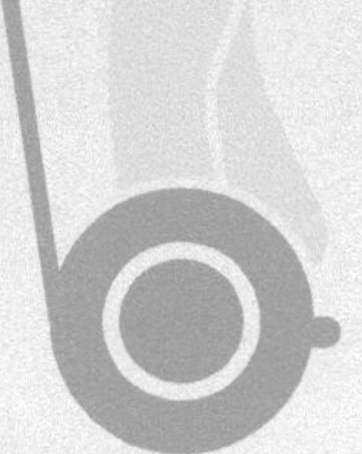

PAYÉ 9 MARS 2019 09h37

Rappel

Pour mettre des événements en ordre

d'abord

ensuite

puis

après (ça)

finalement

Étape 2: Mettre en ordre

Avec votre partenaire, mettez en ordre les activités que vous avez faites à Paris. Quand vous êtes d'accord *(agree)*, écrivez l'activité sur une ligne chronologique.

Modèle

—Qu'est-ce que nous avons fait d'abord?
—Nous sommes allé(e)s à...

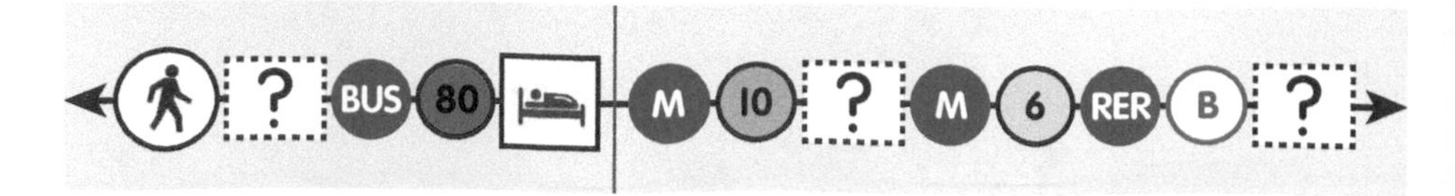

J'avance 3

Une nouvelle page dans mon album

Étape 1: Lire et organiser

Vous regardez les informations d'une journée récente que vous avez passée en ville. Associez chaque image à une description de votre journal.

Étape 2: Créer

Créez une page pour votre album en écrivant une légende ou une petite histoire avec chaque article ou photo.

Étape 3: Partager

Faites voir à un(e) partenaire la nouvelle page de votre album. Posez des questions pour comparer votre journée à la journée de votre partenaire.

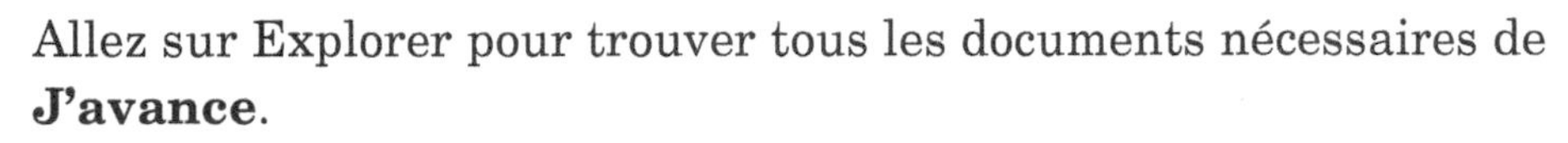

Allez sur Explorer pour trouver tous les documents nécessaires de **J'avance**.

Mon progrès communicatif

I can have a conversation about where I went and what I did.

Le métro à Paris

Synthèse de grammaire

1. Expressing the Most, Least, Best, and Worst: *le superlatif des adjectifs*

When describing places in a city or town, you might want to talk about the places that are best and worst, or to describe the ways in which places stand out in other ways: the most exciting or the least expensive, for example.

plus = *most* *La place qui est la* **plus** *intéressante, c'est la place des Vosges.*

moins = *least* *Ce restaurant est le* **moins** *cher de mon quartier.*

Here is how to form the superlative:

		definite article	plus/moins	adjective	
(m.)	C'est	le	plus	grand	musée.
(f.)	La rue	la	moins	longue	est la rue des Degrés.
(m. pl.)	Les parcs d'attractions sont les endroits	les	moins	relaxants!	
(f. pl.)	Paris a	les	plus	belles	vues.

To express the best or the worst of something, we use ***le/la/les meilleur(e)(s)*** ou ***le/la/les pire(s)***:

Ce musée est ***le meilleur*** *de la ville.*
This museum is the best in the city.

On joue ***les meilleurs*** *matchs de rugby à ce stade.*
They play the best rugby matches in this stadium.

J'ai goûté ***la pire*** *omelette en ville.*
I tasted the worst omelette in the city.

2. Describing What You Did: *le passé composé (I)*

To tell what you did in the past, use the ***passé composé***. The most important thing to notice about the ***passé composé*** is that it has two parts (***composé*** means *compound*).

The first part, immediately after the subject, is always the verb ***avoir*** or the verb ***être*** conjugated in the present tense. Most verbs use ***avoir***, but some, like ***aller***, are formed using ***être***.	The second part, called the past participle, is the part of the ***passé composé*** that looks more like the infinitive. However, it cannot be a verb by itself!
J'ai	***acheté*** *un ticket de métro.*
Je suis	***allé(e)*** *au parc pour jouer au foot.*

3. Telling Where You Went and How You Got There: *le passé composé (II)*

a. The past participle, which is the second part of the ***passé composé,*** is often formed by changing the ending of the infinitive.

There are a few common endings of past participles:

- those that end in ***-é: téléchargé, invité, allé, rentré***;
- those that end in ***-u: vu*** (*saw*, from ***voir***), ***descendu*** (*went down,* from ***descendre***); and,
- others, such as ***pris*** (*took,* from ***prendre***) and ***fait*** (*did,* from ***faire***).

b. When a verb uses ***être*** in the ***passé composé***, the past participle must agree in gender and number with the subject doing the action.

je suis descendu je suis descendue	nous sommes descendus nous sommes descendues
tu es descendu tu es descendue	vous êtes descendu vous êtes descendue vous êtes descendus vous êtes descendues
il est descendu elle est descendue on est descendu(e)(s)	ils sont descendus elles sont descendues

c. When you want to express what you did not do, place ***ne ... pas*** around ***avoir*** or ***être***. ***Ne*** contracts to ***n'*** before a vowel.

Nous ne sommes pas allés au musée. Je n'ai pas acheté de billet.

Vocabulaire

Comment dit-on? 1: I can talk about places people go in a city.

Les endroits en ville	***Places in a city***
l'endroit (m.)	*place*
l'exposition (f.)	*exhibition*
le musée	*museum*
le parc	*park*
le parc d'attractions	*amusement park*
la place	*square, plaza*
le quartier	*neighborhood*
la rue	*street, road*
le spectacle	*show*
le théâtre	*theater (for plays, concerts, etc.)*

Expressions utiles	
Je te conseille de/d'...	*I recommend that you...*
Je vais (à)...	*I'm going (to)..., I go (to)...*
pour s'amuser	*to have fun, for fun*
se trouver	*to be located*

Comment dit-on? 2: I can talk about things people do in a city.

Activités en ville	***City Activities***
aller aux puces	*to go to the flea market*
le billet d'entrée	*entrance fee, ticket*
consulter l'horaire (m.)	*to check the schedule*
envoyer un texto	*to send a text message*
faire de l'accrobranche (f.)	*to go tree trekking*
faire du lèche-vitrine	*to go window shopping*
faire du roller	*to rollerblade*
faire un tour de manège	*to go on a(n) (amusement park) ride*
la fête foraine	*fair*
la gare	*train station*
inviter quelqu'un	*to invite someone*
le plan	*map (of a city, area)*
poster	*to post (online)*
télécharger	*to download*
téléphoner à	*to call*
le ticket	*ticket*
vérifier les heures d'ouverture	*to check opening hours*

Expressions utiles	
l'année (f.) dernière	*last year*
l'appli(cation) (f.)	*app(lication) (digital)*
avant-hier	*the day before yesterday*
déjà	*already*
hier	*yesterday*
mercredi dernier	*last Wednesday*
pas encore	*not yet*
la semaine dernière	*last week*
le week-end dernier	*last weekend*

Comment dit-on? 3: I can talk about how I get to places in a city.

Une journée en ville	***A day in the city***
assister à un match (de foot)	*to attend a (soccer) game*
le bateau	*boat*
louer	*to rent*
le métro	*subway, metro system*
prendre des photos	*to take pictures*
récemment	*recently*
la station de métro	*subway station*

Expressions utiles	
arriver à l'heure	*to arrive on time*
arriver en retard	*to arrive late*
J'ai passé (la journée)...	*I spent (the day)...*
J'ai pris...	*I took...*
J'ai vu...	*I saw...*
Je suis rentré(e) (chez moi).	*I went home (to my house).*

Prendre le métro	**Taking the subway**
le carnet	*booklet, pack of tickets*
la correspondance	*changing trains (or other transportation)*
descendre	*to get out of a vehicle, go down*
en espèces	*in cash*
la ligne	*line (of a train, subway, etc.)*
le tarif	*fee, price*
le tarif réduit	*reduced price*

J'y arrive

Questions essentielles

- What experiences are available to young people in a Francophone city or town?
- How can I access information to make plans?
- How does culture influence where I go and what I do in a Francophone city or town?

Une sortie dans la Ville Lumière

Vous passez une semaine à Paris avec votre professeur et les autres élèves de votre classe. Le premier jour, vous pouvez choisir où vous voulez aller et ce que vous allez voir et faire. À l'hôtel, vous regardez une vidéo avec quelques opinions sur des endroits différents en ville. Ensuite, vous en discutez avec un(e) autre élève pour décider quels endroits visiter. Après avoir fait les activités, écrivez une description de votre journée en ligne pour partager avec de futurs voyageurs.

Avant de commencer, référez-vous à Explorer pour vous familiariser avec les critères d'évaluation de **J'y arrive**.

Interpretive Assessment

Que faire à Paris?

Vous êtes à Paris avec d'autres élèves de votre école. En arrivant à l'hôtel, le propriétaire vous suggère une vidéo en ligne où des jeunes parlent des endroits intéressants à visiter en ville.

a. Regardez la vidéo et répondez aux questions.

b. Priorisez les trois endroits dans l'ordre de vos préférences.

Interpersonal Assessment

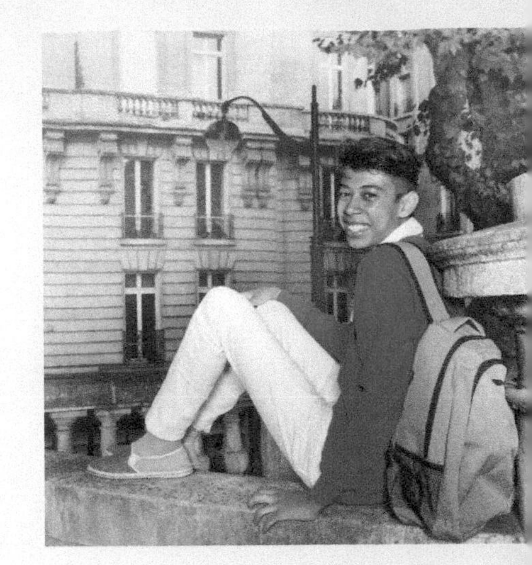

Choisissons un endroit

Après avoir regardé la vidéo, vous parlez avec un(e) autre élève pour choisir un endroit à visiter. Discutez avec votre partenaire de l'endroit que vous voulez visiter.

- Expliquez pourquoi vous préférez cet endroit.
- Expliquez comment vous pouvez y aller.
- Prenez une décision ensemble.

Presentational Assessment

Nos avis sur Paris

Maintenant, écrivez une description de votre journée en ville pour écrire un post en ligne. Donnez votre avis de la journée. Expliquez:

- Où vous êtes allé(e)(s);
- Comment vous y êtes arrivé(e)(s);
- Ce que vous avez vu; et
- Ce que vous avez fait.

UNITÉ 5

Des conseils pour une vie saine

Objectifs de l'unité

Read, view, and listen to informational texts such as websites, infographics, and personal stories about healthy habits.

Discuss with others the ways in which they and others stay healthy.

Research health information in order to make a presentation on adolescent health.

Investigate how people in Francophone cultures maintain their physical as well as social and emotional health.

Questions essentielles

How do people where I live and in Francophone cultures take care of their physical health?

How do people address concerns with their health?

How do people where I live and in Francophone cultures view social and emotional health?

Health and wellness are essential to our daily lives. Our daily habits impact our physical as well as social and emotional health. In this unit, Mathew and Brenda will share information about what they do to stay healthy.

Rencontre interculturelle

Dijon et la Bourgogne-Franche-Comté, France

Nom: Mathew

Langues parlées: français, anglais

Origine: Dijon, France

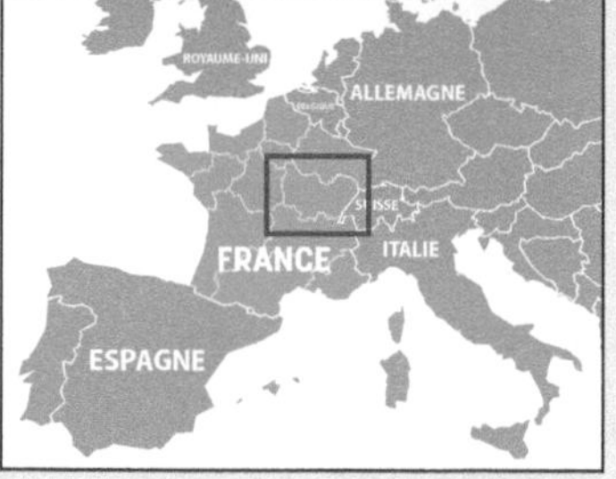

Dijon est une ville administrative de la Bourgogne-Franche-Comté, une des dix-huit régions de France. Riche en art, histoire et gastronomie, c'est une ville parfaite pour explorer la culture française!

En gastronomie, les escargots de Bourgogne ont la meilleure réputation car ils sont gros et préparés avec les cinq mêmes ingrédients depuis des siècles: de l'ail, du persil, du beurre, du sel et du poivre, miam!

Un autre plat emblématique de la Bourgogne est le bœuf bourguignon. Ce plat traditionnel est servi les jours de célébration. Ce sont des morceaux de bœuf cuits dans du vin rouge et des épices.

Dijon donne une place importante au sport. On peut y trouver un skatepark, des terrains de foot, un stade d'athlétisme, des piscines, des gymnases, une salle d'escalade et bien d'autres sites sportifs encore! De plus, Dijon possède 825 hectares d'espaces verts (1 hectare=10 000 m^2), idéal pour faire des marches, du vélo ou même du bateau sur le canal. Le contact avec la nature est très relaxant!

Et quel est l'emblème de Dijon? C'est une petite chouette sculptée et très usée. Elle garde l'église Notre-Dame de Dijon depuis 600 ans! La légende dit qu'il faut la caresser parce qu'elle porte bonheur *(brings good luck)*. C'est chouette, non?

Bourgogne

Le bœuf bourguignon

Les escargots de Bourgogne

Le jardin Darcy, Dijon

Une chouette

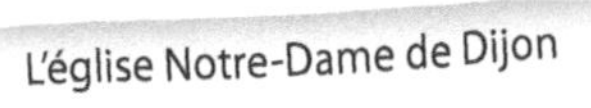

L'église Notre-Dame de Dijon

La chouette sculptée de l'église Notre-Dame

Activité 1

  **De quoi parle Mathew?**

Mathew vous parle de sa région, la Bourgogne-Franche-Comté, et de sa ville natale, Dijon. Pouvez-vous compléter ses descriptions avec les expressions de l'encadré *(box)*?

des escargots	du bœuf	une ville administrative
de sport	d'espaces verts	la petite chouette

1. *Il y a des hectares et des hectares ___________ dans ma ville natale.*
2. *Aujourd'hui, Dijon est ______________ de la Bourgogne-Franche-Comté.*
3. *J'adore quand mes parents cuisinent ___________ avec beaucoup d'ail et de beurre, c'est délicieux!*
4. *Je trouve que ___________ est très mignonne. Je la touche souvent pour avoir de la chance.*
5. *Ce qui est super à Dijon, c'est qu'on peut faire beaucoup ___________. Moi, j'adore le foot!*
6. *Dans ma famille, on sert toujours ___________ bourguignon avec des pommes de terre pour les fêtes. C'est ma viande préférée.*

I can compare how local infrastructure supports the pursuit of a healthy lifestyle in a Francophone city and in my community.

Réflexion interculturelle

Mathew loves Dijon, the city where he is from. He shared several special aspects of his city. In particular, Dijon has infrastructure (e.g., transportation, public places, etc.) that encourages being active and staying in good health. What is the place where you live like? Is there any infrastructure in your community that encourages people to be active and stay healthy? Answer the questions in the discussion forum in Explorer.

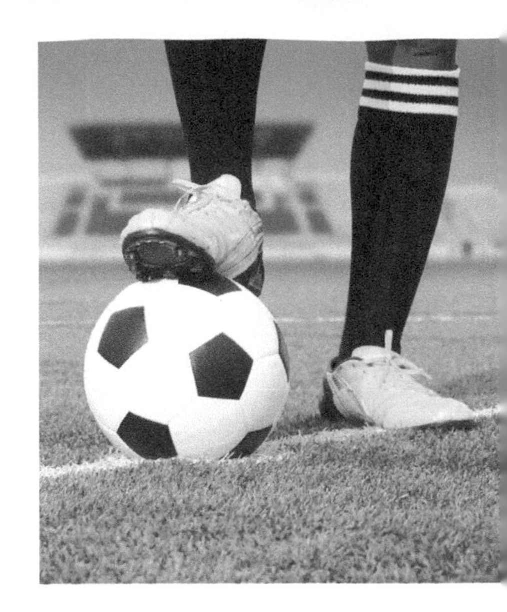

Activité 2

Rendez-vous avec Mathew!

Étape 1: Regarder et lire

Regardez la vidéo de Mathew et complétez le texte avec les mots de l'encadré que vous entendez.

bientôt – une école – apprendre – semaine – Dijon – sortir – en mars – mon père – dix-sept – baccalauréat

Bonsoir, je m'appelle Mathew, j'ai (1)____ ans et je vis à (2)____ avec ma famille. Ma famille est composée de ma mère, (3)____, ma sœur et mon grand frère. Je vais à (4)____ qui donne accès à un diplôme qui s'appelle le (5)____ international. Mes passe-temps sont le football, le volley-ball et (6)____ avec mes amis. Je pratique le football deux fois par (7)____ et le volley-ball (8)____. J'espère vous revoir (9)____ et vous (10)____ beaucoup de choses.

Étape 2: Noter et parler

D'après les informations écrites et les vidéos de Mathew et d'Elisa (de l'**Activité 1 de l'Unité 4**), qu'est-ce qu'ils ont en commun? Notez deux ou trois choses qu'ils ont en commun sur une feuille de papier. Puis, comparez vos réponses avec celles des autres élèves de votre groupe.

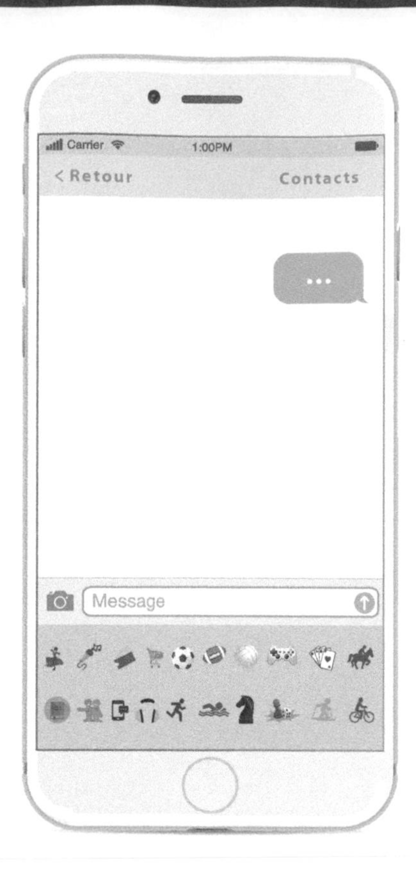

Rappelle-toi

Activité 3

Qu'est-ce que tu fais pendant ton temps libre?

Les activités sont très importantes pour rester en bonne santé.

a. Écrivez des messages à un(e) autre élève pour demander ce qu'il ou elle fait après l'école ou le week-end comme activités.

b. Répondez aux questions et continuez la conversation écrite.

Modèle

Élève A: Qu'est-ce que tu aimes faire après l'école ou le week-end?

Élève B: Je ... Et toi?...

Activité 4

Quels sont les choix responsables?

Étape 1: Écrire

Vous voulez manger mieux cette année. Classez la nourriture que vous aimez dans la catégorie qui correspond. Soyez spécifique.

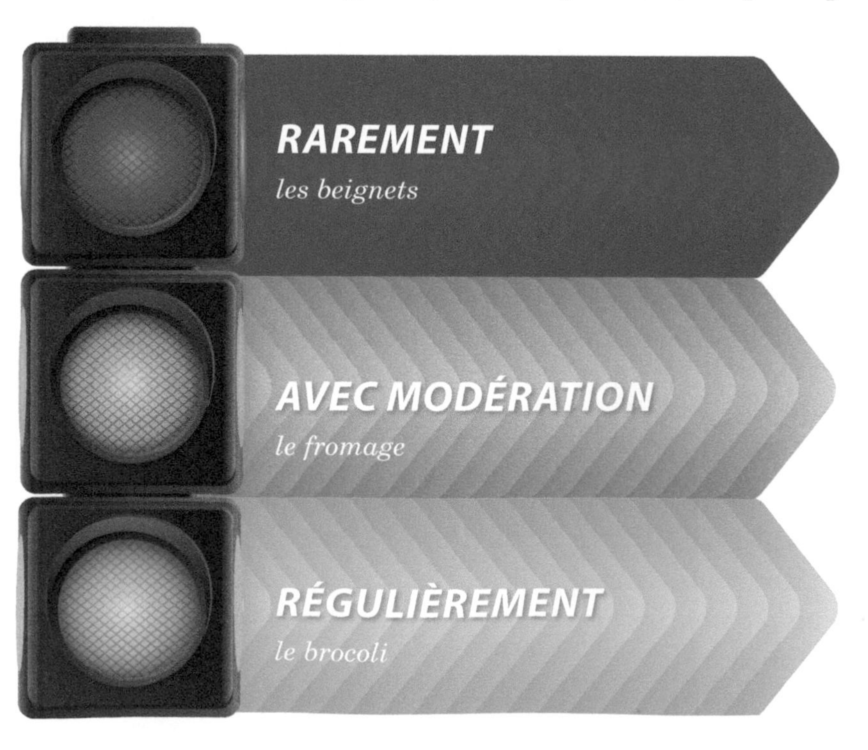

Étape 2: Parler

Vous avez un(e) ami(e) qui fait du sport avec vous, mais il ou elle ne mange pas toujours correctement. Laissez un message sur son répondeur pour expliquer ce que vous allez manger.

Modèle

Coucou! Je mange des aliments différents ce semestre parce que je joue au foot. Je vais manger plus souvent du brocoli. Je vais manger du fromage avec modération, pas tous les jours! Je vais manger rarement des beignets. C'est trop sucré!

Activité 5

Quelles solutions choisir?

Étape 1: Écouter et décider

Regardez le tableau d'affichage *(bulletin board)*. Les conseillers proposent de participer à des clubs pour être en bonne santé. Écoutez les messages de Léa, de Marco, de Marguerite et de Modibo.

Avec un(e) partenaire, décidez quel est le meilleur club pour:

A. Léa
B. Marco
C. Marguerite
D. Modibo

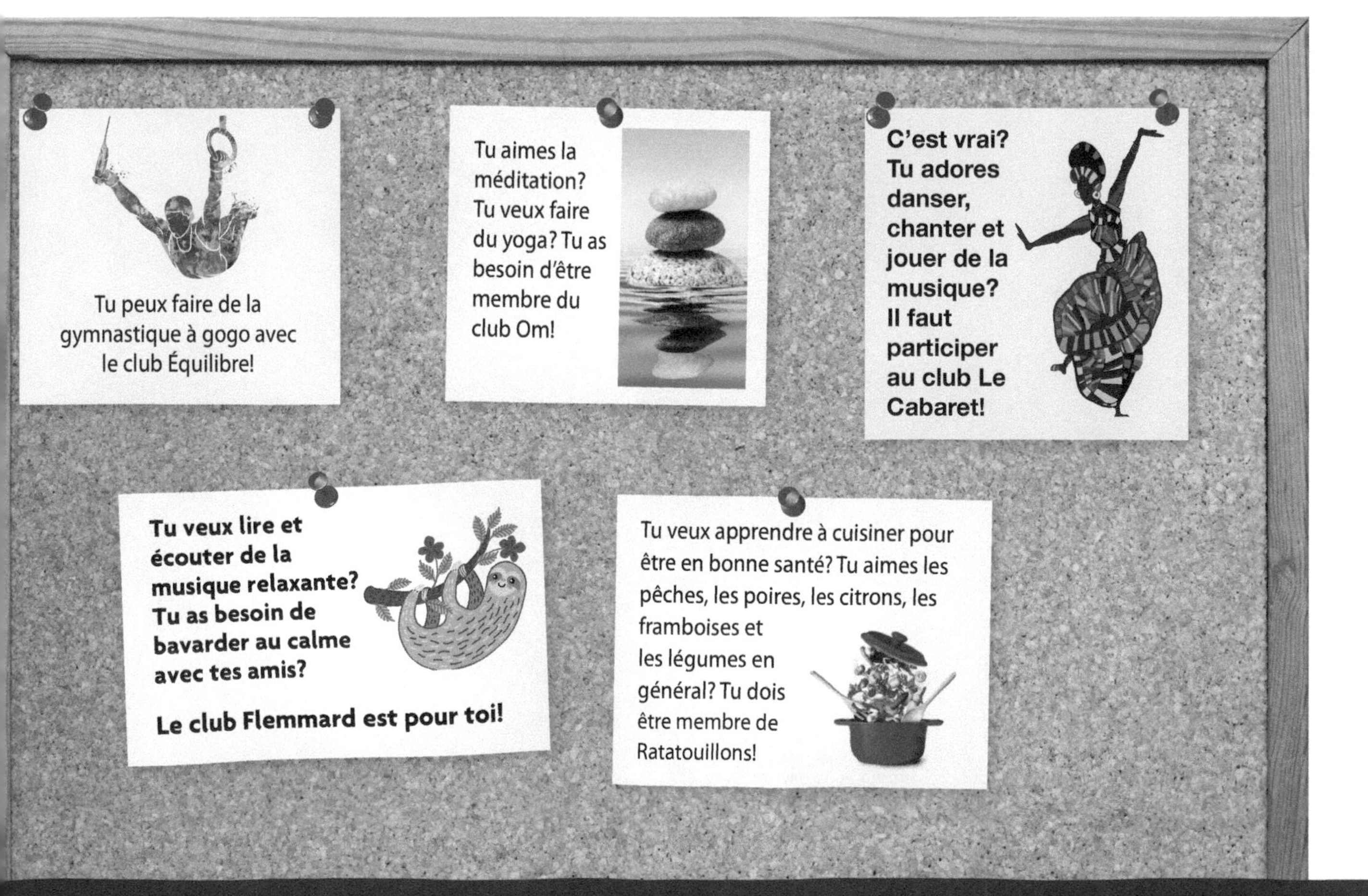

Rappel

Tu as besoin de...

Tu dois...

Il faut...

Étape 2: Réécouter et conseiller

Comment aider vos amis Léa, Marco, Marguerite et Modibo?

a. Réécoutez leurs messages et notez leurs difficultés.

1. Léa
2. Marco
3. Marguerite
4. Modibo

b. Maintenant, donnez des conseils de la liste à chaque personne.

Modèle

Marguerite, tu as besoin de faire du sport.

A. ...aller au cinéma.

B. ...faire de la randonnée à pied ou à vélo.

C. ...faire une grosse salade avec des tomates, des concombres, des oignons, des avocats et de la moutarde.

D. ...participer à un club d'athlétisme.

E. ...passer du temps avec tes amis.

F. ...consulter l'infirmier.

G. ...aller à la pharmacie.

H. ...prendre des médicaments.

I. ...manger des légumes tous les jours.

J. ...faire du sport.

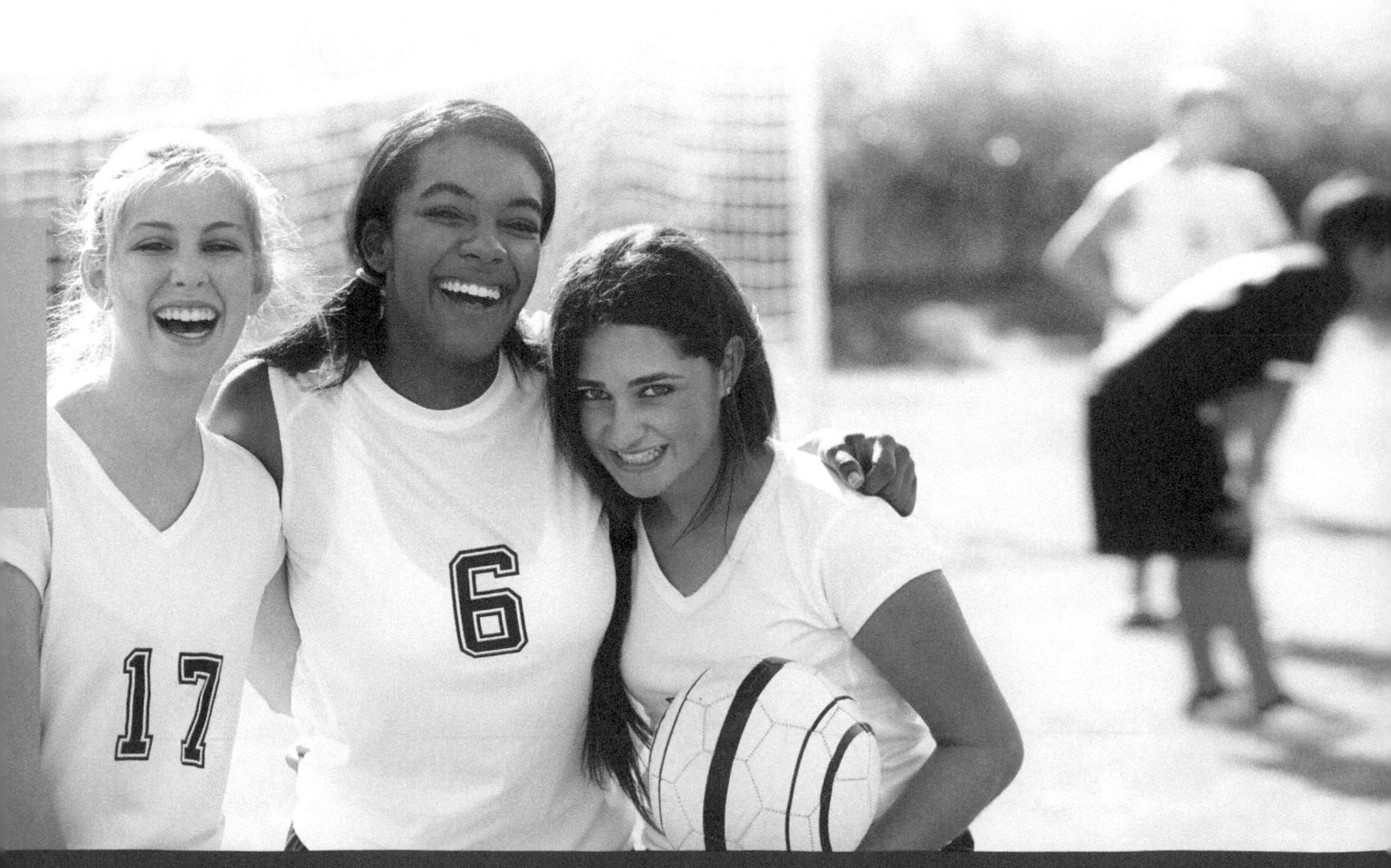

Rappelle-toi

Quelques aliments

l'avocat (m.)
la banane
le citron
le concombre
la framboise
les frites (f. pl.)
le fromage
les fruits (m. pl.)
le gâteau
la glace
la mangue
la moutarde
l'œuf (m.)
l'oignon (m.)
le pain
les pâtes (f. pl.)
la pêche
la poire
le poisson
la pomme de terre
le poulet
le riz
la salade verte
la soupe
le steak
la tarte
la tomate
la viande

Expressions utiles

aller à la pharmacie
à tes/vos souhaits
en bonne santé
mettre de la crème solaire
prendre un médicament

Les activités entre amis

aller au cinéma
bavarder
chanter
danser
écouter de la musique relaxante
envoyer des textos
lire
participer aux clubs
passer du temps avec des amis

faire de la gymnastique
faire une randonnée
faire du sport
faire du vélo

jouer aux échecs
jouer aux jeux vidéo
jouer au/à la/à l'/aux (le nom d'un sport)
jouer de la musique

Rappel

Pour parler de la fréquence

tous les jours
tout le temps
(une) fois par (semaine)
souvent
parfois
de temps en temps
rarement
(ne...) jamais

On peut aussi dire

les boissons (f. pl.) énergisantes
energy drinks
consommer
to consume
le/la dentiste
dentist
fumer/vapoter
to smoke/to vape
grignoter
to snack
le/la kiné(sithérapeute)
physical therapist
l'ophtalmo(logiste) (m./f.)
eye doctor
l'orthodontiste (m./f.)
orthodontist
prendre rendez-vous
to make an appointment
des produits (m. pl.) bio
organic products
le/la psy(chologue)
psychologist
un régime tendance
fad, trendy diet

Communiquons

Comment dit-on? 1

Pour bien vivre, où commencer?

Des habitudes saines

Pour être en bonne santé, il est important de:

dormir assez pour avoir un **sommeil** adéquat

faire de l'exercice

passer du temps au soleil (mais pas trop!)

dire "non" à l'alcool, au tabac et aux drogues

Pour la prévention des maladies, le plus important, c'est de:

passer une visite médicale

prendre rendez-vous chez le dentiste une ou deux fois par an

Pour une alimentation **saine** et **équilibrée**,

<u>il faut **éviter de**</u>

consommer **trop** de matières grasses et de glucides

suivre des régimes tendance

trop grignoter

<u>on devrait **essayer de**</u>

choisir des produits bio

opter pour **des aliments** riches en vitamines et en protéines

limiter les boissons énergisantes

Activité 6

Comment est-ce qu'ils choisissent de rester en forme?

Étape 1: Écouter

Vous écrivez un article sur les stratégies des lycéens français pour rester en bonne santé et vous cherchez des informations.

a. Écoutez les podcasts de Djamila, de Romain et d'Idriss, trois lycéens de Dijon.

b. Cochez (✔) leurs bonnes habitudes dans la représentation schématique sur Explorer.

- dormir assez
- passer du temps au soleil
- faire de l'exercice
- dire "non" à l'alcool, au tabac et aux drogues
- avoir une alimentation saine et équilibrée

Étape 2: Discuter

Est-ce que les élèves de votre groupe et vous avez les mêmes habitudes?

a. Choisissez trois des stratégies mentionnées dans l'**Étape 1**.

b. Discutez-en dans votre groupe. Posez des questions et écrivez les réponses.

Expressions utiles

Il est important de...
Le plus important, c'est (de)...
On devrait...
riche en...
dire "non" à...
prendre son temps

Activité 7

Comment peut-on avoir un cœur en bonne santé?

Étape 1: Discuter et décider

La fondation Cœur et Artères aide à financer la recherche sur les risques cardiovasculaires.

a. Lisez l'infographie de la fondation.

b. Discutez avec un(e) partenaire et décidez si les propositions qui suivent sont vraies ou fausses.

1. Il ne faut pas boire plus de deux verres de jus de fruits par jour.
2. On devrait éviter les produits laitiers, surtout le fromage.
3. Un verre d'alcool par jour est acceptable mais pas plus.
4. Il faut rester actif au moins trente minutes chaque jour. Par exemple, on peut faire du jardinage.
5. Si on fait du sport, on peut consommer des boissons sucrées régulièrement.
6. Il est important de manger au moins cinq portions de fruits et légumes chaque jour.

 Étape 2: Écrire

Oh là là! Après avoir regardé cette infographie, vous êtes un peu préoccupé(e) par les mauvaises habitudes de votre ami, Kévin.

a. Regardez ses messages et ses photos sur son profil.

b. Commentez avec des conseils et posez des questions.

Modèle

Tu ne dois pas manger trop de matières grasses! Est-ce que tu manges des légumes tous les jours?

Il y a une heure

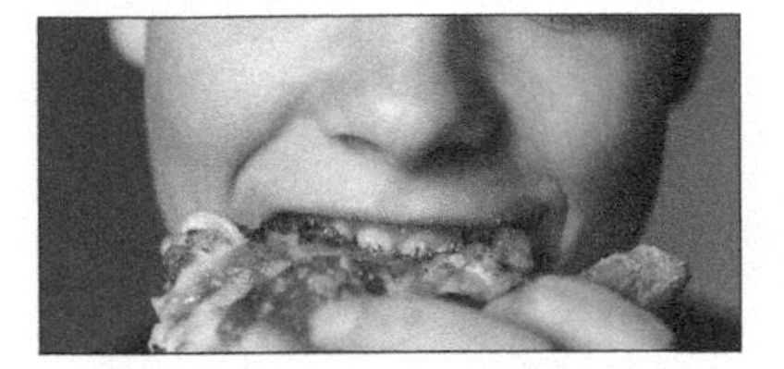

Voici mon déjeuner. Je prends une demi-pizza tous les jours! #record #maîtredelapizza

Il y a quarante-cinq minutes

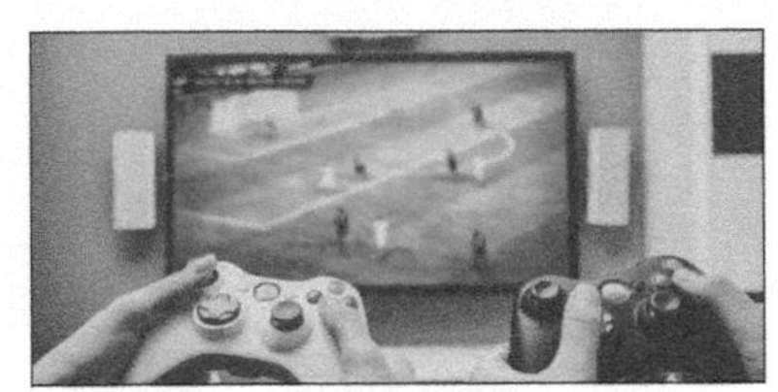

C'est l'heure du sport. Aujourd'hui, c'est moi qui vais gagner contre @mathew2001. #activitéphysique #coupedumondedusofa

Il y a trois minutes

Je préfère mon sucre avec un peu de café. Alors quoi? #monsieurbonbon

Détail grammatical

Trop

Trop est une quantité excessive.

Je mange **trop**. (Je mange excessivement.)

Tu dors 14 heures par jour? C'est **trop**. (Tu dors plus que nécessaire.)

Pour une quantité *de* quelque chose, utilisez **trop de**:

Tu manges **trop de** bonbons! Tu vas avoir besoin d'un dentiste!

Mon père a passé **trop de** temps au soleil et maintenant il est tout rouge!

Présenter des statistiques

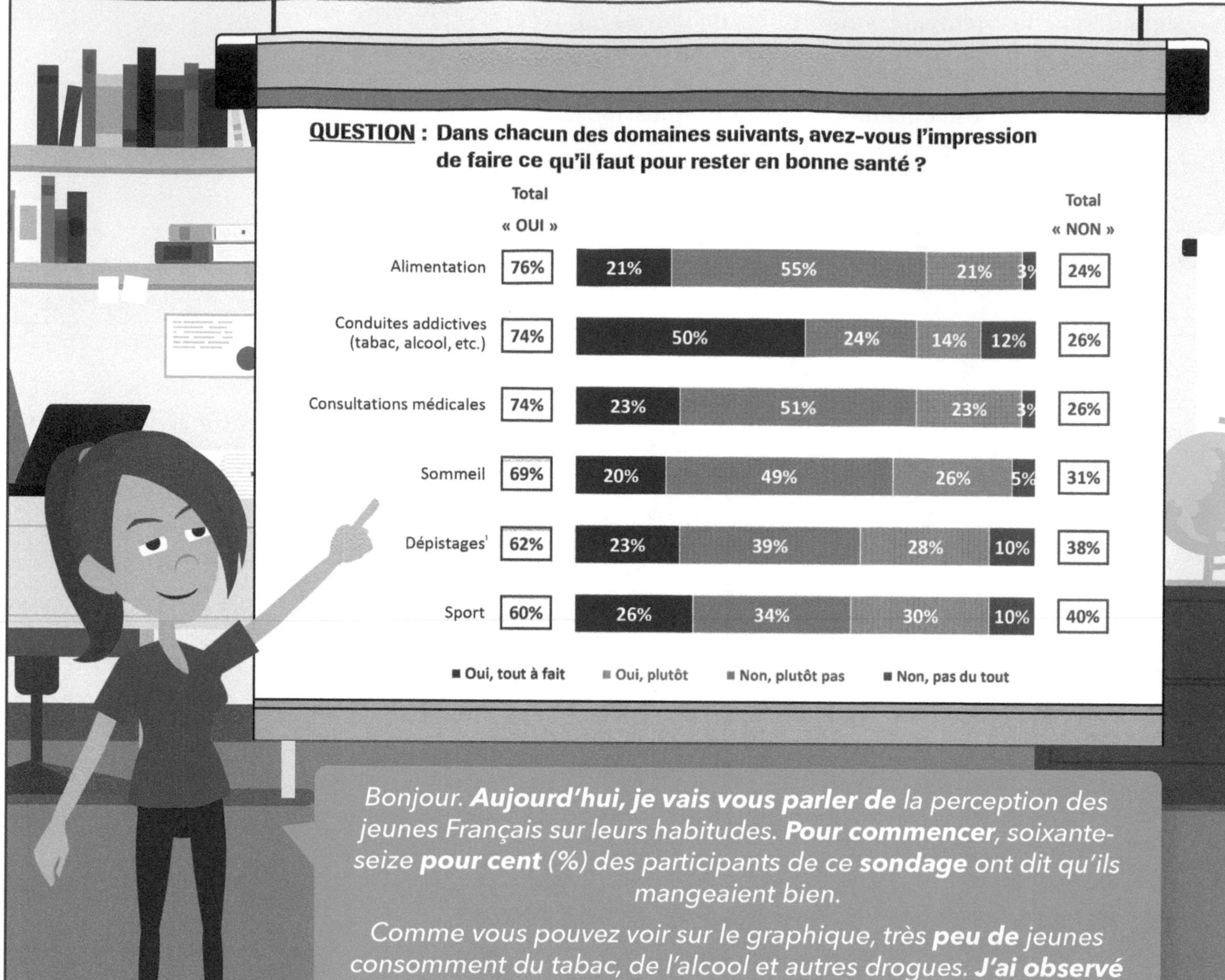

[1] *Screenings*

Expressions utiles

Comme vous pouvez (le) voir
J'ai observé que…
pour cent

Réflexion interculturelle

Look at the graph that Océane is presenting based on a survey of 18–25 year olds in France. Do you get the impression that young people in France have healthy habits? How do you think these answers compare to young people in your community? Answer the questions in the forum in Explorer.

Activité 8

Quelles autres informations peut-on voir?

Regardez le graphique qu'Océane présente.

a. Utilisez le nuage de mots pour écrire des phrases basées sur le graphique.

b. Utilisez les phrases d'Océane comme modèles.

la plupart (de) **dorment assez**
ont passé des consultations médicales
jeunes **soixante-quatorze pour cent (de)**
peu (de) **font des dépistages**

Étape 2: Présenter

Maintenant, organisez vos phrases de l'**Étape 1** et ajoutez des connecteurs. Présentez vos observations sur Explorer.

Dijon, France

I can understand perspectives related to a healthy lifestyle in Francophone countries and compare them to those in my community.

I can summarize the results of a survey in a short, organized presentation.

Stratégies

Delivering a Presentation

Avant de faire une présentation en français, il est important d'organiser et de bien préparer vos idées.

1. Organisez vos idées en quelques phrases avec des détails à l'appui.
2. Créez un support visuel qui vous servira de plan.
3. Utilisez le langage corporel, faites des pauses intentionnelles et maîtrisez le volume et le ton de votre voix.
4. Présentez une introduction et une conclusion solides avec des mots-clés et des transitions.

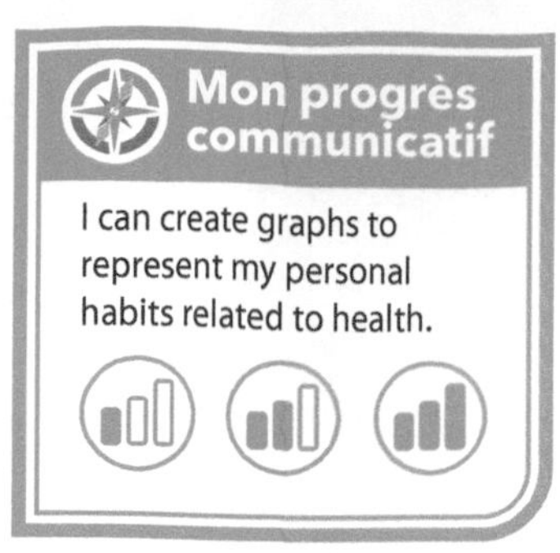

Activité 9

Comment sont mes habitudes à moi?

Étape 1: Réfléchir

Vous réfléchissez à vos habitudes de santé.

a. Pensez à la semaine dernière. Combien de fois avez-vous...?
   - assez dormi
   - passé un peu de temps au soleil
   - fait de l'exercice
   - grignoté

b. Créez un diagramme en bâtons pour représenter vos habitudes.

c. Pensez à votre dernier repas. Estimez les nutriments (par exemple, protéines, glucides, matières grasses, etc.) que vous avez mangés et représentez-les dans un camembert.

un diagramme en bâtons

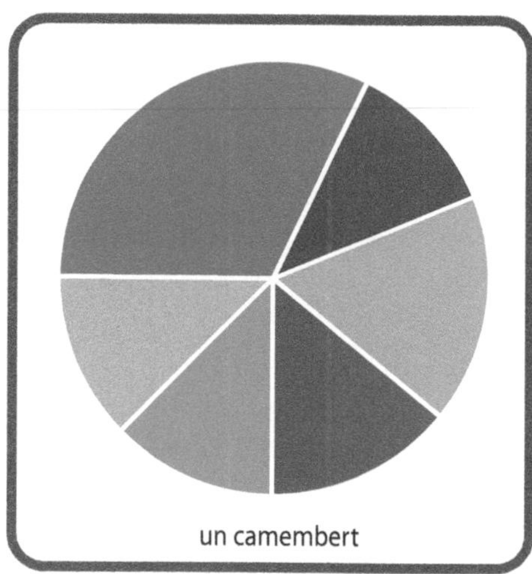
un camembert

Étape 2: Discuter

a. Posez des questions pour savoir les habitudes de votre groupe.

b. Répondez aux questions à l'aide de votre graphique.

c. Écoutez bien les autres élèves pour comparer et pour donner des conseils.

Modèle

–Combien de fois est-ce que tu as assez dormi cette semaine?

–J'ai bien dormi trois fois.

–Oh là là! Pas moi. Moi, je dors bien tous les jours. Il est important d'avoir un sommeil adéquat!

Zoom culture

Pratique culturelle: L'assurance maladie en France

  **Connexions**

When you go to a medical appointment, what kinds of records do you have to bring? How do people in your community pay for medical care?

En France, on considère que la santé, tout comme l'éducation, doit être accessible à tous. Le système de santé français est né après la Seconde Guerre mondiale (*WWII*) et il a été classé meilleur du monde par l'Organisation mondiale de la Santé (OMS) *[World Health Organization (WHO)]* en 2000. Il offre une couverture universelle, ce qui veut dire que toute la population a accès aux services de santé.

Comment ça fonctionne? Toute la population doit payer une assurance maladie obligatoire. Une prime (une somme à payer à l'assurance) est déduite automatiquement du salaire de tous les employés. En 2019, une visite médicale chez un généraliste coûte 25 euros et le système de sécurité sociale couvre la majorité (70% en général) du coût global [100% pour les problèmes médicaux qui durent longtemps *(long-lasting)*]. De plus, en France, il est possible d'avoir la visite du médecin à la maison.

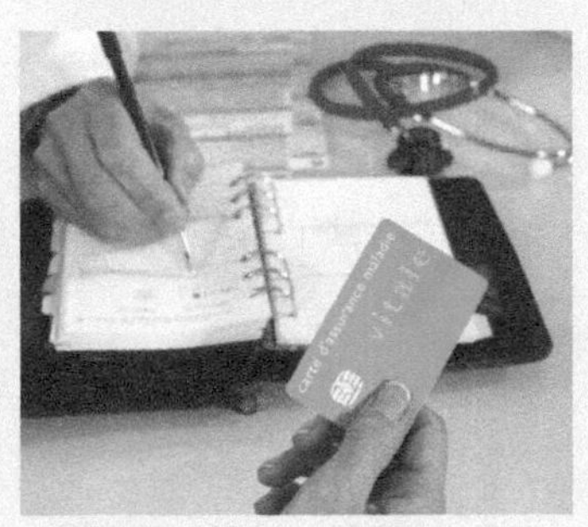
La carte vitale

Depuis 1998, les Français peuvent avoir une carte vitale. Cette carte a une photographie de l'assuré(e) et une puce électronique qui possède toutes les informations des visites médicales pour faciliter les transactions.

  **Réflexion**

For the French, health care is a national responsibility. What do you think about the health care system in your state or community? How does it compare to the one in France?

Découvrons 1

Giving General Advice

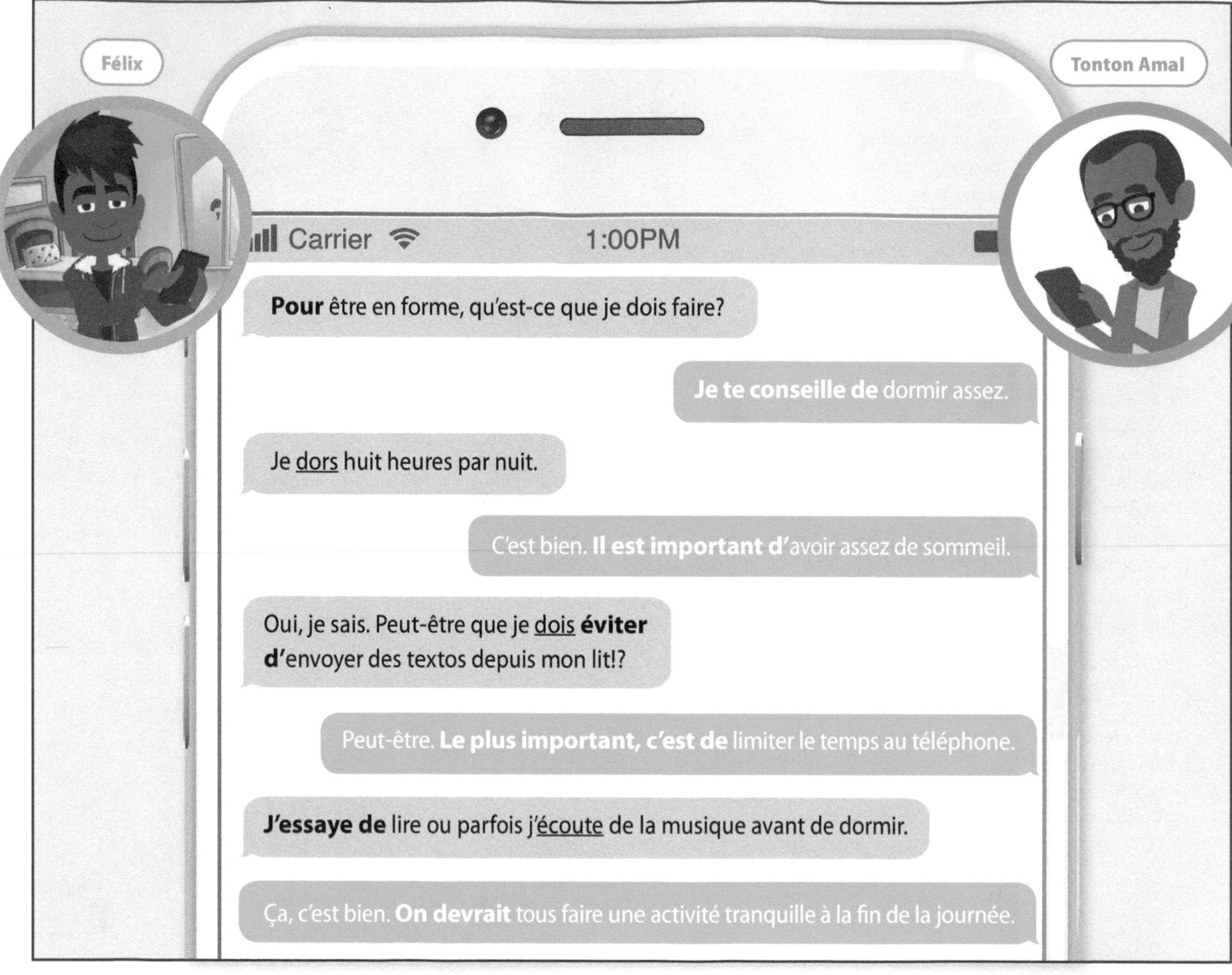

Découvertes

Reflect on what you observe and respond to the following items in the graphic organizer in Explorer.

1. Look at the words immediately following the expressions in bold. Do they have the ***-er, -ir, -re*** endings or are they in other forms?
2. Compare the words you examined in question 1 to the words ***dors, dois*** and ***écoute***. How are these words different?
3. Share your observations with a partner. What else do you notice together or what else can you add to your observations?

Activité 10

Quels sont les facteurs de risque de cancer?

Dans un journal québécois, vous voyez ce graphique qui présente les facteurs de risque de cancer et cela vous inspire pour créer une campagne de sensibilisation *(awareness campaign)*.

Étape 1: Lire

a. Lisez le graphique.

b. Avec un(e) partenaire, complétez chaque phrase avec sa suite logique de la colonne de droite *(right column)*.

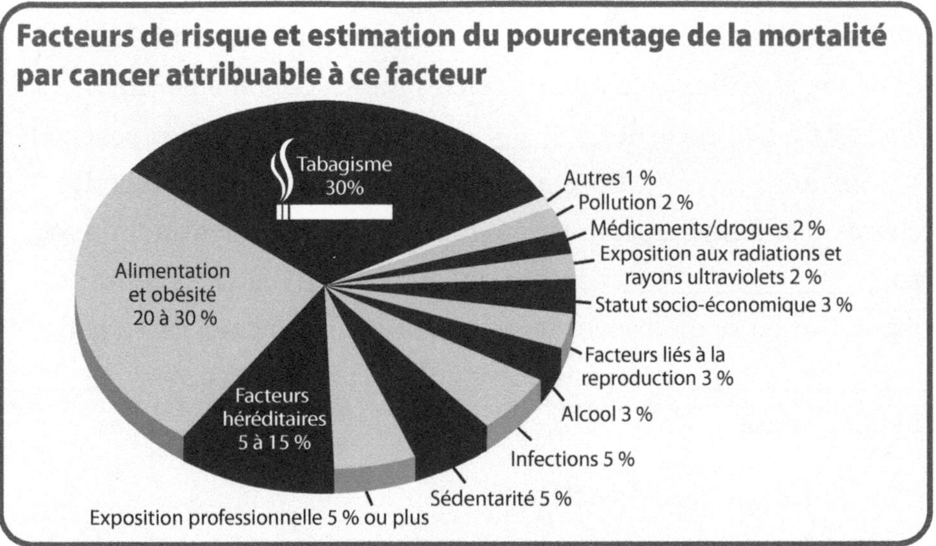

1. Seulement une petite proportion des cancers (15% ou moins) est liée…
2. La plus grande partie des cancers [environ 70%] est liée…
3. Ce camembert représente…
4. Le tabagisme est un facteur…

a. une estimation des facteurs de risque pour le cancer
b. dix fois plus dangereux que l'alcool
c. à l'hérédité (transmission par les gènes).
d. à des habitudes modifiables (par exemple, le tabagisme, l'alimentation, la sédentarité, l'alcool).

Étape 2: Créer une vidéo

a. Avec votre partenaire, choisissez un ou deux facteurs de risque qui vous semblent les plus importants.

b. Créez une vidéo pour donner des conseils à votre public. Utilisez des expressions de **Découvrons 1**.

Activité 11

Comment Mathew reste-t-il en bonne santé?

Étape 1: Écouter

Mathew vous explique comment il reste en bonne santé. Écoutez bien et complétez ce qu'il dit dans la vidéo.

Bonsoir, je suis ravi de vous retrouver aujourd'hui pour un autre vlog. Aujourd'hui, je vais répondre à la question "Que fais-tu pour rester en ________?", le ________ et ma routine. Alors, en ce qui me concerne, j'ai un cycle de ________ très régulier. J'essaye de me coucher aux mêmes heures, aux alentours de 10 à 11h, et de me réveiller aux mêmes heures aussi. Cela me permet d'avoir un bon cycle de ________ et de pouvoir bien me reposer, et d'avoir une ________. En ce qui concerne ma routine, je fais des choses très simples comme manger de bons repas matin, midi et soir, ________________, essayer de ne pas trop rester devant les écrans, et en ce qui concerne les saisons comme l'été, j'essaye de ________________ pour rester hydraté, ce qui me fait être en ________. Merci beaucoup.

Étape 2: Identifier

Louisa, la sœur de Mathew, parle de son frère mais elle invente beaucoup de choses! D'après la vidéo, déterminez si les commentaires de Louisa sont vrais ou faux.

1. Mathew aime rester en bonne santé.
2. Il va dormir régulièrement aux mêmes heures.
3. Il n'a pas un bon cycle de sommeil.
4. Il a trois repas par jour.
5. L'été, il prend beaucoup de boissons sucrées.

AP® Étape 3: Répondre

Mathew pose des questions sur vos habitudes. Répondez à ses questions.

J'avance 1

Et toi? Que fais-tu pour avoir une vie saine?

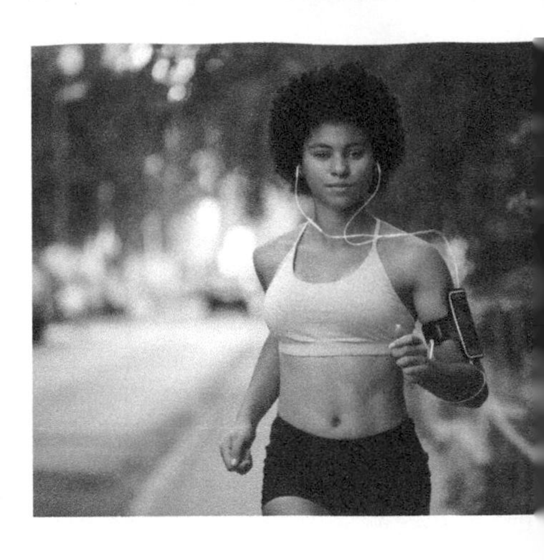

Vous avez trouvé une infographie qui donne des conseils pour une vie saine, mais vous vous demandez *(wonder)* combien d'autres élèves de votre classe suivent ces conseils.

Étape 1: Lire

Associez chaque comportement à un des troncs de l'infographie.

Étape 2: Poser des questions

Posez trois questions pour savoir si d'autres élèves de votre classe suivent ces conseils. Notez les réponses.

Étape 3: Présenter

a. Représentez les résultats de votre questionnaire dans un graphique logique.

b. Présentez vos recherches et expliquez votre graphique à un petit groupe d'élèves.

Allez sur Explorer pour trouver tous les documents nécessaires de **J'avance**.

I can understand recommendations for maintaining a healthy lifestyle from an infographic.

I can ask and answer questions about healthy habits.

I can summarize the results of a survey in a short, organized presentation.

Comment dit-on? 2

Aïe, j'ai mal!

Les parties du corps

Océane, Louis et Félix ne vont pas bien. Ils sont chez l'infirmier.

Expressions utiles

Ça fait mal.

Ça ne va pas du tout!

Qu'est-ce que tu as?

Activité 12

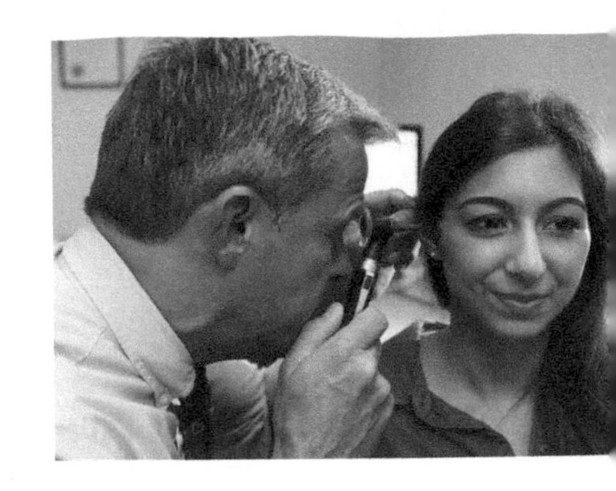

Où ont-ils mal?

Étape 1: Lire

Océane, Félix et Louis sont chez l'infirmier scolaire. Lisez ce qu'ils pensent ou ce qu'ils disent. Pour chaque partie du corps, écrivez le nom de la personne qui y correspond.

a.   b.  c.  d.  e.  f. 

Étape 2: Parler

Quelles sont les solutions que l'infirmier propose? Parlez à un(e) partenaire et donnez deux ou trois exemples.

Zoom culture

Pratique culturelle: Consulter le pharmacien

Connexions

What do you do when you are sick? Do you make an appointment with a doctor? Where do you go to get medicine or home remedies that help you feel better?

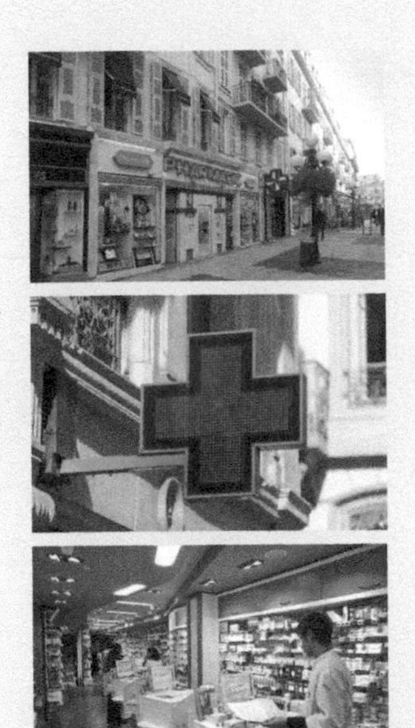

En France, on peut aller à la pharmacie au lieu d'aller chez le médecin. Les pharmaciens peuvent écouter les symptômes et prescrire des médicaments pour des problèmes de santé mineurs. Ils peuvent même vacciner contre la grippe.

Comment trouver une pharmacie en France? Cherchez la grande croix verte!

Avez-vous soif? On ne vend ni boissons, ni bonbons, ni jouets à la pharmacie française. On peut y trouver uniquement des médicaments et des produits de soin personnel. Les médicaments ne coûtent pas trop chers. Dans la plupart des pharmacies on trouve également des remèdes homéopathiques.

Si on est assez malade, on peut toujours prendre rendez-vous chez le médecin ou avoir une consultation de médecin à domicile! En plus, l'option moderne de la téléconsultation permet aux malades de rester au lit. Il y a beaucoup de possibilités pour ceux qui ne se sentent pas bien.

Réflexion

What do you think are the advantages and/or disadvantages of consulting a pharmacist rather than a doctor when you are feeling sick?

Réflexion interculturelle

In its simplest definition, what is a pharmacy? Consider some of the products and services available in pharmacies near where you live that may or may not be in line with that definition. Why do you think pharmacies in different parts of the world offer different products or services? Answer the questions in the discussion forum in Explorer.

Activité 13

On plante les choux avec le pied?

Écoutez cette comptine et identifiez l'ordre des parties du corps mentionnées dans la chanson.

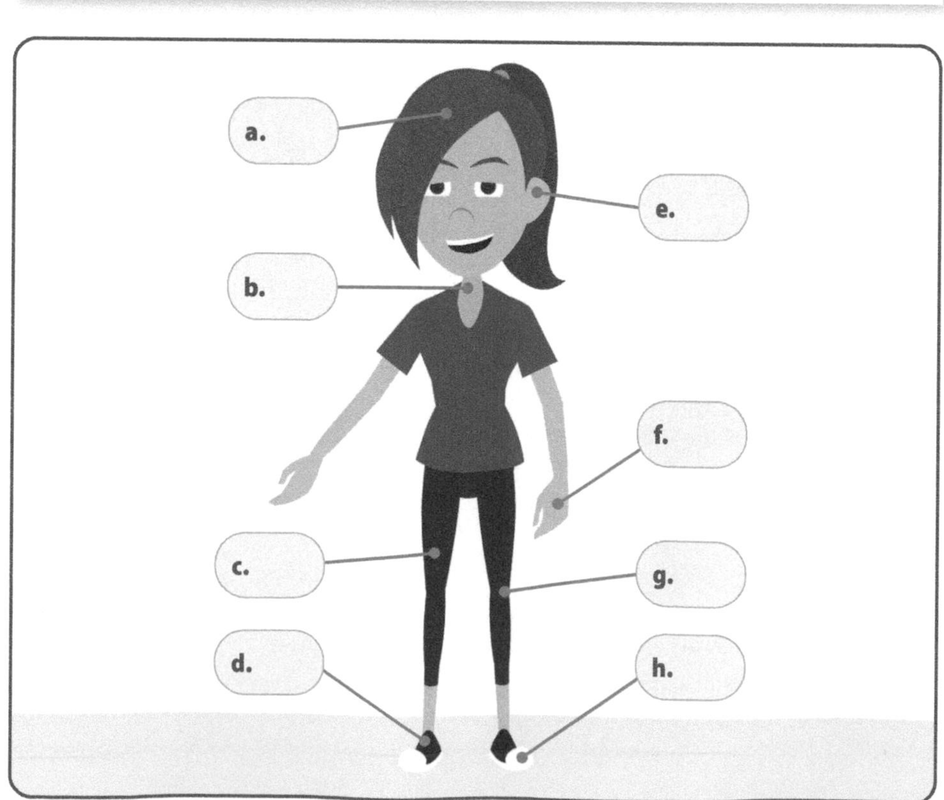

Rappel

Les parties du corps

la main

le pied

On peut aussi dire

la cheville
ankle

le coude
elbow

l'œil (m. s.)/les yeux (m. pl.)
eye/eyes

le poignet
wrist

Activité 14

Tu ne vas pas bien?

Votre ami a joué au foot le week-end dernier et il est tombé *(fell)*. Il vous envoie ces photos. Vous aidez votre ami à écrire un e-mail à l'école:

a. pour expliquer la situation; et

b. dire ce qu'il ne peut pas faire cette semaine à cause de l'accident.

Modèle

Bonjour Monsieur,

J'ai mal à la tête. Je n'arrive pas à faire mes devoirs.
Je ne peux pas aller à l'école.

Prononciation

L'élision

What happens when there are two vowel sounds together in French?

You have probably noticed that the French language tends to preserve a steady stream of alternating consonant and vowel sounds. There are several ways that this happens, including ***l'élision***, the elimination of a vowel sound (when speaking) and replacement of the written vowel with an apostrophe. ***L'élision*** is not the only way of maintaining a consonant-vowel pattern, and there are even some occasions when two vowel sounds *can* exist next to each other.

In the following transcription of a health podcast, see if you can determine the correct option for avoiding too many vowel sounds together. Listen to the recording and complete the pronunciation activity in Explorer.

> Qu'est-ce [que on/qu'on] doit faire pour éviter la maladie? Pour éviter [de être/d'être] malade, on peut adopter des gestes simples, comme faire de [le exercice/l'exercice]. Une personne qui ne tombe jamais malade a un système immunitaire plus fort parce [que elle/qu'elle] a [sa attitude/s'attitude/son attitude] positive et une vie équilibrée. [Si on/S'on] a faim, il est toujours mieux de manger [des aliments/d'aliments] riches en vitamines et [de essayer/d'essayer] de rester hydraté.

Les symptômes d'une maladie

Consultez nos médecins

Des conseils rapides

Je **suis malade**! Je **suis fatiguée**. Je n'ai pas d'énergie. J'**ai un rhume** depuis deux jours. J'**ai le nez qui coule**, j'éternue et je **tousse** sans cesse. Je n'**ai** pas **faim** et je ne peux pas manger. J'**ai de la fièvre** aussi. Ma température est de 38,2 °C! J'**ai chaud**! Est-ce que je devrais aller à l'école demain? Je suis stressée!

@Joséphineguitariste16

Désolée! Si tu as de la fièvre, il est important de dormir.

Ne va pas à l'école pour ne pas infecter les autres. Pour soigner un rhume ou la grippe, une maladie qui a des symptômes similaires, prends de la soupe ou une boisson chaude régulièrement.

Quand tu n'as plus de fièvre, tu peux bouger un peu (faire de l'exercice modéré ou faire une promenade) pour stimuler le système immunitaire. **Reste** bien **hydraté**. Il faut boire assez d'eau. **Consulte le médecin** aujourd'hui pour demander conseil.

Expressions utiles

avoir la grippe
bouger un peu
éternuer
soigner

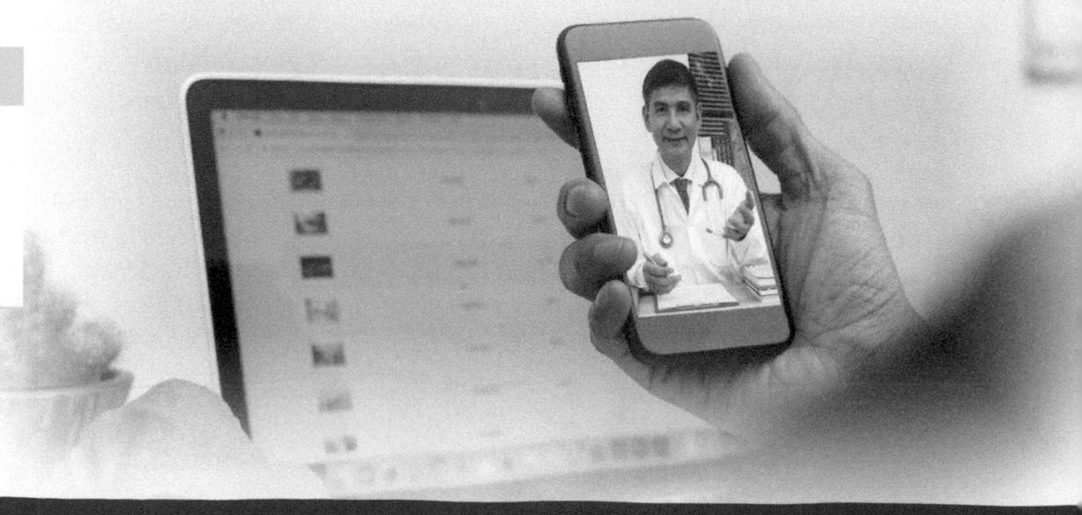

Activité 15

Qu'est-ce que tu as?

Étape 1: Écouter

Les élèves de l'école de Mathew ont des problèmes de santé. Écoutez-les et choisissez le bon conseil à envoyer à chacun.

1. Thuy
2. Christophe
3. Mahdi
4. Janine
5. Manon

a. Il faut bouger un peu et faire de l'exercice modéré.

b. Tu dois dormir. Reste au lit jusqu'au matin.

c. Il faut consulter le médecin aujourd'hui. Prends une boisson chaude.

d. Prends une soupe chaude qui a beaucoup de protéines.

e. Tu ne bois pas assez d'eau. Prends plus d'eau pour rester hydraté.

Étape 2: Converser

Vous voulez savoir ce que font les autres élèves quand ils sont malades.

a. Écrivez ce que vous faites quand vous avez chaque symptôme.

- mal à la tête
- stressé/stressée
- fatigué/fatiguée
- faim
- soif
- un rhume
- mal à la cheville

b. Posez les questions à deux autres élèves et notez leurs réponses.

Modèle

Qu'est-ce que tu fais quand tu es stressé(e)?

J'écoute de la musique ou je joue au basket quand je suis stressé(e). Et toi?

c. Écrivez trois phrases de comparaison entre les autres élèves et vous.

On peut aussi dire

avoir des allergies
to have allergies

l'énergie (f.)
energy

épuisé/épuisée
exhausted

être stressé/stressée
to be stressed

la maladie
illness

le symptôme
the symptom

Détail linguistique

Les expressions avec avoir et être

Many expressions related to health have a form that uses both ***avoir*** and ***être***, although sometimes their meaning is slightly different.

avoir faim
être affamé/affamée

avoir un rhume
être enrhumé/enrhumée

avoir soif
être assoiffé/assoiffée

avoir sommeil
être fatigué/fatiguée

Activité 16

Il a un rhume ou la grippe?

Étape 1: Écrire

Votre ami Pierre vous envoie un texto avant l'école. Il est malade!

a. Lisez l'affiche à côté de l'infirmerie de l'école.

b. Écrivez des questions à Pierre pour lui demander ses symptômes.

Modèle

Pierre, tu as de la fièvre?

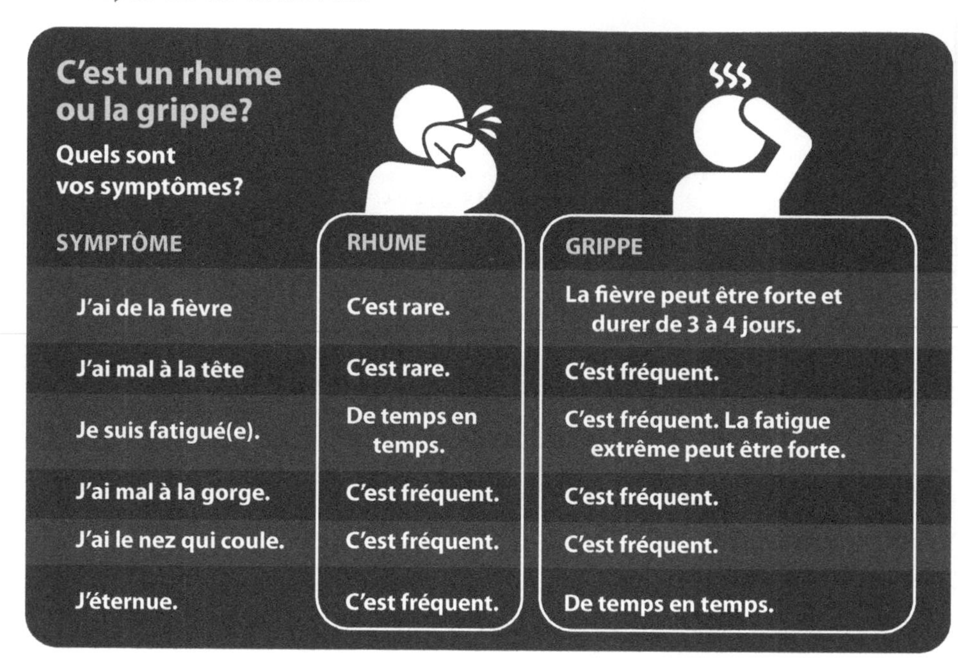

C'est un rhume ou la grippe?
Quels sont vos symptômes?

SYMPTÔME	RHUME	GRIPPE
J'ai de la fièvre	C'est rare.	La fièvre peut être forte et durer de 3 à 4 jours.
J'ai mal à la tête	C'est rare.	C'est fréquent.
Je suis fatigué(e).	De temps en temps.	C'est fréquent. La fatigue extrême peut être forte.
J'ai mal à la gorge.	C'est fréquent.	C'est fréquent.
J'ai le nez qui coule.	C'est fréquent.	C'est fréquent.
J'éternue.	C'est fréquent.	De temps en temps.

Étape 2: Écouter

En réponse à vos textos, Pierre vous laisse un message.

a. Écoutez le message de Pierre.

b. Notez les symptômes de Pierre.

Étape 3: Parler

Vous téléphonez à Pierre, mais il dort. Laissez un message sur son répondeur avec des conseils. Enregistrez votre message sur Explorer.

Modèle

Salut, Pierre! Je pense que tu as... Tu dois...

Découvrons 2

Telling Someone What to Do

Mathew et les autres élèves fêtent la semaine de la santé à l'école.

Découvertes

Reflect on what you observe and respond to the following items in the graphic organizer in Explorer.

1. What do you notice about the words in bold? Who is using these words? To whom are the speakers directing these words?
2. What similarities and differences do you observe between the forms of the words when they are used to talk to different numbers of people?
3. Where is the ***ne...pas*** placed? What do the sentences that use this mean?
4. Share your observations with a partner. What else do you notice together or what else can you add to your observations?

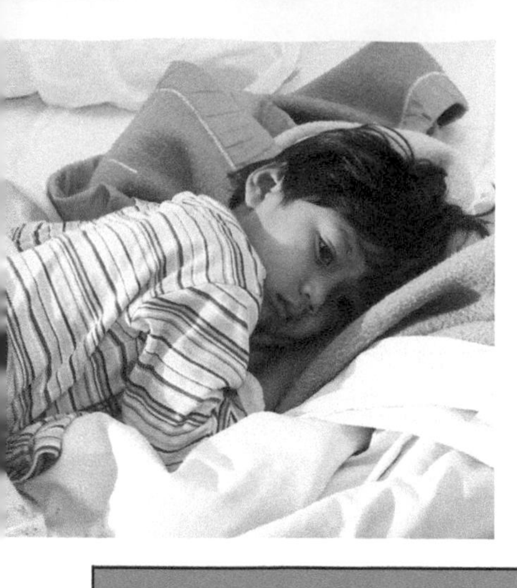

Activité 17

Peut-on éternuer sans contaminer les autres?

Étape 1: Lire et choisir

Lisez l'affiche. Choisissez une activité et faites des gestes pour mimer l'activité. Votre partenaire va deviner l'action. Puis, changez de rôle.

jetez le mouchoir à la poubelle	lavez-vous les mains
couvrez votre nez quand vous éternuez	éternuez dans le pli de votre coude

PROTÉGEZ LA SANTÉ DES AUTRES !

Tousser ou éternuer sans contaminer

1 Couvrez votre bouche et votre nez avec un mouchoir de papier lorsque vous toussez ou éternuez.

2 Jetez le mouchoir de papier à la poubelle.

3 Si vous n'avez pas de mouchoir de papier, toussez ou éternuez dans le pli de votre coude ou le haut de votre bras.

4 Lavez-vous les mains souvent. Si vous n'avez pas accès à de l'eau et du savon, utilisez un produit antiseptique.

SI VOUS ÊTES MALADE, ÉVITEZ DE RENDRE VISITE À VOS PROCHES.

sante.gouv.qc.ca

ENSEMBLE › on fait avancer le Québec

Québec

Étape 2: Classer

Les petits cousins de Mathew ont un rhume. Les pauvres! Décidez si les déclarations de Mathew sont pour:

a) un petit cousin ou b) ses deux petits cousins.

1. Couvre-toi le nez et la bouche avec un mouchoir quand tu tousses.

2. N'éternue pas dans tes mains si tu n'as pas de mouchoir.
3. Jetez le mouchoir à la poubelle.
4. En absence de mouchoir, tousse dans le pli du coude.
5. Éternuez dans le haut du bras.
6. Utilisez un produit antiseptique si ce n'est pas possible de vous laver les mains avec de l'eau et du savon.
7. Évitez le contact avec les autres.
8. Ne rends pas visite aux amis.

Activité 18

C'est un bon conseil ou un mauvais conseil?

Étape 1: Classer

Davinder veut jouer au tennis avec l'équipe de son école. Ses amis lui envoient des textos avec des conseils.

a. Lisez les conseils des amis de Davinder.

b. Avec votre partenaire, décidez si les conseils sont bons ou mauvais et expliquez pourquoi.

Modèle

C'est un bon conseil parce qu'il est important d'avoir un sommeil adéquat. Tu es d'accord?

1. Choisis des plats riches en matières grasses avant l'entraînement de tennis.
2. Ne dors pas moins de huit heures!
3. Fais des exercices de relaxation tous les jours.
4. N'invite pas les amis à jouer avec toi.
5. Ne joue pas au tennis quand tu as de la fièvre!
6. Prends des boissons sucrées avant les matchs pour avoir de l'énergie.

Étape 2: Écrire

Davinder veut envoyer des conseils à tous les membres de son équipe. Avec votre partenaire, aidez Davinder à écrire un e-mail aux membres de son équipe.

Utilisez les conseils de l'**Étape 1** et d'autres conseils créatifs.

Modèle

Pour rester en forme, limitez le temps devant les jeux vidéo.

Rappel

Le verbe dormir

We conjugate ***dormir*** in a similar way to other verbs you have seen.

dormir

je dors	nous dormons
tu dors	vous dormez
il/elle/on dort	ils/elles dorment

mettre

je mets	nous mettons
tu mets	vous mettez
il/elle/on met	ils/elles mettent

servir

je sers	nous servons
tu sers	vous servez
il/elle/on sert	ils/elles servent

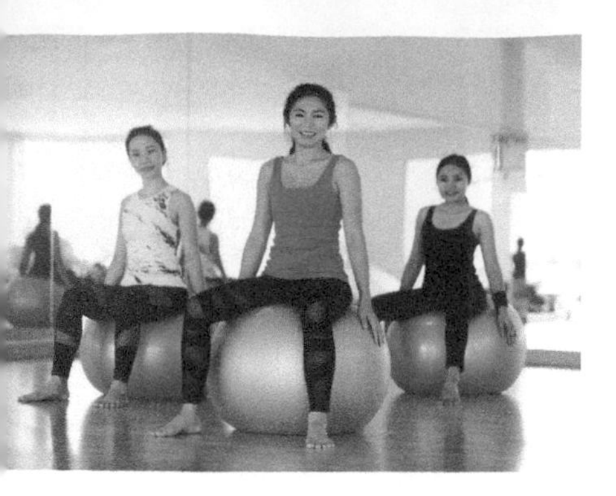

Activité 19

Tu as des idées pour moi?

Étape 1: Écouter et donner des conseils

Badou, Véronique et Paul, des élèves de Dijon, veulent rester en bonne santé. Ils cherchent des conseils.

a. Écoutez les messages des élèves de Dijon et prenez des notes.

b. Utilisez les images des solutions possibles pour écrire un texto de conseils à envoyer à chaque élève ou chaque groupe d'élèves.

1. Badou et Véronique
2. Paul
3. Paul
4. Badou et Véronique
5. Badou et Véronique
6. Paul

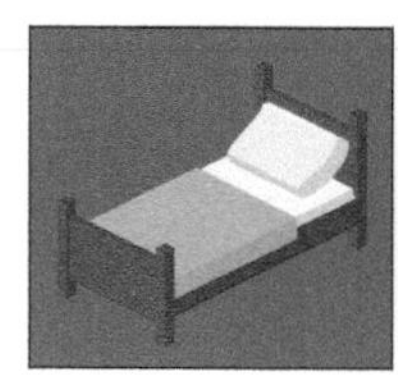    

Étape 2: Écrire

Après les échanges avec les élèves de Dijon, vous voulez créer une affiche pour encourager les membres de votre communauté scolaire à rester en bonne santé.

a. Écrivez trois conseils pour les membres de votre communauté scolaire.

b. Illustrez les conseils sur une affiche.

Modèle

Mangeons des fruits et des légumes tous les jours. Ne consommons pas trop de boissons sucrées.

Rappel

Le verbe manger

Just as we keep the ***e*** in ***je mangeais*** when describing what we used to eat, ***manger*** keeps the ***e*** in the ***nous*** form in ***le présent*** and ***l'impératif***. (E.g., ***Nous mangeons des fruits. Mangeons des produits bio!***) This is to keep the same soft ***g*** sound as in ***je mange***.

J'avance 2

Qu'est-ce que tu as?

Brenda est malade! Elle vous envoie des textos avant l'école. D'abord, répondez à Brenda. Ensuite, lisez un site web sur les symptômes de maladie pour aider Brenda. Finalement, laissez un message à Brenda avec des conseils.

Mon progrès communicatif

I can ask about symptoms and exchange information about what I and others do when we are sick.

  Étape 1: Répondre

Brenda vous envoie des textos avant l'école. Répondez aux textos de Brenda.

Mon progrès communicatif

I can understand recommendations on a website about what to do if one is sick.

  Étape 2: Lire

Pour aider Brenda, vous cherchez des informations en ligne.

a. Lisez un site web.

b. Répondez aux questions.

Mon progrès communicatif

I can give advice about how to feel better to someone who is sick.

Étape 3: Laisser un message

Téléphonez à Brenda et laissez un message. Dans le message, donnez trois conseils à Brenda pour soigner ses symptômes.

Allez sur Explorer pour trouver tous les documents nécessaires de **J'avance**.

Expressions utiles

réduire le stress
la veille

On peut aussi dire

un centre d'intérêt
interest (n.)

consacrer
to dedicate

prendre un bain (chaud)
to take a (hot) bath

un réveil
alarm clock

le sourire
smile

une tisane
herbal tea

Rappel

Pour parler du matin

à l'heure
en retard
le lit

Comment dit-on? 3

Le bien-être, c'est plus que le corps

Ma santé sociale et émotionnelle

Avez-vous un esprit sain dans un corps sain? Évaluez-vous en vous donnant un score de 1 (pas du tout) à 3 (tout le temps)!

LE MATIN

1.

Je **me réveille** à l'heure.

2.

Je **planifie** mes tâches pour la journée.

3.

Je garde le sourire pour réduire le stress et bien commencer la journée.

LA JOURNÉE

4.

Je consacre du temps à mes centres d'intérêts et mes **passe-temps**.

5.

Quand je **me sens** stressé(e) ou **tendu**(e), je **respire** et me concentre sur des pensées positives.

6.

Je **me repose** un peu après l'école.

7.
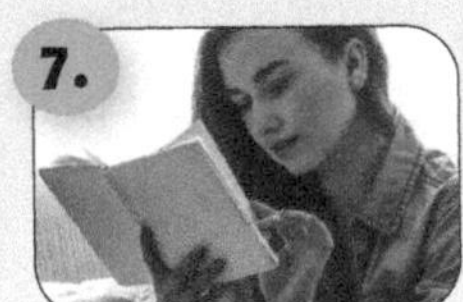
Je fais une activité sportive, je lis un livre, ou je passe du temps avec des amis pour **m'amuser**.

LE SOIR

8.

Je **me promène** après le dîner.

9.

Je **simplifie** ma routine du matin en préparant mes vêtements, mon sac à dos et mon déjeuner la veille.

10.

J'arrête de regarder **les écrans** une heure avant de dormir.

11.

Je prends un bain chaud ou je bois une tisane avant d'aller au lit.

12.

Je **me couche** avant 22h.

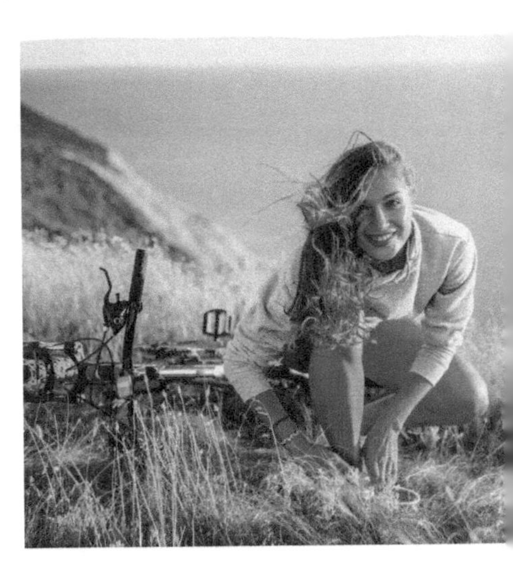

Activité 20

Est-ce que j'ai des habitudes saines pour une vie moins stressante?

Étape 1: Répondre

Complétez le quiz «Avez-vous un esprit sain dans un corps sain».

a. Donnez-vous un score (1–3) pour chaque numéro.

b. Calculez votre total.

c. Réfléchissez: Est-ce que vous avez de bonnes habitudes sociales et émotionnelles?

Étape 2: Écouter

a. Notez les habitudes mentionnées par chaque ami.

- Johann
- Adiouma
- Gabin

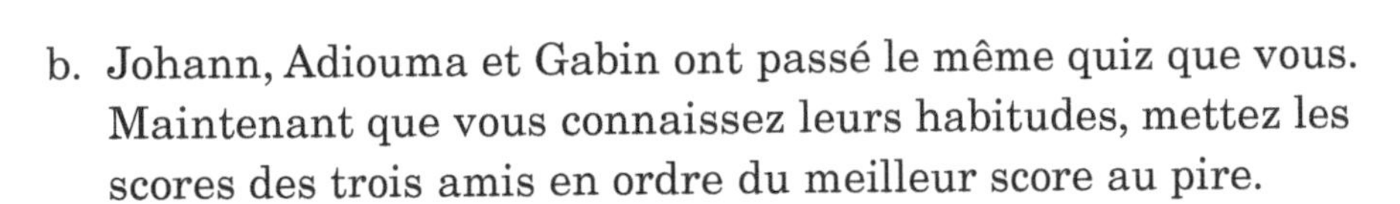

b. Johann, Adiouma et Gabin ont passé le même quiz que vous. Maintenant que vous connaissez leurs habitudes, mettez les scores des trois amis en ordre du meilleur score au pire.

- Qui a le meilleur score?
- Après, c'est qui?
- Qui a le pire score?

Étape 3: Écrire

Choisissez une personne de l'**Étape 2** qui a besoin de vos conseils. Écrivez-lui un e-mail où vous expliquez ce que vous faites pour éviter le stress et rester calme.

Modèle

Bonjour:

Je peux t'aider avec quelques conseils? Voici comment je reste en bonne santé émotionnelle...

Quelles sont leurs habitudes quotidiennes?

Étape 1: Regarder

Mathew et Brenda ont posté des vidéos sur un forum international de la santé sociale et émotionnelle.

a. Regardez leurs vidéos.

b. Cochez (✔) les habitudes de chaque élève.

	Mathew	Brenda
écouter de la musique		
faire beaucoup d'exercice		
limiter le temps devant les écrans		
lire des livres		
bien manger		
rester hydraté/hydratée		
se coucher à 10h ou 11h		
avoir un sommeil adéquat		
planifier sa journée		

Étape 2: Parler

Vous allez inviter des amis de votre classe à passer le week-end chez vous avant les examens. Vous voulez rester en bonne santé sociale et émotionnelle pendant le week-end. Proposez des activités pour le week-end. Acceptez ou refusez gentillement les idées de votre groupe.

Modèle

–Tu veux passer le week-end chez moi? On peut écouter de la musique. En plus, on peut...

–Bonne idée. Et peut-être aussi...

Activité 22

Combien d'heures de sommeil faut-il par nuit?

Étape 1: Lire

Regardez l'infographie et dites si chaque phrase est vraie ou fausse.

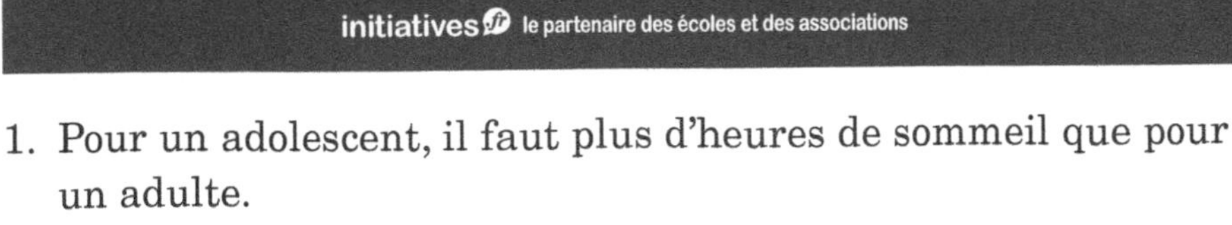

1. Pour un adolescent, il faut plus d'heures de sommeil que pour un adulte.
2. Les personnes âgées ont besoin de plus d'heures de sommeil que les enfants.
3. Pendant qu'on dort, le cerveau range et organise les souvenirs de la journée.
4. Un enfant de dix ans qui se lève à 7h du matin doit se coucher à vingt heures trente.
5. Pendant qu'on dort, une hormone est secrétée pour nous faire rêver *(dream)*.

Étape 2: Présenter

Avec un groupe, présentez les idées principales de l'infographie dans une vidéo. Enregistrez votre présentation sur Explorer.

La vie en ligne

Expressions utiles

communiquer
être accro à
isolé/isolée
J'ai appris (à)...
rire

On peut aussi dire

Quelques activités relaxantes

d'autres points (m. pl.) de vue
other points of view
faire du yoga
to do yoga
lâcher prise
to "let go"
se lever
to get up
méditer
to meditate
passer du temps seul/seule
to spend some time alone
tricoter
to knit

Activité 23

Combien de temps passez-vous devant un écran?

Étape 1: Lire et répondre

Votre professeur veut savoir pourquoi ses élèves sont très fatigués en cours. Utilisez l'infographie pour répondre aux questions de votre professeur.

1. Combien de collégiens se couchent après 22h pendant la semaine?
2. Combien de collégiens veulent dormir ou s'endorment en cours?
3. Combien de collégiens envoient des textos pendant la nuit?
4. Combien de collégiens utilisent des réseaux sociaux pendant la nuit?
5. Combien de collégiens ne passent pas de temps sur un écran après le dîner?

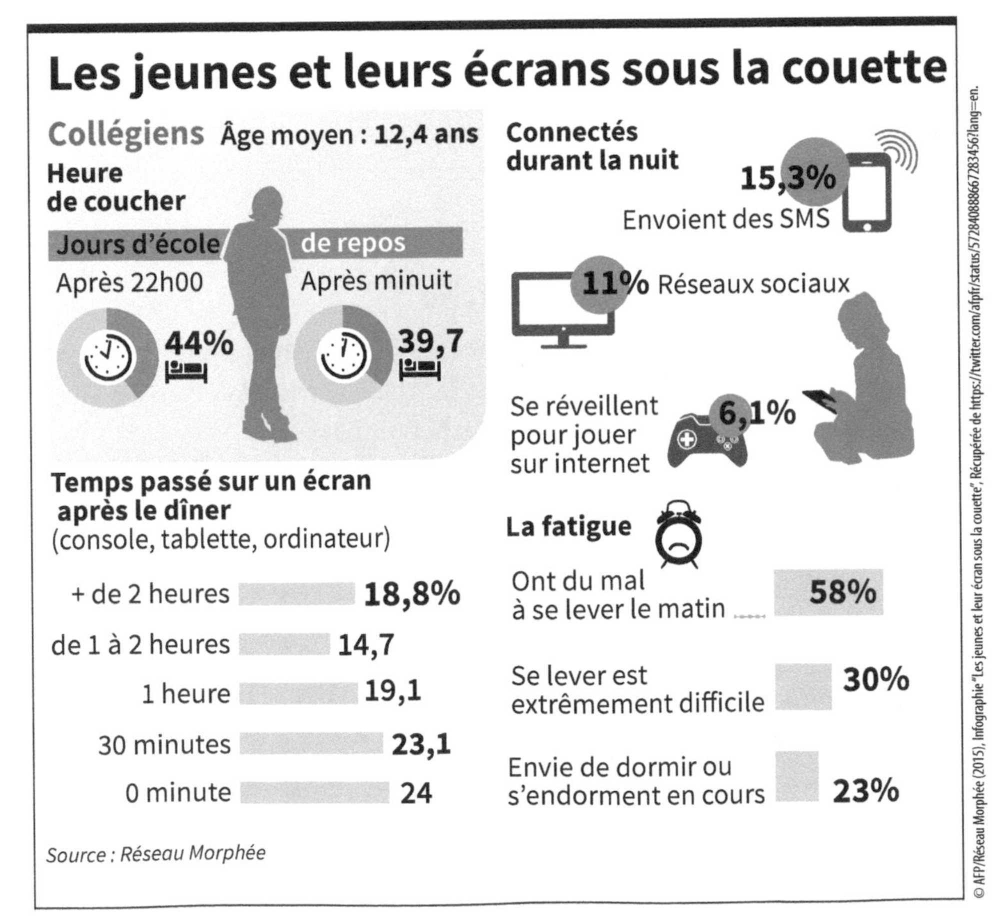

Étape 2: Répondre et demander

Votre professeur cherche plus d'informations sur les habitudes des élèves de votre école.

a. Répondez aux questions en phrases complètes dans la colonne "moi" de la représentation schématique.

b. Posez les questions à votre partenaire.

c. Notez les réponses de votre partenaire dans la colonne "mon/ma partenaire" de la représentation schématique.

	moi	mon/ma partenaire
1. En général, combien de temps passes-tu sur un écran après le dîner?		
2. Est-ce que tu t'endors en cours de temps en temps? En quel cours?		
3. Combien de temps passes-tu sur les réseaux sociaux chaque jour?		
4. Combien de temps passes-tu à envoyer des textos ou à jouer aux jeux vidéos chaque jour?		

Étape 3: Créer une affiche

Le proviseur de votre école veut publier des affiches pour encourager des habitudes saines de temps d'écran. Avec votre partenaire, créez une affiche. Sur l'affiche, mettez:

a. deux conseils utiles pour les élèves de votre école pour encourager de bonnes habitudes devant l'écran; et

b. des images.

Modèle

Passez moins d'une heure devant un écran après le dîner.

Utilisez les écrans pour communiquer avec des amis.

Mon progrès interculturel

I can understand practices and perspectives related to social and emotional health in Francophone cultures and compare them to those in my community.

Réflexion interculturelle

Look again at the infographic ***Les jeunes et leurs écrans sous la couette.*** Which of the statistics do you think would be similar or different if the students at your school were surveyed? What are some measures that you and your family have taken to address this issue? Answer the questions in the discussion forum in Explorer.

Activité 24

Vous êtes accro à votre smartphone?

Vous investiguez si les adolescents utilisent trop des réseaux sociaux et, si oui, comment combattre ce problème.

Étape 1: Regarder

Regardez la vidéo ***Réseaux sociaux, tous accros?*** Associez chaque statistique ou terme à sa définition.

1. la majorité
2. plus de quatre-vingts pour cent
3. 2h19
4. 1h23
5. accro
6. la dopamine

a. le nombre d'adolescents qui consultent leur smartphone avant de s'endormir

b. le temps qu'un Français moyen *(average)* consulte les réseaux sociaux

c. un adjectif qui désigne une personne qui a une addiction

d. le nombre de personnes de 18 à 34 ans qui consultent leur smartphone au réveil

e. le temps moyen qu'une personne regarde son smartphone

f. une molécule biochimique relâchée par nos cerveaux quand on reçoit des notifications ou des likes

Détail linguistique

Famille de mots: tendu

Observez la racine de cette famille de mots:

tendu/**tend**ue ≅ stressé/stressée, anxieux/anxieuse

se dé**tend**re ≅ se reposer

la **ten**sion ≅ le stress

Étape 2: Lire et discuter

Voici ce qu'un blogueur propose pour être moins accro à son smartphone.

a. Avec un(e) partenaire, mettez ses suggestions en ordre de la plus facile à la plus difficile.

b. Expliquez vos motivations et vos limitations pour être moins accro à la technologie.

Modèle

Je pense que supprimer des applications est facile pour moi parce que je veux simplifier ma vie. Et toi?

DÉFI: 7 JOURS POUR DÉCROCHER DE SON SMARTPHONE

JOUR 1 LUNDI – SIMPLIFIER Sur les réseaux sociaux, on se désabonne de tous les comptes qui sont toxiques ou inutiles. On supprime les applications qu'on n'utilise jamais.	**JOUR 2 MARDI – DÉSACTIVER** On désactive les notifications des réseaux sociaux et des mails.	**JOUR 3 MERCREDI – RÉSISTER** On résiste au désir de regarder son téléphone dès le réveil.	**JOUR 4 JEUDI – ÉLOIGNER** On charge notre téléphone en dehors de la chambre la nuit.
JOUR 5 VENDREDI – OUBLIER On va se promener ou faire les courses en laissant son téléphone à la maison.	**JOUR 6 SAMEDI – LIMITER** On passe la journée sans aller ni poster sur les réseaux sociaux.	**JOUR 7 DIMANCHE – DÉCROCHER** On éteint ou on laisse son téléphone dans un tiroir toute la journée.	

Découvrons 3

Describing My Routine

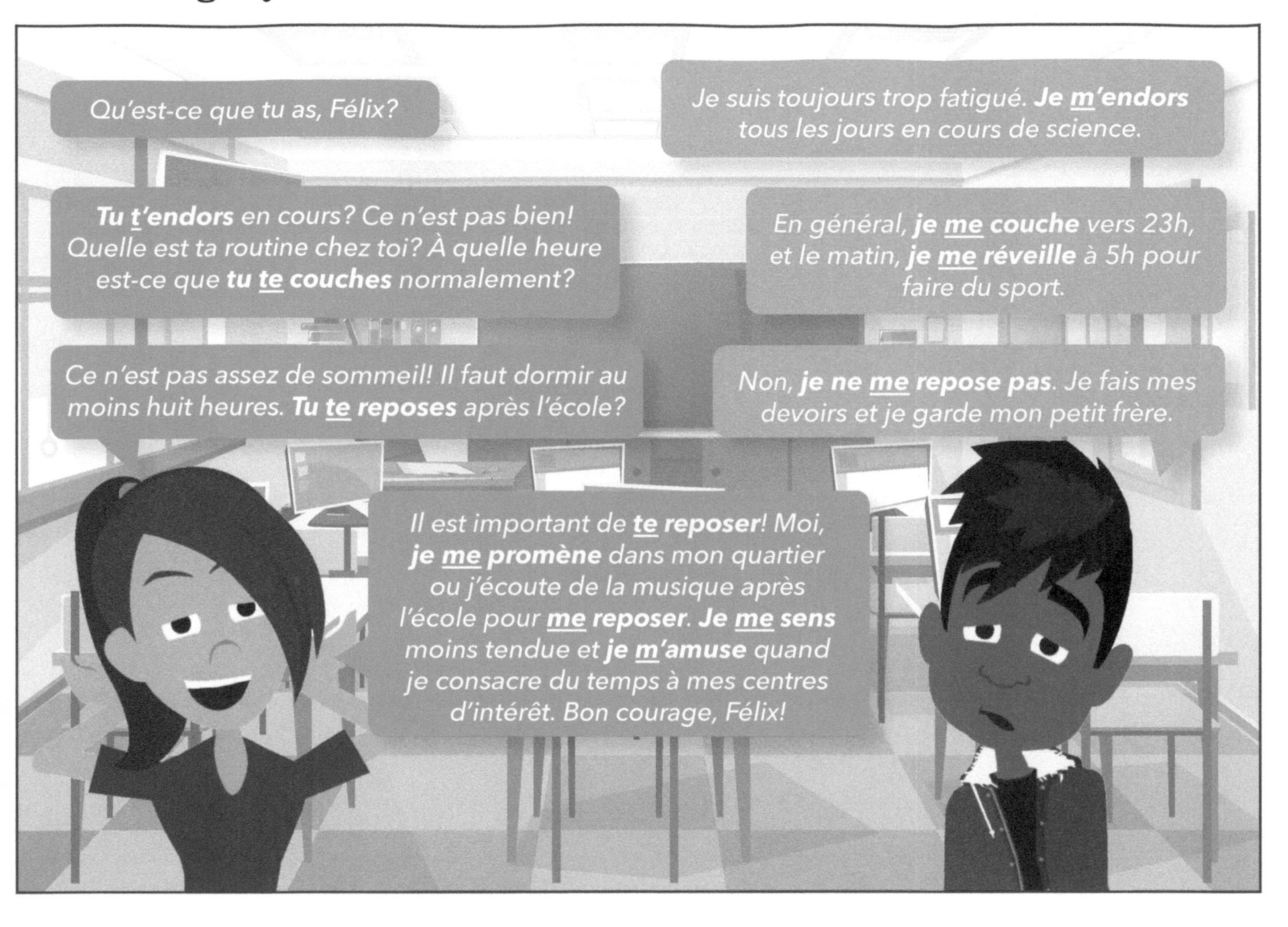

Découvertes

Reflect on what you observe and respond to the following items in the graphic organizer in Explorer.

1. What do you observe about the words in bold? How are they similar to or different from other verbs that you know?
2. Make a list of all of the underlined words that you see. How many are there? Do you notice a pattern between the words and the subjects with which they are used?
3. Look at the way the underlined words are listed in the vocabulary list at the end of the unit. How would you describe the way that they change from that list to the way they are shown here?
4. Share your observations with a partner. What else do you notice together or what else can you add to your observations?

Activité 25

Nous avons la même routine?

Étape 1: Écouter

Pendant un stage *(internship)* cet été, vous allez habiter avec un(e) colocataire *(roommate)*. Pour choisir un(e) colocataire, vous comparez votre routine avec la routine d'un autre élève.

a. Écoutez la routine d'été de Grégoire.

b. Notez l'heure de chaque activité.

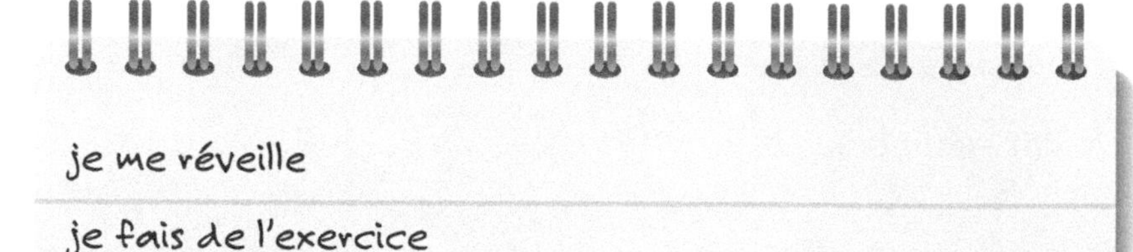

je me réveille

je fais de l'exercice

je prends le petit déjeuner

je travaille à la piscine

je me repose

je me promène

je me couche

je m'endors

Étape 2: Parler

Maintenant, créez une vidéo à envoyer à Grégoire pour parler de votre routine quotidienne en été.

a. À quelle heure est-ce que vous faites les activités?

b. Est-ce que vous voulez être colocataire de Grégoire? Pourquoi ou pourquoi pas?

Activité 26

À quelle heure est-ce que tu te réveilles le week-end?

Étape 1: Lire et indiquer

Est-ce que votre routine du week-end est différente de votre routine pendant la semaine?

Cochez (✔) les activités que vous faites pendant la semaine scolaire et pendant le week-end.

	la semaine (scolaire)	le week-end
Je me réveille avant 7h.		
Je me repose au moins 30 minutes.		
Je me promène tranquillement.		
Je me sens souvent tendu/tendue ou stressé/stressée.		
Je me couche avant 22h.		
Je m'endors rapidement.		

Étape 2: Écrire et poser des questions

Vous faites un sondage sur les habitudes et la routine des autres élèves de votre classe.

a. Choisissez un mot ou un groupe de mots de chaque colonne pour former une question.

b. Écrivez trois questions dans la représentation schématique à poser aux autres élèves.

À quelle heure		te promènes	le week-end
Quand	est-ce que tu	te réveilles	le lundi
Où		te couches	après l'école
Pourquoi		t'endors	à l'école
		te reposes	

Modèle

À quelle heure est-ce que tu te couches le week-end?

question	réponse de l'élève n°1	réponse de l'élève n°2	réponse de l'élève n°3

c. Posez vos questions aux autres élèves et notez leurs réponses dans la représentation schématique.

Activité 27

Quels conseils pour réduire son stress?

Étape 1: Écouter

Vous écoutez une interview dans un podcast où un expert du bien-être présente quelques astuces *(tips)* pour réduire le stress. Complétez les notes que vous avez déjà commencées.

Je simplifie ma vie avant de . . . .

Il est important de . . . . après le travail ou l'école.

. . . . un peu tous les jours

. . . . moins anxieux

Mon progrès communicatif

I can post a response to a podcast about habits related to good social and emotional health.

Étape 2: Écrire

Vous répondez au podcast avec un commentaire en ligne.

a. Expliquez quels conseils de l'expert vous suivez déjà.

b. Identifiez les conseils qui, pour vous, sont difficiles à suivre.

c. Posez au moins une question.

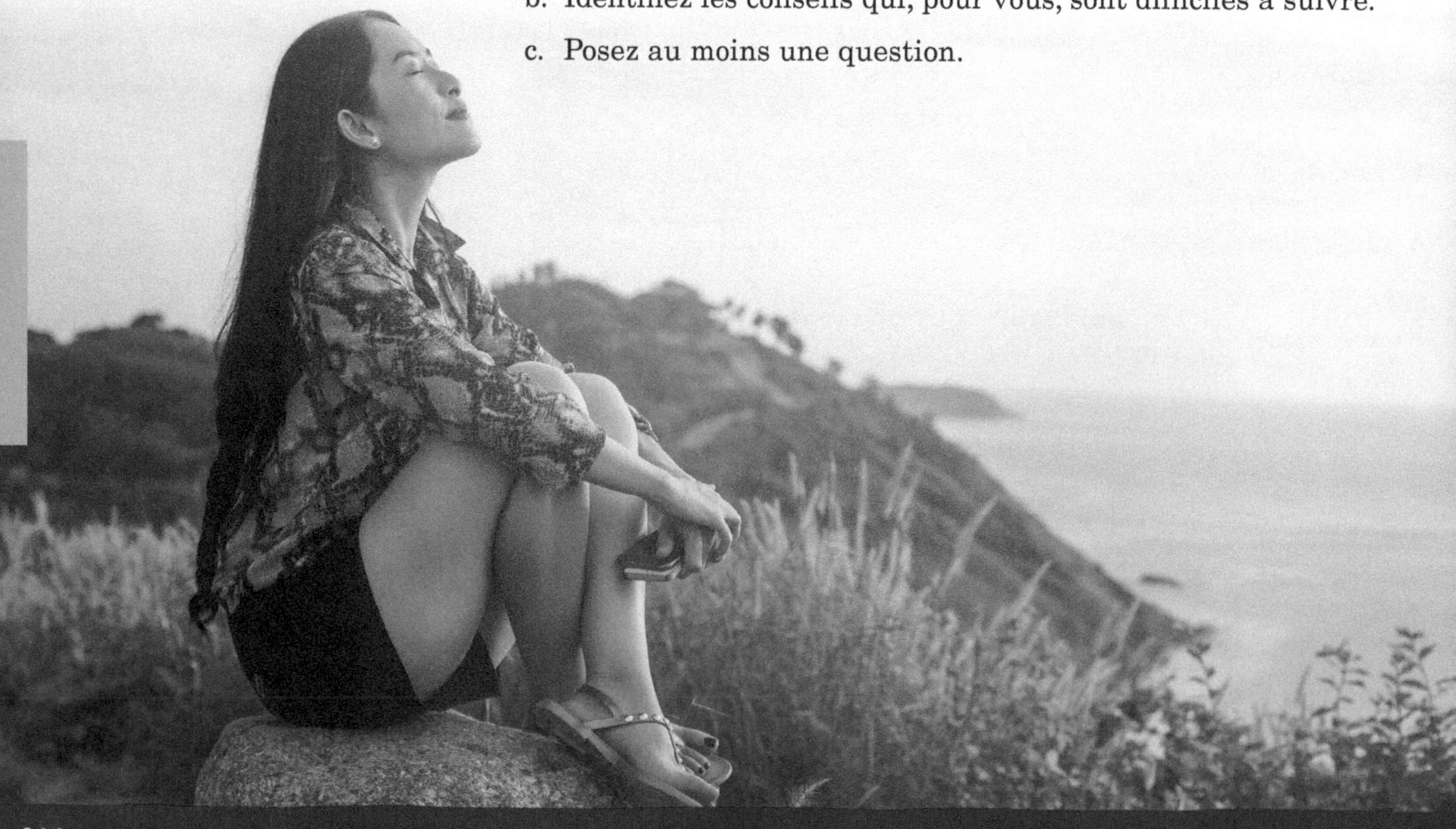

J'avance 3

Des ressources pour la santé sociale et émotionnelle de notre école

Un comité de professeurs veut créer un site sur la santé sociale et émotionnelle pour les élèves de votre école et ils ont demandé votre aide. Le comité veut y mettre des vidéos et une foire aux questions (FAQ).

Mon progrès communicatif

I can understand recommendations for maintaining social and emotional health in a video.

Étape 1: Regarder

Regardez la vidéo professionnelle que le comité de professeurs a choisie.

a. Dans la représentation schématique, identifiez les aspects positifs et négatifs mentionnés dans la vidéo.

b. Puis, donnez votre avis. Est-ce que le comité doit inclure cette vidéo sur le site?

Mon progrès communicatif

I can ask and answer questions about my habits related to social and emotional health.

Étape 2: Discuter

Maintenant, créez une vidéo de la perspective des élèves. Filmez une interview avec un(e) partenaire où vous vous interrogez sur vos habitudes de bonne santé sociale et émotionnelle.

Étape 3: Écrire

Écrivez quelques possibilités pour la page FAQ (foire aux questions) sur le site web. Écrivez des questions et vos réponses.

Allez sur Explorer pour trouver tous les documents nécessaires de **J'avance**.

Mon progrès communicatif

I can write questions and answers related to maintaining social and emotional health for a Frequently Asked Questions (FAQ) page.

Synthèse de grammaire

1. Giving General Advice: *l'infinitif après certaines expressions*

In many cases, verbs must be changed or conjugated according to their subject. On the other hand, there are a number of situations in which the use of the ***infinitif*** or "un-conjugated" form of the verb is the appropriate form to use. You can recognize the ***infinitif*** by its ***-er***, ***-ir***, or ***-re*** ending.

a. After another verb that is conjugated: Je devrais **manger** des produits bio. Tu aimes **faire** de l'exercice?

b. After the word ***pour***: Je fais de l'exercice pour **être** en bonne santé. Elle prend son temps pour bien **digérer**.

c. After certain verbs or expressions followed by the preposition ***de (d')***, such as:

éviter de	Il est important de...
essayer de	Le plus important, c'est de...
conseiller de	

Je te conseille de **consommer** moins de sucre. Il est important d'**éviter** le fast-food.

2. Telling Someone What to Do: *l'impératif*

When telling someone what to do or giving a direct command or advice, use ***l'impératif***. The imperative has just three conjugated forms:

Fais de l'exercice.	*Exercise.*	(tu)
Choisissons un sport actif!	*Let's choose an active sport!*	(nous)
Restez hydratés!	*Stay hydrated!*	(vous)

The formation of ***l'impératif*** is the generally the same as the regular conjugation of the ***tu, nous,*** or ***vous*** forms in the present tense.

For verbs that end in ***-er***, the ***tu*** form of ***l'impératif*** is formed by dropping the ***s*** from the present tense conjugation. The ***nous*** and ***vous*** forms are the same as the present tense conjugation.

Manger tu manges *(you eat)* **Mange!** *Eat!*

To tell someone *not* to do something, place the ***ne...pas*** around the verb in ***l'impératif***.

Ne **dors** pas!	*Don't sleep!*	(tu)
Ne **prenons** pas de boissons sucrées.	*Let's not have sugary drinks.*	(nous)
N'**utilisez** pas votre portable.	*Don't use your cell phone.*	(vous)

3. Describing My Routine: *les verbes pronominaux*

Many activities that are part of our daily habits and routine are expressed through reflexive verbs, which are a type of pronominal verb.

Je me réveille à 6h. — *I wake up at 6:00.*

À quelle heure est-ce que **tu te réveilles**? — *At what time do you wake up?*

Mon frère, **il se réveille** tard, vers 10h. — *My brother wakes up late, around 10:00.*

You form pronominal verbs the same way that you form other verbs in ***le présent, l'imparfait***, ou ***le passé composé*** or ***l'infinitif***. Pronominal verbs, though, have a pronoun that goes directly before the verb. The pronoun must agree with the subject.

je	me	couche
tu	te	couches
il/elle/on	se	couche

The pronouns contract to ***m', t'***, and ***s'*** when followed by a verb that starts with a vowel.

je	m'	amuse
tu	t'	amuses
il/elle/on	s'	amuse

Je me suis réveillé(e) tard hier.

Tu te promènes dans le quartier de temps en temps?

Mon grand-père s'endormait tôt quand il était petit.

J'aime me coucher tard le week-end.

To use a pronominal verb in the negative, place the ***ne*** in front of the pronoun and the ***pas*** after the conjugated verb.

Je ne **m'endors** pas en cours.

Tu ne **te reposes** pas après l'école?

Elle ne **se sent** pas bien.

Vocabulaire

Comment dit-on? 1: I can describe ways that people stay healthy.

Des habitudes saines	***Healthy habits***
l'aliment (m.)	*food*
dormir assez	*to get enough sleep*
équilibré/équilibrée	*balanced*
essayer de	*to try to*
éviter de	*to avoid*
faire de l'exercice	*to exercise*
limiter	*to limit*
sain/saine	*healthy*
le sommeil	*sleep*
trop de	*too much (of)*

Expressions utiles	
Comme vous pouvez (le) voir	*As you can see*
J'ai observé que...	*I observed that...*
pour cent	*percent*

Expressions utiles	
dire "non" à	*to say "no" to*
Il est important de...	*It's important (to)...*
Le plus important, c'est (de)...	*The most important thing is (to)...*
On devrait...	*We should.../People should.../One should...*
riche en...	*rich in...*

Pour faire une présentation	***Giving a presentation***
Aujourd'hui, je vais vous parler de...	*Today, I will speak to you about...*
En somme,	*In summary,*
Merci de votre attention.	*Thank you for your attention., Thank you for listening.*
peu de	*few*
la plupart	*the majority, most*
Pour commencer,	*To begin with,*
le sondage	*survey*

Comment dit-on? 2: I can describe symptoms of sickness and give advice for how to feel better.

Les parties du corps	***Parts of the body***
le cou	*neck*
le genou	*knee*
la gorge	*throat*
la jambe	*leg*
l'oreille (f.)	*ear*
la tête	*head*
le ventre	*tummy, belly*

Pour exprimer la douleur	***Expressing pain***
avoir mal + au/à la/à l'/aux + [partie du corps]	*["body part"] hurts, aches*
ne pas arriver à	*to not be able to*

Expressions utiles	
Ça fait mal.	*That hurts.*
Ça ne va pas du tout.	*It's not going well at all.*
Qu'est-ce que tu as?	*What's wrong?*

Les symptômes	*Symptoms*
avoir chaud	*to feel hot*
avoir de la fièvre	*to have a fever*
avoir faim	*to be hungry*
avoir le nez qui coule	*to have a runny nose*
avoir un rhume	*to have a cold*
avoir soif	*to be thirsty*
être fatigué/fatiguée	*to be tired*
être malade	*to be sick*
tousser	*to cough*

Les conseils	*Advice*
consulter le médecin	*to consult the doctor*
rester hydraté/hydratée	*to stay hydrated*

Expressions utiles	
avoir la grippe	*to have the flu*
bouger un peu	*to move (around) a little bit*
éternuer	*to sneeze*
soigner	*to treat, to take care of*

Comment dit-on? 3: I can discuss ways that people maintain their social and emotional health.

La santé sociale et émotionnelle	*Social and emotional health*
s'amuser	*to have fun*
se coucher	*to go to bed*
l'écran (m.)	*screen*
le passe-temps	*hobby, pastime*
planifier	*to plan*
se promener	*to take a walk*
se reposer	*to relax*
respirer	*to breathe*
se réveiller	*to wake up*
se sentir	*to feel*
simplifier	*to simplify*
tendu(e)	*tense*

La vie en ligne	*Life online*
anxieux/anxieuse	*anxious*
l'appli(cation) (f.)	*app(lication) (on smartphone or tablet)*
s'endormir	*to fall asleep*
le réseau social	*social media*
rester connecté/connectée	*to stay connected*

Expressions utiles	
communiquer	*to communicate*
être accro (à)	*to be addicted (to)*
isolé/isolée	*isolated*
J'ai appris (à)...	I learned (to)...
réduire le stress	*to reduce stress*
rire	*to laugh*
la veille	*the day before*

J'y arrive

Questions essentielles

- How do people where I live and in Francophone cultures take care of their physical health?
- How do people address concerns with their health?
- How do people where I live and in Francophone cultures view social and emotional health?

Une présentation sur la santé des adolescents

Votre classe participe à une conférence virtuelle sur la santé adolescente. D'abord, il faut faire des recherches: vous allez regarder une vidéo. Puis, vous allez présenter un webinaire sur un sujet connecté à la santé. Après la présentation, vous devez répondre aux questions que l'on vous pose.

Avant de commencer, référez-vous à Explorer pour vous familiariser avec les critères d'évaluation de **J'y arrive**.

Interpretive Assessment

Que faut-il faire pour avoir un sommeil adéquat?

Regardez la vidéo de Vulgaris Médical (www.vulgaris-medical.com).

a. Complétez les phrases pour résumer le détail qui correspond à chaque illustration de la vidéo.

b. Notez deux autres détails de la vidéo qui ne sont pas représentés sur les images.

Presentational Assessment

 Je présente les informations

Créez une vidéo où vous présentez des conseils sur la santé adolescente. Organisez bien votre présentation:

- Commencez par une introduction.
- Présentez quelques idées avec des détails ou des statistiques intéressantes.
- Utilisez l'information de la vidéo ou faites des recherches sur un autre sujet de votre choix.
- Utilisez des connecteurs.
- Terminez logiquement.

Interpersonal Assessment

  Encore des questions

Posez des questions aux autres présentateurs de votre classe et répondez aux questions que l'on vous pose suite à votre présentation.

UNITÉ 6

Voyager autrement

Objectifs de l'unité

Read, view, and listen to informational texts such as announcements, videos, and personal stories about world travel.

Participate in an interview in which you discuss your travel plans.

Provide information about yourself in order to apply for a travel scholarship.

Investigate how and why people travel around the world for more than just tourism.

Questions essentielles

What do I need to know to explore another country or culture?

What is the difference between a tourist and a traveler?

How do travel experiences shape our intercultural understanding and respect for the communities we visit?

There's more than one way to travel! Taking pictures and visiting famous sites is certainly fun, but the world has more to offer to those who are willing to go a bit deeper into the culture. In this unit, Brenda will share information about where and how she travels.

Nom: Brenda

Langues parlées: français, éwé, anglais

Origine: Yaoundé, Cameroun

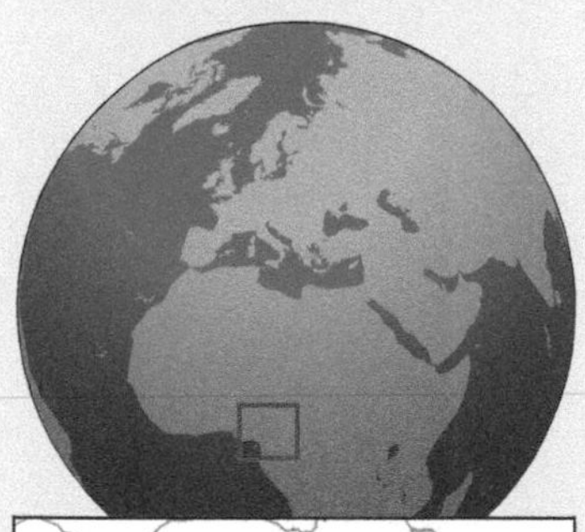

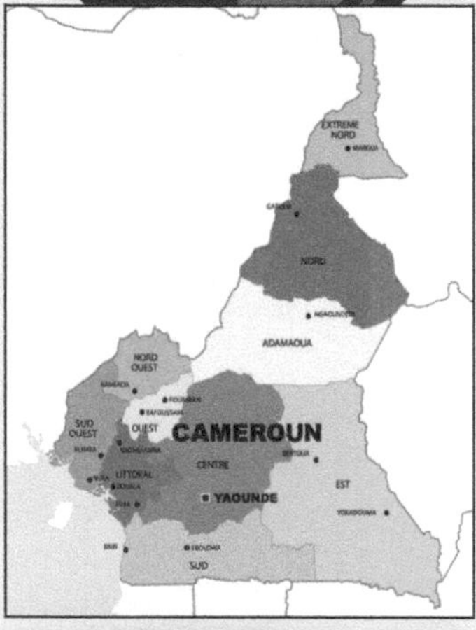

Le drapeau du Cameroun

Rencontre interculturelle

Le Cameroun

Le Cameroun est un pays d'Afrique centrale qui a beaucoup de diversité culturelle et géographique. Il est situé entre le Nigéria, le Tchad, la République centrafricaine, le Gabon, la Guinée équatoriale et la république du Congo. Sa plus grande ville, Douala, est bordée par le golfe de Guinée. L'autre grande ville camerounaise est Yaoundé, la capitale. Il y a plus de 240 langues parlées au Cameroun. Les deux langues officielles sont le français et l'anglais.

Les animaux, tels que les caméléons, les gorilles, les chèvres, les suricates et les girafes, profitent de l'environnement riche et varié du pays.

Mais il n'y a pas seulement de la nature au Cameroun. La population camerounaise apprécie beaucoup les sports, notamment le football, la boxe, l'athlétisme et le handball. Il y a également un tour cycliste tous les ans. Et pour les plus courageux, il y a l'ascension du mont Cameroun!

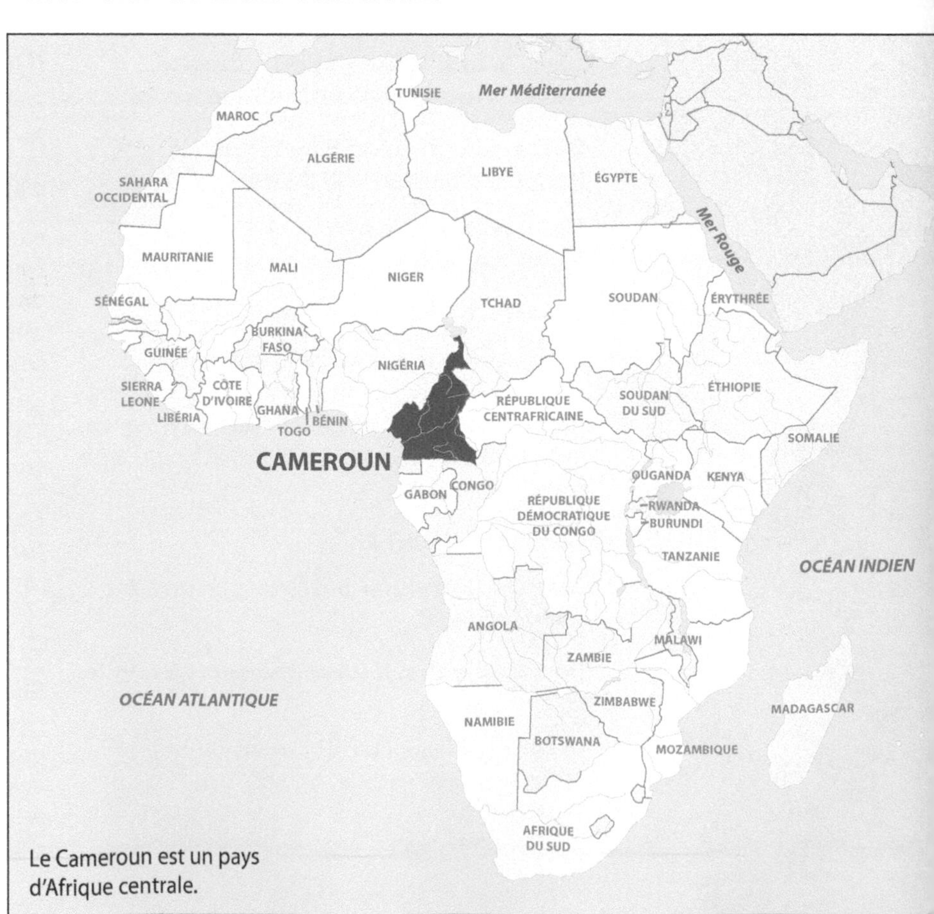

Le Cameroun est un pays d'Afrique centrale.

Le football est un sport très important au Cameroun.

Un caméléon feuille (bien camouflé!) sur une branche

blickwinkel / Alamy Stock Photo

L'équipe de foot camerounaise s'appelle les Lions indomptables *(untamable)*.

Alan Smith / Alamy Stock Photo

Olivier Asselin / Alamy Stock Photo

Au Cameroun, il y a des plages, des montagnes, des volcans, des chutes d'eau, des fleuves et des forêts. Grâce à sa beauté et à sa diversité naturelle, il y a beaucoup d'écotourisme au Cameroun, centré sur la découverte et la protection de la nature.

Les plages de Douala

Les chutes d'Ekom dans la forêt tropicale.

Le mont et le lac Oku

Des suricates curieux

Limbé, Cameroun

Activité 1

Le pays de Brenda

Lisez les informations dans la **Rencontre interculturelle** et notez les informations importantes dans les catégories de la représentation schématique sur Explorer.

le Cameroun	
catégorie	**informations mentionnées**
pays voisins	
villes	
nature	
animaux	
langues	
activités	

Je m'appelle Brenda.

Je suis née le 29 décembre.

Je parle le français, l'éwé et l'anglais.

J'aime l'école.

Je joue du piano à la maison.

Brenda et sa famille viennent du Cameroun. Elle a aussi habité au Togo. Elle parle trois langues. Elle a une petite sœur et un petit frère. Elle aime la musique, alors elle joue du piano.

Yaoundé, Cameroun

Activité 2

Bonjour, Brenda!

Étape 1: Lire et écrire

Lisez les informations de Brenda et regardez sa vidéo. Notez ce qu'elle dit dans les catégories qui correspondent dans la représentation schématique sur Explorer.

catégorie	ce que dit Brenda
âge	
famille	
activités	
pays d'origine	

Étape 2: Écouter et écrire

Parlez avec un(e) partenaire sur les aspects que Brenda a en commun avec les autres blogueurs. Notez les similarités dans la représentation schématique sur Explorer. Choisissez un ou deux blogueurs ou tous les cinq.

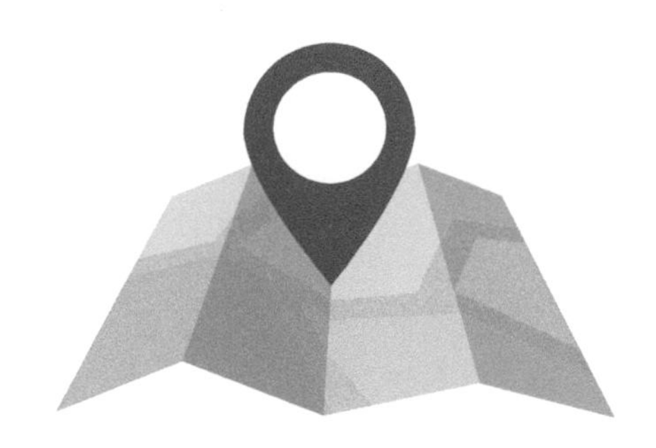

Réflexion interculturelle

If anything were possible, to which destinations in the Francophone world would you prefer to travel and why? What would you hope to gain from traveling to those destinations? What similarities and differences would you expect to notice? Answer the questions in the discussion forum in Explorer.

Rappelle-toi

Activité 3

 **Quel temps fait-il?**

Vous considérez des destinations pour les vacances à différents moments de l'année prochaine.

a. Regardez les photos.

b. Écrivez le temps qui correspond à chaque destination.

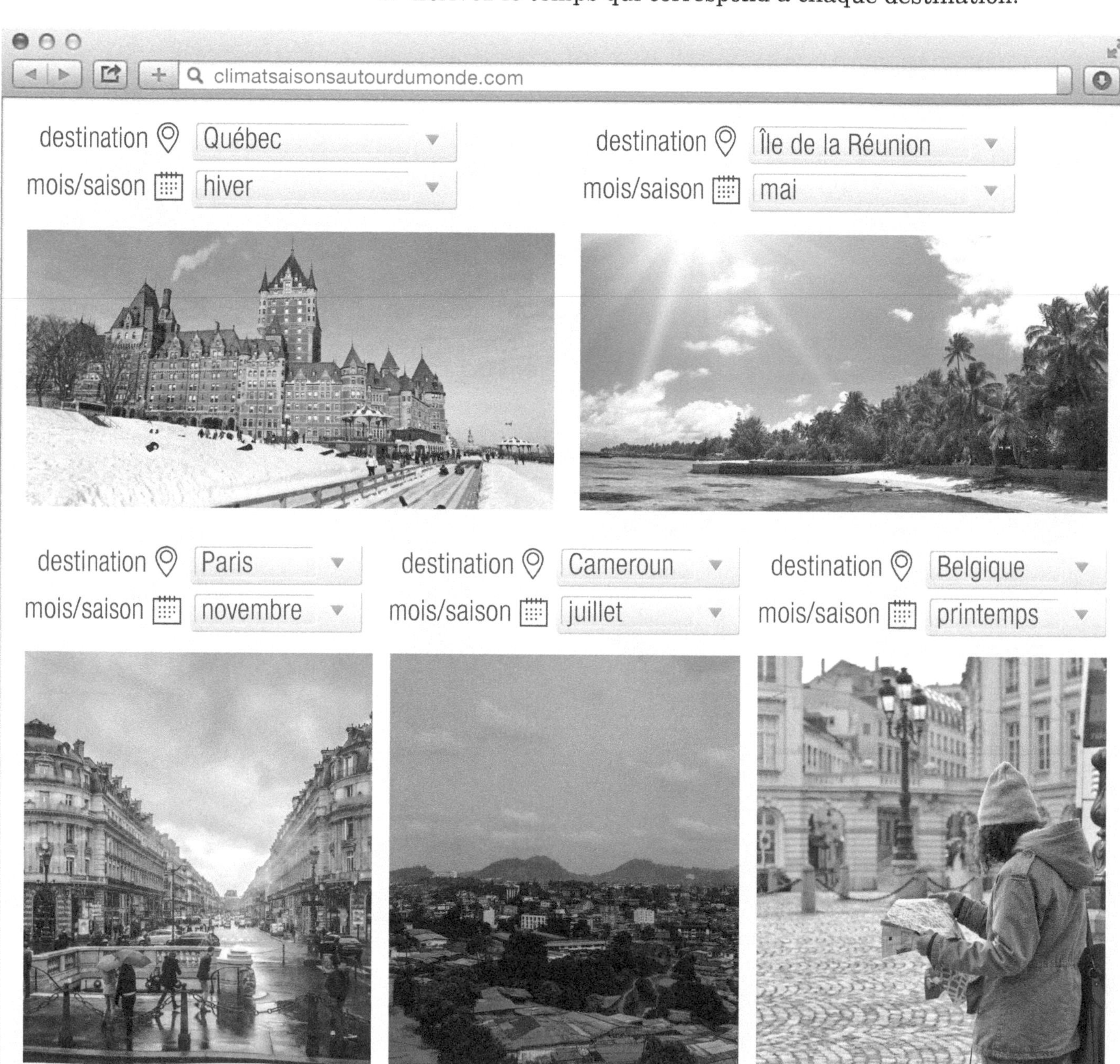

Activité 4

Comment étaient leurs vacances?

Vos amis Alizée et Thibault décrivent leurs vacances. Écoutez ce qu'ils disent et notez les éléments dans les catégories qui conviennent.

Détails de leurs vacances	Alizée	Thibault
où		
quand		
temps		
vêtements		
transports		

Activité 5

Tu es allé(e) où et c'était comment?

Étape 1: Noter

Pensez à un voyage que vous avez fait (près ou loin de chez vous). Notez vos idées dans les catégories de la représentation schématique sur Explorer.

Modèle

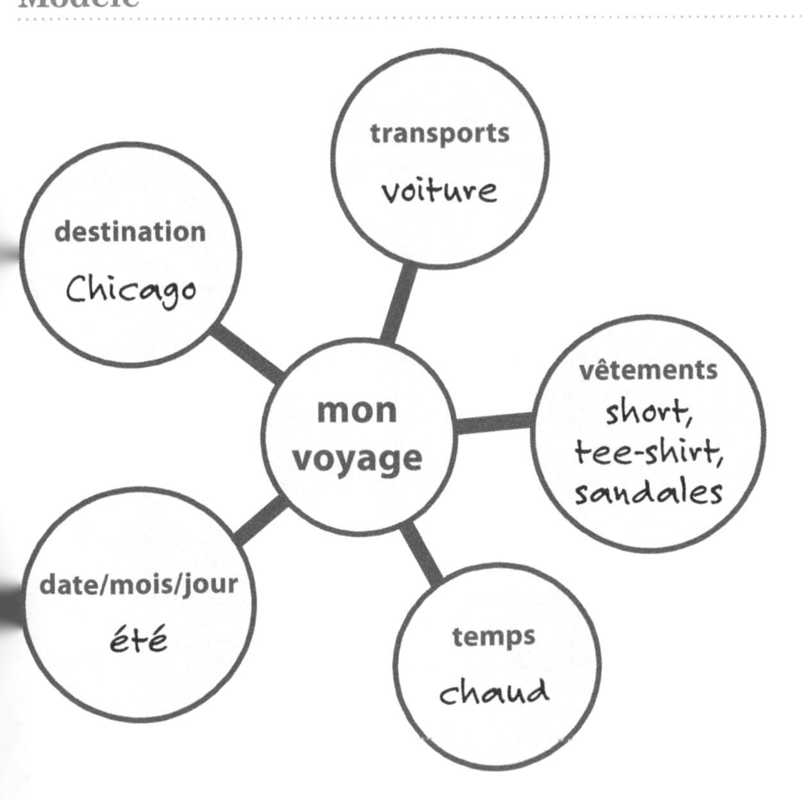

Rappel

Pour décrire le passé

C'était…

Il y avait…

Étape 2: Écrire

À l'aide de vos notes, écrivez une description de votre voyage.

Modèle

Je suis allé(e) à Chicago. Il y avait du vent et il faisait très chaud. Il y avait une piscine à l'hôtel, alors j'ai fait de la natation. Je portais un short, un tee-shirt et des sandales. C'était un voyage intéressant.

Étape 3: Parler

Parlez de votre voyage avec un(e) partenaire. Puis posez une ou deux questions au sujet de son voyage.

Modèle

Pourquoi est-ce que tu as voyagé ________ ? Quelle était la date?

Rappelle-toi

Les vêtements

des bottes (f. pl.)
un chapeau
des chaussures (f. pl.)
une chemise
un chemisier
une écharpe
des gants (m. pl.)
un jean
une jupe
des lunettes (f. pl.) de soleil
un maillot de bain
un manteau
un pantalon
un pull
des sandales (f. pl.)
un short
un tee-shirt
un uniforme
une veste

Les endroits et les activités

à la montagne
à la piscine
bavarder
faire de la natation
faire du ski
rendre visite à quelqu'un

Le temps

Il fait chaud.
Il fait frais.
Il fait froid.
Il neige.
Il pleut.
Il y a du soleil.

On peut aussi dire

la baie
bay

le golfe
gulf

le parc national
national park

la savane
savanna

le volcan
volcano

Communiquons

Comment dit-on? 1

Explorons les possibilités!

Choisir sa destination

Choisissez votre destination!

Bonjour et bienvenue à l'agence Grand'Escapade! Cette saison, nous vous proposons quatre destinations de voyage. Êtes-vous prêts à partir?

Vous voulez explorer un **pays** froid?

le Canada

Son **climat** est froid et **humide**.
Ces endroits **se trouvent** au Canada:

- la **forêt** Montmorency et le lac Saint-Jean
- les **chutes** du Niagara
- les **îles** de la Madeleine
- le golfe de Saint-Laurent

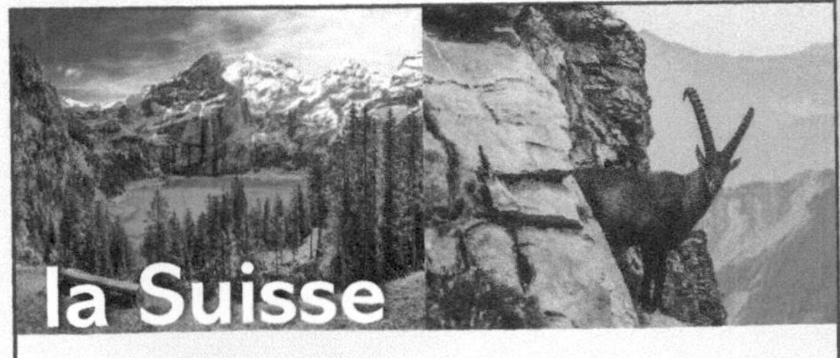

la Suisse

Son **climat** est **alpin**.
Ces endroits **se trouvent** en Suisse:

- des montagnes, des **lacs** et des rivières
- les **chutes** du Rhin
- la **forêt** du Parc national suisse

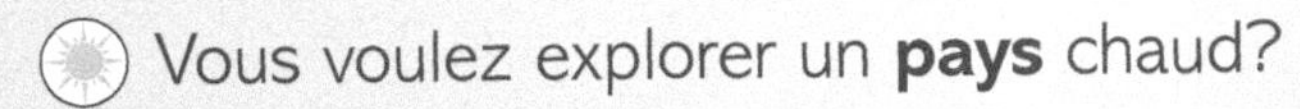

Vous voulez explorer un **pays** chaud?

le Cameroun

Son **climat** est chaud et **humide** au sud, et chaud et sec au nord.
Ces endroits **se trouvent** au Cameroun:

- la savane de l'Adamaoua
- les **forêts** denses des parcs
- la **côte** et ses plages
- la **région** volcanique du mont Cameroun

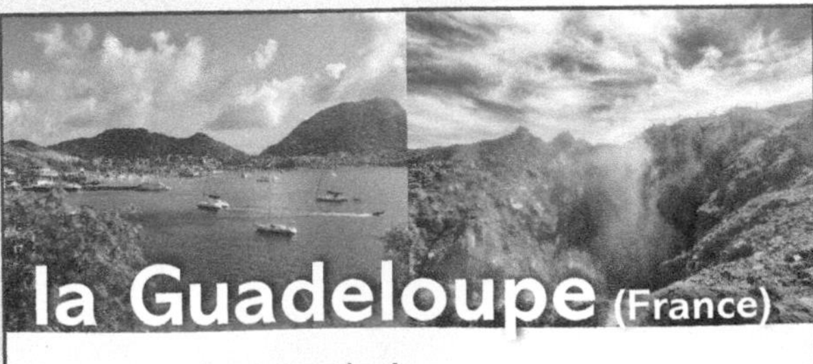

la Guadeloupe (France)

Son **climat** est **tropical**.
Ces endroits **se trouvent** à la Guadeloupe:

- la baie des Saintes
- le parc national de Guadeloupe
- la Soufrière, un volcan actif
- les **chutes** du Carbet

Réflexion interculturelle

How far do you have to go to see a mountain, seashore, or desert? What natural phenomena would you be interested in seeing? Where in the French-speaking world could you go to see them? Answer the questions in the discussion forum in Explorer.

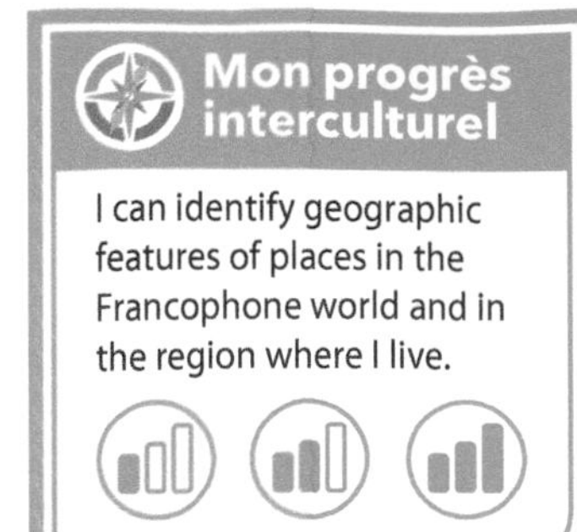

Activité 6

Où se trouvent les excursions?

L'agence Grand'Escapade vous propose des excursions. Écoutez les annonces de l'agence et la description de leurs excursions. Décidez quel pays va avec chaque excursion: le Canada, le Cameroun, la Suisse, ou la Guadeloupe?

Étape 2: Parler

Quelle excursion voudriez-vous faire? Quel pays vous intéresse? Enregistrez votre réponse dans le forum sur Explorer.

Modèle

Je voudrais aller...parce que...

Activité 7

Où est-ce que tu veux voyager?

Étape 1: Décrire

Quel pays ou quelle région est-ce que vous voulez visiter? Posez des questions à votre partenaire pour découvrir une région qu'il ou elle aime. Notez ses réponses dans la représentation schématique.

Modèle

Où est-ce que tu veux voyager? Moi, je voudrais aller en Suisse. Il y fait froid, mais avec le climat alpin, on peut faire du ski.

	région/pays	climat	géographie
moi			
mon/ma partenaire			

Détail grammatical

Le pronom "y"

Le pronom **y** peut vous aider à éviter la répétition d'un endroit. On le met juste devant le verbe.

Tu vas en Europe cet été?

Oui, j'**y** vais.

Nous allons en Afrique. On va **y** voir des déserts, des plages et des forêts.

Vous allez à l'aéroport?

Non, on n'**y** va pas. On prendra le train.

Expressions utiles

Ce sera...
Il y aura...
J'aurai...
Je ferai...
J'irai...
Je passerai (du temps)...

Étape 2: Écrire et écouter

a. Écrivez une description détaillée d'une région ou d'un pays que vous voulez visiter.

b. Puis écoutez quelqu'un lire les descriptions. Pouvez-vous deviner *(guess)* de quelle région du monde on parle?

Modèle

C'est une région/une province/un État/un pays. Il y a...

Vive les vacances alternatives!

Blog de mon séjour au Maroc

Salut, les amis! Je suis bien arrivée à l'aéroport de Casablanca aujourd'hui, donc **mon séjour** au Maroc commence. Voici mon programme pour le reste de l'été:

Lydia Herrmann/ SuSanA Flickr

- Je passerai la première semaine sur **un chantier** international **de bénévoles**. Nous travaillerons en **zone rurale** dans le **désert** pour donner accès à l'eau potable à plus de maisons.

- Après ça, j'irai en **famille d'accueil** pendant deux semaines. Voici une photo du père qui sert du thé. J'aurai aussi des cours de langue en français et en arabe.

- À la fin de mon séjour, je ferai **un stage** où j'aiderai une coopérative de femmes qui font de l'artisanat marocain.

Ce sera super! Il y aura beaucoup à faire et en plus, j'aurai pas mal de temps pour voir ce beau pays!

Zoom culture

Pratique culturelle: Voyager autrement

  **Connexions**

What kinds of travel are you familiar with? Have you (or someone you know) participated in a trip where you really got a chance to experience a new culture?

Le tourisme, ce n'est pas la seule manière de voyager. Il y a plusieurs options pour ceux qui désirent s'intégrer dans une culture et se faire de bons amis pour la vie. Si on veut améliorer son français (ou une autre langue), on peut faire **un séjour linguistique**. On peut en même temps suivre des cours de langue et visiter le pays où la langue est parlée. D'habitude, pendant un séjour linguistique, on loge en **famille d'accueil**. C'est une famille qui aime bien inviter des élèves internationaux. On mange avec la famille et on participe à ses activités quotidiennes.

Si on veut travailler pendant un voyage, on peut aller à **un chantier de bénévoles** ou **faire un stage**. Il y a plein de programmes pour les jeunes bénévoles qui veulent s'engager dans l'agriculture, combattre la pauvreté et construire des maisons dans le monde francophone. Si on veut de l'expérience professionnelle, on peut chercher **un stage** selon ses centres d'intérêt: le commerce, la mode, la médecine, etc.

  **Réflexion**

How might the type of travel you engage in affect your impressions of the culture of the place where you are traveling? What are the pros and cons of traveling as a "tourist" versus seeking out a more immersive experience?

Réflexion interculturelle

Look at the ***Stan & Alphone*** cartoon. Do you agree with the claim being presented? Why or why not? Answer the questions in the discussion forum in Explorer.

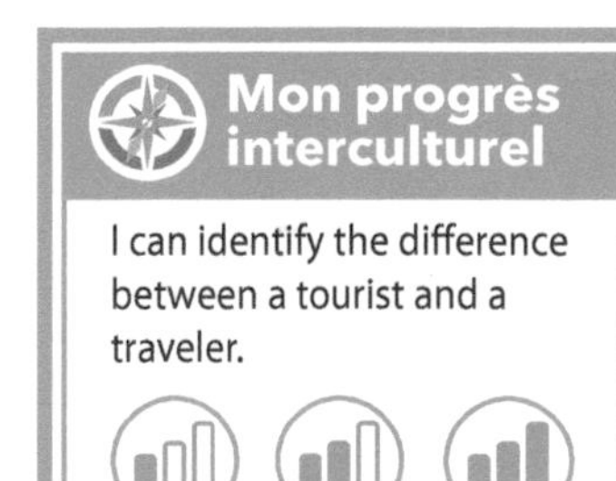

STAN, ALPHONE ET LE TOURISME

Mon progrès communicatif

I can understand the main ideas and some details in an informational video about a travel destination.

Activité 8

Serez-vous bénévole au Tour de France?

Étape 1: Écouter

Vous vous intéressez au cyclisme et vous voulez en savoir un peu plus sur les régions de France. Vous avez trouvé cette vidéo sur la ville de Nîmes. Regardez-la et cochez (✔) les mots que vous entendez.

découvrir
pendant trois semaines
des lacs
le Tour de France
des villes
la forêt
le grand départ
dans le sud-est
le monument
des îles
les Romains
une ville fortifiée
le parc national
les beautés architecturales

Étape 2: Lire

Voici un appel à bénévoles pour le Tour de France. Lisez l'annonce et répondez aux questions avec un(e) partenaire.

Tour de France: la Ville recherche 500 bénévoles

En juillet, le départ du Tour de France sera donné de Vendée. Du 13 mars au 30 avril, la municipalité de La Roche-sur-Yon lance un appel à bénévoles. Ils seront chargés d'accueillir la présentation des équipes, qui se déroulera le 5 juillet, et l'arrivée de la deuxième étape du Tour (le 8 juillet). Les futurs bénévoles se verront proposer plusieurs missions: poste de signaleurs sur le parcours; fléchage et signalétique; gestion des flux de voitures dans les parkings; distribution de goodies sur la ligne d'arrivée; accueil et information du public.

Une réunion de coordination sera organisée au mois de juin. 500 bénévoles seront recrutés.

a. Quelle ville cherche des bénévoles?
b. Quelle étape du Tour de France sera dans cette ville?
c. Avant quelle date faut-il se présenter comme bénévole?
d. Identifiez et dessinez deux rôles possibles pour des bénévoles.

Étape 3: Écrire

Complétez le formulaire en ligne pour devenir bénévole au Tour de France.

- Pourquoi voulez-vous visiter cette région de France?
- Quel rôle voulez-vous prendre comme bénévole?

Nom

Prénom

Pourquoi voulez-vous être bénévole au Tour de France?

Mon progrès communicatif

I can express my interest in a volunteer opportunity.

Prononciation

Les combinaisons "au," "ou" et "eu"

What is the difference between certain vowel combinations?

You have probably noticed that there are many different vowel combinations in French. You have likely also noticed that each vowel combination has its own sound, but each combination is consistent. When trying to decipher new and unfamiliar words or place names, it is especially helpful to rely on the patterns you know. Can you think of some French words that include the combinations ***au, ou,*** and ***eu***? How do they sound in those words?

In the following radio weather report, see if you can correctly predict the sounds in the underlined words. Listen to the recording and complete the pronunciation activity in Explorer.

> Voici la météo internationale pour aujourd'hui. À Ya**ou**ndé, au Camer**ou**n, il y a du soleil et il fait chaud avec une température de 32°C. Il fait beaucoup plus froid en Europe! À **Lau**sanne et à Montr**eux** en Suisse, le temps est nuageux avec une température de 3°C. En Belgique, à **Au**denarde, la température se maintient à 4°C. Il fait meilleur à T**ou**l**ou**se au sud de la France avec une température de 8°C et un grand soleil. Finalement, au Québec, à Saint-Jean-sur-Richel**ieu**, il fait froid avec une température de -6°C. Mais il fait très beau à Port-**au**-Prince, en Haïti où la température est de 31°C.

Découvrons 1

Describing What Will Happen/What You Will Do (Part 1)

Découvertes

Reflect on what you observe and respond to the following items in the graphic organizer in Explorer.

1. Can you identify which of the words in bold are forms of the following words: ***faire, aller, être, voir,*** and ***avoir***?
2. Are Océane and Félix talking about the past, the present, or the future?
3. What do you notice about the beginnings of the words in bold? The endings?
4. How are these words similar to or different from other verb forms you have seen?
5. Share your observations with a partner. What else do you notice together or what else can you add to your observations?

Activité 9

Quelle sorte de séjour feras-tu?

Étape 1: Écouter et déterminer

Vous recevez un message vocal d'une agence qui organise des voyages linguistiques et multiculturels.

a. Écoutez le message.

b. Avec un(e) partenaire, déterminez si les informations sont vraies ou fausses.

Vrai ou faux? L'agence propose...

1. un séjour sportif.
2. de progresser en français au Cameroun.
3. de découvrir la culture et la région de Yaoundé.
4. d'écouter des musiciens camerounais.
5. de dormir à l'hôtel.
6. de voyager en hiver.
7. de visiter un parc pour voir des animaux.

c. Répondez aux questions dans la représentation schématique de l'**Étape 2**.

Étape 2: Lire

Lisez l'annonce et complétez la représentation schématique.

Vous avez entre 14 et 18 ans? Vous voulez voyager autrement pendant deux semaines au printemps? Vous aimez la nature? Vous voulez faire du bénévolat et rencontrer des gens fantastiques? Le chantier solidaire «Les amis du foufou» a besoin de vous pour créer des jardins! Notre objectif est de planter une bonne variété de légumes, fruits et plantes médicinales biologiques. Nous plantons aussi beaucoup de fleurs pour deux raisons: Elles sont belles et elles protègent le foufou, le colibri de la Guadeloupe (le foufou a besoin du nectar des fleurs!). Tous nos bénévoles seront en familles d'accueil et il y aura une participation financière de 700 euros.

Pour plus d'informations, envoyez vos questions à amisdufoufou@mail.fr

	étape 1	étape 2
Qui fera ce voyage?		
Que feront les participants?		
Quand sera ce voyage?		
Combien de temps durera *(will last)* le séjour?		
Combien coûtera le voyage?		

Mon progrès communicatif

I can exchange information about what I and others will do during a vacation.

Étape 3: Parler

Vous avez l'occasion de partir en voyage et vous devez choisir une destination. Est-ce que vous irez au Cameroun ou à la Guadeloupe? Que ferez-vous dans ces endroits? Discutez-en avec un(e) partenaire.

Modèle

Moi, j'irai au/à la ________ et je verrai/je ferai/j'irai ________.

On peut aussi dire

Les continents

l'Afrique (f.)/en Afrique
l'Amérique (f.) du Nord/en Amérique du Nord
l'Amérique (f.) du Sud/en Amérique du Sud
l'Antarctique (f.)/en Antarctique
l'Asie (f.)/en Asie
l'Australie (f.)/en Australie
l'Europe (f.)/en Europe
l'Océanie (f.)/en Océanie

Activité 10

Et si tu gagnes au loto?

Quelle chance! Vous recevez 1 000 000 $! Que ferez-vous de tout cet argent? En groupe, décrivez le voyage que vous ferez. Vous pouvez employer ces expressions ou d'autres.

Nous irons... **intéressant** **Il y aura...** **en Suisse** **au Canada** **Nous aurons...** **génial** **à la Guadeloupe** **au Cameroun** **super** **des forêts** **Ce sera...** **des îles**

Activité 11

Que faire avec la narration?

Étape 1: Regarder et noter

1. Cette vidéo présente quel genre de séjour?
2. Où peut-on aller avec cet organisme?
3. Quelles sont les caractéristiques d'un séjour avec cet organisme?

 ### Étape 2: Écrire

Oups! Quelqu'un a oublié d'écrire une narration pour cette vidéo avant de l'avoir postée sur internet. Écrivez des descriptions où vous expliquez ce que les voyageurs feront avec cet organisme.

Activité 12

C'est quoi, le stage idéal?

 ### Étape 1: Présenter

Créez une vidéo où vous proposez le stage idéal pour vous. Dans votre vidéo, expliquez:

- quelle sorte de stage vous ferez (e.g., photographie, théâtre, etc.);
- où vous irez; et
- quelles activités vous ferez.

Postez votre vidéo dans le forum sur Explorer.

Étape 2: Écrire des commentaires

Regardez quelques vidéos des autres élèves de votre classe. Écrivez des questions ou des réactions dans le forum sur Explorer.

Rappel

Des professions

acteur/actrice
créateur/créatrice de mode
danseur/danseuse
photographe
scientifique

On peut aussi dire

Je ferai un stage de/d'...

commerce
informatique
marketing
mode
photographie
science
théâtre

Mon progrès communicatif

I can exchange information about what I and others will do during a vacation.

Mon progrès communicatif

I can understand the main ideas and some details in an informational video about a travel destination.

Mon progrès communicatif

I can express my interest in a volunteer opportunity.

J'avance 1

Je ferai un séjour génial!

Vous cherchez un séjour "pas ordinaire" à faire pendant vos vacances d'été.

Étape 1: Parler

Vous voulez savoir ce que les autres élèves de votre classe feront pendant les vacances pour chercher des idées. Posez des questions aux autres élèves et numérotez leurs réponses dans l'ordre de vos préférences.

Étape 2: Écouter

Votre professeur vous envoie *(sends you)* une vidéo qui présente encore une option pour l'été. Regardez la vidéo et répondez aux questions.

Étape 3: Écrire

Écrivez un e-mail à monsieur Ferey, qui s'occupe des bénévoles pour cet événement.

- Exprimez votre intérêt.
- Posez des questions.

Allez sur Explorer pour trouver tous les documents nécessaires de **J'avance**.

Comment dit-on? 2

Je fais ma valise!

Se préparer au voyage

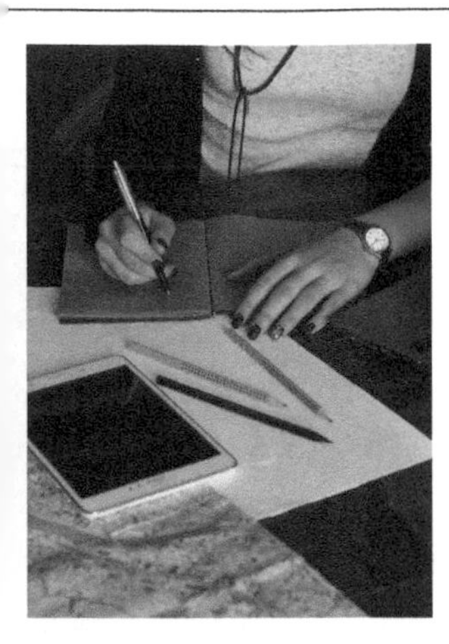

Avant de voyager, il faut toujours bien **se renseigner** sur la destination. Quand je pars **à l'étranger**, j'organise toujours mon séjour. D'abord, je me renseigne: Est-ce que je dois obtenir **un passeport** ou un visa? Je dois ensuite **établir un budget**. Puis, je **réserve un vol**. Je peux **imprimer** ma confirmation de vol. Finalement, je fais toujours une liste des endroits que je veux visiter.

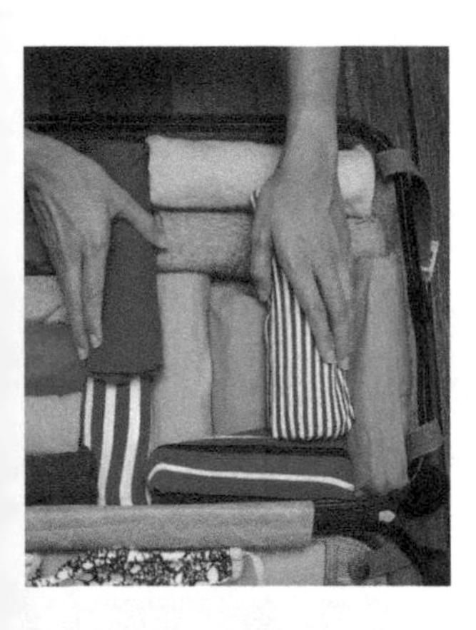

D'habitude, je **fais ma valise** deux jours avant mon départ. J'y mets toujours mes vêtements, un **pyjama** confortable et **un cadeau** pour ma famille d'accueil. Je n'oublie jamais mes écouteurs et ma **brosse à dents**. Je les mets dans mon **bagage à main** avec mon passeport et mon **portefeuille**.

À **l'aéroport**, il sera nécessaire de passer la sécurité. Si je passe une frontière, il sera aussi nécessaire de **passer la douane**  et de **changer mon argent**.

Rappel

Dans la valise on peut mettre:

la crème solaire
les écouteurs (m. pl.)
le journal
le livre
le magazine
les médicaments (m. pl.)

Expressions utiles

le départ
la frontière

On peut aussi dire

la brosse à cheveux
hair brush
le dentifrice
toothpaste
les lentilles (f. pl.)
contact lenses
la lotion anti-moustiques
mosquito repellent
le sac de voyage
travel bag
la trousse de toilette
toiletry bag

Activité 13

Qu'est-ce qu'on doit faire avant de partir en voyage?

Brenda et son cousin Roger vont voyager ensemble à la Guadeloupe.

Étape 1: Lire et écrire

Regardez les posts de Brenda sur un réseau social. Avec un(e) partenaire, écrivez une liste des tâches qu'elle fait pour préparer son voyage.

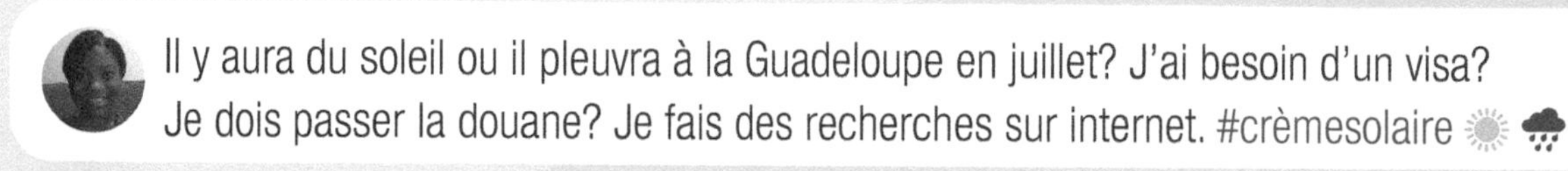
Il y aura du soleil ou il pleuvra à la Guadeloupe en juillet? J'ai besoin d'un visa? Je dois passer la douane? Je fais des recherches sur internet. #crèmesolaire

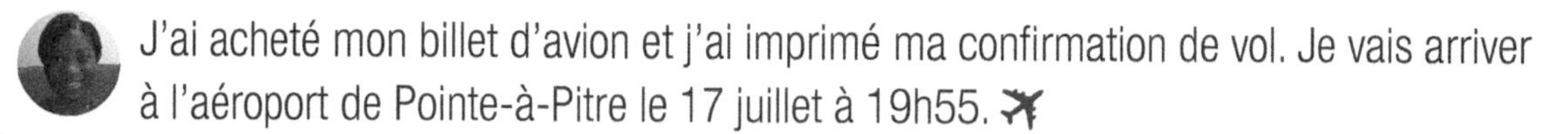
J'ai acheté mon billet d'avion et j'ai imprimé ma confirmation de vol. Je vais arriver à l'aéroport de Pointe-à-Pitre le 17 juillet à 19h55.

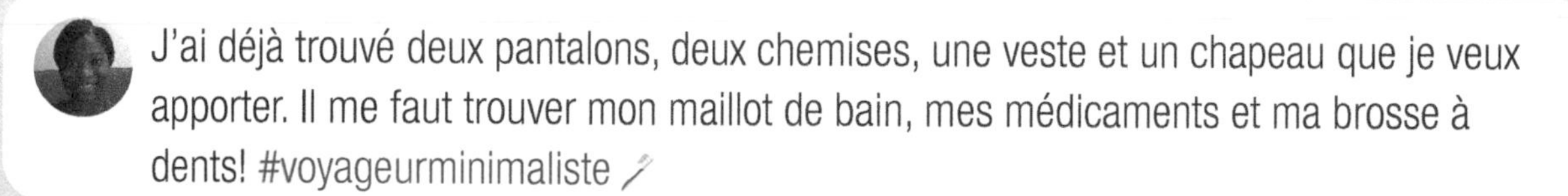
J'ai déjà trouvé deux pantalons, deux chemises, une veste et un chapeau que je veux apporter. Il me faut trouver mon maillot de bain, mes médicaments et ma brosse à dents! #voyageurminimaliste

Je suis allée à la banque pour chercher des euros. 1 euro = 656 francs CFA!!

À la Guadeloupe, combien coûte un ticket de bus? Je pense dépenser 20 € par jour pour manger. Je veux aussi visiter les musées et acheter des cadeaux pour ma famille. Je dois économiser maintenant pour avoir assez d'argent pour les petites excursions! #portefeuillefermé

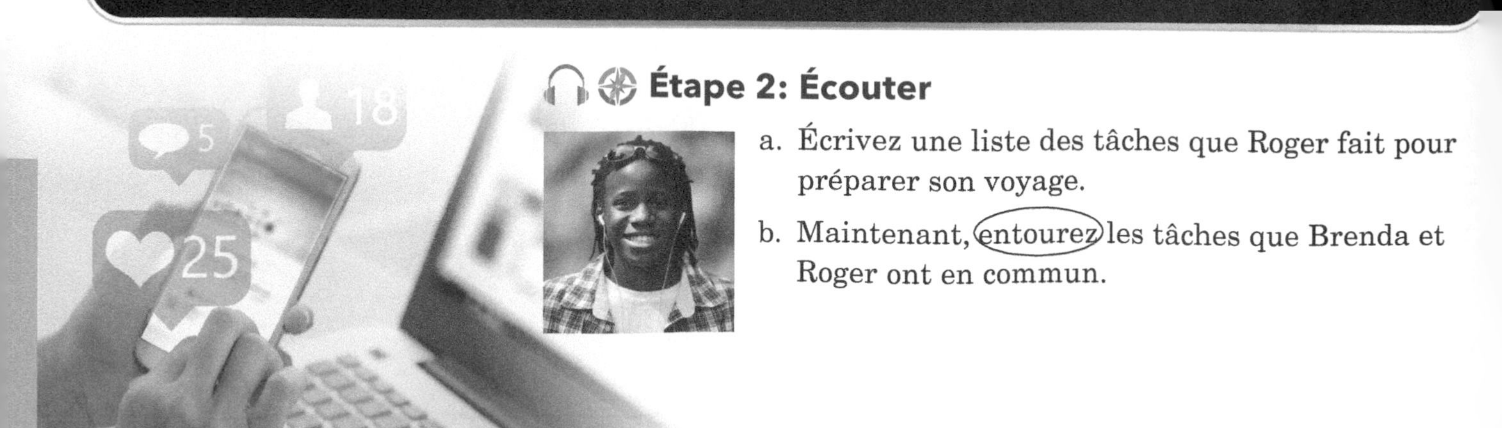

Étape 2: Écouter

a. Écrivez une liste des tâches que Roger fait pour préparer son voyage.

b. Maintenant, entourez les tâches que Brenda et Roger ont en commun.

Activité 14

Où mettre ma brosse à dents?

Brenda voyage de temps en temps au Togo. Regardez la vidéo et notez si elle met chaque objet dans sa valise ou dans son bagage à main.

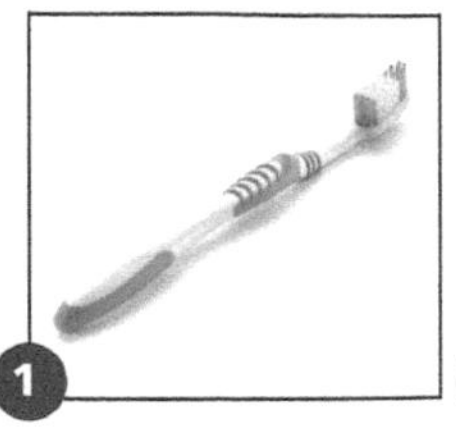
1

2

3

4

Dans la valise:

Dans le bagage à main:

Zoom culture

Pratique culturelle: Voyager à l'étranger

  **Connexions**

Have you ever met someone who has traveled to a country other than that where they live? Have you ever been to another country? What do you think might be important to do before traveling to another country?

En général, les voyageurs qui partent à l'étranger doivent avoir un passeport. Dans certains cas, on a besoin aussi d'un visa dans le passeport. La nécessité de demander un visa dépend de votre citoyenneté, du pays où vous allez, de la durée de votre voyage et des activités que vous allez faire pendant le voyage (tourisme, bénévolat, stage, études).

Quand on arrive dans un autre pays, il faut passer la douane. À la douane, il faut présenter vos documents (passeport, visa) aux agents des douanes. Les agents vous posent des questions sur le voyage. Il faut aussi déclarer les objets que vous transportez à votre destination, surtout les produits alimentaires, les plantes et les animaux. Souvent, ces objets ne peuvent pas passer la douane.

Avant ou après votre arrivée à votre destination, il faut changer de l'argent au bureau de change ou à la banque. La monnaie utilisée dépend du pays: le franc CFA au Cameroun ou au Togo; l'euro en France ou en Belgique; le franc suisse en Suisse; le dirham marocain au Maroc; et le dollar canadien au Canada, par exemple. Le taux de change *(exchange rate)* varie chaque jour.

  **Réflexion**

What are the benefits of or disadvantages of declaring at customs items that travelers bring into or out of a country when crossing a border? Other than security, why do you think some products are limited or controlled when traveling from country to country?

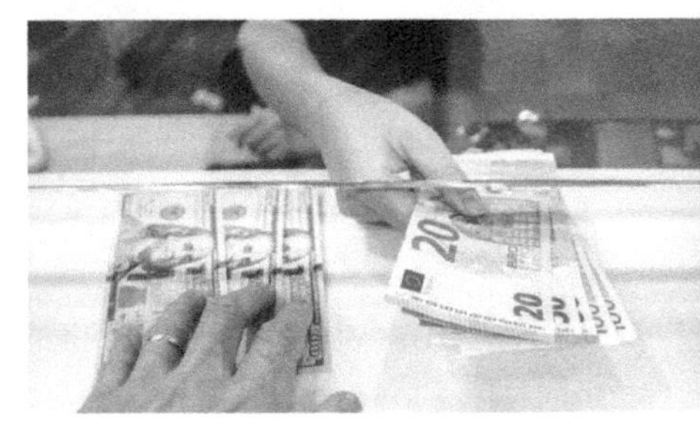

Activité 15

Qu'est-ce qu'il y a dans votre bagage à main?

Vous avez un stage à l'aéroport cet été. Vous allez travailler à l'accueil et parler avec des voyageurs francophones qui veulent se renseigner sur l'aéroport et les voyages internationaux.

 **Étape 1: Lire**

Comme préparation pour le stage, vous lisez les renseignements sur les objets autorisés et interdits dans les bagages à main.

a. Lisez les informations.

b. Répondez aux textos de votre ami qui va bientôt voyager.

Que mettre dans mon bagage à main? Qu'est-ce qui est autorisé en cabine d'avion?

Guide Pratique: Conseils et astuces pour voyageurs

Les aliments

Avez-vous envie de manger dans l'avion?

Des sandwichs, des bretzels, du pain, des biscuits et des fruits sont de bons choix.

On ne permet pas les aliments liquides en général.

Les yaourts, les crèmes, les soupes, les confitures, les pâtés, le fromage à pâte molle (camembert, fromage blanc) et tout type de boissons ne peuvent pas passer la sécurité. Cependant, vous pouvez les acheter dans les boutiques de l'aéroport pour les transporter à bord de l'avion.

Exception: Vous pouvez transporter en cabine sans restrictions de quantité:

- les aliments et les boissons pour les bébés; et
- les aliments nutritionnels sans lesquels vous ne pouvez pas voyager.

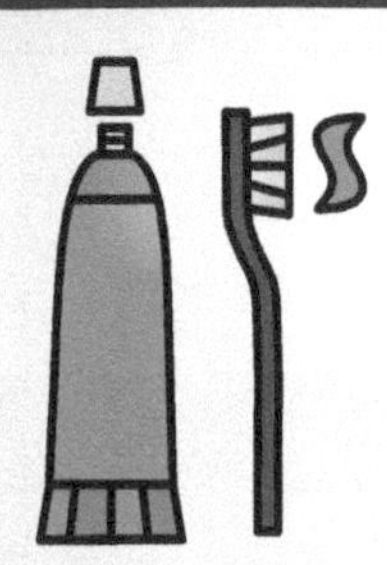

Les objets de toilette

Les objets coupants sont interdits en cabine. On ne peut jamais transporter les ciseaux, les couteaux ou les rasoirs dans le bagage à main.

Les liquides sont limitées en cabine pour des raisons de sécurité. On peut transporter les liquides en cabine (par ex., shampooing, crème solaire, parfums) mais il faut les mettre dans de petits contenants. Chaque contenant ne doit pas dépasser 100 ml. Il faut mettre les liquides dans un sac plastique transparent.

Exception: Vous pouvez transporter en cabine sans restrictions de quantité:

- les médicaments, accompagnés d'une ordonnance du médecin.

Divertissements

On peut transporter en cabine:

- les livres, les magazines et les journaux;
- les lecteurs MP3, les appareils-photo numériques, les ordinateurs portables, les tablettes et les téléphones portables; et
- les objets achetés dans les boutiques des aéroports (après avoir passé la sécurité).

 **Mon progrès communicatif**

I can respond to questions to give advice about preparing for an international trip.

1. Salut! Je fais mon bagage à main et j'ai des questions. Je peux voyager avec ma crème solaire?
2. Je veux prendre de la confiture pour ma famille d'accueil. C'est possible?
3. Mon petit frère de huit mois a besoin de beaucoup de lait dans l'avion. On peut mettre du lait dans le bagage à main pour lui?
4. Mon voyage en avion est long. Qu'est-ce que je peux mettre dans mon bagage à main pour m'amuser pendant le vol?

Étape 2: Identifier

Pendant votre premier jour du stage, deux passagers perdent *(lose)* leurs bagages à main à l'aéroport.

a. Écoutez les messages de monsieur Tremblay et de madame Gauthier.

b. Identifiez le bagage à main de chaque passager.

Étape 3: Parler

Vous remarquez dans les bagages à main que chaque passager a un objet non autorisé dans l'avion. Téléphonez aux deux passagers (monsieur Tremblay et madame Gauthier) et laissez un message.

a. Dites aux deux voyageurs que vous avez trouvé leurs bagages à main.

b. Expliquez-leur qu'ils ont chacun un objet non autorisé dans leurs bagages à main.

Modèle

Bonjour, monsieur Tremblay. Nous avons votre bagage à main. Attention, vous ne pouvez pas avoir…

Activité 16

Ça vous dit de faire un séjour linguistique en Suisse?

Étape 1: Lire

Vous lisez la brochure d'un séjour linguistique en Suisse. Votre prof de français vous pose des questions pour expliquer le séjour aux autres élèves de la classe. Avec un(e) partenaire, répondez aux questions de votre prof.

ÉCOLE BARILLON

Séjour linguistique en Suisse

L'école Barillon vous propose un séjour d'une à six semaines en immersion française. Située dans la région francophone de la Suisse et près d'une grande station de ski, notre école vous offre un contexte idéal pour apprendre et vous amuser. On accueille des élèves internationaux de partout dans le monde pour une expérience enrichissante. Chaque élève fera un stage dans une organisation ou entreprise de la région pendant la semaine.

Âges:
11-18 ans

Dates:
de septembre à mai

Prix par semaine*:
1.500 CHF / semaine
(1.318 € / semaine)

*Bourses disponibles

Une journée typique**

6h30	On se réveille
7h00	Petit déjeuner
8h00 - 11h00	Cours (conversation, grammaire, culture)
11h30	Déjeuner
13h00 - 16h30	Stage (individuel)
15h30 - 17h00	Grands projets (excursions, arts, sports, ateliers culturels)
17h00 - 18h30	Étude
19h00	Repas du soir

** Le week-end, les élèves partent en station de ski pour pratiquer le snowboard ou le ski.

1. Le séjour dure combien de semaines?
2. À quelle heure est-ce que les élèves se réveillent chaque jour?
3. On fait le stage combien de temps chaque jour?
4. Il y a des activités sportives ou culturelles?
5. Quelle langue est-ce qu'on parle avec les profs et les autres élèves internationaux?
6. Il faut établir un budget. Combien coûte le séjour?

Mon progrès communicatif

I can understand the main ideas and some details in a brochure about alternative travel.

Étape 2: Laisser un message

Une autre élève de votre classe s'intéresse au séjour linguistique en Suisse. Elle vous envoie un e-mail avec des questions.

a. Lisez l'e-mail de l'élève.

b. Notez ses questions et préparez vos réponses.

c. Laissez un message à l'élève avec les renseignements sur les préparatifs du séjour.

> Bonjour!
>
> Ça serait super de partir en Suisse pour étudier le français avec d'autres élèves internationaux. Mais, je n'ai jamais fait de séjour linguistique et je n'ai jamais voyagé à l'étranger. Alors, j'ai des questions. J'ai besoin d'un passeport pour voyager en Suisse? Est-ce que je dois passer la douane quand j'arrive à l'aéroport? Que faut-il mettre dans mon sac de voyage? Est-ce que je dois mettre quelque chose de spécial dans mon bagage à main?

Mon progrès communicatif

I can describe how to prepare for an international trip.

Étape 3: Parler

Votre partenaire et vous voulez participer au séjour linguistique. Posez des questions et répondez à votre partenaire pour faire des projets. Considérez ce qu'il faut faire:

-avant le voyage;

-à l'aéroport; et

-pendant le séjour linguistique.

Modèle

Qu'est-ce que tu dois faire avant le voyage? Moi, je dois réserver un vol et chercher mon passeport.

Découvrons 2

Avoiding Repetition Using *le*, *la*, and *les*

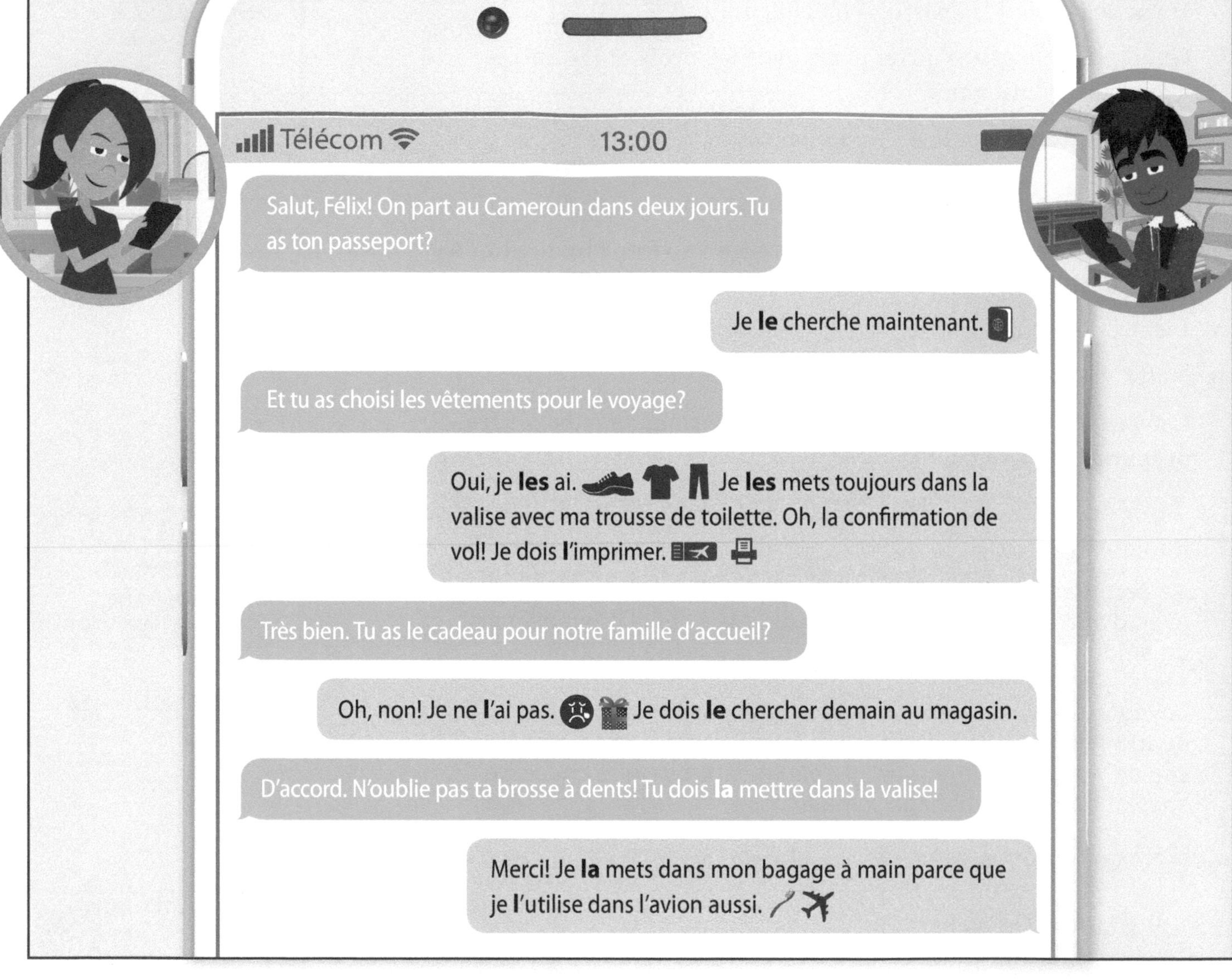

Découvertes

Reflect on what you observe and respond to the following items in the graphic organizer in Explorer.

1. Make a list of all of the different words in bold that you see in the above conversation.
2. Where in each sentence are the words in bold placed?
3. What do each of the words in bold refer to? Explain how the words change based on what is being described.
4. Share your observations with a partner. What else do you notice together or what else can you add to your observations?

Activité 17

Est-ce que tu peux les apporter?

Vous allez rester en famille d'accueil à Douala pendant un séjour linguistique. La famille vous envoie des textos avant le voyage.

a. Lisez les messages de la famille.

b. Choisissez la réponse logique à chacun des textos de la famille.

1. Bonjour! Tu as déjà ta confirmation de vol?
2. Et attention à ton passeport. Ne le mets pas dans ta valise. Garde-le avec toi.
3. Tu as regardé les sites web sur notre région que nous avons recommandés?
4. N'oublie pas d'apporter ton maillot de bain pour la plage!
5. Est-ce que tu peux apporter tes lunettes de soleil?
6. Nous avons un vieux vélo que nous pouvons réparer pour toi.
7. S'il te plaît, regarde les photos que tu recevras dans ton e-mail pour pouvoir nous reconnaître à l'aéroport.

---

a. D'accord! Je vais le mettre dans mon sac de voyage maintenant.

b. Oui, je l'ai. Je vais l'imprimer demain. J'arriverai le 17 juin.

c. Bonne idée! Je vais les regarder et les imprimer avant mon départ.

d. Oui, je veux bien l'utiliser pour aller à mon cours de français. Merci.

e. Merci. Je les porte toujours quand je suis dehors.

f. Oui, merci. Je le garde dans mon bagage à main ou dans ma poche.

g. Tout à fait! Je les explore maintenant! J'apprends beaucoup de choses.

Une école à Douala

Douala, Cameroun

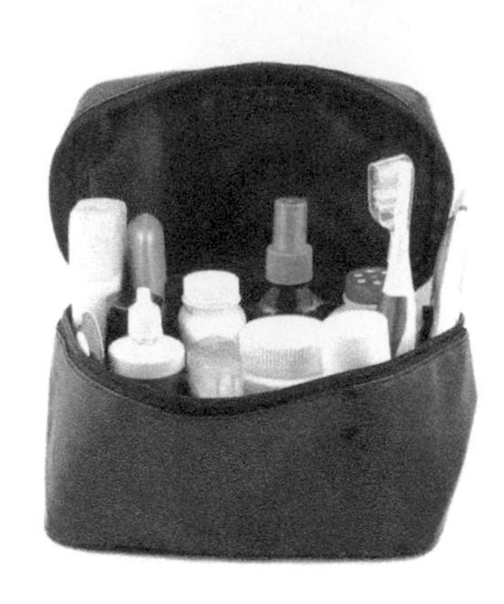

Activité 18

Tu les mets dans ta valise ou dans ton bagage à main?

Vous allez voyager à l'étranger avec un autre élève de votre classe. L'élève vous envoie des textos quelques jours avant le voyage. Utilisez un pronom objet direct (le, la, les, l') et une phrase complète pour répondre à ses questions.

Modèle

Tu as ta valise?

Oui, je l'ai.

1. Tu mets ta brosse à dents dans ta valise ou dans ton bagage à main?
2. Et où est-ce que tu mets ton pantalon?
3. Et ton passeport? Où est-ce que tu le mets?
4. Tu achètes le cadeau pour ta famille d'accueil au magasin ou au marché?
5. Tu changes l'argent à la banque ou à l'aéroport?
6. Tu imprimes ta confirmation de vol ou tu l'as sur ton portable?

Activité 19

Tu le mets où?

Vous préparez vos bagages pour un séjour, mais vous voulez comparer ce que vous faites avec un(e) ami(e).

a. "Préparez" vos bagages: Dessinez cinq à sept articles dans la valise ou dans le petit sac.
b. "Téléphonez" à votre partenaire pour savoir où il ou elle met chaque objet.
c. Notez les différences.

Modèle

—Ton sandwich, tu le mets dans la valise ou dans ton bagage à main?

—Je le mets dans mon bagage à main. Peut-être que j'aurai faim dans l'avion!

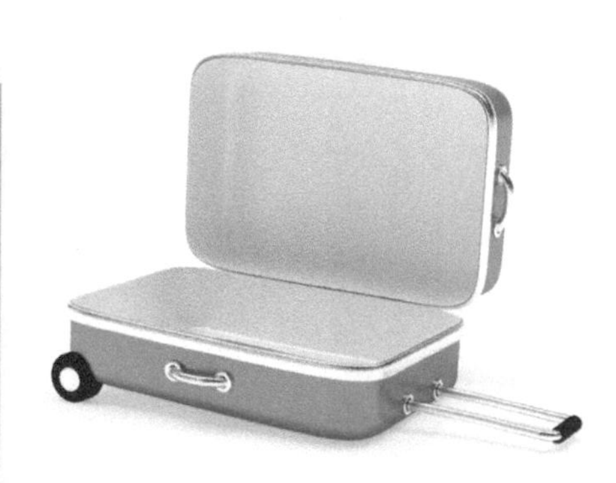

J'avance 2

Préparons-nous pour un voyage au Cameroun!

Vous allez voyager au Cameroun cet été avec un groupe d'élèves internationaux. Avant de partir, vous communiquez avec Jean-Claude, un élève suisse qui va aussi voyager avec le groupe.

Étape 1: Parler

Publiez une vidéo sur le site de réseau social de l'agence de voyages. Décrivez les tâches que vous allez faire pour préparer le voyage au Cameroun.

Étape 2: Écouter

Jean-Claude publie un message audio sur une page de réseau social de l'agence de voyages. Il décrit ce qu'il fait pour se préparer avant le voyage au Cameroun. Cochez (✔) les activités de préparation que Jean-Claude a déjà faites.

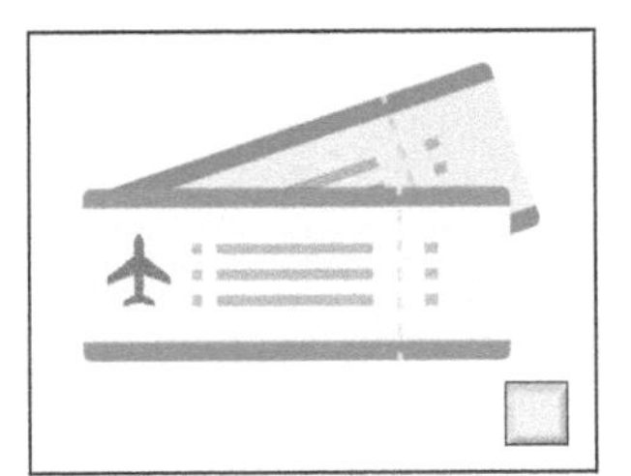

Étape 3: Répondre

Pour Jean-Claude, c'est son premier voyage à l'étranger. Il est un peu nerveux. Écrivez des textos pour répondre à ses questions sur les voyages à l'étranger.

Allez sur Explorer pour trouver tous les documents nécessaires de **J'avance**.

On peut aussi dire

aller à un festival

aller à une foire

une location à court terme, une location de courte durée

Expressions utiles

l'hébergement (m.)

l'hôtel (m.)

Comment dit-on? 3

Que ferai-je en voyage?

Les hébergements et les activités de voyage

J'irai ***flâner*** *pour découvrir la ville lentement ou je* ***découvrirai une activité culturelle****?*

Je dormirai dans ***une auberge de jeunesse****, je réserverai une chambre dans un hôtel ou je* ***louerai un appart en courte durée*** *(2 ou 3 semaines)?*

Je ***visiterai un site historique*** *ou un parc naturel?*

J'écrirai dans ***mon carnet de voyage*** *ou je* ***bloguerai*** *mes expériences en ligne?*

Activité 20

Quel hébergement choisir?

Vous allez faire un séjour linguistique à Douala. Vous considérez les hébergements qui sont proposés aux élèves.

Étape 1: Lire

a. Lisez les options d'hébergement proposées par le directeur du séjour linguistique.

Séjour linguistique à Douala: Quel hébergement choisir?

famille d'accueil

- À partir de 112€ la semaine.
- Chambre individuelle ou double.
- Repas en famille.
- La meilleure façon de découvrir la culture et les gens.
- Participez à des activités culturelles et vivez l'immersion au quotidien en famille.

résidence étudiante

- À partir de 150€ la semaine.
- Chambre individuelle.
- Accès à une cuisine commune.
- En pleine ville: Pas nécessaire de prendre le bus pour flâner, découvrir la ville ou faire des achats.
- Rencontrez d'autres étudiants de toutes nationalités.

appart en courte durée

- À partir de 125€ la semaine.
- Chambre individuelle, douche, toilettes et cuisine.
- Les apparts à louer se trouvent en banlieue, près de deux sites historiques à 10-15 minutes en bus ou tramway du centre-ville.

auberge de jeunesse

- À partir de 105€ la semaine.
- Une chambre de neuf lits à partager avec d'autres étudiants.
- Salle de bains commune.
- Petit-déj inclus.
- Wi-fi gratuit - Prenez le temps de bloguer ou vérifier vos e-mails.

b. Répondez aux questions.

1. Quelle est l'option la moins chère?
2. Quel est le meilleur hébergement pour quelqu'un qui veut se promener en centre-ville?
3. Quel hébergement est préférable pour un élève qui aime visiter les sites historiques?
4. Quelle option doit-on choisir si on n'aime pas préparer le petit-déjeuner?
5. Quelles sont les meilleures options pour ceux qui aiment habiter avec d'autres personnes?

Des appartements au Cameroun

Étape 2: Écouter

Trois élèves du séjour linguistique doivent choisir leurs hébergements. Écoutez leurs préférences et suggérez une option d'hébergement pour chacun.

élève	préférences	hébergement suggéré
Marie		
Ousman		
Tristan		

Étape 3: Écrire

Écrivez un message au directeur du séjour linguistique.

a. Présentez-vous.

b. Indiquez l'hébergement que vous préférez.

c. Expliquez votre choix.

Modèle

Cher directeur,

Je m'appelle… Je préfère rester… parce que…

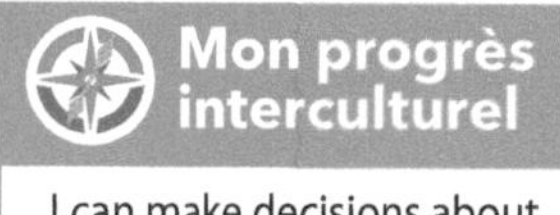

Mon progrès interculturel

I can make decisions about international travel options to meet my needs.

Réflexion interculturelle

This is the last ***Réflexion interculturelle*** in ***EntreCultures 2***. What are some things you have learned about international travel? Which of the options for immersive travel would you consider? Why or why not? Answer the questions in the discussion forum in Explorer.

Activité 21

Quelles activités est-ce que les voyageurs préfèrent?

Vous faites un stage dans une organisation belge qui accueille des voyageurs internationaux.

Étape 1: Analyser

Une de vos responsabilités est de faire des recherches sur les activités préférées des voyageurs de différents pays. Utilisez le graphique pour répondre aux questions de votre maître de stage.

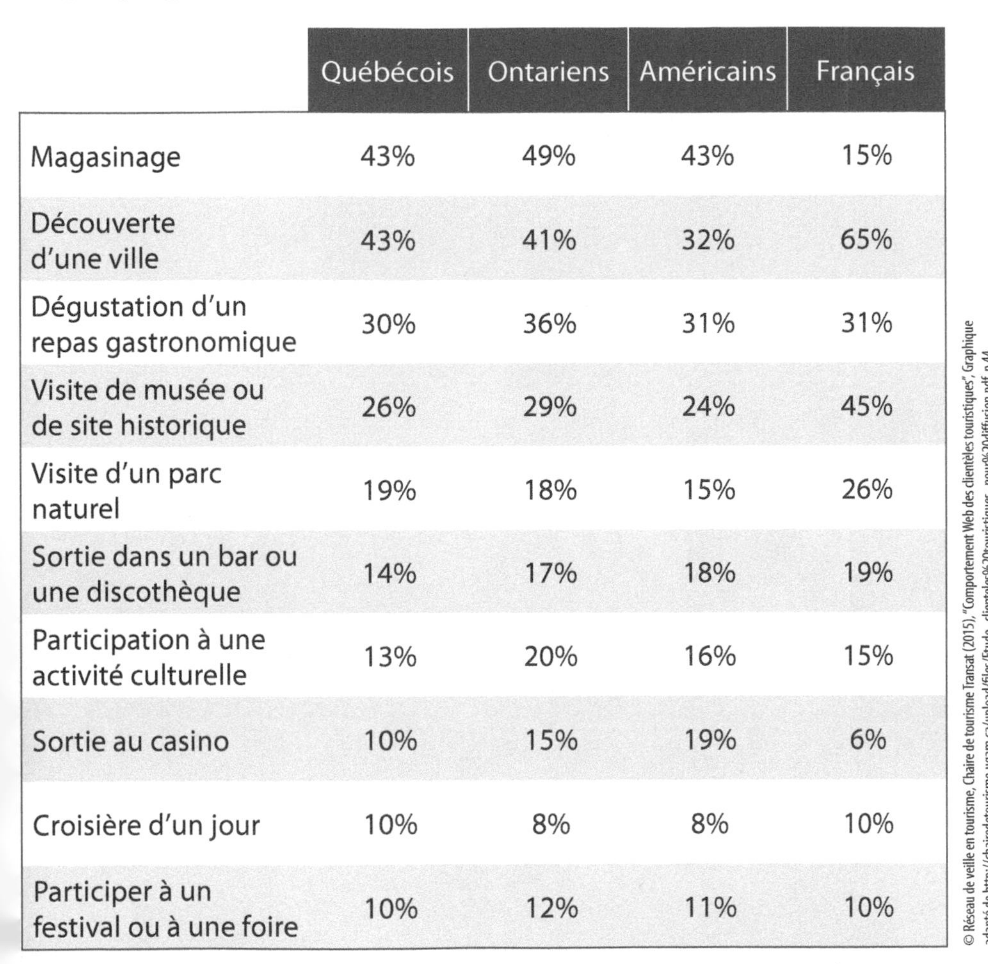

	Québécois	Ontariens	Américains	Français
Magasinage	43%	49%	43%	15%
Découverte d'une ville	43%	41%	32%	65%
Dégustation d'un repas gastronomique	30%	36%	31%	31%
Visite de musée ou de site historique	26%	29%	24%	45%
Visite d'un parc naturel	19%	18%	15%	26%
Sortie dans un bar ou une discothèque	14%	17%	18%	19%
Participation à une activité culturelle	13%	20%	16%	15%
Sortie au casino	10%	15%	19%	6%
Croisière d'un jour	10%	8%	8%	10%
Participer à un festival ou à une foire	10%	12%	11%	10%

*Sondage de 5520 répondants du Québec, de l'Ontario, de la France et du Nord-Est des États-Unis du 17 novembre au 7 décembre 2014.

1. Combien d'Américains font du shopping au cours d'un voyage? Et combien de Français?
2. Quelles sont les activités préférées des voyageurs américains?
3. Quelles activités sont peu populaires chez les voyageurs américains?
4. Quelle est l'activité pratiquée par la plupart des Français?
5. Est-ce que beaucoup de voyageurs aiment faire du shopping?

Nice, France

Pointe à la Renommée, Québec, Canada

Étape 2: Parler

Faites un sondage pour avoir des informations sur les élèves de votre classe.

a. Choisissez deux des activités présentées sur le graphique.

b. Demandez quelle activité les élèves préfèrent et pourquoi.

Modèle

Est-ce que tu préfères visiter un parc naturel ou déguster un repas gastronomique?

Moi, je préfère visiter un parc naturel pour découvrir la nature et les animaux du pays et parce que j'aime être actif.

Étape 3: Présenter

Présentez les résultats de votre sondage.

a. Créez une représentation visuelle des résultats du sondage.

b. Présentez les résultats à un petit groupe d'élèves.

Activité 22

Pour ou contre la famille d'accueil?

Étape 1: Regarder

Vous faites des recherches sur internet pour voir ce que pensent les autres élèves qui sont restés en famille d'accueil pendant un séjour linguistique. Décidez si chaque phrase est vraie ou fausse selon la vidéo. Si elle est fausse, corrigez-la!

1. Ça coûte plus cher de rester chez l'habitant (en famille d'accueil) que dans d'autres types d'hébergements.
2. Généralement, quand on est en famille d'accueil, la famille vous prépare des repas.
3. Rester en famille d'accueil vous immerge dans la culture.
4. Le jeune homme de la vidéo dit que la culture de la famille d'accueil n'est pas accessible.
5. La famille peut vous aider à apprendre la langue.
6. La maison de la famille peut être un peu loin de l'école.
7. D'habitude, la maison de la famille d'accueil est au centre de la ville.

Étape 2: Discuter

Avec un(e) partenaire, décidez si chaque phrase de l'**Étape 1** constitue un avantage ou un inconvénient.

Modèle

Moi, je préfère rester en famille d'accueil parce que...

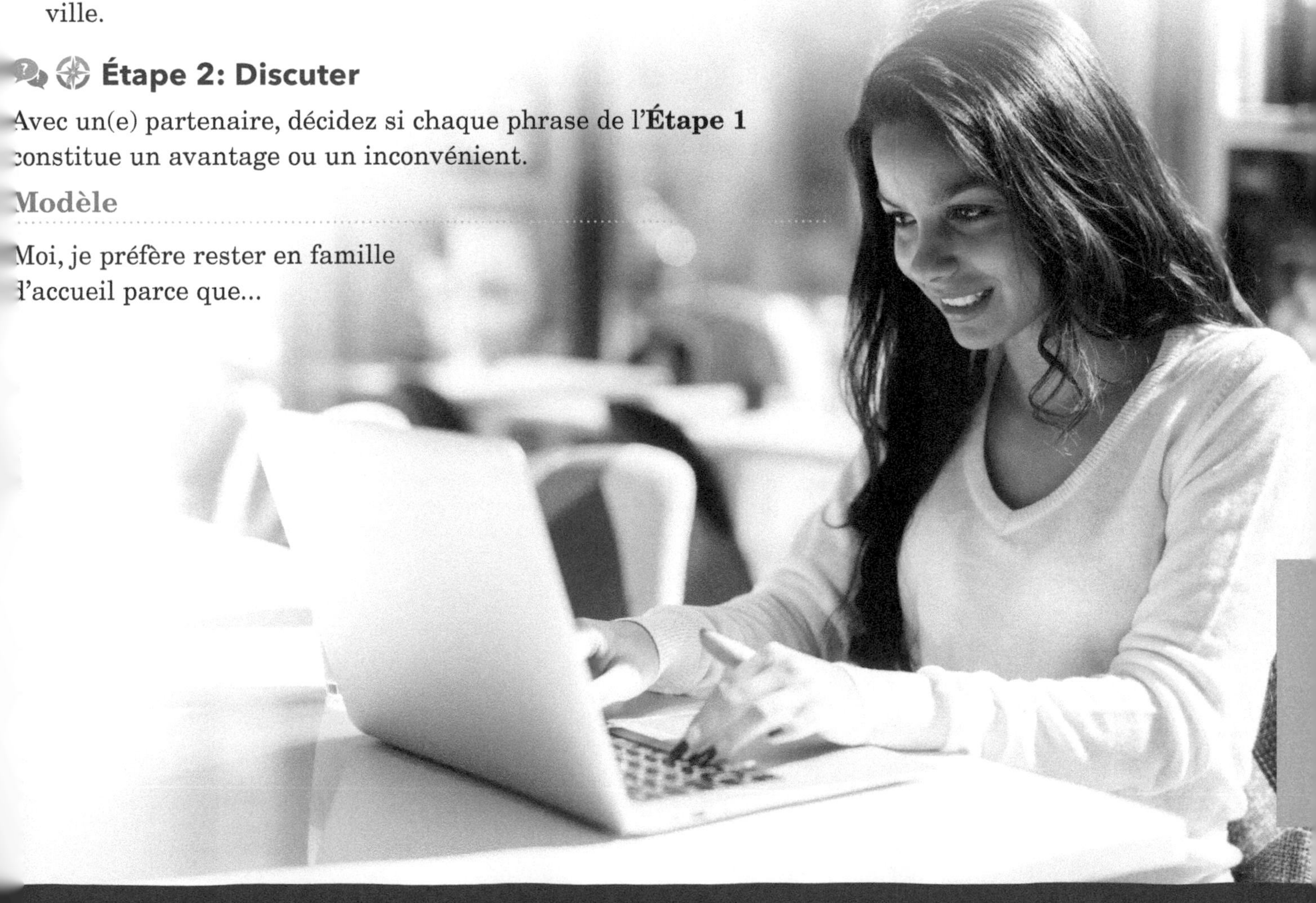

Zoom culture

Pratique culturelle: Rester en famille d'accueil

  Connexions

Have you ever stayed in another person's home or hosted someone in your home? If you were hosting a student from another country, what would you consider important for the student to see, learn, or experience while staying with you?

Les élèves qui voyagent à l'étranger ont souvent l'option de rester en famille d'accueil pendant leur séjour. Un séjour en famille d'accueil donne l'occasion d'un échange entre cultures, mais il faut être flexible et s'adapter! En famille, on peut apprendre intimement la culture de la région visitée et utiliser la langue en pleine immersion. On peut aussi participer à la routine quotidienne de la famille, comme la préparation des repas et l'entretien de la maison. Et avec un peu de chance, on est présent lors de célébrations telles que les festivals, ou les fêtes d'anniversaire, de mariage ou autres. Il y a des organismes qui aident les élèves à trouver des familles d'accueil à l'étranger. Ensuite, les élèves doivent remplir (*to fill in*) un dossier d'inscription avec leurs informations personnelles, leurs passe-temps et leur niveau de langue. C'est assez simple à organiser et avec cette option, on a vraiment une expérience unique et authentique.

  Réflexion

What are some things you would look forward to when staying in a home in various places in the French-speaking world? What would you hope for in a host family?

 Des conseils pour les voyageurs

Guide de voyage pour les élèves internationaux

Quand on étudie dans un autre pays, on n'est pas touriste! Voici quelques conseils pour être responsable et respectueux pendant votre séjour.

Essayez toujours de **préserver** les ressources naturelles. Il ne faut pas utiliser trop d'eau quand vous vous lavez. Ne **gaspillez** pas l'électricité; éteignez la lumière quand vous ne l'utilisez pas.

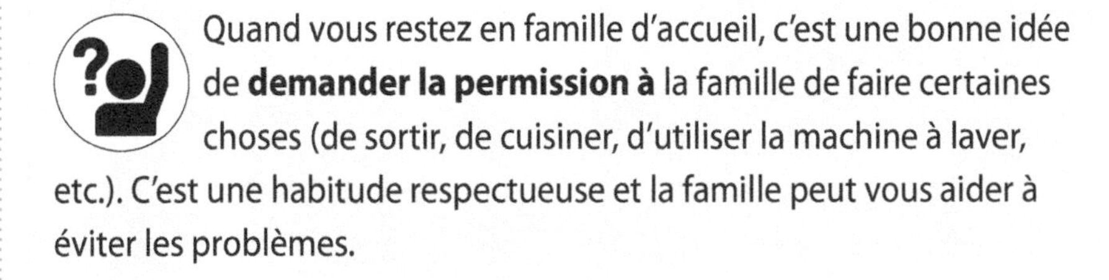

Quand vous restez en famille d'accueil, c'est une bonne idée de **demander la permission à** la famille de faire certaines choses (de sortir, de cuisiner, d'utiliser la machine à laver, etc.). C'est une habitude respectueuse et la famille peut vous aider à éviter les problèmes.

Gardez l'esprit ouvert! Vos expériences seront sûrement différentes de votre quotidien. Voyager à l'étranger donne l'occasion de **tenter de nouvelles choses:** goûter un nouveau plat, sentir de nouvelles odeurs, rencontrer de nouveaux amis.

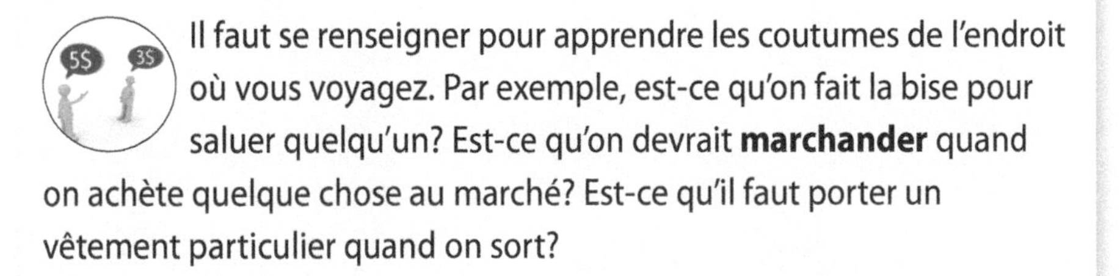

Il faut se renseigner pour apprendre les coutumes de l'endroit où vous voyagez. Par exemple, est-ce qu'on fait la bise pour saluer quelqu'un? Est-ce qu'on devrait **marchander** quand on achète quelque chose au marché? Est-ce qu'il faut porter un vêtement particulier quand on sort?

On peut aussi dire

la coutume
custom

éteindre la lumière
turn out the light

particulier/particulière
particular

respectueux/respectueuse
respectful

Activité 23

Êtes-vous un voyageur responsable?

Étape 1: Identifier

Vous vous préparez pour un voyage à l'étranger. Votre prof vous envoie un article sur les voyages responsables.

a. Lisez les conseils pour devenir un voyageur responsable.

b. Identifiez trois habitudes que vous avez déjà dans votre vie quotidienne.

c. Identifiez une habitude que vous voulez essayer d'incorporer dans votre vie quotidienne ou quand vous voyagerez à l'avenir.

Détail grammatical

L'impératif des verbes pronominaux

To give direct advice or tell someone what to do when using a pronominal verb, place the pronoun after the verb in the imperative form.

Renseignez-vous sur votre destination.

Renseigne-toi sur le budget de voyage.

Renseignons-nous sur les objets autorisés en cabine d'avion.

When telling someone what *not* to do, place the pronoun *before* the verb.

Ne te lève pas tard.

Suivez ces conseils pour devenir un voyageur responsable

Avec les habitants

1. Renseignez-vous au maximum sur les coutumes de votre destination.
2. Apprenez quelques expressions de la langue locale.
3. Réfléchissez aux vêtements que vous emportez.
4. Privilégiez l'authenticité et les rencontres locales (rituels ou traditions).
5. Évitez d'exposer des signes de richesse (de l'argent, des appareils numériques, des accessoires chics, etc.).
6. Marchandez si cela fait partie des habitudes locales, mais ne devenez pas agressif.
7. Choisissez les restaurants locaux.
8. Demandez la permission avant de prendre une photo.
9. Respectez les lieux sacrés (églises, mosquées, temples, etc.) et ne vous amusez pas à les piétiner ou à les escalader.

Avec la nature:

1. Ne jetez pas vos déchets dans la nature; emportez toujours avec vous un sac-poubelle.
2. N'approchez pas les animaux; restez à une distance raisonnable. Ne donnez pas à manger aux animaux.
3. Chut! Ne troublez pas la tranquillité de la nature et de ses habitants.
4. Utilisez les transports en commun pour moins polluer.
5. Avant d'acheter un produit, renseignez-vous sur son origine. N'achetez surtout pas de produits issus d'espèces animales ou végétales en danger.
6. N'abusez pas des ressources limitées, comme l'eau et l'électricité.
7. Achetez de la nourriture locale plutôt qu'importée.

Étape 2: Discuter

Avec votre partenaire, discutez:

a. Quelles habitudes sont les plus importantes, à votre avis? Pourquoi?

b. Quelles habitudes sont les plus difficiles à avoir, à votre avis? Pourquoi?

c. Quelles habitudes sont les plus faciles à avoir, à votre avis? Pourquoi?

Modèle

À mon avis, c'est difficile de ne pas approcher les animaux parce que j'adore les animaux.

Stratégies

Culturally Sensitive Travel

Voici quelques stratégies pour faire un voyage sensible aux différences culturelles.

1. Apprenez du nouveau vocabulaire.
2. Renseignez-vous sur la destination.
3. Goûtez la nourriture de la région.
4. Demandez avant de prendre une photo.
5. Préservez les ressources.

Activité 24

Comment sont les voyageurs?

Étape 1: Lire

Vous lisez des messages dans un forum pour les voyageurs à l'étranger. Choisissez le(s) bon(s) commentaire(s) pour répondre à leurs messages.

a. Bravo, tu gardes l'esprit ouvert!

b. C'est bon! Tu es super respectueux/respectueuse!

c. Super! Tu préserves les ressources naturelles!

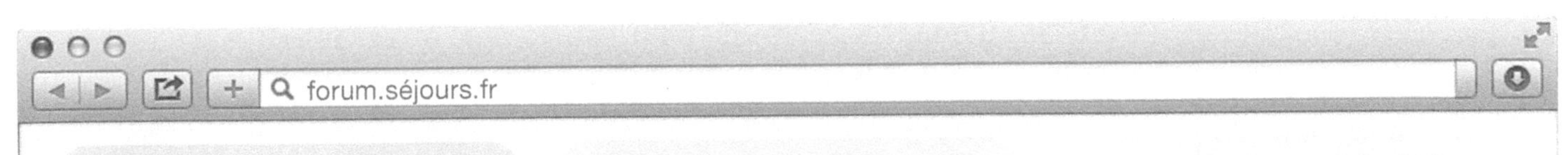

Aujourd'hui, j'ai goûté un nouveau plat préparé par ma famille d'accueil… les tripes ti-nain de la Martinique. C'est à base de bananes (pas mon fruit préféré), mais le plat était très bon!

Ce matin, j'ai acheté un sac à main au marché de Rabat. J'ai marchandé avec le vendeur pendant cinq minutes. C'était un peu stressant parce que c'était ma première fois au marché et j'hésitais à marchander. Le vendeur était sympa!

Hier, je me suis lavé très vite dans la douche à l'auberge de jeunesse. Chez moi, je me lave pendant dix minutes, mais hier j'ai fini en une minute! Je ne voulais pas gaspiller l'eau et les autres voyageurs attendaient la douche aussi.

Je loue un appart en courte durée en ville. J'utilise l'électricité seulement pour cuisiner et pour voir le soir. Aujourd'hui je suis allé à un festival et j'ai appris à danser le zouk, une danse des Caraïbes. C'est tellement amusant de tenter de nouvelles choses!

Hier soir, je suis allé au musée de sculpture avec d'autres élèves internationaux que j'ai rencontrés. Je n'avais jamais visité un musée comme ça! Avant de sortir, j'ai demandé la permission à ma mère d'accueil. Elle m'a donné un plan de la ville et m'a expliqué comment utiliser le métro.

Étape 2: Écouter

Anouk et David se préparent pour un voyage au Cameroun. Ça sera leur premier voyage à l'étranger et ils sont un peu nerveux. Ils publient des messages audio dans le forum de voyages.

a. Écoutez les messages d'Anouk et de David et notez leurs qualités et leurs préférences dans la représentation schématique.

élève	qualités	préférences
Anouk		
David		

b. Avec un(e) partenaire, identifiez les activités de voyage qui seront peut-être difficiles pour chacun.

marchander
tenter de nouvelles choses
rester en famille d'accueil
se renseigner sur la culture de sa destination

Modèle

Je pense que marchander sera difficile pour… parce que…

Étape 3: Écrire

Écrivez un message à Anouk ou à David pour l'encourager et pour lui donner des conseils pour son voyage à l'étranger.

Mon progrès communicatif

I can write a message to give travel advice to someone.

Découvrons 3

Describing What Will Happen/What You Will Do (Part 2)

Séjours Agence Yenga
Accord entre Félix et l'agence Yenga

Nom: Félix
Destination: Cameroun
Durée de séjour: 3 semaines

Avant le séjour:

- Je **me renseignerai** sur l'histoire et la culture du pays.
- Je **mettrai** dans ma valise seulement les affaires indispensables et j'**éviterai** le luxe.
- Je **choisirai** un cadeau pour ma famille d'accueil.

Pendant le séjour:

- Mes amis et moi, nous **parlerons** autant que possible la langue locale.
- Je **visiterai** des sites historiques et culturels.
- J'**écrirai** dans mon carnet de voyage.

Après le séjour:

- Je **dirai** "merci" à ma famille d'accueil.
- Ma famille d'accueil **gardera** un bon souvenir de moi.
- Chez moi, mes amis **apprendront** de mes expériences.

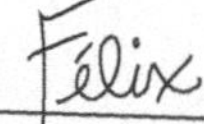

Découvertes

Reflect on what you observe and respond to the following items in the graphic organizer in Explorer.

1. What can you apply here from your understanding of ***Découvrons 1***? What do you notice that is consistent between what you see in ***Découvrons 1*** and what you see here?
2. What is different here compared to ***Découvrons 1***? Is it easier or harder to identify the verbs being used?
3. Share your observations with a partner. What else do you notice together or what else can you add to your observations?

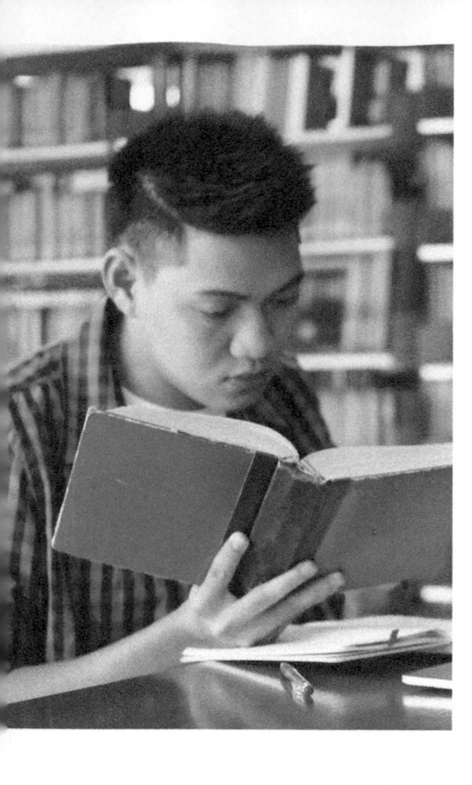

Activité 25

Qu'est-ce que vous ferez pendant la journée libre?

Étape 1: Sélectionner

Le proviseur de votre école a annoncé une journée libre surprise pour la semaine prochaine. Le proviseur veut savoir ce que les élèves feront pendant cette journée libre. Cochez (✔) les activités que vous ferez pour répondre au sondage du proviseur.

____ Je lirai un livre ou un magazine.

____ Je ferai de l'exercice.

____ J'irai au musée.

____ Je prendrai le train, le bus ou le métro pour faire une sortie avec mes amis.

____ Je flânerai dans mon quartier.

____ Je choisirai un nouveau plat à cuisiner.

____ Je me réveillerai très tôt.

____ J'écrirai dans mon journal.

D'autres activités?: ____________________

Étape 2: Parler

Vous voulez planifier votre journée libre.

a. Écrivez les activités que vous ferez le matin, l'après-midi et le soir.

b. Posez des questions à votre partenaire pour apprendre son horaire.

	mes activités	les activités de mon/ma partenaire
le matin		
l'après-midi		
le soir		

Étape 3: Écrire

Notez deux similarités et deux différences entre votre horaire et celui de (*that of*) votre partenaire pour la journée libre.

Modèle

L'après-midi, mon/ma partenaire et moi, nous ferons du sport. Mon/Ma partenaire jouera au basket, mais je ferai de la natation.

Activité 26

Que fera Brenda pendant son voyage?

Étape 1: Écouter

Écoutez la description d'un voyage futur de Brenda. Indiquez si les phrases sont vraies ou fausses et corrigez les phrases qui sont fausses.

1. Brenda ira en France.
2. Brenda voyagera avec sa mère et son chien.
3. Brenda rendra visite à sa grand-mère.
4. Pendant ses vacances, Brenda fera beaucoup de balades pour explorer sa destination.

Étape 2: Écrire des questions

Brenda n'a pas beaucoup parlé des activités qu'elle fera pendant son voyage. Vous voulez en savoir plus sur ses projets. Utilisez les mots dans l'encadré et vos propres idées pour poser des questions à Brenda dans un e-mail sur son futur voyage.

Modèle

Brenda, est-ce que tu loueras un appart en courte durée? Choisiras-tu une sortie au musée ou au stade?

rester dans une auberge de jeunesse
louer un appart en courte durée
découvrir la ville
écrire dans ton carnet de voyage
bloguer
visiter un site historique
tenter de nouvelles choses
flâner
préserver les ressources naturelles
gaspiller l'électricité
garder l'esprit ouvert

Activité 27

Êtes-vous prêt(e) à vivre entre cultures?

Étape 1: Regarder

a. Cochez (✔) les mots que vous entendez dans la vidéo.

- économie
- environnement
- séjour
- culture
- ouvrir au monde
- linguistique
- préservation de l'environnement
- alimentaire
- durable et responsable
- un impact positif
- des coopératives
- le commerce
- d'hommes et de femmes engagés
- patrimoine culturel
- solidaire
- générateur de revenu pour les populations locales

b. Avec un(e) partenaire, expliquez l'idée principale de cette vidéo en répondant aux questions:

- Cette vidéo a été créée par le ministère du Tourisme de quel pays francophone?
- Quels sont les objectifs des projets de tourisme durable?

Étape 2: Discuter

Menez une enquête sur l'attitude des élèves de votre classe. Que feront-ils quand ils voyageront? Notez leurs réponses dans la représentation schématique.

Modèle

Qu'est-ce que tu feras pour contribuer à l'économie locale?
-J'achèterai des produits de la population locale.

	élève 1	élève 2	élève 3
économie locale			
environnement			
culture locale			

Étape 3: Déclarer

Dans une vidéo, faites une déclaration de votre philosophie comme voyageur. Quand vous voyagerez dans le monde francophone et ailleurs *(elsewhere)*, qu'est-ce que vous ferez et qu'est-ce que vous ne ferez pas? Enregistrez votre vidéo sur Explorer.

Détail linguistique

Le patrimoine

Quand on parle du **patrimoine** culturel, qu'est-ce que ça veut dire? Le mot **patrimoine** vient du latin et sa définition est "l'héritage du père."

Le **patrimoine** désigne les éléments fondamentaux au cœur d'une culture. Ce sont les sources de la fierté *(pride)* et de l'identité. Le **patrimoine** peut être composé de l'architecture, la gastronomie, la langue, les fêtes et les traditions d'un peuple ou d'un pays.

J'avance 3

Comment sera mon séjour?

Mon progrès communicatif

I can understand guidelines for responsible travel.

Étape 1: Lire et associer

Vous allez faire un séjour linguistique de deux semaines au Cameroun. Vous avez réservé un lit dans l'auberge de jeunesse Les Flâneurs de Douala.

a. Lisez l'accueil de la page web de l'auberge de jeunesse Les Flâneurs de Douala.

b. Associez chaque image à une règle de l'auberge.

1

2

3

4

5

6

AP® Étape 2: Répondre aux questions

Maintenant, appelez l'auberge de jeunesse et répondez aux questions de l'employé.

Étape 3: Écrire

Écrivez un message à un(e) ami(e) pour expliquer où vous logerez et ce que vous ferez pendant votre voyage. Décrivez aussi comment vous ferez un voyage qui sera respectueux de la culture et de l'environnement.

Allez sur Explorer pour trouver tous les documents nécessaires de **J'avance**.

Le mont Cameroun

Synthèse de grammaire

1. Describing What Will Happen/What You Will Do (I): *le futur simple des verbes irréguliers*

When you want to describe events that will happen in the future, especially if those events are weeks, months, or even years away, use ***le futur simple***:

Je **ferai** un stage de journalisme. *I will do a journalism internship.*

Nous **irons** en Espagne. *We will go to Spain*

To say what someone *will have,* start your verb with the stem ***aur-***. For *will be,* use ***ser-***. For *will do / make,* use ***fer-***. For *will go,* use ***ir-,*** and for *will see,* use ***verr-.*** The expressions ***il y a*** and ***c'est*** become ***il y aura*** and ***ce sera*** in the future.

Then, you just need to add to appropriate ***futur simple*** ending to the stem:

je fer**ai**	nous fer**ons**
tu fer**as**	vous fer**ez**
il/elle/on fer**a**	ils/elles fer**ont**

2. Avoiding Repetition Using *le, la,* and *les: les pronoms "le," "la," "les"*

When having a conversation or writing several sentences in a row, you may find that you keep referring back to the same person or object. Once you have introduced a specific person or thing, you can later avoid repetition by replacing the specific noun with a direct object pronoun:

Tu vois mon passeport? Oui, je le vois.
Do you see my passport? Yes, I see **it**.

The typical placement of the pronouns ***le, la, les*** is just before the relevant verb.

When referring back to something that is masculine, singular, use ***le***:
Je **le** prends. (**mon sac de voyage**)

When referring back to something that is feminine, singular, use ***la***:
Tu **la** mets dans la valise? (**ta brosse à dents**)

When referring back to something that is plural, whether masculine or feminine, use ***les***:
Mon père **les** oublie tout le temps! (**les billets**)

Other notes;

- ***Le*** and ***la*** change to ***l'*** if they occur before a vowel sound:
  Je l'utilise souvent.
- When the pronouns ***le, la,*** or ***les*** occur in a negative sentence, they stay inside the ***ne...pas***:
  Tu vois mon passeport? Non, je **ne** le vois **pas**.

3. Describing What Will Happen/What You Will Do (II): *le futur simple des verbes réguliers*

For most verbs, the stem for the ***futur simple*** is simply the infinitive of the verb–in other words, the whole verb. For example, if you wanted to say that someone *will travel*, simply add the ***futur simple*** endings to the stem ***voyager-***:

je voyager**ai**	nous voyager**ons**
tu voyager**as**	vous voyager**ez**
il/elle/on voyager**a**	ils/elles voyager**ont**

Many other verbs just need one small change in order to have that distinctive look and sound of the ***futur simple***. There must always be a letter "R" just before the ending, so if you have a verb that ends in an "e" (other than those listed in ***Découvrons 1***) you will need to remove the "e." For example, for "will take," the verb ***prendre*** looks like this in the ***futur simple***:

je prendr**ai**	nous prendr**ons**
tu prendr**as**	vous prendr**ez**
il/elle/on prendr**a**	ils/elles prendr**ont**

Vocabulaire

Comment dit-on? 1: I can talk about the places I will go and the trips I will take.

La géographie	*Geography*
alpin/alpine	*alpine, mountainous*
les chutes (f. pl.)	*(water)falls*
le climat	*climate*
la côte	*coast*
le désert	*desert*
la forêt	*forest*
humide	*humid, wet*
l'île (f.)	*island*
le lac	*lake*
le pays	*country*
la région	*region*
rural/rurale	*rural*
se trouver	*to be located*
tropical/tropicale	*tropical*
la zone	*zone, area*

Expressions utiles	
Ce sera...	*It will be...*
Il y aura...	*There will be...*
J'aurai...	*I will have...*
Je ferai...	*I will do...*
J'irai...	*I will go...*
Je passerai (du temps)...	*I will spend (time)...*

Les voyages alternatifs	*Alternative travel*
le chantier de bénévoles	*volunteer work site*
la famille d'accueil	*host family*
le séjour	*stay (n.)*
le stage	*internship, apprenticeship*

Comment dit-on? 2: I can talk about how I prepare to travel.

Se préparer au voyage	*Preparing for a trip*
l'aéroport (m.)	*airport*
le bagage à main	*carry-on bag*
la brosse à dents	*toothbrush*
le cadeau	*gift*
changer de l'argent	*to exchange currency*
établir un budget	*to establish a budget*
à l'étranger	*abroad, in a different country*
faire sa valise	*to pack one's suitcase*
imprimer	*to print*
le passeport	*passport*
passer la douane	*to go through customs*
le portefeuille	*wallet*
le pyjama	*pyjamas*
se renseigner	*to get information*
réserver un vol	*to reserve a flight*

Expressions utiles

le départ	*departure*
la frontière	*border*

Comment dit-on? 3: I can talk about where I stay and what I do as a responsible traveler.

Les hébergements et les activités de voyage	*Lodging and travel activities*
l'auberge (f.) de jeunesse	*youth hostel*
bloguer	*to blog*
le carnet de voyage	*travel journal*
découvrir une activité culturelle	*to discover a cultural activity*
flâner	*to stroll*
louer un appart(ement) en courte durée	*to rent an apartment for a short term*
visiter un site historique	*to visit an historic site*

Des conseils pour les voyageurs	*Advice for travelers*
demander la permission	*to ask permission*
garder l'esprit ouvert	*to keep an open mind*
gaspiller	*to waste*
marchander	*to haggle, to negotiate price*
préserver	*to conserve*
tenter de nouvelles choses	*to try new things*

Expressions utiles

l'hébergement (m.)	*accommodations / lodging*
l'hôtel (m.)	*hotel*

Bafut, Cameroun

J'y arrive

Questions essentielles

- What do I need to know to explore another country or culture?
- What is the difference between a tourist and a traveler?
- How do travel experiences shape our intercultural understanding and respect for the communities we visit?

Un voyage à l'étranger

Une organisation à but non lucratif *(not-for-profit organization)* dans votre région propose des bourses *(scholarships)* à des élèves qui veulent voyager à l'étranger. D'abord, considérez les trois offres de voyages. Ensuite, choisissez une offre et complétez un formulaire de candidature pour recevoir la bourse. Finalement, posez-vous des questions avec un(e) partenaire pour vous préparer avant l'interview officielle avec le comité de sélection.

Avant de commencer, référez-vous à Explorer pour vous familiariser avec les critères d'évaluation de **J'y arrive**.

Interpretive Assessment

Choisir une destination à l'étranger

Lisez les brochures sur les offres de voyage cet été. Notez les détails de chaque offre pour en choisir une.

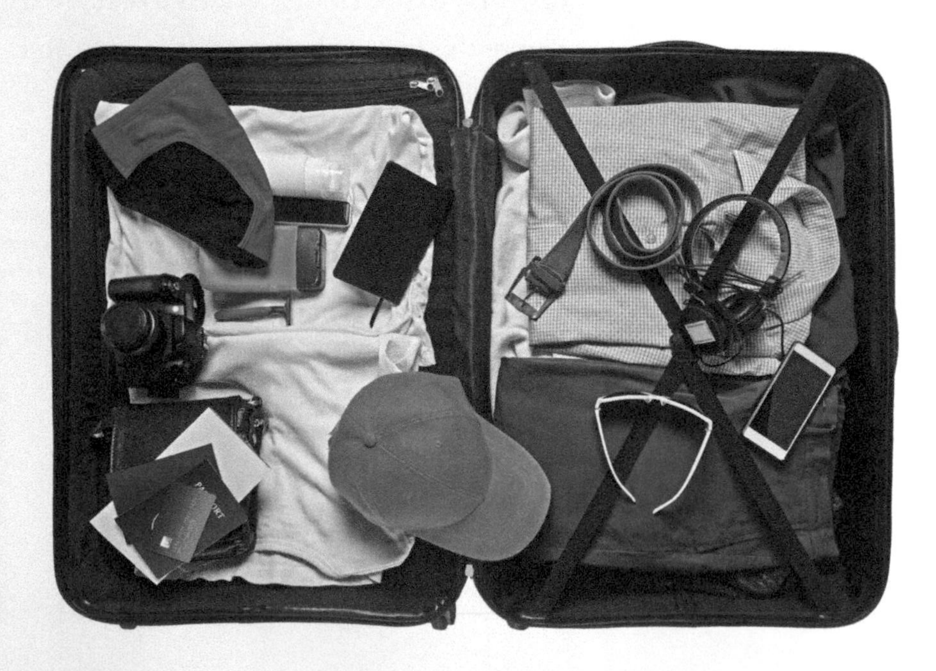

Presentational Assessment

 Moi, je suis candidat(e)!

Complétez le formulaire de candidature pour la bourse. Indiquez l'offre de voyage que vous préférez et répondez aux questions.

Interpersonal Assessment

 Préparons-nous avant l'interview

Vous allez passer une interview avec le comité de sélection. Avec un(e) autre élève, préparez-vous pour l'interview. Posez des questions sur le voyage et répondez-y:

- Comment est-ce que vous vous préparerez pour le voyage?
- Que ferez-vous pendant le voyage?
- Qu'est-ce que vous ne ferez pas pendant le voyage?
- Comment est-ce que vous avez fait votre choix?

Enregistrez votre conversation sur Explorer.

Bruxelles, Belgique

Can-Do Statements

Unité 1

Mon progrès communicatif

- ❑ I can identify some information about a school schedule related to times of day. (19, 27)
- ❑ I can share information about class preferences. (25)
- ❑ I can share information about what I am going to do this school year. (26)
- ❑ I can ask and answer questions about my class schedule. (27)
- ❑ I can write a description of the ideal school calendar. (27)
- ❑ I can understand descriptions of places in school buildings and compare them to my school. (29)
- ❑ I can describe some places in a school, the people who work there, and what students do in those places. (31, 37)
- ❑ I can understand simple descriptions of people who work at a school. (33)
- ❑ I can describe the jobs and the characteristics of the people who work in the school community. (35)
- ❑ I can exchange information about school staff related to their roles and personal qualities. (35, 37)
- ❑ I can understand descriptions of some places in a school, who works there, and what students do in those places. (37)
- ❑ I can exchange advice about ways to be successful in school. (40, 49)
- ❑ I can understand basic information about how often students prepare for classes. (40, 49)
- ❑ I can present tips on how to be successful in school. (42, 49)
- ❑ I can understand some facts about extracurricular activities from short texts. (42)
- ❑ I can exchange texts with a friend comparing my schedule to one in a Francophone school. (47)

Mon progrès interculturel

- ❑ I can identify some similarities and differences between a Francophone teen and myself related to school life. (9)
- ❑ I can identify some elements of the school-year calendar in ***la Réunion*** and how they reflect the culture. (18)
- ❑ I can identify some of the school course offerings that students take in a Francophone culture and why these courses are selected for them. (23)
- ❑ I can identify some extracurricular activities and the role they play in Francophone cultures. (45)

Unité 2

Mon progrès communicatif

- ❏ I can exchange information about ingredients in a traditional dish. (70)
- ❏ I can exchange information about foods I would like to try, providing reasons and simple details. (71, 80)
- ❏ I can understand someone's food preferences in order to suggest menu items. (72)
- ❏ I can write about some foods that I used to eat when I was young. (78, 80)
- ❏ I can understand someone describing what they used to eat. (79, 80)
- ❏ I can identify activities that people did in the past. (82)
- ❏ I can ask and answer questions about childhood eating habits. (88, 91, 94)
- ❏ I can write descriptions for photo captions about what people used to do, cook, or eat in the past. (89, 94)
- ❏ I can identify what and how often people used to prepare, cook, and eat in the past. (90, 94)
- ❏ I can understand text messages about what people used to eat. (91)
- ❏ I can understand the main ideas in announcements about culinary events. (95, 105)
- ❏ I can ask someone which culinary event they prefer to attend and give reasons for my preferences. (96)
- ❏ I can create an invitation to invite others to a Francophone culinary event. (97)
- ❏ I can understand and respond to text messages about an event. (98, 105)
- ❏ I can persuade a friend to attend a community event. (99)
- ❏ I can create and present a simple advertisement to persuade others to attend a community event. (105)

Mon progrès interculturel

- ❏ I can identify a Francophone teen's family members and interests, describe where he or she lives, and compare the teen's interests to my own. (61)
- ❏ I can compare traditional dishes from my community to traditional dishes in Belgium. (73)
- ❏ I can identify some produce that is grown locally in Belgium and in my community and explain why people buy seasonal produce. (83)
- ❏ I can identify why community members organize an event, that includes food, to benefit a cause in Francophone cultures and in my community. (100)

Unité 3

Mon progrès communicatif

- ❑ I can understand when people talk about the chores they do. (126, 134)
- ❑ I can understand an infographic about chores in the home. (127)
- ❑ I can write short messages to tell people which chores they will do. (127, 134)
- ❑ I can record a message to tell people which chores they have to do. (130)
- ❑ I can answer some questions about the types of chores that need to be done. (133, 134)
- ❑ I can select a volunteer opportunity based on my interests. (136)
- ❑ I can write a recommendation for someone and give reasons. (138, 146)
- ❑ I can identify key information about what volunteers are like and what they are willing to do. (139)
- ❑ I can respond to text messages with recommendations. (139)
- ❑ I can ask and answer questions about traits and preferences related to volunteering. (143, 146)
- ❑ I can understand an announcement about a volunteer opportunity. (146)
- ❑ I can recommend volunteer locations based on preferences. (149)
- ❑ I can understand the reasons people give for volunteering. (150)
- ❑ I can select a volunteer opportunity from an online description. (151, 157)
- ❑ I can tell someone where to volunteer and why. (152, 157)
- ❑ I can understand the main idea of a poem. (155)
- ❑ I can participate in an online discussion about a volunteer opportunity. (156, 157)

Mon progrès interculturel

- ❑ I can identify how a Francophone teen uses free time and why. (117)
- ❑ I can identify some ways that culture, gender, and age affect the types of chores people do. (129)
- ❑ I can identify ways people in my community and Francophone cultures respond to challenges and give reasons why. (141)
- ❑ I can identify and locate volunteer sites in my community and in a Francophone community. (147)

Unité 4

Mon progrès communicatif

- ❑ I can give advice about places to go in a city or town. (176, 185)
- ❑ I can understand when someone describes his or her preferred activities and where they take place. (176, 185)
- ❑ I can understand information about a city in a poem. (179)
- ❑ I can give a description of the area where I live. (179, 185)
- ❑ I can create and present a short podcast to give reasons for visiting a favorite place. (180)
- ❑ I can exchange online messages to trade opinions about the best places to visit in a city or town. (183)
- ❑ I can understand how someone spent a day in Paris and the places he or she visited. (187)
- ❑ I can understand visitor information on a website. (190, 197)
- ❑ I can ask and answer questions about activities my friends and I have done. (192, 196, 197)
- ❑ I can describe my activities from the past weekend. (192, 196)
- ❑ I can invite others to an event. (196, 197)
- ❑ I can understand key details in a video blog about where someone went and how he or she arrived there. (199)
- ❑ I can leave a voicemail telling how I will get somewhere. (202)
- ❑ I can tell where I went and what I did during a day in the city. (209, 211)
- ❑ I can understand key details from visitor information. (210, 211)
- ❑ I can have a conversation about where I went and what I did. (210, 211)

Mon progrès interculturel

- ❑ I can compare daily life in my town to that of a Francophone teen in his or her city. (169)
- ❑ I can give some reasons why people choose various places to spend their free time in Francophone cities and in my own community. (175)
- ❑ I can identify and compare where young people go to gather socially in Francophone cultures and in my community. (194)
- ❑ I can identify similarities and differences in cultural factors that affect teenage independence in Francophone cultures and in my community. (200)

Unité 5

Mon progrès communicatif

- ❑ I can ask and answer questions about healthy habits. (229, 239)
- ❑ I can understand recommendations for maintaining a healthy lifestyle from an infographic. (230, 239)
- ❑ I can summarize the results of a survey in a short, organized presentation. (233, 239)
- ❑ I can create graphs to represent my personal habits related to health. (234)
- ❑ I can understand the main ideas and some details in a video about healthy habits. (238)
- ❑ I can understand people talking about health problems and choose the best advice. (245)
- ❑ I can exchange information about what I and others do when we are sick. (245)
- ❑ I can ask someone about his or her symptoms. (246)
- ❑ I can give advice about how to feel better to someone who is sick. (246, 251)
- ❑ I can ask about symptoms and exchange information about what I and others do when we are sick. (251)
- ❑ I can understand recommendations on a website about what to do if one is sick. (251)
- ❑ I can describe my healthy social and emotional habits in an email. (253)
- ❑ I can understand recommendations for maintaining social and emotional health in a video. (254, 265)
- ❑ I can ask and answer questions about my habits related to social and emotional health. (258, 265)
- ❑ I can describe my daily routine in a video. (262)
- ❑ I can post a response to a podcast about habits related to good social and emotional health. (264)
- ❑ I can write questions and answers related to maintaining social and emotional health for a Frequently Asked Questions (FAQ) page. (265)

Mon progrès interculturel

- ❑ I can compare how local infrastructure supports the pursuit of a healthy lifestyle in a Francophone city and in my community. (222)
- ❑ I can understand perspectives related to a healthy lifestyle in Francophone countries and compare them to those in my community. (233)
- ❑ I can compare the role of pharmacies in Francophone cultures and in my community. (242)
- ❑ I can understand practices and perspectives related to social and emotional health in Francophone cultures and compare them to those in my community. (258)

Unité 6

Mon progrès communicatif

- ❑ I can understand the main ideas and some details in an informational video about a travel destination. (286, 290, 292)
- ❑ I can express my interest in a volunteer opportunity. (287, 292)
- ❑ I can understand the main ideas in an advertisement for a volunteer opportunity. (289)
- ❑ I can exchange information about what I and others will do during a vacation. (290, 292)
- ❑ I can describe where I will go and what I will do during a vacation. (291)
- ❑ I can understand when someone describes his or her preparations for an international trip. (295, 303)
- ❑ I can respond to questions to give advice about preparing for an international trip. (296, 303)
- ❑ I can understand the main ideas and some details in a brochure about alternative travel. (299)
- ❑ I can describe how to prepare for an international trip. (299, 303)
- ❑ I can ask and answer questions about how to prepare for international travel. (299)
- ❑ I can understand guidelines for responsible travel. (312, 319)
- ❑ I can write a message to give travel advice to someone. (314)
- ❑ I can ask and answer questions about travel plans. (316, 318)
- ❑ I can answer questions about my travel plans. (319)
- ❑ I can describe my plans for responsible travel. (319)

Mon progrès interculturel

- ❑ I can predict some similarities and differences I might find between Francophone cultures and my community when traveling abroad. (277)
- ❑ I can identify geographic features of places in the Francophone world and in the region where I live. (283)
- ❑ I can identify the difference between a tourist and a traveller. (285)
- ❑ I can make decisions about international travel options to meet my needs. (306)

Douala, Cameroun

Rubrics

Level 2 *EntreCultures* Analytic Growth Rubric

Interpretive Reading, Listening, Audiovisual, and Viewing

Level 2 Target: Novice High - Intermediate Low

DOMAINS	NOVICE MID	NOVICE HIGH	INTERMEDIATE LOW	INTERMEDIATE MID
How well do I understand? ***Main Idea and/or Details***	I can recognize and understand some basic information with memorized words and phrases.	I can identify pieces of information and sometimes the main idea(s) without explanation when the idea is familiar, short, and simple.	I can identify the main idea(s) and some details when the idea is familiar, short, and simple.	I can identify the main idea(s) and a few supporting details when the idea is related to everyday life, personal interests, and studies.
What words and structures do I understand? ***Vocabulary and Structures in Context***	I can recognize words and phrases, including cognates, and borrowed words in text or speech from well-practiced topics.	I can understand words, phrases, simple sentences, and some structures in short, simple texts or sentence-length speech, one utterance at a time, with support, related to familiar topics of study.	I can identify words, phrases, high-frequency expressions, and some learned structures in short, simple, loosely connected texts or sentence-length speech, one utterance at a time, related to familiar topics of study.	I can identify some words, phrases, and structures in various time frames (e.g., past, future) in simple, loosely connected texts or straightforward speech related to everyday life and personal interests and studies.
How well can I understand unfamiliar language? ***Context Clues***	I can understand some basic meaning when authentic texts or speech on very familiar topics include cognates and/or visual clues.	I can understand basic meaning when short, non-complex authentic texts or speech include cognates and visual clues, on familiar topics.	I can understand literal meaning from authentic texts or speech on familiar topics and from highly predictable texts related to daily life.	I can understand literal meaning from authentic texts on familiar topics and from predictable texts related to daily life and personal interests or studies.

DOMAINS	NOVICE MID	NOVICE HIGH	INTERMEDIATE LOW	INTERMEDIATE MID
How well can I infer meaning beyond what I read or hear? ***Inferences***	I can make limited inferences based on visual clues, organizational layout, background knowledge, keywords, intonation and/or body language.	I can make a few inferences based on visual clues, organizational layout, background knowledge, keywords, intonation and/or body language.	I can make some inferences based on the main idea and information such as visual clues, organizational layout, background knowledge, keywords, intonation and/or body language.	I can make inferences based on the main idea and information such as visual clues, organizational layout, background knowledge, keywords, intonation and/or body language.
How intercultural am I? ***Interculturality***	I can identify a few cultural products, practices, and perspectives, including cultural behaviors and expressions related to daily life.	I can identify some cultural products, practices, and perspectives, including cultural behaviors and expressions related to daily life.	I can describe cultural products, practices, and perspectives, including cultural behaviors and expressions related to daily life.	I can compare cultural products, practices, and perspectives, including cultural behaviors and expressions related to daily life.

*Based on classroom tasks/activities/ intercultural reflections and outside classroom experiences.

Adapted from Jefferson County Public Schools World Languages: Performance Assessment Rubrics (Kentucky), Howard County Public Schools World Languages (Maryland).

Level 2 *EntreCultures* Analytic Growth Rubric

Interpersonal Communication: Speaking and Writing

Level 2 Target: Novice High - Intermediate Low

DOMAINS	NOVICE MID	NOVICE HIGH	INTERMEDIATE LOW	INTERMEDIATE MID
How well do I maintain the conversation? ***Quality of Interaction***	I have some difficulty maintaining simple conversation by using isolated words and memorized phrases. I speak with frequent hesitation, pauses, and/or repetition.	I can participate in short social interactions by asking and answering simple questions and relying heavily on learned phrases and short or incomplete sentences. I speak with hesitation, pauses, and/or repetition.	I can sustain the conversation by relying on phrases, simple sentences and a few appropriate questions. I attempt to self-correct but speak with hesitation, pauses, and/or repetition.	I can start and sustain the conversation by asking appropriate questions and responding with a series of sentences. I can rephrase, self-correct and use circumlocution. I speak with some hesitation, pauses, and/or repetition.
What language/ words do I use? ***Vocabulary in Context***	I can use a limited number of highly practiced words and expressions to identify familiar objects and actions.	I can use learned words and phrases to interact with others in tasks and activities on familiar topics.	I can use a variety of new and previously learned words and phrases to interact with others on a range of familiar topics.	I can use a variety of words, expressions, and personalized vocabulary to interact with others on a wide range of topics and begin to expand vocabulary within a topic.
How do I use language? ***Function and Text Type***	I can ask and respond to highly predictable questions with words, lists, and memorized phrases. I am beginning to communicate beyond the word level, but my errors often interfere with the message.	I can use phrases, simple sentences, and questions. I am beginning to create original sentences with simple details, but errors sometimes interfere with the message.	I can combine words and phrases to create original sentences in present time with a few details on familiar topics. I can sometimes vary the time frames (e.g., past, future), but errors may interfere with the message.	I can use a series of sentences to describe or explain with details, using a variety of time frames (e.g., past, future), but I make frequent errors in complex structures. I can combine simple sentences using connectors or transitions.

DOMAINS	NOVICE MID	NOVICE HIGH	INTERMEDIATE LOW	INTERMEDIATE MID
How well am I understood ? ***Comprehensibility***	I am somewhat understood by someone accustomed to a language learner.	I am often understood by someone accustomed to a language learner.	I am usually understood by someone accustomed to a language learner.	I am easily understood by someone accustomed to a language learner.
How well do I understand? ***Comprehension***	I can understand some familiar language, one phrase at a time. I rely on visual clues, repetition, and/or a slowed rate of speech.	I can understand pieces of information and sometimes the main idea in straightforward language that uses familiar structures. I occasionally rely on visual clues, repetition, and/or a slowed rate of speech.	I can understand the main idea in short, simple messages and conversations and in sentence-length speech that uses familiar structures. I rely on restatement, paraphrasing, and/or contextual clues.	I can understand the main ideas in messages and conversations on a variety of everyday topics and personal interests. I can understand extended speech but with frequent gaps in comprehension.
How intercultural am I? ***Interculturality*** *Based on classroom tasks/ activities/intercultural reflections and outside classroom experiences.	I can apply my knowledge of cultural products, practices, and perspectives in order to interact with respect and understanding.	I can apply my knowledge of cultural products, practices, and perspectives in order to interact with respect and understanding.	I can apply my knowledge of cultural products, practices, and perspectives in order to interact with respect and understanding.	I can apply my knowledge of cultural products, practices, and perspectives in order to interact with respect and understanding.

Adapted from Jefferson County Public Schools World Languages: Performance Assessment Rubrics (Kentucky), Howard County Public Schools World Languages (Maryland).

Level 2 *EntreCultures* Analytic Growth Rubric

Presentational Speaking

Level 2 Target: Novice High - Intermediate Low

DOMAINS	NOVICE MID	NOVICE HIGH	INTERMEDIATE LOW	INTERMEDIATE MID
What language/ words do I use? *Vocabulary in Context*	I can use a limited number of words and expressions to identify objects and actions in familiar contexts.	I can use words and expressions that I have practiced to present familiar topics.	I can use a variety of new and previously learned words and phrases to present a range of familiar topics.	I can use a variety of words, expressions, and personalized vocabulary to present a wide range of familiar topics. I am beginning to use expanded vocabulary within a topic of study.
How do I use language? *Function and Text Type*	I can use highly predictable words, lists, and memorized phrases in very familiar contexts.	I can use phrases, simple sentences, and questions. I am beginning to create original sentences with some simple details in familiar contexts.	I can use a series of simple sentences by combining words and phrases to create original sentences with some details and elaboration in familiar contexts.	I can use a series of sentences to describe or explain with some detail and elaboration using connector words to create original sentences in contexts related to familiar topics and studies.
How well am I understood ? *Comprehensibility*	I am somewhat understood by someone accustomed to a language learner.	I am often understood by someone accustomed to a language learner.	I am usually understood by someone accustomed to a language learner.	I am easily understood by someone accustomed to a language learner.
How accurate am I? *Structures*	I can use mostly memorized words and some basic structures with frequent errors.	I can use basic structures in present time with some errors, relying on memorized phrases.	I can use basic structures with some variety in time frames (e.g., past, future) with some errors.	I can use basic structures in a variety of time frames (e.g., past, future), including some complex structures with connectors and transitions but may have frequent errors.
How well do I deliver my message? *Delivery, Fluency, Visuals, Impact on Audience*	I can deliver my message using isolated words and memorized phrases, speaking with frequent hesitation, pauses, and/or repetition.	I can deliver my message by relying on learned phrases and short or incomplete sentences, speaking with hesitation, pauses, and/or repetition.	I can deliver my message by relying on phrases and simple sentences, speaking with hesitation, pauses, and/or repetition.	I can deliver my message by using a series of sentences. I can self- correct some of the time, speaking with some hesitation, pauses, and/or repetition.
How intercultural am I? *Interculturality* *Based on classroom tasks/ activities/ intercultural reflections and outside classroom experiences.	I can apply my knowledge of cultural products, practices, and perspectives in order to interact with respect and understanding.	I can apply my knowledge of cultural products, practices, and perspectives in order to interact with respect and understanding.	I can apply my knowledge of cultural products, practices, and perspectives in order to interact with respect and understanding.	I can apply my knowledge of cultural products, practices, and perspectives in order to interact with respect and understanding.

Adapted from Jefferson County Public Schools World Languages: Performance Assessment Rubrics (Kentucky), Howard County Public Schools World Languages (Maryland).

Level 2 *EntreCultures* Analytic Growth Rubric

Presentational Writing

Level 2 Target: Novice High - Intermediate Low

DOMAINS	NOVICE MID	NOVICE HIGH	INTERMEDIATE LOW	INTERMEDIATE MID
What language/ words do I use? *Vocabulary in context*	I can use a limited number of memorized words and phrases in context.	I can use words and expressions that I have practiced on familiar topics.	I can use a variety of new and previously learned words and phrases on a range of familiar topics.	I can use a variety of words, expressions, and personalized vocabulary on a wide range of familiar topics. I am beginning to use expanded vocabulary within a topic.
How do I use language? *Function and Text Type*	I can supply information in a form, chart, or organizer. I can write lists and memorized phrases on familiar topics.	I can write short messages, postcards, and simple notes on familiar topics related to everyday life. I can use learned vocabulary and structures to create simple sentences and questions on very familiar topics. I can add simple details.	I can write a series of simple sentences on familiar topics. I can create original sentences and questions using some connectors. I can describe or explain with some detail and elaboration.	I can write on a wide variety of familiar topics using connected sentences in paragraphs. I can describe or explain events and experiences with details and elaboration. I am beginning to provide clarification or justification.
How well am I understood ? *Comprehensibility*	I am somewhat understood by someone accustomed to a language learner.	I am often understood by someone accustomed to a language learner.	I am usually understood by someone accustomed to a language learner.	I am easily understood by someone accustomed to a language learner.
How well do I use the language? *Language Control*	I am beginning to use basic structures with frequent errors.	I can use basic structures in present time with some errors.	I can use basic structures with some variety in time frames (e.g., past, future) but more errors may occur.	I can use basic structures in a variety of time frames. I can use some connectors and transitions to combine sentences including complex structures but with frequent errors.
How well do I complete the task? *Ideas and Organization*	I can complete the task with familiar content. My ideas are minimally developed and lack organization.	I can complete the task with familiar content and some examples. My ideas are somewhat developed and organized.	I can complete the task with familiar content using some details and examples. My ideas are mostly developed and organized.	I can complete the task with appropriate content, details, and adequate examples. My ideas are adequately developed and organized.
How intercultural am I? *Interculturality* *Based on classroom tasks/ activities/ intercultural reflections and outside classroom experiences.	I can apply my knowledge of cultural products, practices, and perspectives in order to convey respect and understanding in writing.	I can apply my knowledge of cultural products, practices, and perspectives in order to convey respect and understanding in writing.	I can apply my knowledge of cultural products, practices, and perspectives in order to convey respect and understanding in writing.	I can apply my knowledge of cultural products, practices, and perspectives in order to convey respect and understanding in writing.

dapted from Jefferson County Public Schools World Languages: Performance Assessment Rubrics (Kentucky), Howard County Public Schools World Languages (Maryland).

Level 2 *EntreCultures* Holistic Rubric

Interpretive Reading, Listening, and Viewing: Written, Print, Audio, Visual and Audio Visual Resources

Level 2 Target: Novice High - Intermediate Low

Daily work, formative assessments

1 This is still a goal.
2 Can do this with help.
3 Can do this independently.[1]

	INTERPRETIVE: Reading, Listening, and Viewing	1	2	3
NM	• Recognizes and understands memorized words, phrases, and basic information in text or speech in familiar contexts. • Makes limited inferences from visual and/or contextual clues and cognates or may use other interpretive strategies. • Identifies a few cultural products, practices, and perspectives related to daily life, including cultural behaviors and expressions.*			
NH	• Understands and identifies words, phrases, questions, simple sentences, and sometimes the main idea in short pieces of informational text or speech in familiar contexts. • Makes a few inferences from visual and/or contextual clues, cognates, and keywords or uses other interpretive strategies. • Identifies some cultural products, practices, and perspectives related to daily life, including cultural behaviors and expressions.*			
IL	• Understands and identifies the main idea and key details in short, simple, loosely connected texts or speech in familiar contexts. • Makes some inferences from visual and/or contextual clues, cognates, and keywords or uses other interpretive strategies. • Describes cultural products, practices, and perspectives related to daily life, including cultural behaviors and expressions.**			
IM	• Identifies main ideas and a few supporting details in various time frames (e.g., past, future) in loosely connected texts or speech related to personal interests and studies. • Makes appropriate inferences from visual and/or contextual clues, cognates, keywords, and some details or uses other interpretive strategies. • Compares cultural products, practices, and perspectives related to daily life, including cultural behaviors and expressions.**			

Based on classroom tasks/activities/ intercultural reflections and outside classroom experiences.

LEARNER SELF-REFLECTION:
What interpretive strategies can I use to help me understand what I read/heard/viewed?

READING

What strategies can I use to make myself understood?

- ❑ I preview titles, photos, layout, and visuals, etc.
- ❑ I skim the text for cognates and familiar words and phrases.
- ❑ I scan the text for specific details.
- ❑ I make predictions based on context, prior knowledge, and/or experience.

LISTENING/VIEWING

What strategies did I use to help me understand what I heard?

- ❑ I listen/watch for emotional reactions.
- ❑ I listen for time/time frames.
- ❑ I listen for intonation.
- ❑ I listen for cognates, familiar words, phrases, and word-order patterns.

Adapted from Jefferson County Public Schools World Languages: Performance Assessment Rubrics (Kentucky).

[1] LinguaFolio®, NCSSFL. (2014). Interculturality. Retrieved from http://ncssfl.org/secure/index.php?interculturality, March 6, 2016.
* Novice range: using appropriate gestures, imitating appropriate etiquette, simple interactions in stores and restaurants.
** Intermediate range: demonstrating how to be culturally respectful, forms of address, appropriate interactions in everyday life.

Level 2 *EntreCultures* Holistic Rubric

Interpersonal Communication: Speaking, Listening, and Writing

Level 2 Target: Novice High - Intermediate Low

Daily class work, participation, class discussions, pair work, group work, and formative assessments

1 This is still a goal.
2 Can do this with help.
3 Can do this independently.[1]

	INTERPERSONAL COMMUNICATION: Speaking, Listening, and Writing	1	2	3
NM	• Communicates with some memorized words and expressions in familiar contexts, but needs continual repetition. Some interference from first language. • Maintains limited simple conversations with frequent hesitation, pauses, and/or repetition. • Makes limited inferences from visual and/or contextual clues, or cognates. • Applies knowledge of cultural products, practices, and perspectives in order to interact with respect and understanding.*			
NH	• Communicates and exchanges information with learned words, phrases, simple sentences, and sometimes the main idea/simple details in familiar contexts. Some interference from first language. • Participates in short social interactions by asking and answering simple questions with hesitation, pauses, and/or repetition, using a few communication strategies. • Makes a few inferences from visual and/or contextual clues, cognates, or other language features. • Applies knowledge of cultural products, practices, and perspectives in order to interact with respect and understanding.*			
IL	• Communicates and exchanges information with a variety of new and learned words, phrases, and original sentences in present tense with some details in familiar contexts. Limited interference from first language. • Participates in social interactions by asking and answering a few appropriate questions with hesitation, pauses, and/or repetition, using some communication strategies. • Makes some inferences from visual and/or contextual clues, cognates, or other language features. • Applies knowledge of cultural products, practices, and perspectives in order to interact with respect and understanding.**			
IM	• Communicates with a variety of expressions and personalized vocabulary with a series of sentences to describe details in a variety of time frames in daily life. A few errors may interfere with the message. • Participates in conversations by asking and answering a variety of questions with some hesitation, pauses, and/or repetition, using a variety of communication strategies. • Makes appropriate inferences from visual and/or contextual clues, cognates, or other language features. • Applies knowledge of cultural products, practices, and perspectives in order to interact with respect and understanding.**			

Based on classroom tasks/activities/ intercultural reflections and outside classroom experiences.

LEARNER SELF-REFLECTION:
What communication strategies can I use to help me understand and make myself understood?

SPEAKING/WRITING

What strategies can I use to make myself understood?

- ❑ I repeat words and phrases.
- ❑ I use facial expressions, gestures, and appropriate openings and closings.
- ❑ I self-correct when I am not understood.
- ❑ I imitate modeled words.
- ❑ I restate and rephrase using different words.
- ❑ I build upon what I've heard/read and elaborate in my response.
- ❑ I use level-appropriate vocabulary in familiar and contextualized situations.

LISTENING

What strategies did I use to help me understand what I heard?

- ❑ I ask for clarification or repetition.
- ❑ I repeat statements as questions for clarification.
- ❑ I listen for intonation.
- ❑ I listen for cognates, familiar words, phrases, and word-order patterns.
- ❑ I indicate lack of understanding.
- ❑ I ask questions.

Adapted from Jefferson County Public Schools World Languages: Performance Assessment Rubrics (Kentucky).

LinguaFolio®, NCSSFL. (2014). Interculturality. Retrieved from http://ncssfl.org/secure/index.php?interculturality, March 6, 2016.
Novice range: using appropriate gestures, imitating appropriate etiquette, simple interactions in stores and restaurants.
* Intermediate range: demonstrating how to be culturally respectful, forms of address, appropriate interactions in everyday life.

Level 2 *EntreCultures* Holistic Rubric

Presentational Speaking

Level 2 Target: Novice High - Intermediate Low

Daily class work, participation, share out or present to class, present to a group, formative assessments, and using Explorer audio and video recording feature

1 This is still a goal.
2 Can do this with help.
3 Can do this independently.[1]

	PRESENTATIONAL SPEAKING	1	2	3
NM	• Uses some memorized words and expressions in familiar contexts. Some interference from first language. • Delivers message using some highly practiced basic structures with frequent errors. Speaks with frequent hesitation, pauses, and/or repetition. • Makes limited use of gestures, self-correction, and examples/visuals to support the message. • Applies knowledge of cultural products, practices, and perspectives in order to interact with respect and understanding.*			
NH	• Uses most highly practiced/learned words, phrases, and simple sentences in familiar contexts. Some interference from first language. • Delivers message using present time frame with some errors and some memorized new structures. Speaks with hesitation, pauses, and/or repetition. • Makes some use of gestures, self-correction, and examples/visuals to support the message, or a few other communication strategies. • Applies knowledge of cultural products, practices, and perspectives in order to interact with respect and understanding.*			
IL	• Uses new and previously learned words and phrases in a series of simple sentences/ questions to describe or explain with some details and elaboration in familiar contexts. Limited interference from first language. • Delivers message using basic structures with some variety in time frames (e.g., past, future) with some errors. Speaks with hesitation, pauses, and/or repetition. • Makes appropriate use of gestures, self-correction, and examples/visuals to support the message, or other communication strategies. • Applies knowledge of cultural products, practices, and perspectives in order to interact with respect and understanding.**			
IM	• Uses a variety of expressions and personalized vocabulary in a series of sentences to describe or explain with details and elaboration in familiar contexts. A few errors may interfere with the message. • Delivers message using a variety of basic time frames (e.g., past, future) using connectors and transitions, including complex structures with frequent errors. Speaks with some hesitation, pauses, and/or repetition. • Makes consistent use of gestures, self-correction, and examples/visuals to support the message, and other communication strategies. • Applies knowledge of cultural products, practices, and perspectives in order to interact with respect and understanding.**			

Based on classroom tasks/activities/ intercultural reflections and outside classroom experiences.

LEARNER SELF-REFLECTION:
What communication strategies did I use to make myself understood to my audience?

PRESENTATIONAL SPEAKING

- ❑ I organize my presentation in a clear manner.
- ❑ I use facial expressions and gestures.
- ❑ I self-correct when I make mistakes.
- ❑ I present my own ideas.
- ❑ I use examples to support my message.
- ❑ I use visuals to support meaning.
- ❑ I include a hook to gain the audience's attention.
- ❑ I notice the reaction of the audience during the presentation.
- ❑ I repeat or rephrase if the audience doesn't understand.
- ❑ I project my voice so the audience can hear me.
- ❑ I practice my presentation before I present to the audience.

apted from Jefferson County Public Schools World Languages: Performance Assessment Rubrics (Kentucky).

nguaFolio®, NCSSFL. (2014). Interculturality. Retrieved from http://ncssfl.org/secure/index.php?interculturality, March 6, 2016.
ovice range: using appropriate gestures, imitating appropriate etiquette, simple interactions in stores and restaurants.
ntermediate range: demonstrating how to be culturally respectful, forms of address, appropriate interactions in everyday life.

Level 2 *EntreCultures* Holistic Rubric

Presentational Writing

Level 2 Target: Novice High - Intermediate Low

Daily written class work, forms, organizers, charts, messages, notes, formative assessments, and using Explorer tasks, surveys, discussion forums, and more

1 This is still a goal.
2 Can do this with help.
3 Can do this independently.[1]

	PRESENTATIONAL WRITING	1	2	3
NM	• Uses memorized words, expressions, and short sentences in somewhat organized and familiar contexts. Frequent interference from first language. • Completes the task with some highly practiced basic structures with frequent errors. Ideas lack development and organization. • Makes limited use of presentational writing strategies. • Applies knowledge of cultural products, practices, and perspectives in order to convey respect and understanding in writing.*			
NH	• Uses highly practiced/learned words, phrases, questions, and simple sentences to write short, simple messages with simple details in familiar contexts. Some interference from first language. • Completes the task using present time frame and some memorized new structures. Ideas are partially developed and somewhat organized. • Makes some use of drafting, outlining, or peer review, or other presentational writing strategies. • Applies knowledge of cultural products, practices, and perspectives in order to convey respect and understanding in writing.*			
IL	• Uses new and previously learned words and phrases in a series of original and simple sentences/questions to describe or explain in some detail, using supporting examples and elaboration in familiar contexts. Limited interference from first language. • Completes the task using basic structures with some variety in time frames (e.g., past, future) with significant errors. Ideas are mostly developed and organized. • Makes appropriate use of drafting, outlining, peer review, or other presentational writing strategies. • Applies knowledge of cultural products, practices, and perspectives in order to convey respect and understanding in writing.**			
IM	• Uses a variety of expressions and personalized vocabulary and connected sentences in paragraphs to describe with details, supporting examples, and elaboration; beginning to provide clarification or justification on a wide variety of familiar topics. A few errors may interfere with the message. • Completes the task using a variety of basic time frames (e.g., past, future), using connectors and transitions, including complex structures, with frequent errors. Ideas are adequately developed and organized. • Makes consistent use of drafting, outlining, peer review, and other presentational writing strategies. • Applies knowledge of cultural products, practices, and perspectives in order to convey respect and understanding in writing.**			

Based on classroom tasks/activities/ intercultural reflections and outside classroom experiences.

LEARNER SELF-REFLECTION:
What communication strategies can I use to make my message understood to the reader?

PRESENTATIONAL WRITING

- ❑ I organize my presentation in a clear manner.
- ❑ I include a hook to gain the reader's attention.
- ❑ I present my own ideas.
- ❑ I write an outline before I begin to write.
- ❑ I cite my sources if I have done research on the topic.
- ❑ I write a draft of my message.
- ❑ I use examples to support my message.
- ❑ I ask someone to peer edit my draft before I submit it.
- ❑ I check all spelling and grammar before I submit it.
- ❑ I make sure my writing is clear and my handwriting is legible.

Adapted from Jefferson County Public Schools World Languages: Performance Assessment Rubrics (Kentucky).

[1] LinguaFolio®, NCSSFL. (2014). Interculturality. Retrieved from http://ncssfl.org/secure/index.php?interculturality, March 6, 2016.
* Novice range: using appropriate gestures, imitating appropriate etiquette, simple interactions in stores and restaurants.
** Intermediate range: demonstrating how to be culturally respectful, forms of address, appropriate interactions in everyday life.

Rubrics

EntreCultures 2 – General *J'avance* Rubric

DOMAINS	BEGINNING	DEVELOPING	MEETING
Task Completion	Minimal completion of the task. Ideas are not developed. Responses display minimal/no understanding of the information presented.	Partial completion of the task. Ideas are minimally developed. Responses display a limited understanding of the information presented.	Adequate completion of the task. Ideas are appropriately developed. Responses display an adequate understanding of the information presented.
Structures (Grammar) in Context	Minimal use of target language structures. Errors make comprehension difficult.	Limited accuracy with target language structures. Errors may impede comprehension.	Generally accurate use of target language structures with a few errors. Errors do not impede comprehension.
Vocabulary in Context	Vocabulary used is inaccurate and repetitive and minimally includes essential unit vocabulary.	Vocabulary is limited to highly practiced words and expressions and includes some essential unit vocabulary.	Vocabulary is adequate and mostly relevant to the task and includes essential unit vocabulary.
Comprehensibility & Pronunciation	Message may be comprehensible with great difficulty. Pronunciation impedes ability to understand.	Message is somewhat comprehensible. Pronunciation may interfere with ability to understand.	Message is generally comprehensible. Pronunciation facilitates understanding.
Quality of Interaction or Presentation	Insufficient language to communicate message; reverts to English. Requires prompting or teacher assistance to maintain interaction/presentation. Frequent hesitations.	Limited language to communicate message and may revert to English. Requires some prompting or teacher assistance to maintain interaction/presentation. Some hesitations.	Attempts creative use of language to communicate message. May require prompting or teacher assistance to maintain interaction/presentation. Occasional hesitations.

Not all domains will apply to every mode. There is also a single-point rubric available in Explorer for each ***J'avance*** assessment.

	Scores:		
EXCEEDING	**INTERPRETIVE**	**INTERPERSONAL**	**PRESENTATIONAL**
Exceeds task expectations. Ideas are well developed. Responses display a complete understanding of the information presented, including details.			
Very accurate use of target language structures with minimal errors. Errors do not impede comprehension.			
Vocabulary is varied and relevant to the task and may exceed essential unit vocabulary.			
Message is fully comprehensible. Pronunciation enhances understanding.			
Creative use of language to communicate message. Little to no prompting needed to maintain interaction/ presentation. Few to no hesitations.			

Rubrics

Integrated Performance Assessment Rubric

Unité 1 – *Un échange scolaire*

Domains	Task Components	NOVICE LOW
INTERPRETIVE ASSESSMENT **Interpretive Audiovisual Part A**	**Recognizes key words** Student checks the key words and phrases he/she hears about how a student from ***La Réunion*** approaches the school year.	Correctly recognizes one or two memorized target vocabulary words related to the topic.
Interpretive Audiovisual Part B	**Identifies words to complete main ideas** Student completes statements based on the main ideas of the video by selecting the appropriate word or phrase.	Correctly identifies one or two of the words or phrases to complete statements based on the main ideas of the video.
INTERPERSONAL ASSESSMENT **Interpersonal Speaking**	**Participates in a phone conversation** Student individually answers a series of questions about resources in his/her school, extracurricular activities, and study habits.	Contributes very limited relevant content using only memorized words and phrases. Speaks with frequent hesitation, pauses, and/or repetition that inhibit communication. Frequent errors interfere with understanding.
PRESENTATIONAL ASSESSMENT **Presentational Writing**	**Creates a visual representation of his/her school** Student creates a visual guide to introduce his/her school to a visiting student from ***La Réunion***, including: • information important for a student visiting from a Francophone culture • locations of classes • locations where students spend time • locations of school resources and support • school activities that build community	The visual representation includes few of the task's components. Uses some familiar words, unit vocabulary, and memorized phrases. **Interculturality** Does not demonstrate understanding of similarities and/or differences between his/her school life and that of a student from ***La Réunion***.

NOVICE MID	NOVICE HIGH	INTERMEDIATE LOW
Correctly recognizes a few memorized target vocabulary words related to the topic.	Correctly recognizes some of the target vocabulary related to the topic.	Correctly recognizes most of the unit target vocabulary related to the topic.
Correctly identifies a few of the words or phrases to complete statements based on the main ideas of the video.	Correctly identifies some of the words or phrases to complete statements based on the main ideas of the video.	Correctly identifies most of the words or phrases to complete statements based on the main ideas of the video.
Contributes limited relevant content or irrelevant content using only memorized words and phrases. May attempt simple sentences. Speaks with frequent hesitation, pauses, and/or repetition. Somewhat understood despite frequent errors.	Contributes some relevant content and simple details using mostly familiar words and phrases in simple sentences. Relies heavily on learned phrases and short or incomplete sentences. Speaks with hesitation, pauses, and/or repetition. Often understood despite frequent errors.	Contributes mostly relevant content with some details using a variety of unit vocabulary and expressions in simple, original sentences. Attempts to self-correct. Speaks with hesitation, pauses, and/or repetition. Usually understood despite a few errors.
The visual representation includes some of the task's components. Uses some familiar words, unit vocabulary, and memorized phrases and attempts simple sentences. **Interculturality** Minimally demonstrates understanding of similarities and/or differences between his/her life school life and that of a student from ***La Réunion***.	The visual representation includes most of the task's components with a few original ideas, some simple details, and minimal elaboration. Uses learned vocabulary and structures in simple sentences. **Interculturality** Adequately demonstrates understanding of similarities and/or differences between his/her life school life and that of a student from ***La Réunion***.	The visual representation includes all or almost all of the task's components with some original ideas, some details and elaboration. Uses the unit vocabulary and structures with ease in a series of simple and some original sentences using some connectors. **Interculturality** Adequately demonstrates understanding of similarities and/or differences between his/her life school life and that of a student from ***La Réunion***.

Rubrics

Integrated Performance Assessment Rubric

Unité 2 – *Un goût de chez vous*

Domains	Task Components	NOVICE LOW
INTERPRETIVE ASSESSMENT **Interpretive Print Part A**	**Identifies details from one or both texts.** Student chooses which food blog (or both) contains a given detail.	Correctly pairs a few of the details with the source text.
Interpretive Print Part B	**Identifies key words.** Student checks pictures of ingredients necessary for two recipes.	Correctly identifies a few of the keywords that apply to each text.
INTERPERSONAL ASSESSMENT **Interpersonal Speaking**	**Participates in a conversation with classmates.** Students in pairs or small groups ask and answer questions about their memories related to food and special occasions.	Provides a few short answers to direct questions, using words or phrases.
PRESENTATIONAL ASSESSMENT **Presentational Speaking**	**Creates a video invitation.** Student creates a video invitation inviting blogger and his family to a traditional Belgian meal. Video must include: • an appropriate greeting or introduction • a description of the traditional dishes he/she will serve • an explanation of his/her choice of the side dish that references the memories that the food bloggers shared with their recipes • time and place of the meal • an appropriate sign-off or conclusion	The visual representation includes a few of the task's components. Uses some familiar words, unit vocabulary, and memorized phrases. **Interculturality** Does not demonstrate understanding of the connection between food and community.

NOVICE MID	NOVICE HIGH	INTERMEDIATE LOW
Correctly pairs some of the details with the source text.	Correctly pairs most of the details with the source text.	Correctly pairs all or almost all of the details with the source text.
Correctly identifies some of the keywords that apply to each text.	Correctly identifies most of the keywords that apply to each text.	Correctly identifies all or almost all of the keywords that apply to each text.
Provides some short answers to questions, using words or phrases. Attempts to use simple sentences and ask a few questions. Contributes limited relevant content or irrelevant content using only memorized words and phrases. May attempt simple sentences. Speaks with frequent hesitation, pauses, and/or repetition. Somewhat understood despite frequent errors.	Asks several simple questions and responds appropriately to a classmate, using some unit vocabulary and expressions in simple sentences. Speaks with some hesitations, pauses, and/or repetition. Often understood despite some errors.	Asks several questions and responds appropriately to classmate, using a variety of unit vocabulary and expressions in simple, original sentences. Attempts to self-correct when necessary. May speak with hesitation, pauses, and/or repetition. Usually understood despite a few errors.
The visual representation includes some of the task's components. Uses some familiar words, unit vocabulary, and memorized phrases and attempts simple sentences. **Interculturality** Minimally demonstrates an understanding of the connection between food and community.	The visual representation includes most of the task's components with a few original ideas, some simple details, and minimal elaboration. Uses learned vocabulary and structures in simple sentences. Student language/presentation is somewhat comprehensible, requiring some listener interpretation. **Interculturality** Adequately demonstrates an understanding of the connection between food and community.	The invitation includes all or almost all of the task's components with some original ideas, some details and elaboration. Uses the unit vocabulary and structures with ease in a series of simple and some original sentences using some connectors. Student language/presentation is mostly comprehensible, requiring some listener interpretation. **Interculturality** Adequately demonstrates an understanding of the connection between food and community.

Rubrics

Integrated Performance Assessment Rubric

Unité 3 – *Être bénévole à Montréal*

Domains	Task Components	NOVICE LOW
INTERPRETIVE ASSESSMENT **Interpretive Print Part A**	**Associates images with the appropriate text.** Student selects which posting about a volunteer opportunity is associated with each image.	Correctly associates one or none of the images with the appropriate text.
Interpretive Print Part B	**Classifies key words.** Student classifies key words from volunteer postings as places, tasks, or personal qualities.	Correctly classifies one or none of the keywords.
INTERPERSONAL ASSESSMENT **Interpersonal Speaking**	**Participates in a conversation with classmates.** Student discusses with a partner his or her preferred volunteer opportunity and gives reasons for his or her preferences.	Provides a few short answers to direct questions, using words or phrases.
PRESENTATIONAL ASSESSMENT **Presentational Writing**	**Completes a volunteer application.** Student completes a volunteer application, providing basic information about himself or herself, and answering some questions about why he or she wants to volunteer and what qualities and talents he or she can bring to a volunteer position.	Provides short responses that include words or phrases, with little or no elaboration. Student uses some familiar words, unit vocabulary, and memorized phrases. Student language requires much reader interpretation. **Interculturality** Does not demonstrate understanding of belonging to a community through volunteerism.

NOVICE MID	NOVICE HIGH	INTERMEDIATE LOW
Correctly associates a few of the images with the appropriate text.	Correctly associates some of the images with appropriate text.	Correctly associates most of the images with the appropriate text.
Correctly classifies some of the keywords.	Correctly classifies most of the keywords.	Correctly classifies all or almost all of the keywords.
Provides some short answers to questions, using words or phrases. Attempts to use simple sentences and ask a few questions. Contributes limited relevant content or irrelevant content using only memorized words and phrases. Speaks with frequent hesitation, pauses, and/or repetition. Somewhat understood despite frequent errors.	Asks several simple questions and responds appropriately to a classmate, using some unit vocabulary and expressions in simple sentences. Speaks with some hesitations, pauses, and/or repetition. Often understood despite some errors.	Asks several questions and responds appropriately to classmate, using a variety of unit vocabulary and expressions in simple, original sentences. Attempts to self-correct when necessary. May speak with hesitation, pauses, and/or repetition. Usually understood despite a few errors.
Provides responses that include words and phrases, and may attempt simple sentences with minimal elaboration. Student uses some familiar words, unit vocabulary, and memorized phrases. Student language often requires reader interpretation. **Interculturality** Minimally demonstrates understanding of belonging to a community through volunteerism.	Provides responses that include simple sentences, with some elaboration. Uses learned vocabulary and structures in simple sentences. Student language is somewhat comprehensible, requiring some reader interpretation. **Interculturality** Adequately demonstrates understanding of belonging to a community through volunteerism.	Provides responses that include a series of simple and some original sentences using some connectors and elaboration. Uses the unit vocabulary and structures with ease. Student language is mostly comprehensible, requiring some reader interpretation. **Interculturality** Adequately demonstrates understanding of belonging to a community through volunteerism.

Rubrics

Integrated Performance Assessment Rubric

Unité 4 – *Une sortie dans la Ville Lumière*

Domains	Task Components	NOVICE MID
INTERPRETIVE ASSESSMENT **Interpretive Audiovisual**	**Identifies key details from a tourism video.** Student identifies the place mentioned in each of three segments of the video, as well as activities to do at each site and how to get there.	Correctly identifies a few of the details from the video.
INTERPERSONAL ASSESSMENT **Interpersonal Speaking**	**Participates in a conversation with classmates.** Student discusses with a partner the place that he or she would like to visit, explaining why the student prefers this place and how the pair can get there (transportation). Student reaches an agreement with partner.	Provides some short answers to questions, using words or phrases. Attempts to use simple sentences and ask a few questions. Contributes limited relevant content or irrelevant content using only memorized words and phrases. May attempt simple sentences. Speaks with frequent hesitation, pauses, and/or repetition. Somewhat understood despite frequent errors.
PRESENTATIONAL ASSESSMENT **Presentational Writing**	**Writes a description of his or her day.** Student writes a description of the day spent in Paris. Student explains: • where he or she went; • how he or she arrived there; • what he or she saw; and, • what he or she did.	The written description includes some of the task's components. Uses some familiar words, unit vocabulary, and memorized phrases and attempts simple sentences. Student language frequently requires reader interpretation. **Interculturality** Minimally demonstrates understanding of life in a Francophone city.

NOVICE HIGH	INTERMEDIATE LOW	INTERMEDIATE MID
Correctly identifies some of the details from the video.	Correctly identifies most of the details from the video.	Correctly identifies all or almost all of the details from the video.
Asks several simple questions and responds appropriately to a classmate, using some unit vocabulary and expressions in simple sentences. Speaks with some hesitations, pauses, and/or repetition. Often understood despite some errors.	Asks several questions and responds appropriately to classmate, using a variety of unit vocabulary and expressions in simple, original sentences. Attempts to self-correct when necessary. May speak with hesitation, pauses, and/or repetition. Usually understood despite a few errors.	Asks several questions and responds appropriately to a classmate, using a variety of unit vocabulary in original sentences. Self-corrects when necessary. May speak with some hesitation, pauses, and/or repetition. Almost always understood despite a few errors.
The written description includes most of the task's components with a few original ideas, some simple details, and minimal elaboration. Uses learned vocabulary and structures in simple sentences. Student language is somewhat comprehensible, requiring some reader interpretation. **Interculturality** Adequately demonstrates understanding of life in a Francophone city.	The written description includes almost all of the task's components with some original ideas, some details and elaboration. Uses the unit vocabulary and structures with ease in a series of simple and some original sentences using some connectors. Student language is mostly comprehensible, requiring some reader interpretation. **Interculturality** Adequately demonstrates understanding of life in a Francophone city.	The written description includes all of the task's components with original ideas, details, and elaboration. Uses the unit vocabulary and structures with ease in original sentences using connectors. Student language is comprehensible, requiring minimal reader interpretation. **Interculturality** Clearly demonstrates understanding of life in a Francophone city.

Rubrics

Integrated Performance Assessment Rubric

Unité 5 – *Une présentation sur la santé des adolescents*

Domains	Task Components	NOVICE MID
INTERPRETIVE ASSESSMENT **Interpretive Audiovisual Part A**	**Identifies key details from a video about health and sleep.** Student completes the sentences to summarize key information that corresponds to the illustrations of the video.	Correctly identifies a few of the details from the video.
Interpretive Audiovisual Part B	Student identifies two additional details not mentioned in the previous task.	Mentions one or two incomplete ideas or repeats information from previous task.
PRESENTATIONAL ASSESSMENT **Presentational Speaking**	**Creates a video to inform on adolescent health.** Student creates a video presenting information and advising on adolescent health. Video must include: • an introduction • ideas to promote health based on pertinent details/ data • information from the source or from his/ her choice of health topic • sentence connectors • an appropriate sign-off or conclusion	The audiovisual presentation includes some of the task's components. Uses some familiar words, unit vocabulary, and memorized phrases and attempts simple sentences. Student language frequently requires listener interpretation. **Interculturality** Minimally demonstrates understanding of how people in different communities maintain their health.
INTERPERSONAL ASSESSMENT **Interpersonal Writing**	**Participates in a Q/A with classmates.** Student asks questions to presenters and answers questions about his or her own presentation.	Asks a few memorized questions and provides a few short answers to questions, using a few words or phrases from the unit. Student language frequently requires reader interpretation.

NOVICE HIGH	INTERMEDIATE LOW	INTERMEDIATE MID
Correctly identifies some of the details from the video.	Correctly identifies most of the details from the video.	Correctly identifies all or almost all of the details from the video.
Identifies one detail or mostly complete details and/or much of what is stated is repetition of details from previous task.	Identifies two complete ideas but may have some element of repetition of details from previous task.	Clearly identifies two complete ideas not mentioned in the previous task.
The audiovisual presentation includes most of the task's components with some simple details, and minimal elaboration. Uses learned vocabulary and structures in simple sentences. Student language/presentation is somewhat comprehensible, requiring some listener interpretation. **Interculturality** Adequately demonstrates understanding of how people in different communities maintain their health.	The audiovisual presentation includes almost all of the task's components with some original ideas, some details and elaboration. Uses the unit vocabulary and structures with ease in a series of simple sentences using some connectors. Student language/presentation is mostly comprehensible, requiring some listener interpretation. **Interculturality** Adequately demonstrates understanding of how people in different communities maintain their health.	The audiovisual presentation includes almost all of the task's components with original ideas, some details and elaboration. Uses the unit vocabulary and structures with ease in a series of simple and some original sentences using some connectors. Student language/presentation is mostly comprehensible. **Interculturality** Clearly demonstrates understanding of how people in different communities maintain their health.
Asks several simple questions and responds appropriately to some messages, using some unit vocabulary and expressions in simple sentences. Student language is somewhat comprehensible, requiring some reader interpretation.	Asks several questions and responds appropriately to messages, using a variety of unit vocabulary and expressions in simple, original sentences. Student language is mostly comprehensible, requiring some reader interpretation.	Asks several pertinent questions and responds appropriately to messages, using a variety of unit vocabulary and expressions in original sentences. Student language is comprehensible, requiring minimal reader interpretation.

Rubrics

Integrated Performance Assessment Rubric

Unité 6 – *Un voyage à l'étranger*

Domains	Task Components	NOVICE MID
INTERPRETIVE ASSESSMENT **Interpretive Print**	**Identifies key details from a travel brochure.** Student identifies relevant information from a travel brochure in a chart. Student answers questions to help determine which travel opportunity is best suited for him/her.	Correctly identifies a few of the relevant details from the brochure to complete the chart and answers a few questions.
PRESENTATIONAL ASSESSMENT **Presentational Writing**	**Completes a scholarship application form.** Student completes the application form which includes the travel option chosen and short answer questions.	Provides responses that include words and phrases, and may attempt simple sentences with minimal elaboration. Student uses some familiar words, unit vocabulary, and memorized phrases. Student language often requires reader interpretation.
INTERPERSONAL ASSESSMENT **Interpersonal Speaking**	**Prepares for an interview to obtain a scholarship.** Student prepares for an interview with a scholarship committee. With a partner, he or she will practice asking and answering the following questions about traveling: How will you prepare for the trip? What will you do during the trip? What will you avoid during the trip? How did you make your choice?	Provides some short answers to questions, using words or phrases. Attempts to use simple sentences and ask a few questions. Contributes limited relevant content or irrelevant content using only memorized words and phrases. May attempt simple sentences. Speaks with frequent hesitation, pauses, and/or repetition. Somewhat understood despite frequent errors. **Interculturality** Minimally demonstrates understanding of how to travel responsibly.

NOVICE HIGH	INTERMEDIATE LOW	INTERMEDIATE MID
Correctly identifies some of the relevant details from the brochure to complete the chart and answers some questions.	Correctly identifies most of the relevant details from the brochure to complete the chart and answers most questions.	Correctly identifies all or almost all of the relevant details from the brochure to complete the chart and answers all of the questions.
Provides responses that include simple sentences, with some elaboration. Uses learned vocabulary and structures in simple sentences. Student language is somewhat comprehensible, requiring some reader interpretation.	Provides responses that include a series of simple and some original sentences using some connectors and elaboration. Uses the unit vocabulary and structures with ease. Student language is mostly comprehensible, requiring some reader interpretation.	Provides responses that include a series of original sentences, some details, connectors, and elaboration. Uses a variety of unit vocabulary and structures with ease. Student language is mostly comprehensible, requiring minimal interpretation.
Asks questions and responds appropriately to a classmate, using some unit vocabulary and expressions in simple sentences. Speaks with some hesitations, pauses, and/or repetition. Often understood despite some errors. **Interculturality** Adequately demonstrates understanding of how to travel responsibly.	Asks questions and responds appropriately to classmate, using a variety of unit vocabulary and expressions in simple, original sentences. Attempts to self-correct when necessary. May speak with hesitation, pauses, and/or repetition. Usually understood despite a few errors. **Interculturality** Adequately demonstrates understanding of how to travel responsibly.	Asks questions and responds appropriately to a classmate, using a variety of unit vocabulary in original sentences. Self-corrects when necessary. May speak with some hesitation, pauses, and/or repetition. Almost always understood despite a few errors. **Interculturality** Clearly demonstrates understanding of how to travel responsibly.

EntreCultures 2
AP® and IB Correlation Guide

AP® Theme	Unit 1	Unit 2	Unit 3	Unit 4	Unit 5	Unit 6
Les défis mondiaux						
La tolérance						✔
L'économie		✔				
L'environnement	✔		✔			✔
La santé		✔			✔	
Les droits de l'être humain						
L'alimentation		✔			✔	
La paix et la guerre						
La science et la technologie						
La recherche et ses nouvelle frontières					✔	
Les découvertes et les inventions						
Les choix moraux			✔		✔	✔
L'avenir de la technologie					✔	
La propriété intellectuelle						
Les nouveaux moyens de communication				✔	✔	
La technologie et ses effets sur la société				✔	✔	
La vie contemporaine						
La publicité et le marketing						✔
L'éducation et l'enseignement	✔		✔			✔
Les fêtes		✔				
Le logement			✔			✔
Les loisirs et le sport	✔	✔	✔	✔	✔	✔
Le monde du travail			✔			✔
Les rites de passage	✔		✔	✔		✔
Les voyages	✔			✔		✔

AP® Theme	Unit 1	Unit 2	Unit 3	Unit 4	Unit 5	Unit 6
La quête de soi						
L'aliénation et l'assimilation			✔			
Les croyances et les systèmes de valeurs			✔			
La sexualité						
L'identité linguistique		✔				✔
Le pluriculturalisme		✔				✔
Le nationalisme et le patriotisme	✔	✔	✔			✔
La famille et la communauté						
Les rapports sociaux	✔	✔	✔			
L'enfance et l'adolescence	✔	✔	✔	✔	✔	
La citoyenneté	✔	✔	✔			
Les coutumes	✔	✔	✔			
La famille	✔	✔				✔
L'amitié et l'amour		✔		✔		
L'esthétique						
L'architecture				✔		
Le patrimoine		✔		✔		✔
Le beau				✔		
Les arts littéraires			✔	✔		
La musique	✔					
Les arts du spectacle	✔					
Les arts visuels		✔		✔		

IB Theme	Unit 1	Unit 2	Unit 3	Unit 4	Unit 5	Unit 6
1. Identités	✔	✔	✔	✔	✔	✔
2. Expériences	✔	✔	✔	✔	✔	✔
3. Ingéniosité humaine				✔		
4. Organisation sociale	✔	✔				
5. Partage de la planète		✔	✔			

Glossary French-English

LEGEND

f. - feminine

f. pl. - feminine plural

m. - masculine

m. pl. - masculine plural

l' abri (m.) shelter (3)

accéder à la plate-forme de la classe to access the class learning platform (1)

l' accueil (m.) reception area (1)

accueillir to welcome (3)

acheter to buy (4)

actif/active active (3)

les activités (f. pl.) d'une organisation activities in an organization (3)

les activités (f. pl.) en ville city activities (4)

les activités (f. pl.) périscolaires extracurricular activities (1)

les ados (m./f. pl.) teens (3)

l' aéroport (m.) airport (6)

l' Afrique (f.)/en Afrique Africa/in or to Africa (6)

âgé/âgée old (3)

l' agenda (m.) scolaire school planner (1)

aider to help (1, 3)

l' ail (m.) garlic (2)

l' aire (f.) de jeux playground (4)

ajouter to add (2)

à l'étranger (m.) abroad, in a different country (6)

à l'heure (f.) on time (5)

à la montagne in the mountains (6)

à la piscine at the pool (6)

à la recherche de in search of (3)

l' algèbre (f.) algebra (1)

les aliments (m. pl.) foods (2, 5)

l' allemand (m.) the German language (1)

aller au cinéma to go to the movies (5)

aller à un festival to go to a festival (6)

aller à une foire to go to a fair (6)

aller aux puces to go to the flea market (4

aller voir... to go see... (1)

alpin/alpine alpine, mountainous (6)

ambitieux/ambitieuse ambitious (3)

améliorer to improve (3)

l' Amérique (f.) du Nord/en Amérique du Nord North America/in or to North America (6)

l' Amérique (f.) du Sud/en Amérique du Sud South America/in or to South America (6)

s' amuser to have fun (5)

ancien/ancienne old, ancient (4)

l' anglais (m.) the English language (1)

l' année (f.) scolaire school year (1)

l' Antarctique (f.)/en Antarctique Antarctica/in or to Antarctica (6)

anxieux/anxieuse anxious (5)

à pied on foot (4)

l' appartement (m.) apartment (3)

l' appli(cation) (f.) (mobile) app(lication) (4

apprendre to learn (3)

après l'école after school (1)

l' aquarium (m.) aquarium (4)

À quelle heure? At what time? (1)

l' arabe (m.) the Arabic language (1)

l' arrondissement (m.) administrative district of a city (4)

arroser to water (3)

les arts (m. pl.) plastiques visual arts (1)

l' Asie (f.)/en Asie Asia/in or to Asia (6)

l' assiette (f.) plate (2)

assister à un match (de foot) to attend a (soccer) game (4)

attendre au dernier moment (pour) to wait until the last minute (to) (1)

l' auberge (f.) de jeunesse youth hostel (6)

Aujourd'hui, je vais vous parler de... Today, I will speak to you about... (5)

l' Australie (f.)/en Australie Australia/in or to Australia (6)

l' autobus (m.) bus (4)

avant l'école before school (1)

l' avenir (m.) the future (3)

l' avocat (m.) avocado (5)

avoir chaud to feel hot (5)

avoir de la fièvre to have a fever (5)

avoir des allergies to have allergies (5)

avoir faim to be hungry (5)

avoir le nez qui coule to have a runny nose (5)

avoir mal + au/à la/à l'/aux + (partie du corps) (body part) hurts, aches (5)

avoir soif to be thirsty (5)

avoir un rhume to have a cold (5)

le bagage à main carry-on bag (6)

la baguette baguette (2)

la baie bay (6)

la banane banana (2, 5)

la banque alimentaire food bank (3)

bas/basse low (4)

le bateau boat (4)

bavarder to chat (5, 6)

beaucoup de monde lots of people (4)

les beignets congolais (m. pl.) Congolese donuts (2)

le/la bénévole volunteer (3)

les betteraves (f. pl.) beets (2)

le beurre butter (2)

le billet d'entrée entrance fee, ticket (4)

la billetterie ticket window, online ticket sales (4)

la biologie biology (1)

bloguer to blog (6)

les boissons (f. pl.) beverages (2)

les boissons (f. pl.) énergisantes energy drinks (5)

le bol bowl (2)

les bottes (f. pl.) boots (6)

la boucherie butcher's shop (4)

la boulangerie bakery (4)

le bouquet garni bundle of herbs for flavoring soups or sauces (2)

la boutique boutique (4)

le bowling bowling alley (4)

la brosse à cheveux hairbrush (6)

la brosse à dents toothbrush (6)

le bureau central main office (1)

le bus bus (4)

le cadeau gift (6)

le café coffee (2)

au café to the café (4)

le cahier notebook (1)

la calculatrice calculator (1)

le calendrier scolaire school calendar (1)

canadien/canadienne Canadian (3)

le canard duck (2)

la cantine cafeteria (1)

la carbonnade flamande Belgian beef stew (2)

le carnet booklet, pack of tickets (4)

le carnet de voyage travel journal (6)

la carotte carrot (2)

la carte menu (2)

le casier locker (1)

Ça vous dit (de...) Are you interested (in...) (2)

le céleri celery (2)

le centre d'intérêt interest (5)

au centre-ville downtown (4)

les cerises (f. pl.) cherries (2)

le cerveau brain (1)

C'est quelqu'un de ___ He/she's a ___ person. (1)

chaleureux/chaleureuse warm, welcoming (2)

la chambre (à coucher) bedroom (3)

changer de l'argent to exchange currency (6)

chanter to sing (5)

le chantier work site (3)

le chantier de bénévoles volunteer work site (6)

le chapeau hat (6)

la charcuterie delicatessen (deli) (4)

chauffer to heat, to warm (2)

les chaussures (f. pl.) shoes (6)

le/la chef leader (3)

la chemise shirt (6)

le chemisier blouse (6)

cher/chère expensive (4)

la cheville ankle (5)

le chocolat chaud hot chocolate (2)

la chorale chorus (1)

le chou cabbage (2)

les chutes (f. pl.) (water)falls (6)

au cinéma to the movie theater (4)

cinquième (5e) fifth (5th) (1)

les ciseaux (m. pl.) scissors (1)

le citoyen/la citoyenne citizen (3)

le citron lemon (2, 5)

le classeur binder (1)

le climat climate (6)

le club théâtre, le club cinéma, le club de___ theater club, film club, _____ club (1)

la collecte drive (as in blood drive, food drive, etc.) (3)

le collège middle school (1)

Combien? How many? (3)

Comment? How? (3)

le commerce business (6)

les compétences (f. pl.) d'un bénévole abilities of a volunteer (3)

le complexe sportif sports complex (1)

composer (un poème, une chanson, etc.) to compose (a poem, a song, etc.) (1)

la compote applesauce (or other fruit compote) (2)

compréhensif/compréhensive understanding (3)

le concert concert (4)

le concombre cucumber (5)

la confiture jam, jelly (2)

consacrer to dedicate (5)

conseiller to give advice to (3)

le conseiller/la conseillère d'orientation school counselor (1)

les conseils (m. pl.) advice (5)

consommer to consume (5)

consulter le médecin to consult the doctor (5)

consulter l'horaire (m.) to check the schedule (4)

le continent continent (6)

contribuer à to contribute to (3)

convivial/conviviale friendly, lively (2)

la correspondance changing trains (or other transportation) (4)

la côte coast (6)

le cou neck (5)

se coucher to go to bed (5)

le coude elbow (5)

le couloir hallway (1)
couper to cut (2)
courageux/courageuse courageous (3)
le cours class, course (1)
le cours commence à... The class begins at... (2)
le cours termine à... The class ends at... (2)
court/courte short (4)
le cousin/la cousine cousin (2)
le couteau knife (2)
la coutume custom (6)
le crayon pencil (1)
créatif/créative creative (1, 3)
créer to create (3)
créer un robot to create a robot (1)
la crème cream (2)
la crème solaire sunblock (6)
la crèmerie dairy, creamery (4)
la crêpe beurre-sucre crepe with butter and sugar (2)
le croissant croissant (2)
le croque-monsieur hot ham and melted cheese sandwich (2)
croustillant/croustillante crispy, crunchy (2)
cueillir (les fruits, les fleurs) to pick (fruit, flowers) (2)
la cuillère spoon (2)
d'abord first (of all) (2)
danser to dance (5)
d'autres points (m. pl.) de vue other points of view (5)
débarrasser to clear, to empty (3)
de bonnes habitudes (f. pl.) good habits (1)
découvrir une activité culturelle to discover a cultural activity (6)
déjeuner to eat lunch (1)
le déjeuner lunch (1)
demander la permission to ask permission (6)
de mauvaises habitudes (f. pl.) bad habits (1)
le dentifrice toothpaste (6)
le/la dentiste dentist (5)
dernier/dernière last (1)
descendre to get out of a vehicle, go down (4)
le désert desert (6)
le dessert dessert (2)
de temps en temps from time to time (1)
deuxième (2e) second (2nd) (1)
devenir to become (3)
dévoué/dévouée dedicated (1)
le dictionnaire dictionary (1)
le dîner dinner (2)
dixième (10e) tenth (10th) (1)
le/la documentaliste library media specialist (1)
donner du sang to give blood (3)
les dons (m. pl.) donations (3)
dormir to sleep (5)
dormir assez to get enough sleep (5)
dormir tard to sleep late (1)
du temps libre free/unscheduled time (1)
dynamique dynamic (1, 3)
l' eau (f.) plate/gazeuse/minérale flat/sparkling/mineral water (2)
l' écharpe (f.) scarf (6)
l' économie (f.) economics (1)
écouter de la musique relaxante to listen to relaxing music (5)
les écouteurs (m. pl.) headphones (6)
l' écran (m.) screen (5)
l' éducation (f.) physique et sportive physical education (1)
efficace efficient (1)
l' emploi (m.) du temps schedule (1)

en début de journée at the beginning of the day (1)

s' **endormir** to fall asleep (5)

l' **endroit (m.)** place (4)

les **endroits (m. pl.) de l'école** places at school (1)

les **endroits (m. pl.) en ville** places in a city (4)

l' **énergie (f.)** energy (5)

énergique energetic (1, 3)

en espèces in cash (4)

l' **enfant (m. or f.)** child (2)

en fin de journée at the end of the day (1)

engagé/engagée actively involved (3)

en retard late (5)

enseigner to teach (1)

En somme In summary (5)

ensuite next, then (2)

l' **entraîneur** coach/trainer (1)

envoyer un texto/des textos to send a text message/text messages (4, 5)

l' **épicerie (f.)** small grocery store (for produce) (4)

les **épices (f. pl.)** spices (2)

l' **éponge (f.)** sponge (3)

épuisé/épuisée exhausted (5)

équilibré/équilibrée balanced (5)

l' **équipe (f.) de (foot, volley, basket, etc.)** (soccer, volleyball, basketball, etc.) team (1)

l' **espagnol (m.)** the Spanish language (1)

essayer de to try to (5)

essayer quelque chose de nouveau to try something new (3)

établir un budget to establish a budget (6)

éteindre la lumière turn out the light (6)

être fatigué/fatiguée to be tired (5)

être malade to be sick (5)

être stressé/stressée to be stressed (5)

étroit/étroite narrow (4)

étudier des fiches de révision to study notecards (1)

l' **Europe (f.)/en Europe** Europe/in or to Europe (6)

l' **événement (m.)** event (2)

l' **événement (m.) spécial** special event (2)

éviter (de) to avoid (5)

exigeant/exigeante demanding, challenging (1)

expérimenté/expérimentée experienced (3)

l' **exposition (f.)** exhibition (4)

faire to do, make (4)

faire attention to pay attention (1)

faire de l'accrobranche (f.) to go tree trekking (4)

faire de l'exercice (m.) to exercise (5)

faire de la natation to swim (6)

faire des exercices (m. pl.) to do exercises (1)

faire deux choses en même temps to do two things at once (1)

faire du bénévolat to volunteer, to do volunteer work (3)

faire du lèche-vitrine to go window shopping (4)

faire du roller to rollerblade (4)

faire du ski to ski (6)

faire du sport to play sports (5)

faire du vélo to ride a bike (5)

faire du yoga to do yoga (5)

faire les devoirs to do homework (1)

faire sa valise to pack one's suitcase (6)

faire une/des pause(s) to take a break, to take breaks (1)

faire un tour de manège to go on a(n) (amusement park) ride (4)

faire une randonnée to go hiking (5)

la **famille d'accueil** host family (6)

la **farine** flour (2)

le fast-food fast food restaurant (4)
la ferme farm (2)
le festival festival (4)
la fête party, holiday (2)
la fête d'anniversaire birthday party (2)
la fête foraine fair (4)
la fête religieuse religious holiday (2)
la feuille de papier sheet of paper (1)
fidèle loyal (3)
le filet américain steak tartare (raw, seasoned beef) (2)
la fille daughter (2)
le fils son (2)
finalement finally, lastly (2)
flâner to stroll (6)
le fleuve river (4)
(une) fois par semaine (one) time per week (1)
la fondation foundation (3)
les fonds (m. pl.) funds (3)
la forêt forest (6)
le four oven (2)
la fourchette fork (2)
la fourniture scolaire school supply (1)
le foyer student lounge (1)
le foyer de soins nursing home (3)
la fraise strawberry (2)
la framboise raspberry (2, 5)
le français the French language (1)
fréquenté/fréquentée busy, popular (for a place) (4)
le frère brother (2)
les frites (f. pl.) fries (2, 5)
le fromage cheese (2, 5)
les fruits (m. pl.) fruit (2, 5)
les fruits (m. pl.) de mer seafood (2)
fumer to smoke (5)
les gants (m. pl.) gloves (6)
garder to keep, look after, babysit (3)
garder l'esprit ouvert to keep an open mind (6)
la garderie daycare facility (3)
la gare train station (4)
gaspiller to waste (6)
le gâteau cake (2, 5)
la gaufre waffle (2)
généreux/généreuse generous (3)
le genou knee (5)
gentil/gentille nice, kind (1, 3)
la géographie (géo) geography (1, 6)
gérer to manage (3)
la glace ice cream (2, 5)
le golfe gulf (6)
la gorge throat (5)
le goût taste (n.) (2)
goûter to taste (2)
la grand-mère grandmother (2)
le grand-père grandfather (2)
les grands-parents (m. pl.) grandparents (2)
gratter to scrape (3)
grignoter to snack (5)
le guichet ticket window, counter (4)
le gymnase gymnasium (1, 4)
les habitudes (f. pl.) saines healthy habits (5)
les haricots (verts) (m. pl.) (green) beans (2)
haut/haute high (4)
l' histoire (f.) history (1)
l' histoire-géo (f.) history-geography (1)
l' hôpital (m.) hospital (3)
humide humid (6)
huitième (8e) eighth (8th) (1)
l' île (f.) island (6)
impatient/impatiente impatient (1)
imprimer to print (6)
l' infirmerie (f.) nurse's office (1)
l' infirmier/l'infirmière nurse (1)

l' informatique (f.) computer science (1)

intelligent/intelligente smart, intelligent (3)

inviter quelqu'un to invite someone (4)

(ne...) jamais never (1, 5)

la jambe leg (5)

le jardin garden (3)

le jardinage gardening (3)

le jardin communautaire community garden (3)

le jean (pair of) jeans (6)

jeune young (3)

Je vais suivre un cours de/d' ___ . I'm going to take a ___ class. (1)

Je vous invite (à...) I'm inviting you (to...) (2)

Je vous propose I'm suggesting [to you] (2)

jouer au basket (au volley, etc.) to play basketball (volleyball, etc.) (1)

jouer aux échecs to play chess (5)

jouer aux jeux vidéo to play video games (5)

jouer au/à la/à l'/aux + (un nom d'un sport) to play a specific sport (5)

jouer de la guitare (du piano, etc.) to play the guitar (the piano, etc.) (1)

jouer de la musique to play music (5)

le jour férié holiday (1)

le journal newspaper (6)

la journée en ville the day in the city (4)

la jupe skirt (6)

le jus d'orange/de pomme orange/apple juice (2)

le/la kiné(sithérapeute) physical therapist (5)

le labo(ratoire) laboratory (1)

le lac lake (6)

lâcher prise to "let go" (5)

le lait milk (2)

lancer de nouvelles idées to introduce, to initiate new ideas (3)

les langues (f. pl.) vivantes modern languages (1)

le lapin rabbit (2)

les lardons (m. pl.) cubed ham, bacon pieces (2)

large wide (4)

le latin the Latin language (2)

laver to wash (2)

laver le linge to wash laundry (3)

le lave-vaisselle dishwasher (3)

les légumes (m. pl.) vegetables (2)

les lentilles (f. pl.) contact lenses (6)

se lever to get up (5)

la ligne line (of a train, subway, etc.) (4)

limiter to limit (5)

lire to read (1, 5)

la littérature literature (1)

le livre book (1, 6)

le lit bed (5)

la location rental, renting (4)

la location à court terme, la location de courte durée short-term rental (6)

long/longue long (4)

la lotion anti-moustiques mosquito repellent (6)

louer to rent (4)

louer un appart(ement) en courte durée to rent an apartment for a short term (6)

la lumière light (4)

les lunettes (f. pl.) de soleil sunglasses (6)

le lycée high school (1)

le magasin store (4)

le magazine magazine (6)

le maillot de bain swimsuit (6)

la main hand (5)

la maison house (3, 4)

manger to eat (5)

la mangue mango (2, 5)

le manteau coat (6)
marchander to haggle, to negotiate price (6)
le mariage civil civil marriage (2)
le marketing marketing (6)
les mathématiques (f. pl.) (maths) mathematics (1)
les matières (f. pl.) school subjects (1)
la médiathèque media center (1, 4)
les médicaments (m. pl.) medications (6)
méditer to meditate (5)
mélanger to mix (2)
le menu fixed-price menu (2)
Merci de votre attention. Thank you for your attention. Thank you for listening (5)
la mère mother (2)
le métro subway, metro system (4)
mettre to put or place (2)
mettre la table to set the table (2, 3)
mettre le couvert to set the table (3)
la mode fashion (6)
les moments (m. pl.) de la journée times of the day (1)
la monnaie change (money) (4)
les montagnes (f. pl.) russes roller coaster (4)
motivé/motivée motivated (3)
la moto motorbike (4)
la moule mussel (2)
le moule baking mold or pan (2)
les moules-frites (f. pl.) mussels served with fries (2)
la moutarde mustard (5)
le mur d'escalade climbing wall (4)
les mûres (f. pl.) blackberries (2)
le musée museum (4)
la musique music (1)
ne pas arriver à to not be able to (5)
neuvième (9e) ninth (9th) (1)
l' Océanie (f.)/en Océanie Oceania/in or to Oceania (6)
l' œil (m.) eye (5)
l' œuf (m.) egg (2, 5)
l' oignon (m.) onion (2, 5)
l' omelette (f.) omelette (2)
l' oncle (m.) uncle (2)
onzième (11e) eleventh (11th) (1)
l' opéra (m.) opera (4)
l' ophtalmo(logiste) (m./f.) eye doctor (5)
l' orchestre (m.) orchestra (1)
l' ordinateur (m.) computer (1)
l' oreille (f.) ear (5)
organisé/organisée organized (3)
organiser to organize (1)
organiser son emploi du temps to organize one's schedule (3)
un organisme à but non-lucratif (OBNL) not-for-profit organization (NPO) (3)
l' orthodontiste (m./f.) orthodontist (5)
Où?/D'où? Where?/From where? (3)
le pain bread (2, 5)
le pantalon (pair of) pants (6)
par terre on the floor (3)
le parc park (4)
le parc d'attractions amusement park (4)
le parc national national park (6)
les parents (m. pl.) parents (2)
parfois sometimes (1)
le parking parking lot (1)
partager des ressources en ligne to share online resources (1)
participer to participate (1)
participer à des activités périscolaires to participate in extracurricular activities (1)
participer aux clubs to participate in clubs (5)

particulier/particulière particular (6)
les **parties (f. pl.) du corps** parts of the body (5)
le **passeport** passport (6)
passer la douane to go through customs (6)
le **passe-temps** hobby, pastime (5)
la **pâtisserie** pastry shop, bakery (4)
passer du temps avec des amis to spend time with friends (5)
passer du temps seul/seule to spend time alone (5)
passer l'aspirateur to vacuum (3)
la **pâte** dough (2)
les **pâtes (f. pl.)** pasta (2, 5)
patient/patiente patient (1, 3)
le **pays** country (6)
la **pêche** peach (5)
peindre to paint (3)
le **père** father (2)
la **permanence ("perm")** study hall (1)
le **personnel de l'école** school staff (1)
le **petit déjeuner** breakfast (2)
les **petits pois (m. pl.)** peas (2)
peu de few (5)
la **pharmacie** pharmacy (4)
la **photo(graphie)** photography (6)
la **physique** physics (1)
la **physique-chimie** physics-chemistry (1)
le **pied** foot (5)
la **piscine** swimming pool (4)
le **pion** (*slang*) hallway monitor, cafeteria monitor (1)
la **place** square, plaza (4)
le **plan** map (of a city, area) (4)
planifier to plan (5)
plier le linge to fold laundry (3)
la **plupart** the majority (5)
le **poignet** wrist (5)
le **poireau** leek (2)
les **poires (f. pl.)** pears (2, 5)
le **poisson** fish (2, 5)
les **poivrons (m. pl.)** peppers (2)
les **pommes (f. pl.)** apples (2)
les **pommes de terre (f. pl.)** potatoes (2, 5)
le **portable** cell phone (1)
le **portefeuille** wallet (6)
positif/positive positive (1, 3)
poster to post (online) (4)
le **poulet** chicken (2, 5)
le **poulet moamba** chicken cooked in palm oil with vegetables (2)
le **poulet rôti** roast chicken (2)
Pour commencer, To begin with, (5)
pour exprimer la douleur in order to express pain (5)
pour faire une présentation in order to give a presentation (5)
Pourquoi? Why? (3)
premier (1er)/première (1re) first (1st) (1)
prendre des notes to take notes (1)
prendre des photos to take photos (4)
prendre le métro to take the subway (4)
prendre un bain (chaud) to take a (hot) bath (5)
se **préparer au voyage** to prepare for a trip (6)
préserver to conserve (6)
presser to press (2)
le **principal/la principale** principal (1)
des **produits (m. pl.) bio** organic products (5)
le/la **professeur (prof)** teacher (1)
le **projet** project, plan (3)
se **promener** to take a walk (5)
le **proviseur/la proviseure** high school principal (1)

le proviseur-adjoint/la proviseure-adjointe assistant principal (1)

la psychologie psychology (1)

le/la psy(chologue) psychologist (5)

le pull sweater (6)

la purée mashed (potatoes) (2)

le pyjama pyjamas (6)

le quai platform, paved riverbank (4)

les qualités d'un bénévole traits of a volunteer (3)

Quand? When? (3)

quatrième (4e) fourth (4th) (1)

le quartier neighborhood (4)

Que/qu'? What? (3)

québécois/québécoise from Quebec (3)

Quelle heure est-il? What time is it? (1)

Qui? Who? (3)

la quiche quiche (2)

ramasser les déchets to pick up the trash (3)

ranger to tidy up, put away (3)

rarement rarely (1, 5)

réaliser to make something a reality (3)

récemment recently (4)

réconforter (quelqu'un) to comfort (someone) (3)

la récréation (récré) recess (1)

le refuge pour animaux animal shelter (3)

le refuge pour sans-abris homeless shelter (3)

regarder to look (4)

regarder des films to watch films (1)

regarder mon portable au lieu de dormir to look at my phone instead of sleeping (1)

le régime tendance fad, trendy diet (5)

la région region (6)

régulièrement regularly (1)

rencontrer de nouveaux amis to meet new friends (3)

rendre visite à quelqu'un to visit someone (6)

se renseigner to get information (6)

la rentrée back-to-school (1)

le repas meal (2)

le repas familial family meal (2)

repasser to iron (3)

repeindre to repaint (3)

se reposer to relax (5)

le RER (Réseau Express Régional) a commuter rail service serving Paris and its suburbs (4)

le réseau network (3)

le réseau social social network (4, 5)

réserver un vol to reserve a flight (6)

respectueux/respectueuse respectful (6)

respirer to breathe (5)

le restaurant restaurant (4)

rester connecté/connectée to stay connected (5)

rester hydraté/hydratée to stay hydrated (5)

la réunion meeting (3)

le réveil alarm clock (5)

se réveiller to wake up (5)

réviser to review (1)

le riz rice (2, 5)

la rue street, road (4)

rural/rurale rural (6)

le sac à dos backpack (1)

le sac de voyage travel bag (6)

sain/saine healthy (5)

la salade verte salad (2, 5)

la salle à manger dining room (3)

la salle de bains bathroom (3)

la salle de concert concert hall (4)

la salle de classe classroom (1)

la salle d'informatique computer room (1)
le salon living room (3)
les sandales (f. pl.) sandals (6)
le sandwich jambon-fromage ham and cheese sandwich (2)
la santé émotionnelle emotional health (5)
la santé sociale social health (5)
la saucisse sausage (2)
la savane savanna (6)
sec/sèche dry (6)
les sciences (f. pl.) sciences (1)
les sciences (f. pl.) de la vie et de la Terre (SVT) life and earth science (1)
les sciences (f. pl.) sociales social sciences (1)
le scooter scooter (4)
second/seconde (2^d^/2de) second (2nd) (final of two) (1)
le secrétaire/la secrétaire secretary (1)
le séjour stay (n.) (6)
se sentir to feel (5)
septième (7e) seventh (7th) (1)
la serviette napkin (2)
servir to serve (2, 3)
le short (pair of) shorts (6)
simplifier to simplify (5)
sixième (6e) sixth (6th) (1)
la sœur sister (2)
la soirée party, gathering in the evening (2)
la soirée chez des amis party, gathering in the evening at a friends' home (2)
le sommeil sleep (n.) (5)
le sondage survey (5)
sortir to take out (3)
la soupe soup (2, 5)
le sourire smile (5)
soutenir to support (3)
souvent often (1)
Soyez les bienvenu(e)s (à...) You are welcome to come (to...) (2)
le spectacle show (4)
le sport physical education (1)
sportif/sportive athletic (3)
le stade stadium (4)
le stage internship, apprenticeship (6)
la station de métro subway station (4)
le steak steak (2, 5)
le steak-frites steak and French fries (2)
strict(e) strict (1)
le stylo pen (1)
le supermarché supermarket (4)
le surveillant/la surveillante hall monitor, cafeteria monitor (1)
le symptôme symptom (5)
la tablette tablet (1)
les tâches (f. pl.) ménagères household tasks (3)
la tante aunt (2)
le tarif fee, price (4)
le tarif réduit reduced price (4)
la tarte pie, tart (2, 5)
la tarte au riz rice pie (2)
le taxi taxi (4)
le tee-shirt t-shirt (6)
télécharger to download (4)
tendu/tendue tense (5)
terminal/terminale last (1)
téléphoner à to call (4)
tenter de nouvelles choses to try new things (6)
le terrain de sport sports field (1, 4)
la tête head (5)
le thé tea (2)
le théâtre theater (for plays, concerts, etc.) (4)
le ticket ticket (4)
la tisane herbal tea (5)
les toilettes (f. pl.) toilets (1, 3)
la tomate tomato (5)

tous les jours every day (1)

tousser to cough (5)

tout le temps all the time (1)

le trajet route, trip (4)

travailleur/travailleuse hard-working (3)

tricoter to knit (5)

troisième (3e) third (3rd) (1)

trop de too much (of) (5)

tropical/tropicale tropical (6)

la trousse pencil case (1)

la trousse de toilette toiletry bag (6)

l' uniforme (m.) uniform (6)

utiliser to use (1)

utiliser mon portable en classe to use my phone in class (1)

les vacances (f. pl.) vacation (1)

la valise suitcase (6)

vapoter to vape (5)

la veille the day before (1, 5)

le vélo bike (4)

Venez nombreux (à...) Come one and all (to...) (2)

le ventre tummy, belly (5)

vérifier les heures d'ouverture to check opening hours (4)

verser to pour (2)

la veste jacket (6)

les vêtements (m. pl.) clothing (6)

la viande meat (2, 5)

la vie en ligne life online (5)

visiter to visit (4)

visiter un site historique to visit an historic site (6)

la voiture car (4)

les voyages (m. pl.) alternatifs alternative travel (6)

le voyageur/la voyageuse traveller (6)

la ville city (3)

la visite guidée guided visit (4)

visiter to visit (4)

le volcan volcano (6)

le waterzooï meat or fish stew with a cream sauce (2)

les yeux (m. pl.) eyes (5)

la zone zone, area (6)

le zoo zoo (4)

Expressions utiles French-English

à côté de next to, beside (3, 4)
à droite de to the right of (4)
à gauche de to the left of (4)
aller à la pharmacie to go to the pharmacy (5)
aller voir... to go see... (1)
l' **année (f.) dernière** last year (4)
arriver à l'heure to arrive on time (4)
arriver en retard to arrive late (4)
à tes/vos souhaits bless you (5)
avant-hier the day before yesterday (4)
Avec plaisir! With pleasure!, Gladly! (2)
avoir la grippe to have the flu (5)
Bonne idée! Good idea! (1, 3)
bouger un peu to move (around) a little bit (5)
Ça, c'est... This is... (1)
Ça fait mal. That hurts. (5)
Ça ne va pas du tout. It's not going well at all. (5)
Ce sera... It will be... (6)
C'est important de... It's important to... (3)
C'était... It was... (2)
chercher quelque chose to look for something, to go get something (1)
Comme vous pouvez (le) voir As you can see (5)
communiquer to communicate (5)
construire des maisons to build houses (3)
cuit(e)(s) avec cooked with (2)
d'accord OK (1)
dans in (3, 4)
déjà already (4)
délicieux/délicieuse delicious (1)
demander conseil à.... to ask for advice from... (1)
le **départ** departure (6)
derrière behind (4)
Désolé/Désolée, mais je ne peux pas. Sorry, but I can't. (2)
devant in front of, before (4)
dire "non" à... to say "no" to... (5)
donner à manger to feed (3)
donner un coup de main to lend a helping hand (3)
en bonne santé in good health (5)
en face de (quelqu'un, quelque chose) opposite, across from (somebody, something) (4)
épicé/épicée spicy (2)
éternuer to sneeze (5)
être accro (à) to be addicted (to) (5)
faire le lit to make the bed (3)
fait(e)(s) avec made with (2)
la **frontière** border (6)
gratuit/gratuite free, no cost (2)
hebdomadaire weekly (3)
l' **hébergement (m.)** accommodations, lodging (6)
hier yesterday (4)
l' **hôtel (m.)** hotel (6)
Ici, on peut... Here, you can... (1)
Il est important de... It's important (to)... (5)
Il fait chaud. It is hot outside. (6)
Il fait frais. It is cool outside. (6)
Il fait froid. It is cold outside. (6)
Il fallait... It was necessary (to)... (2)
Il neige. It is snowing. (6)
Il pleut. It is raining. (6)
Il y a... There is..., There are... (1)
Il y a du soleil. It is sunny outside. (6)
Il y aura... There will be... (6)
Il y avait... There was..., There were... (2)
isolé/isolée isolated (5)
J'ai appris (à)... I learned (to)... (5)

J'ai fait... I did... (4)

J'ai observé que... I observed that... (5)

J'ai passé (la journée)... I spent (the day)... (4)

J'ai pris... I took... (4)

J'ai vu... I saw... (4)

J'aurai... I will have... (6)

Je ferai... I will do... (6)

J'irai... I will go... (6)

Je ne dois pas... I must not... (1)

Je ne suis pas d'accord (avec toi). I don't agree (with you). (1)

Je passerai (du temps)... I will spend (time)... (6)

Je suis allé(e) à... I went to... (4)

Je suis d'accord (avec toi). I agree (with you). (1, 3)

Je suis rentré(e) (chez moi). I went home (to my house). (4)

Je te conseille de/d'... I recommend that you... (4)

Je vais (à)... I am going (to)..., I go (to)... (4)

Je vais y réfléchir. I'll think about it. (1, 3)

léger/légère light (2)

le plus important, c'est (de)... The most important thing, is (to)... (5)

loin de far (away) from (4)

mensuel/mensuelle monthly (3)

mercredi dernier last Wednesday (4)

mettre de la crème solaire to put on sunblock (5)

un monde meilleur a better world (3)

nature plain (referring to food) (2)

On devrait... We should..., People should..., One should... (5)

On va se régaler! We're really going to savor this! (2)

Oui, je veux bien. Yes, I'd really like to. (2)

parce que/qu' because (1)

Parlez-en à vos amis! Tell your friends about it! (2)

pas encore not yet (4)

passer du temps to spend time (1)

planifier to plan (3)

planter des arbres to plant trees (3)

pour cent percent (5)

Pour réussir à l'école, je dois... to be successful at school, I must... (1)

pour s'amuser to have fun, for fun (4)

prendre un médicament to take medication (5)

prendre son temps to take one's time (5)

près de close to, near (4)

Qu'est-ce que tu as? What's wrong? (5)

Quand j'étais petit/petite... When I was little... (2)

quotidien/quotidienne daily (3)

réduire le stress to reduce stress (5)

répondre au téléphone to answer the telephone (3)

réserver to reserve (2)

riche rich, fatty (2)

riche en... rich in... (5)

rire to laugh (5)

salé/salée salty (2)

la **semaine** week (1)

la **semaine dernière** last week (4)

servi(e)(s) avec served with (2)

soigner to treat, take care of (5)

sucré/sucrée sweet (2)

sur on (3)

trier et distribuer le courrier to sort and hand out, distribute the mail (3)

se **trouver** to be located (4)

Voici... Here is... (1)

le **week-end** weekend (1)

le **week-end dernier** last weekend (4)

Glossary English-French

LEGEND

f. - feminine

f. pl. - feminine plural

m. - masculine

m. pl. - masculine plural

abilities of a volunteer les compétences (f. pl.) d'un bénévole (3)

abroad à l'étranger (6)

(body part) aches avoir mal + au/à la/à l'/aux + (partie du corps) (5)

to **access the class learning platform** accéder à la plate-forme de la classe (1)

active actif/active (3)

actively involved engagé/engagée (3)

activities in an organization les activités (f. pl.) d'une organisation (3)

to **add** ajouter (2)

administrative district of a city l'arrondissement (4)

advice les conseils (m. pl.) (5, 6)

Africa/in or to Africa l'Afrique (f.)/en Afrique (6)

after school après l'école (1)

airport l'aéroport (m.) (6)

alarm clock le réveil (5)

algebra l'algèbre (f.) (1)

all the time tout le temps (1)

alpine alpin/alpine (6)

alternative travel les voyages (m. pl.) alternatifs (6)

ambitious ambitieux/ambitieuse (3)

amusement park le parc d'attractions (4)

ancient ancien/ancienne (4)

ankle la cheville (5)

animal shelter le refuge pour animaux (3)

Antarctica/in or to Antarctica l'Antarctique (f.)/en Antarctique (6)

anxious anxieux/anxieuse (5)

apartment l'appartement (m.) (3)

apple juice le jus de pomme (1)

apples les pommes (f. pl.) (2)

applesauce (or other fruit compote) la compote (2)

app(lication) l'appli(cation) (f.) (mobile) (4, 5)

apprenticeship le stage (6)

aquarium l'aquarium (m.) (4)

the **Arabic language** l'arabe (m.) (1)

area la zone (6)

Are you interested (in...) Ça vous dit (de...) (2)

Asia/in or to Asia l'Asie (f.)/en Asie (6)

to **ask permission** demander la permission (6)

assistant principal le proviseur-adjoint/la proviseure-adjointe (1)

athletic sportif/sportive (3)

to **attend a (soccer) game** assister à un match (de foot) (4)

at the beginning of the day en début de journée (1)

at the end of the day en fin de journée (1)

at the pool à la piscine (6)

At what time? À quelle heure? (1)

aunt la tante (2)

Australia/in or to Australia l'Australie (f.)/en Australie (6)

avocado l'avocat (m.) (5)

to **avoid** éviter (de) (5)

to **babysit** garder (des enfants) (3)

backpack le sac à dos (1)

back-to-school la rentrée (1)

bacon pieces les lardons (m. pl.) (2)

bad habits de mauvaises habitudes (f. pl.) (1)

baguette la baguette (2)

bakery la boulangerie (4)

baking mold or pan le moule (2)

balanced équilibré/équilibrée (5)

banana la banane (2, 5)

bathroom la salle de bains (3)

bay la baie (6)

(green) beans les haricots (verts) (m. pl.) (2)

to become devenir (3)

bed le lit (5)

bedroom la chambre (à coucher) (3)

beets les betteraves (f. pl.)

before school avant l'école (1)

To begin with, Pour commencer, (5)

to be hungry avoir faim (5)

to be sick être malade (5)

to be stressed être stressé/stressée (5)

to be thirsty avoir soif (5)

to be tired être fatigué/fatiguée (5)

Belgian beef stew la carbonnade flamande (2)

belly le ventre (5)

beverages les boissons (f. pl.) (2)

bike le vélo (4)

binder le classeur (1)

biology la biologie (1)

birthday party la fête d'anniversaire (2)

blackberries les mûres (f. pl.) (2)

to blog bloguer (6)

blouse le chemisier (6)

boat le bateau (4)

book le livre (1, 6)

booklet le carnet (4)

boots les bottes (f. pl.) (6)

boutique la boutique (4)

bowl le bol (2)

bowling alley le bowling (4)

brain le cerveau (1)

bread le pain (2, 5)

breakfast le petit déjeuner (2)

to breathe respirer (5)

brother le frère (2)

bundle of herbs for flavoring soups or sauces le bouquet garni (2)

bus l'autobus (m.), le bus (4)

business le commerce (6)

busy (for a place) fréquenté/fréquentée (4)

butcher's shop la boucherie (4)

butter le beurre (2)

to buy acheter (4)

cabbage le chou (2)

to the café au café (4)

cafeteria la cantine (1)

cafeteria monitor le surveillant, la surveillante, le pion (*slang*) (1)

cake le gâteau (2, 5)

calculator la calculatrice (1)

to call téléphoner à (4)

Canadian canadien/canadienne (3)

car la voiture (4)

carrot la carotte (2)

carry-on bag le bagage à main (6)

celery le céleri (2)

cell phone le portable (1)

challenging exigeant/exigeante (1)

change (money) la monnaie (4)

changing trains (or other transportation) la correspondance (4)

to chat bavarder (5, 6)

to check opening hours vérifier les heures d'ouverture (4)

to check the schedule consulter l'horaire (4)

cheese le fromage (2, 5)

cherries les cérises (f. pl.) (2)

chicken le poulet (2, 5)

chicken cooked in palm oil with vegetables le poulet moamba (2)

child l'enfant (m. or f.) (2)

chorus la chorale (1)

citizen le citoyen/la citoyenne (3)

city la ville (3)

city activities les activités (f. pl.) en ville (4)

civil marriage le mariage civil (2)

class le cours (1)

the class begins at... le cours commence à... (1)

the class ends at... le cours termine à... (1)

classroom la salle de classe (1)

to clear débarrasser (3)

climate le climat (6)

climbing wall le mur d'escalade (4)

clothing les vêtements (m. pl.) (6)

_____ **club** le club de _____ (1)

coach l'entraîneur (1)

coast la côte (6)

coat le manteau (6)

coffee le café (2)

Come one and all (to...) Venez nombreux (à...) (2)

to comfort (someone) réconforter (quelqu'un) (3)

community garden le jardin communautaire (3)

commuter rail service serving Paris and its suburbs le RER (Réseau Express Régional) (4)

to compose (a poem, a song, etc.) composer (un poème, une chanson, etc.) (1)

computer l'ordinateur (m.) (1)

computer room la salle d'informatique (1)

computer science l'informatique (1)

concert le concert (4)

concert hall la salle de concert (4)

Congolese donuts les beignets congolais (m. pl.) (2)

to conserve préserver (6)

to consult the doctor consulter le médecin (5

to consume consommer (5)

contact lenses les lentilles (f. pl.) (6)

continent le continent (6)

to contribute to contribuer à (3)

to cough tousser (5)

country le pays (6)

courageous courageux/courageuse (3)

course le cours (1)

cousin le cousin/la cousine (2)

cream la crème (2)

creative créatif/créative (1, 3)

to create créer (3)

to create a robot créer un robot (1)

creamery la crèmerie (4)

crepe with butter and sugar la crêpe beurre-sucre (2)

crispy croustillant/croustillante (2)

croissant le croissant (2)

crunchy croustillant/croustillante (2)

cubed ham les lardons (m. pl.) (2)

cucumber le concombre (5)

custom la coutume (6)

to cut couper (2)

dairy (store) la crèmerie (4)

to dance danser (5)

daughter la fille (2)

the day before la veille (1, 5)

the day in the city la journée en ville (4)

daycare facility la garderie (3)

to dedicate consacrer (5)

delicatessen (deli) la charcuterie (4)

demanding exigeant/exigeante (1)

dentist le/la dentiste (5)

desert le désert (6)

dessert le dessert (2)

dictionary le dictionnaire (1)

dining room la salle à manger (3)

dinner le dîner (2)

to discover a cultural activity découvrir une activité culturelle (6)

dishwasher le lave-vaisselle (3)

to do faire (4)

to do exercises faire des exercices (m. pl.) (1)

to do homework faire les devoirs (1)

to do yoga faire du yoga (5)

donations les dons (m. pl.) (3)

dough la pâte (2)

to download télécharger (4)

downtown au centre-ville (4)

drive (as in blood drive, food drive, etc.) la collecte (3)

dry sec/sèche (6)

duck le canard (2)

dynamic dynamique (1, 3)

ear l'oreille (f.) (5)

to eat manger (5)

to eat lunch déjeuner (1)

economics l'économie (f.) (1)

efficient efficace (1)

egg l'œuf (m.) (2, 5)

eighth (8th) huitième (8e) (1)

elbow le coude (5)

eleventh (11th) onzième (11e) (1)

emotional health la santé emotionnelle (5)

to empty débarrasser (3)

energetic énergique (1, 3)

energy l'énergie (5)

energy drinks les boissons (f. pl.) énergisantes (5)

the English language l'anglais (m.) (1)

entrance fee le billet d'entrée (4)

to establish a budget établir un budget (6)

Europe/in or to Europe l'Europe (f.)/en Europe (6)

event l'événement (m.) (2)

every day tous les jours (1)

to exchange currency changer de l'argent (6)

to exercise faire de l'exercice (m.) (5)

exhausted épuisé/épuisée (5)

exhibition l'exposition (f.) (4)

expensive cher/chère (4)

experienced expérimenté/expérimentée (3)

in order to express pain pour exprimer la douleur (5)

extracurricular activities les activités (f. pl.) périscolaires (1)

eye l'œil (m.) (5)

eye doctor l'ophtalmo(logiste) (m./f.) (5)

eyes les yeux (m. pl.) (5)

fad diet le régime tendance (5)

fair la fête foraine (4)

(water)falls les chutes (f. pl.) (6)

to fall asleep s'endormir (5)

family meal le repas familial (2)

farm la ferme (2)

fashion la mode (6)

fast food restaurant le fast-food (4)

father le père (2)

fee le tarif (4)

to feel se sentir (5)

to feel hot avoir chaud (5)

festival le festival (4)

few peu de (5)

fifth (5th) cinquième (5e) (1)

film club le club cinéma (1)

finally finalement (2)

first (1st) premier (1er)/première (1re) (1)
first (of all) d'abord (2)
fish le poisson (2, 5)
fixed-price menu le menu (2)
flat water l'eau (f.) plate (2)
flour la farine (2)
to fold laundry plier le linge (3)
food bank la banque alimentaire (3)
foods les aliments (m. pl.) (2, 5)
foot le pied (5)
forest la forêt (6)
fork la fourchette (2)
foundation la fondation (3)
fourth (4th) quatrième (4e) (1)
free/unscheduled time du temps libre (1)
the French language le français (1)
friendly convivial/conviviale (2)
fries les frites (f. pl.) (2, 5)
from time to time de temps en temps (1)
fruit les fruits (m. pl.) (2, 5)
funds les fonds (m. pl.) (3)
the future l'avenir (m.) (3)
garden le jardin (3)
gardening le jardinage (3)
garlic l'ail (m.) 2)
gathering in the evening la soirée (2)
gathering in the evening at a friends' home la soirée chez des amis (2)
generous généreux/généreuse (3)
geography la géographie (géo) (1, 6)
the German language l'allemand (m.) (1)
to get enough sleep dormir assez (5)
to get information se renseigner (6)
to get out of a vehicle descendre (4)
to get up se lever (5)
gift le cadeau (6)
to give advice to conseiller (3)
to give blood donner du sang (3)
in order to give a presentation pour faire une présentation (5)
gloves les gants (m. pl.) (6)
to go down descendre (4)
to go hiking faire une randonnée (5)
good habits de bonnes habitudes (f. pl.) (1)
to go on a(n) (amusement park) ride faire un tour de manège (4)
to go through customs passer la douane (6)
to go to a fair aller à une foire (6)
to go to a festival aller à un festival (6)
to go to bed se coucher (5)
to go to the flea market aller aux puces (4)
to go to the movies aller au cinéma (5)
to go tree trekking faire de l'accrobranche (f.) (4)
to go window shopping faire du lèche-vitrine (4)
grandfather le grand-père (2)
grandmother la grand-mère (2)
grandparents les grands-parents (m. pl.) (2)
guided visit la visite guidée (4)
gulf le golfe (6)
gymnasium le gymnase (1, 4)
to haggle marchander (6)
hairbrush la brosse à cheveux (6)
hall monitor le surveillant/la surveillante (le pion *slang*) (1)
hallway le couloir (1)
ham and cheese sandwich le sandwich jambon-fromage (2)
hand la main (5)
hard-working travailleur/travailleuse (3)
hat le chapeau (6)

to have a cold avoir un rhume (5)

to have a fever avoir de la fièvre (5)

to have allergies avoir des allergies (5)

to have a runny nose avoir le nez qui coule (5)

to have fun s'amuser (5)

head la tête (5)

headphones les écouteurs (m. pl.) (6)

healthy sain/saine (5)

healthy habits les habitudes (f. pl.) saines (5)

to heat chauffer (2)

He/she's a ____ person. C'est quelqu'un de ____ (1)

to help aider (1, 3)

herbal tea la tisane (5)

high haut/haute (4)

high school le lycée (1)

history l'histoire (f.) (1)

history-geography l'histoire-géo (f.) (1)

hobby le passe-temps (5)

homeless shelter le refuge pour sans-abris (3)

holiday le jour férié (1), la fête (2)

hospital l'hôpital (m.) (3)

host family la famille d'accueil (6)

hot chocolate le chocolat chaud (2)

hot ham and melted cheese sandwich le croque-monsieur (2)

house la maison (3, 4)

household tasks les tâches (f. pl.) ménagères (3)

How? Comment? (3)

How many? Combien (3)

humid humide (6)

(body part) hurts avoir mal + au/à la/à l'/aux + (partie du corps) (5)

I'm going to take a ___ class. Je vais suivre un cours de/d' ___ . (1)

I'm inviting you (to)... Je vous invite (à)... (2)

I'm suggesting (to you) Je vous propose (2)

ice cream la glace (2, 5)

impatient impatient/impatiente (1)

to improve améliorer (3)

in a different country à l'étranger (6)

in cash en espèces (4)

in search of à la recherche de (3)

In summary En somme (5)

in the mountains à la montagne (6)

to initiate new ideas lancer de nouvelles idées (3)

intelligent intelligent/intelligente (3)

interest le centre d'intérêt (5)

internship le stage (6)

to introduce new ideas lancer de nouvelles idées (3)

to invite someone inviter quelqu'un (4)

to iron repasser (3)

island l'île (f.) (6)

It is cold outside. Il fait froid. (6)

It is cool outside. Il fait frais. (6)

It is hot outside. Il fait chaud. (6)

It is raining. Il pleut. (6)

It is snowing. Il neige. (6)

It is sunny outside. Il y a du soleil. (6)

jacket la veste (6)

jam la confiture (2)

(pair of) jeans le jean (6)

jelly la confiture (2)

to keep garder (3)

to keep an open mind garder l'esprit ouvert (6)

kind gentil/gentille (1, 3)

knee le genou (5)

knife le couteau (2)

to knit tricoter (5)

laboratory le labo(ratoire) (1)

lake le lac (6)
last dernier/dernière, terminal(e) (1)
lastly finalement (2)
late en retard (5)
the Latin language le latin (1)
leader le/la chef (3)
to learn apprendre (3)
leek le poireau (2)
leg la jambe (5)
lemon le citron (2, 5)
to "let go" lâcher prise (5)
library media specialist le/la documentaliste (1)
life and earth science les sciences (f. pl.) de la vie et de la Terre (SVT) (1)
life online la vie en ligne (5)
light la lumière (4)
to limit limiter (5)
line (of a train, subway, etc.) la ligne (4)
to listen to relaxing music écouter de la musique relaxante (5)
literature la littérature (1)
lively convivial/conviviale (2)
living room le salon (3)
locker le casier (1)
long long/longue (4)
to look regarder (4)
to look after garder (3)
to look at my phone instead of sleeping regarder mon portable au lieu de dormir (1)
lots of people beaucoup de monde (4)
low bas/basse (4)
loyal fidèle (3)
lunch le déjeuner (1)
magazine le magazine (6)
main office le bureau central (1)
the majority la plupart (5)
to make faire (4)
to make something a reality réaliser (3)
to manage gérer (3)
mango la mangue (2, 5)
map (of a city, area) le plan (4)
marketing le marketing (6)
mathematics les mathématiques (f. pl.) (maths) (1)
mashed (potatoes) la purée (2)
meal le repas (2)
meat la viande (2, 5)
meat or fish stew with a cream sauce le waterzooï (2)
media center la médiathèque (1, 4)
medications les médicaments (m. pl.) (6)
to meditate méditer (5)
meeting la réunion (3)
to meet new friends rencontrer de nouveaux amis (3)
menu la carte (2)
metro system le métro (4)
middle school le collège (1)
milk le lait (2)
mineral water l'eau (f.) minérale (2)
to mix mélanger (2)
modern languages les langues (f. pl.) vivantes (1)
mosquito repellent la lotion anti-moustiques (6)
mother la mère (2)
motivated motivé/motivée (3)
motorbike la moto (4)
mountainous alpin/alpine (6)
to the movie theater au cinéma (4)
museum le musée (4)
music la musique (1)
mussel la moule (2)
mussels served with fries les moules-frites (f. pl.) (2)
mustard la moutarde (5)

napkin la serviette (2)
narrow étroit/étroite (4)
national park le parc national (6)
neck le cou (5)
to **negotiate price** marchander (6)
neighborhood le quartier (4)
network le réseau (3)
never (ne...) jamais (1, 5)
newspaper le journal (6)
next ensuite (2)
nice gentil/gentille (1, 3)
ninth (9th) neuvième (9e) (1)
North America/in or to North America l'Amérique (f.) du Nord/en Amérique du Nord (6)
to **not be able to** ne pas arriver à (5)
notebook le cahier (1)
not-for-profit organization (NPO) un organisme à but non-lucratif (OBNL) (3)
nurse l'infirmier/l'infirmière(1)
nurse's office l'infirmerie (f.) (1)
nursing home le foyer de soins (3)
Oceania/in or to Oceania l'Océanie/en Océanie (6)
often souvent (1)
old âgé/âgée (3), ancien/ancienne (4)
omelette l'omelette (f.) (2)
on foot à pied (4)
onion l'oignon (m.) (2, 5)
online ticket sales la billetterie (4)
on the floor par terre (3)
on time à l'heure (5)
opera l'opéra (4)
orange juice le jus d'orange (2)
orchestra l'orchestre (m.) (1)
organic products des produits (m. pl.) bio (5)
to **organize** organiser (1)
to **organize one's schedule** organiser son emploi du temps (3)
organized organisé/organisée (3)
orthodontist l'orthodontiste (m./f.) (5)
other points of view d'autres points (m. pl.) de vue (5)
oven le four (2)
pack of tickets le carnet (4)
to **pack one's suitcase** faire sa valise (6)
to **paint** peindre (3)
(pair of) pants le pantalon (6)
parents les parents (m. pl.) (2)
park le parc (4)
parking lot le parking (1)
to **participate** participer (1)
to **participate in clubs** participer aux clubs (5)
to **participate in extracurricular activities** participer à des activités périscolaires (1)
particular particulier/particulière (6)
parts of the body les parties (f. pl.) du corps (5)
party la fête (2), la soirée (2)
party in the evening at a friends' home la soirée chez des amis (2)
passport le passeport (6)
pasta les pâtes (f. pl.) (2, 5)
pastime le passe-temps (5)
pastry shop, bakery la pâtisserie (4)
patient patient/patiente (3)
paved riverbank le quai (4)
to **pay attention** faire attention (1)
peach la pêche (5)
pears les poires (f. pl.) (2, 5)
peas les petits pois (m. pl.) (2)
pen le stylo (1)
pencil le crayon (1)
pencil case la trousse (1)
peppers les poivrons (2)
pharmacy la pharmacie (4)

photography la photo(graphie) (6)

physical education le sport, l'éducation (f.) physique et sportive (1)

physical therapist le/la kiné(sithérapeute) (5)

physics la physique (1)

physics-chemistry la physique-chimie (1)

to pick (fruit, flowers) cueillir (les fruits, les fleurs) (2)

to pick up the trash ramasser les déchets (3)

pie la tarte (2, 5)

place l'endroit (m.) (4)

to place mettre (2)

places in a city les endroits (m. pl.) en ville (4)

places at school les endroits (m. pl.) à l'école (1)

plan le projet (3)

to plan planifier (5)

plate l'assiette (f.) (2)

platform le quai (4)

to play a specific sport jouer au/à la/à l'/aux + (le nom d'un sport) (5)

to play basketball (volleyball, etc.) jouer au basket (au volley, etc.) (1)

to play chess jouer aux échecs (5)

playground l'aire (f.) de jeux (4)

to play music jouer de la musique (5)

to play sports faire du sport (5)

to play the guitar (the piano, etc.) jouer de la guitare (du piano, etc.) (1)

to play video games jouer aux jeux vidéos (5)

plaza la place (4)

popular (for a place) fréquenté/fréquentée (4)

positive positif/positive (1, 3)

to post (online) poster (4)

potatoes les pommes de terre (f. pl.) (2, 5)

to pour verser (2)

to prepare for a trip se préparer au voyage (6)

to press presser (2)

price (for ticket, for entry) le tarif (4)

principal le principal/la principale (for middle school), le proviseur/la proviseure (for high school) (1)

to print imprimer (6)

project le projet (3)

psychologist le/la psy(chologue) (5)

psychology la psychologie (1)

to put mettre (2)

to put away ranger (3)

pyjamas le pyjama (6)

from Quebec québécois/québécoise (3)

quiche la quiche (2)

rabbit le lapin (2)

rarely rarement (1, 5)

raspberry la framboise (2, 5)

to read lire (1, 5)

recently récemment (4)

recess la récréation (récré) (1)

reception area l'accueil (m.) (1)

reduced price le tarif réduit (4)

region la région (6)

regularly regulièrement (1)

to relax se reposer (5)

religious holiday la fête religieuse (2)

to rent louer (4)

to rent an apartment for a short term louer un appart(ement) en courte durée (6)

rental la location (4)

renting la location (4)

to repaint repeindre (3)

to reserve a flight réserver un vol (6)

respectful respectueux/respectueuse (6)

restaurant le restaurant (4)

to review réviser (1)

rice le riz (2, 5)

rice pie la tarte au riz (2)

to ride a bike faire du vélo (5)
river le fleuve (4)
road la rue (4)
roast chicken le poulet rôti (2)
roller coaster les montagnes (f. pl.) russes (4)
to rollerblade faire du roller (4)
route le trajet (4)
rural rural/rurale (6)
salad la salade verte (2, 5)
sandals les sandales (f. pl.) (6)
sausage la saucisse (2)
savanna la savane (6)
scarf l'écharpe (f.) (6)
schedule l'emploi (m.) du temps (1)
school calendar le calendrier scolaire (1)
school counselor le conseiller/la conseillère d'orientation (1)
school planner l'agenda (m.) scolaire (1)
school staff le personnel de l'école (1)
school subjects les matières (f. pl.) (1)
school supply la fourniture scolaire (1)
school year l'année (f.) scolaire (1)
sciences les sciences (f. pl.) (1)
scissors les ciseaux (m. pl.) (1)
scooter le scooter (4)
to scrape gratter (3)
screen l'écran (m.) (5)
seafood les fruits de mer (m. pl.) (2)
second (2nd) (final of two) second/seconde (2^{d}/2de) (1)
second (2nd) deuxième (2e) (1)
secretary le secrétaire/la secrétaire (1)
to send a text message /text messages envoyer un texto/des textos (4, 5)
to serve servir (2, 3)
to set the table mettre le couvert (3), mettre la table (2, 3)
seventh (7th) septième (7e) (1)
to share online resources partager des ressources en ligne (1)
sheet of paper la feuille de papier (1)
shelter l'abri (m.) (3)
shirt la chemise (6)
shoes les chaussures (f. pl.) (6)
short court/courte (4)
(pair of) shorts le short (6)
short-term rental la location à court terme, la location de courte durée (6)
show le spectacle (4)
to simplify simplifier (5)
to sing chanter (5)
sister la sœur (2)
sixth (6th) sixième (6e) (1)
to ski faire du ski (6)
skirt la jupe (6)
sleep (n.) le sommeil (5)
to sleep dormir (5)
to sleep late dormir tard (1)
small grocery store (for produce) l'épicerie (f.) (4)
smart intelligent/intelligente (3)
smile le sourire (5)
to smoke fumer (5)
to snack grignoter (5)
social health la santé sociale (5)
social network le réseau social (4, 5)
social sciences les sciences (f. pl.) sociales (1)
sometimes parfois (1)
son le fils (2)
soup la soupe (2, 5)
South America/in or to South America l'Amérique (f.) du Sud/en Amérique du Sud (6)
the Spanish language l'espagnol (m.) (1)
sparkling water l'eau (f.) gazeuse (2)

to spend time alone passer du temps seul/seule (5)

to spend time with friends passer du temps avec des amis (5)

special event l'événement (m.) spécial (2)

spices les épices (f. pl.) (5)

sponge l'éponge (3)

spoon la cuillère (2)

sports complex le complexe sportif (1)

sports field le terrain de sport (1, 4)

square la place (4)

stadium le stade (4)

stay (n.) le séjour (6)

to stay connected rester connecté/connectée (5)

to stay hydrated rester hydraté/hydratée (5)

steak le steak (2, 5)

steak and French fries le steak-frites (2)

steak tartare (raw, seasoned beef) le filet américain (2)

store le magasin (4)

strawberry la fraise (2)

street la rue (4)

to stroll flâner (6)

student lounge le foyer (1)

study hall la permanence ("perm") (1)

to study notecards étudier des fiches de révision (1)

subway le métro (4)

subway station la station de métro (4)

suitcase la valise (6)

sunblock la crème solaire (6)

sunglasses les lunettes (f. pl.) de soleil (6)

supermarket le supermarché (4)

to support soutenir (3)

survey le sondage (5)

sweater le pull (6)

to swim faire de la natation (6)

swimming pool la piscine (4)

swimsuit le maillot de bain (6)

symptom le symptôme (5)

tablet la tablette (1)

to take a break, to take breaks faire une/de pause(s) (1)

to take a (hot) bath prendre un bain (chaud) (5)

to take a walk se promener (5)

to take notes prendre des notes (1)

to take out sortir (3)

to take photos prendre des photos (4)

to take the subway prendre le métro (4)

tart la tarte (2, 5)

taste (n.) le goût (2)

to taste goûter (2)

taxi le taxi (4)

tea le thé (2)

to teach enseigner (1)

teacher le/la professeur (prof) (1)

team (soccer, volleyball, basketball, etc. l'équipe (f.) de (foot, volley, basket, etc.) (1

teens les ados (m./f. pl.) (3)

tense tendu/tendue (5)

tenth (10th) dixième (10e) (1)

Thank you for listening. Merci de votre attention. (5)

Thank you for your attention. Merci de votre attention. (5)

theater (for plays, concerts, etc.) le théâtre (4)

theater club le club théâtre (1)

then ensuite (2)

third (3rd) troisième (3e) (1)

throat la gorge (5)

ticket le billet d'entrée, le ticket (4)

ticket counter le guichet (4)

ticket window la billetterie, le guichet (4)

to tidy up ranger (3)

(one) time per week (une) fois par semaine (1)

times of the day les moments (m. pl.) de la journée (1)

Today, I will speak to you about... Aujourd'hui, je vais vous parler de... (5)

toiletry bag la trousse de toilette (6)

toilets les toilettes (f. pl.) (1, 3)

tomato la tomate (5)

too much (of) trop de (5)

toothbrush la brosse à dents (6)

toothpaste le dentifrice (6)

trainer l'entraîneur (1)

train station la gare (4)

traits of a volunteer les qualités d'un bénévole (3)

travel bag le sac de voyage (6)

travel journal le carnet de voyage (6)

traveller le voyageur/la voyageuse (6)

trendy diet le régime tendance (5)

trip le trajet (4), le voyage (6)

tropical tropical/tropicale (6)

to **try new things** tenter de nouvelles choses (6)

to **try something new** essayer quelque chose de nouveau (3)

to **try to** essayer de (5)

t-shirt le tee-shirt (6)

tummy le ventre (5)

turn out the light éteindre la lumière (6)

uncle l'oncle (m.) (2)

understanding compréhensif/compréhensive (3)

uniform l'uniforme (m.) (6)

to **use** utiliser (1)

to **use my phone in class** utiliser mon portable en classe (1)

vacation les vacances (f. pl.) (1)

to **vacuum** passer l'aspirateur (3)

to **vape** vapoter (5)

vegetables les légumes (m. pl.) (1)

to **visit** visiter (4)

to **visit an historic site** visiter un site historique (6)

to **visit someone** rendre visite à quelqu'un (6)

visual arts les arts (m. pl.) plastiques (1)

volcano le volcan (6)

volunteer le/la bénévole (3)

to **volunteer, to do volunteer work** faire du bénévolat (3)

volunteer work site le chantier de bénévoles (6)

waffle la gaufre (2)

to **wake up** se réveiller (5)

to **wait until the last minute (to)** attendre le dernier moment (pour) (1)

wallet le portefeuille (6)

warm chaleureux/chaleureuse (2)

to **warm** chauffer (2)

to **wash** laver (2)

to **wash laundry** laver le linge (3)

to **waste** gaspiller (6)

to **watch films** regarder des films (1)

to **water** arroser (3)

to **welcome** accueillir (3)

welcoming chaleureux/chaleureuse (2)

What? Que/qu'? (3)

What time is it? Quelle heure est-il? (1)

When? Quand? (3)

Where?/From where? Où?/D'où? (3)

Who? Qui? (3)

Why? Pourquoi? (3)

wide large (4)

work site le chantier (3)

wrist le poignet (5)

You are welcome to come (to...) Soyez les bienvenu(e)s (à...) (2)

young jeune (3)

youth hostel l'auberge (f.) de jeunesse (6)

zone la zone (6)

zoo le zoo (4)

Expressions utiles English-French

accommodations l'hébergement (m.) (6)

across from (somebody, something) en face de (quelqu'un, quelque chose) (4)

already déjà (4)

to answer the telephone répondre au téléphone (3)

to arrive late arriver en retard (4)

to arrive on time arriver à l'heure (4)

to ask for advice from... demander conseil à... (1)

As you can see Comme vous pouvez le voir (5)

to be addicted (to) être accro (à) (5)

because parce que/qu' (1)

before devant (4)

behind derrière (4)

to be located se trouver (4)

beside à côté de (3)

to be successful at school, I must... Pour réussir à l'école, je dois... (1)

a better world un monde meilleur (3)

bless you à tes/vos souhaits (5)

border la frontière (6)

to build houses construire des maisons (3)

close to près de (4)

to communicate communiquer (5)

cooked with cuit(e)(s) avec (2)

daily quotidien/quotidienne (3)

day before yesterday avant-hier (4)

delicious délicieux/délicieuse (2)

departure le départ (6)

far (away) from loin de (4)

fatty riche (2)

to feed donner à manger (3)

for fun pour s'amuser (4)

free gratuit/gratuite (2)

Gladly! Avec plaisir (2)

to go get something chercher quelque chose (1)

to go see... aller voir... (1)

to go to the pharmacy aller à la pharmacie (5)

Good idea! Bonne idée! (1, 3)

to have fun pour s'amuser (4)

to have the flu avoir la grippe (5)

Here is... Voici... (1)

Here, you can... Ici, on peut... (1)

hotel l'hôtel (6)

I agree (with you). Je suis d'accord (avec toi). (1, 3)

I don't agree (with you). Je ne suis pas d'accord (avec toi). (1, 3)

I did... J'ai fait... (4)

I learned (to)... J'ai appris (à)... (5)

I'll think about it. Je vais y réfléchir. (1)

I'm going (to)..., I go (to)... Je vais (à)... (4)

I must not... Je ne dois pas... (1)

in dans (3, 4)

in good health en bonne santé (5)

in front of devant (4)

I observed that... J'ai observé que... (5)

I recommend that you... Je te conseille de/d'... (4)

I saw... J'ai vu... (4)

isolated isolé/isolée (5)

I spent (the day)... J'ai passé (la journée)... (4)

I took... J'ai pris... (4)

It's important to... C'est important de... (3); Il est important de... (5)

It's not going well at all. Ça ne va pas du tout. (5)

I went to... Je suis allé(e) à... (4)

I went home (to my house) Je suis rentré(e) (chez moi). (4)

I will do... Je ferai... (6)

I will go... J'irai... (6)

I will have... J'aurai... (6)

I will spend (time)... Je passerai (du temps)... (6)

It was... C'était... (2)

It was necessary (to)... Il fallait... (2)

It will be... Ce sera... (6)

last Wednesday mercredi dernier (4)

last week la semaine dernière (4)

last weekend le week-end dernier (4)

last year l'année (f.) dernière (4)

to laugh rire (5)

to the left of à gauche de (4)

to lend a helping hand donner un coup de main (3)

light léger/légère (2)

lodging l'hébergement (m.) (6)

to look for something chercher quelque chose (1)

made with fait(e)(s) avec (2)

to make the bed faire le lit (3)

monthly mensuel/mensuelle (3)

he most important thing, is (to)... le plus important, c'est (de)... (5)

to move (around) a little bit bouger un peu (5)

near près de (4)

next to à côté de (3, 4)

no cost gratuit/gratuite (2)

not yet pas encore (4)

OK d'accord (1)

on sur (3)

One should... On devrait (5)

opposite (somebody, something) en face de (quelqu'un, quelque chose) (4)

People should... On devrait (5)

percent pour cent (5)

plain (referring to food) nature (2)

to plan planifier (3)

to plant trees planter des arbres (3)

to put on sunblock mettre de la crème solaire (5)

to reduce stress réduire le stress (5)

to reserve réserver (2)

rich riche (2)

rich in riche en... (5)

to the right of à droite de (4)

salty salé/salée (2)

to say "no" to... dire "non" à... (5)

served with servi(e)(s) avec (2)

to sneeze éternuer (5)

Sorry, but I can't. Désolé/Désolée, mais je ne peux pas. (2)

to sort and hand out, distribute the mail trier et distribuer le courrier (3)

to spend time passer du temps (1)

spicy épicé/épicée (2)

sweet sucré/sucrée (2)

to take care of soigner (5)

to take one's time prendre son temps (5)

to take medication prendre un médicament (5)

Tell your friends about it! Parlez-en à vos amis! (2)

That hurts. Ça fait mal. (5)

There is..., There are... Il y a... (1)

There was..., There were... Il y avait... (2)

There will be... Il y aura... (6)

This is... Ça, c'est... (1)

to treat soigner (5)

We're really going to savor this! On va se régaler (2)

week la semaine (1)

weekend le week-end (1)

weekly hebdomadaire (3)

We should... On devrait (5)

What's wrong? Qu'est-ce que tu as? (5)

When I was little... Quand j'étais petit/petite... (2)

With pleasure! Avec plaisir (2)

Yes, I'd really like to. Oui, je veux bien. (2)

yesterday hier (4)

Credits

Every effort has been made to determine the copyright owners. In case of any omissions, the publisher will be happy to make suitable acknowledgements in future editions. All credits are listed in the order of appearance.

All images are © Shutterstock and © Thinkstock, except as noted below.

Unité 1

© Morin, Philippe, "Notre emploi du temps / Présentation du collège Senghor - Ifs", Recréée de https://fr.slideshare.net/phmorin/prsentation-du-collge-senghor-ifs. 16 nov. 2012.

© Radenne, Jérôme, "Lycée Bellepierre: fiche de vœux entrée en 2nde", Recupérée de http://college-lamontagne.ac-reunion.fr/2017/05/22/lycee-bellepierre-fiche-de-voeux-entree-en-2nde/. 22 mai 2017.

© Ministère de l'Éducation Nationale, "Activités spécifiques organisées pendant les TAP", Récupérée de http://www.education.gouv.fr/cid103212/des-activites-periscolaires-de-qualite-pour-tous-les-enfants.html. 10 octobre 2016.

© Mylène La Ferrière, "Qu'est-ce que vous allez faire cette année?". 2008.

© Ministère de l'Éducation Nationale, "La Restauration scolaire", Récupérée de http://www.education.gouv.fr/cid45/la-restauration-a-l-ecole.html. 2017.

© *Le Parisien étudiant*, "Bac 2016: Les chiffres clés des épreuves", Récupérée de http://etudiant.aujourdhui.fr/etudiant/info/bac-2016-les-chiffres-cles-des-epreuves.html. 14 juin 2016.

© Ville de Saint-Louis et La Rivière, "Au quotidien: restauration scolaire", Récupérée de http://saintlouis.re/. 2017.

Images Unité 1

p. 3 (Photo) © Éloïse*, Maxime*, Mathew*, Élisa*, Brenda*, Lou-Ann*. 2018.

p. 6, 8, 24 (Photo) © Lou-Ann*. 2018.

p. 6 (Map showing the island of la Réunion off the east coast of Madagascar) © TUBS, "Reunion in France", CC BY-SA 3.0, https://creativecommons.org/licenses/by-sa/3.0/legalcode, Récupérée de https://commons.wikimedia.org/wiki/File:Reunion_in_France.svg.

Unité 2

© Lors de l'assemblée générale du groupement interprofessionnel pour la valorisation de la pomme de terre (GIPT), Planétoscope, "Consommation mondiales de frites" Information récupérée de https://www.planetoscope.com/restauration/463-consommation-de-frites-dans-le-monde.html. 2012.

© INSEE, "ÉVOLUTION DE LA CONSOMMATION MOYENNE DE PRODUITS ALIMENTAIRES de 1970 à 2008, agriculteurs inclus, en kg par personne", Tableaux de l'Économie Française, Récréé de http://viepaysanneautrefois.free.fr/chapitres/ch05/560_EvolConsoViandesRecomm_618a634.pdf, page 622. Juillet 2010.

© L'équipe Ça m'intéresse, "Origine des frites France ou Belgique?", Information récupérée de https://www.caminteresse.fr/histoire/origine-des-frites-france-ou-belgique-1158184/. 5 juillet 2017.

© Fabian Gallet, "5 choses que vous ignoriez peut-être sur les frites", Information récupérée de https://femmes.orange.fr/cuisine/nutrition-et-gourmandise/article-5-choses-que-vous-ignoriez-peut-etre-sur-les-frites-CNT000000Q4lK0/photos/-3b175f9907dab75fc19f5db80e3d34ef.html. 2018.

© McCain Foods, Be Good. Do Good., "Les baraques à frites une histoire belge très sérieuse", Information récupérée de http://mccain.begooddogood.fr/une-breve-histoire-des-baraques-a-frites/. 3 mars 2014.

© Lors de l'assemblée générale du groupement interprofessionnel pour la valorisation de la pomme de terre (GIPT), Planétoscope, "Consommation mondiales de frites" Information récupérée de https://www.planetoscope.com/restauration/463-consommation-de-frites-dans-le-monde.html. 2012.

© Sophie Charlier, "Calendrier des fruits et légumes de saison – Belgique", Recréée de http://www.tomate-cerise.be/fruits-et-legumes-de-saisons. 9 novembre 2015.

© La libre, Rédaction lifestyle, "Alimentation : les nouvelles habitudes de consommation en Belgique", Information récupérée de http://www.lalibre.be/lifestyle/food/alimentation-les-nouvelles-habitudes-de-consommation-en-belgique-58d13c26cd70a15c9a47f1cd. 21 mars 2017.

© Weber Shandwick, "TENDANCES ALIMENTAIRES EN BELGIQUE", Information récupérée de http://

*To protect the privacy of these generous French speakers, we have changed or omitted their last names.

webershandwick.be/wp-content/uploads/2017/03/2017-Tendances-Alimentaires-en-Belgique.pdf. Février 2017.

© Le Vif, De Standaard, "Les boulangeries de moins en moins fréquentées", Information récupérée de http://www.levif.be/actualite/belgique/les-boulangeries-de-moins-en-moins-frequentees/article-normal-674851.html. 8 juin 2017.

© Frédéric Solvel, Brussels Life, "Le chocolat belge", Information récupérée de https://www.brusselslife.be/fr/article/chocolat-belge. 3 avril 2013.

© FOURNISSEUR BREVETÉ DE LA COUR DE BELGIQUE, "À l'origine de la praline belge", Information récupérée de https://www.neuhauschocolates.com/fr/a-origine-de-la-praline-belge/.

© Eco Congo, "Le cacao, première source de revenus et de devises durables pour la RDC à l'horizon 2050?", Information récupérée de http://www.ecocongo.cd/fr/system/files/f-pj-a3-1.pdf. Mai 2011.

© Oliver Nieburg, Confectionary News, "Cocoa in the Congo: Emerging origin for organic chocolate makers", Information récupérée de https://www.confectionerynews.com/Article/2017/07/20/Cocoa-in-the-Congo-Emerging-origin-for-organic-chocolate-makers. 20 juillet 2017.

© SudPresse de Hannut, "Souper aux moules", Récupérée de http://hannut.blogs.sudinfo.be/archive/2015/11/04/aujourd-hui-dernier-jour-de-reservation-pour-le-souper-au-x-m-168382.html. 4 novembre 2015.

© Tennis de Table de Tiège, "Grand Souper Moules", Récupérée de http://www.ctttiege.be/2013/01/traditionnel-souper-moules-au-tt-tiege-samedi-9-fevrier-2013/. 9 janvier 2013.

© Miguel Vanhove, «Stoemp de carottes et saucisses», Adapté de http://faimdumonde.kyuran.be/2006/02/21/stoemp-de-carottes-et-saucisses/. 2006.

© Didier Vandeskelde, «Le Chou Rouge aux Pommes», Récupérée de http://didiervandeskelde.be/mes-recettes-de-cuisine/. 11 janvier 2011.

Images Unité 2

pp. 58, 60, 68, 73 (Photo) © Maxime*. 2018.

p. 59 (Photo) © Michael Thaidigsmann, "Philippe, roi des Belges, et son épouse la reine Mathilde, saluent le public après la prestation de serment du nouveau roi devant le Parlement belge", CC BY 3.0, https://creativecommons.org/licenses/by/3.0/legalcode, Récupérée de https://commons.wikimedia.org/w/index.php?curid=27426119.

p. 59 (Photographic Reproduction of Painting) © Geheugen van Nederland, Basile de Loose, "Making Waffles", Domaine public, https://commons.wikimedia.org/w/index.php?curid=16796071.

p. 65 (Curry dish) © Plume_d_argent de monilemapassion.com, "Carry LaRéunion", CC BY-SA 3.0, https://creativecommons.org/licenses/by-sa/3.0/legalcode, Récupérée de https://commons.wikimedia.org/wiki/File:Carry_LaRéunion.jpg.

p. 78 (Image) © Wouter Hagens, "A friterie in Oud-Heverlee, Belgium", CC BY-SA 3.0, https://creativecommons.org/licenses/by-sa/3.0/legalcode, Récupérée de https://commons.wikimedia.org/w/index.php?curid=10969695.

p. 93 Jean-Paul Nsimba Mika © 2018 Artists Rights Society (ARS), New York / ADAGP, Paris.

p. 104 (Photo) © A. Savin, "Late-September 2009 aerial view of Liège", CC BY-SA 3.0, https://creativecommons.org/licenses/by-sa/3.0/legalcode, Récupérée de https://commons.wikimedia.org/wiki/File:Liege_View_03.jpg.

Unité 3

© Terrafemina, "Les ados et la parité: les filles repassent et les garçons lavent la voiture", Récréée de https://www.terrafemina.com/societe/societe/articles/39170-les-ados-et-la-parite-les-filles-cuisinent-les-garcons-jardinent-infographie.html. 4 mars 2014

© Silvia Galipeau, "Partage des tâches domestiques: La parité, quelle parité?", Adaptée de http://plus.lapresse.ca/screens/aa5c9949-4fa9-4ac9-a67a-0fee377f65ca__7C___0.html.

© Institut de recherche et d'informations socio-économiques, "Travail masculin, travail féminin – un peu d'histoire", Adaptée de https://iris-recherche.s3.amazonaws.com/uploads/publication/file/14-01239-IRIS-Notes-Taches-domestiques_WEB.pdf. Octobre 2014.

© Chantiers jeunesse, "Devenir bénévole", Information récupérée de https://www.cj.qc.ca/sengager/devenir-benevole/.

© Statistique Canada, "Évolution de la participation des parents aux tâches domestiques et aux soins des enfants de 1986 à 2015", Adaptée de http://www.statcan.gc.ca/pub/89-652-x/89-652-x2017001-fra.pdf. 1 juin 2017.

© Statistique Canada, "Taux de participation selon le type d'activité bénévole, bénévoles âgés de 15 ans et plus, 2010", Information récupérée de https://www.statcan.gc.ca/pub/11-008-x/2012001/c-g/11638/c-g08-fra.htm. 2010.

© Réseau de l'Action Bénévole du Québec, "Le bénévolat en chiffres", Information récupérée de https://www.rabq.ca/benevolat-en-chiffres.php. 2018.

© Centre d'action bénévole de Montréal, "Association récréative Milton-Parc", Information récupérée de http://cabm.net/v/30811.

© Immigrant Québec, "Bénévolat: une clé d'intégration", Adaptée de https://immigrantquebec.com/fr/consulter/conseils-d-experts/benevolat-une-cle-dintegration. 30 septembre 2012.

© Auteur inconnu, "Définitions du bénévolat", Poem récupéré de: http://www.jumafred.com/ema/txtdiv147.php.

Unité 3 Images

pp. 114, 116, 122 (Photo) © Éloïse*. 2018.

p. 116 (Michaëlle Jean) © Roosewelt Pinheiro/ABr, "Michaëlle Jean, 27e Gouverneure générale du Canada, en Brasil", CC BY 3.0 BR, https://creativecommons.org/licenses/by/3.0/br/deed.en, Récupérée de https://en.wikipedia.org/wiki/Micha%C3%ABlle_Jean#/media/File:Micha%C3%ABlle_Jean_1_11072007.jpg. 11 juillet 2007.

Unité 4

© Salut Paris, "Le top des arrondissements de Paris", Récréée de http://www.salutparis.fr/infographie-le-top-des-arrondissements-de-paris. 2016.

Best Efforts Made © Jacques Charpentreau, "L'école", Récupérée de *La ville enchantée: poèmes pour les enfants*. Paris: L'École. 1976.

© OpenStreetMap contributors, "Plan de Paris", CC BY-SA, https://www.openstreetmap.org/copyright, Récupérée de https://www.openstreetmap.org/#map=18/50.63694/3.06322.

© M0tty - Own work, "Plan de la ligne 10 du métro de Paris", CC BY-SA 3.0, https://creativecommons.org/licenses/by-sa/3.0/legalcode, Récupérée de https://commons.wikimedia.org/w/index.php?curid=4353368.

© OpenStreetMap contributors, "Alma-Marceau", CC BY-SA, https://www.openstreetmap.org/copyright, Récupérée de https://www.openstreetmap.org/#map=18/48.86432/2.30301.

© OpenStreetMap contributors, "Arc de triomphe", CC BY-SA, https://www.openstreetmap.org/copyright, Récupérée de https://www.openstreetmap.org/#map=18/48.87369/2.29562.

© OpenStreetMap contributors, "Trocadéro", CC BY-SA, https://www.openstreetmap.org/copyright, Récupérée de https://www.openstreetmap.org/#map=19/48.86326/2.28734.

© Centre Pompidou, "Informations pratiques", Récupérée de https://www.centrepompidou.fr/fr/Visite/Informations-pratiques.

Best Efforts Made © Vélib', Nom du Vélib', Récupéré de https://www.velib-metropole.fr/en/crc.

Unité 4 Images

pp. 166, 168, 174, 193, 198 (Photos) © Élisa*. 2018.

p. 167 (Image, Pièce d'or) © The Met, "Gold Coin of the Parisii", CC0 1.0 Universal, https://creativecommons.org/publicdomain/zero/1.0/, Récupérée de https://www.metmuseum.org/art/collection/search/464811.

p. 174 (Photo) © Airair - Own work, "Palais des Sports de Paris, 1 place de la Porte-de-Versailles, Paris, 15e ", CC BY-SA 3.0, https://creativecommons.org/licenses/by-sa/3.0/, Récupérée de https://fr.wikipedia.org/wiki/D%C3%B4me_de_Paris_-_Palais_des_Sports#/media/File:Palais_des_Sports_de_Paris.jpg. 28 décembre 2008.

p. 183 (Photo) © Guilhem Vellut, "Auberge Nicolas Flamel, Paris 11 February 2017", CC BY 2.0, https://creativecommons.org/licenses/by/2.0/, Récupérée de https://commons.wikimedia.org/wiki/File:Auberge_Nicolas_Flamel,_Paris_11_February_2017.jpg. 11 février 2017.

p. 183 (Photo) © Athaniel - Own work, " La rue la plus courte de Paris : La rue des degrés sur le 2ème arrondissement", CC BY-SA 3.0, https://creativecommons.org/licenses/by-sa/3.0/, Récupérée de https://commons.wikimedia.org/wiki/File:Ruesdesdegres.jpg. 17 juillet 2009.

pp. 188, 193 (Photos) © Élisa* & Lola*. 2018.

p. 191 (Photo) © Élisa* & Corentin*. 2018.

p. 194 (Photo) © Francesco Dazzi, "St. Germain des Prés - Café Le Procope", CC BY-SA 2.0, https://creativecommons.org/licenses/by-sa/2.0/, Récupérée de https://www.flickr.com/photos/checco/2862479787/in/photolist-8DfZd7-m1gkUJ-6k21No-5mWXvM-stJpC-68dA3V-68hN4U-3g5Lgj-dBf7S8-B5R1b8. 6 août 2007.

p. 198 (Photo) © Mike & Betsy Marron, "Metro Porte d'Auteuil", Récupérée de http://www.marronsinparis2014.org/marmottan-16.html. 2014.

Unité 5

© Fondation Cœur et Artères, "Pour un cœur en pleine santé!!!", Infographie récupérée de http://www.fondacoeur.com/un-coeur-en-pleine-sante.

© Fondation Roche, "L'autoperception du maintien de sa bonne santé", Information adaptée de http://www.fondationroche.org/home/actualites/2017/enquete-sante-jeunes-france.html, p.6. 2017.

© Une production originale du Centre intégré de santé et de services sociaux de Chaudière-Appalaches, "Facteurs de risque et estimation du pourcentage de la mortalité par cancer attribuable à ce facteur", Récréé de https://www.cisss-ca.gouv.qc.ca/rapportdspcancer/consulter-le-rapport-en-ligne/1-un-apercu-de-la-situation-des-cancers/11-les-causes-et-les-mecanismes-associes-au-developpement-du-cancer/111-les-facteurs-de-risque-du-cancer/. 2010.

© Gouvernement du Québec, "Tousser ou éternuer sans contaminer", Affiche récupérée de http://publications.msss.gouv.qc.ca/msss/fichiers/2017/17-207-02F.pdf. 2017.

© Initiatives.fr, partenaire des écoles et des associations, "Tout savoir sur le sommeil", Infographie récupérée de https://www.initiatives.fr/leblog/infographie-une-bonne-nuit-de-sommeil-on-vous-explique-tout-12043.

© AFP/Réseau Morphée, "Les jeunes et leur écran sous la couette", Infographie récupérée de https://twitter.com/afpfr/status/572840888667283456?lang=en. 3 mars 2015.

© Blog du dimanche, Infographie "Défi: 7 jours pour décrocher de son smartphone", Infographie adaptée de https://www.blogdudimanche.fr/defi-7-jours-decrocher-smartphone/.

Unité 5 Images

pp. 220, 223, 238 (Photo) © Mathew*. 2018.

Unité 6

© Ouest-France, "Tour de France: la Ville recherche 500 bénévoles", Récupérée de https://www.ouest-france.fr/pays-de-la-loire/la-roche-sur-yon-85000/tour-de-france-la-ville-recherche-500-benevoles-5624008. 14 mars 2018.

© Air France, "Que puis-je transporter?", Information adaptée de https://www.airfrance.fr/FR/fr/common/guidevoyageur/pratique/produits-interdits-et-reglementes-airfrance.htm.

© Réseau de veille en tourisme, Chaire de tourisme Transat, "Comportement Web des clientèles touristiques", Graphique adapté de http://chairedetourisme.uqam.ca/upload/files/Etude_clienteles%20touristiques_pour%20diffusion.pdf, p.44. Mars 2015.

© Laura, Blog Evaneous, "Comment devenir un voyageur responsable?", Information adaptée de http://blog.evaneos.com/comment-devenir-voyageur-responsable/. 25 janvier 2012.

Unité 6 Images

pp. 274, 276, 304 (Photo) © Brenda*. 2018.

p. 275 (Cameleon feuille) blickwinkel / Alamy Stock Photo

p. 273 (Ghana vs. Cameroon, Africa Cup of Nations, 2008) Olivier Asselin / Alamy Stock Photo

p. 275 (Close up of the Cameroon national team football kit) Alan Smith / Alamy Stock Photo

p. 277 (Photos) © Lou-Ann*, Éloïse*, Mathew*, Maxime*, Élisa*. 2018

p. 284 (Photo) © Lydia Herrmann/ SuSanA Flickr, "Préparation du jardin d'essay", CC BY 2.0, https://creativecommons.org/licenses/by/2.0/, Récupérée de https://www.flickr.com/photos/gtzecosan/9948037766/in/album-72157635841689246/. 4 juin 2013.

p. 284 (Photo) © Rain Rannu, "Tea- Our host pouring Moroccan tea", CC BY 2.0, https://creativecommons.org/licenses/by/2.0/, Récupérée de https://www.flickr.com/photos/rainrannu/2110854798/in/album-72157603453348436/. 1 décembre 2007.

p. 287 (Bande dessinée) Best Efforts Made © HelloKids, "Stan, Alphone et le tourisme". Récupérée de http://r.hellokids.com/c_1833/lire-et-apprendre/bd-pour-enfant/nots-et-themes-d-actualite-expliquees-en-bd/tourisme. 2016.